# Francis Huxley and the Human Condition

Focused on the life and work of Francis Huxley (1923–2016), this book offers an exploration of the search to understand the human condition, one which is simultaneously biographical, philosophical, cultural, historical, political and epistemological.

A member of the illustrious Huxley dynasty, Francis Huxley forged an unusual and innovative career, making key contributions to social anthropology, mental health care and the protection of indigenous peoples. His story reveals how the production and dissemination of ideas can be understood in an intergenerational context which is familial and sociological. The book reflects on the contemporary relevance of Huxley's work, forging links between the central philosophical, cultural, scientific and political themes that dominate the turbulent early 21st century and the enduring questions that have driven human beings in the search to understand themselves and their place in the world. It will be of interest to scholars from across the social sciences and humanities.

**Ron Roberts** is a chartered psychologist and Associate Fellow of the British Psychological Society with over 30 years' experience in higher education. www.ronroberts.co.uk

**Theodor Itten** is a psychotherapist based in Switzerland. He studied social anthropology with Francis Huxley, who became his mentor and friend. www.ittentheodor.ch

# Francis Huxley and the Human Condition
Anthropology, Ancestry and Knowledge

**Ron Roberts and Theodor Itten**

LONDON AND NEW YORK

First published 2021
by Routledge
2 Park Square, Milton Park, Abingdon, Oxon OX14 4RN

and by Routledge
52 Vanderbilt Avenue, New York, NY 10017

*Routledge is an imprint of the Taylor & Francis Group, an informa business*

© 2021 Ron Roberts and Theodor Itten

The right of Ron Roberts and Theodor Itten to be identified as authors of this work has been asserted by them in accordance with sections 77 and 78 of the Copyright, Designs and Patents Act 1988.

All rights reserved. No part of this book may be reprinted or reproduced or utilised in any form or by any electronic, mechanical, or other means, now known or hereafter invented, including photocopying and recording, or in any information storage or retrieval system, without permission in writing from the publishers.

*Trademark notice*: Product or corporate names may be trademarks or registered trademarks, and are used only for identification and explanation without intent to infringe.

*British Library Cataloguing-in-Publication Data*
A catalogue record for this book is available from the British Library

*Library of Congress Cataloging-in-Publication Data*
Names: Roberts, Ron, 1955– author. | Itten, Theodor, author.
Title: Francis Huxley and the human condition : anthropology, ancestry and knowledge / Ron Roberts and Theodor Itten.
Description: Abingdon, Oxon ; New York, NY : Routledge, 2021.
Identifiers: LCCN 2020017197 (print) | LCCN 2020017198 (ebook) | ISBN 9780367553692 (hardback) | ISBN 9781003093190 (ebook)
Subjects: LCSH: Huxley, Francis. | Anthropologists–Great Britain–Biography.
Classification: LCC GN21.H89 R63 2021 (print) | LCC GN21.H89 (ebook) | DDC 301.092 [B]–dc23
LC record available at https://lccn.loc.gov/2020017197
LC ebook record available at https://lccn.loc.gov/2020017198

ISBN: 978-0-367-55369-2 (hbk)
ISBN: 978-1-003-09319-0 (ebk)

Typeset in Times New Roman
by Newgen Publishing UK

For
Irina (RR)
and
Brian Evans (TI)

# Contents

*List of figures*   ix
*Acknowledgements*   x
*Prelude: disturbing the river*   xiii

**PART I**
**Introduction**   1

1   Chronology and family tree   3

**PART II**
**Family life, ancestry and haunting**   9

2   Parents   11

3   Uncle Aldous   31

4   Haunting   50

**PART III**
**The facts of life**   75

5   Gordonstoun   77

6   In the Royal Navy   88

7   Oxford   93

8   Love and history   108

## PART IV
**Social anthropology: in search of the world**     141

9   Anthropology and its challenges     143

10   The Ka'apor     147

11   Saskatchewan     151

12   Haiti fieldwork     167

13   St Catherine's Oxford     174

14   Survival International: anthropology and social justice     188

15   Cosmology and the sacred     195

## PART V
**The human condition**     213

16   The Philadelphia Association     215

17   The late Francis Huxley     239

18   Francis Huxley and the human condition     265

    *Appendix 1: Huxley's bibliography*     275
    *Appendix 2: General bibliography*     285
    *Appendix 3:* Affable Savages *and Monique Lévi-Strauss*     290
    *Index*     292

# Figures

| | | |
|---|---|---|
| 0.1 | Francis Huxley | xi |
| 1.1 | Family tree | 4 |
| 4.1 | Francis, Julian and Anthony 1952 | 56 |
| 5.1 | Francis Huxley. Photographed by Howard Coster. Photograph reproduced with the kind permission of Gordonstoun School | 81 |
| 5.2 | Julian, Juliette, Anthony and Francis on holiday 1938 | 83 |
| 6.1 | Francis Huxley as a sub-lieutenant in the Navy, walking the streets of Hong Kong with two similarly uniformed friends 1944 | 91 |
| 7.1 | Francis Huxley. Gambia expedition 1949 | 100 |
| 8.1 | Painting given to Francis by Ferelyth Howard | 110 |
| 8.2 | Adrianna Santa Cruz 1971 | 127 |
| 8.3 | Francis with Mel Huxley 1975 | 130 |
| 10.1 | Darcy Riberio and Francis with the Ka'apor 1951 | 149 |
| 13.1 | Joan Westcott 1967 | 184 |
| 14.1 | Francis Huxley with Karaya children, Santa Isabel, Aragonia River 1972. Courtesy John Hemming | 191 |
| 16.1 | Poster for the Philadelphia Association 1977 | 223 |
| 17.1 | Francis Huxley with Albert Hofmann 1982, Zurich | 242 |
| 17.2 | Wedding Picture of Francis and Adele, London 1986 | 255 |
| 17.3 | Francis' cabin in Wagnon Road and Grave 2020. Courtesy Dawn Heumann | 261 |

# Acknowledgements

We would like to express our deep thanks and appreciation to the following persons for their time, collaboration, honesty, openness, help, generosity and support:

*Family*: Susan Ray Huxley and Anthony Ray, Victoria Huxley, Trevenen Huxley, Adele Getty Huxley, Meloma Balaskas Huxley, Michael Williams.

*Hosting in Sebastopol:* Adele Getty and Michael Williams.

*Literary support and writing coach*: Deirdre Bair.

*Connecting in his network and encouragement*: John Hemming.

*Interviews in England*: Bettina and Norbert Blume, Marcus Colchester, Audrey Butt Colson, Stephen Corray, Brian Evans, Robin Hanbury-Tenison, John Hemming, John Jones, Stephen Hugh-Jones, Adam Kuper, Thomas Neurath, Chris Oakley, Mina Semyon, Jill Purce, Leon Redler, Rupert Sheldrake, Cosmo Sheldrake, Fiona Watson, Paul Zeal.

*Interviews in Switzerland*: René Fuerst, David Napier, Jeremy Narby, Anatol Itten, Dimitrij Itten, Raphael Itten.

*Interviews in the USA:* Michael Stuart Ani, Diana Conn Darling, Francesco Gaona, Diana Joos, J. Lévy, Cal Peacock, Michael G. Schwab, Loren Eugen White.

*Interviews in Canada:* Andrew Feldmar.

*Additional invaluable support came from*: Vinzent Allen, Jonathan Benthall, David Buckman, Tina Campanella, Barbara Costa, Emily Ellis, Ljiljana Filipovic, Joseph Gomes, Evelyne Gottwalz-Itten, Monique Lévi-Strauss, Emmanuelle Loyer, Marguerite Mignon-Quibel, Thomas Neurath, Alice Raymond, Anna Sander, Lucia Santa Cruz, Merry Cross.

*Translations*: Angéla Szalontainé Krasznai (Hungarian into German) Penny Langton (French into English) Sergio Lenoir (Portuguese into German) Jutta Orth (French into German), Rosmarie Rodwell (French into English).

*Routledge*: Katherine Ong (Editor, Anthropology), Marc Stratton (general support), Kangan Gupta (editorial assistant).

*Institutions*: Balliol College Oxford (John Jones, Anna Sander), *Bognor Regis Post* and *Chichester Post* newspapers (Kevin Smith), Gordonstoun School (Louise Avery), Survival International (Kate Holberton, Alice Raymond), Philadelphia Association, Thames & Hudson, Plon (Marguerite Mignon-Quibel), Rice University (Woodson Research Center: Rebecca Russell and our proxy researcher Trevor Egerton), St Catherine's College (Barbara Costa, Emily Ellis, Nathalie Perret), Zoological Society of London (Tina Campanella, Lyndsey Isaac), Völkerkundemuseum Zürich (Dr. Peter Gerber), World Museum Liverpool (Marion Servat-Fredericq).

Thanks also to John Hemming and Adele Getty for providing permission to use photos.

Finally, we must thank the man himself, the late Francis Huxley, who never dreamt of this book, but made possible the very real privilege of writing it.

*Figure 0.1* Francis Huxley.

## Official sources

FHA   Francis Huxley Archive, 1105 Wagnon Road, Sebastopol, CA.
JHP   Juliette Huxley papers, 1895–1994, MS 474, Woodson Research Center, Fondren Library, Rice University.
JSH   The Papers of Julian Sorell Huxley, Woodson Research Center, Fondren Library, Rice University.
SCC   St Catherine's College Oxford Archive Staff File.
TLD   Theodor Itten's London Diaries

# Prelude
## Disturbing the river

"Scientist Huxley's whereabouts a mystery," is the front-page title in a Brazilian newspaper. Where is Francis Huxley? Lost, it seems, in the Brazilian Jungle. All we know is, that together with the French linguist, Boudin, and Brazilian anthropologist, Darcy Riberio, he was on his way from Belem, via Pará, up the Gurupi river in the dense Amazonian rain forest, to conduct his first ethnographic fieldwork with the Ka'apor – descendants of the Tupinamba tribes – their name literally means forest dwellers. So, had he now vanished without a trace?

According to the newspaper *Folha Verspertina*, on 14 November 1951, Huxley had last been seen on 24 October.[1] The National Directorate of Serviço de Proteção aos Indios (SPI)[2] sent a telegram to the Regional inspectorate, begging them to inquire as to the whereabouts of the 28-year-old English ethnologist. It had all begun so well. When Huxley came to Brazil in November 1950, the recipient of a government grant to pursue his sociological and anthropological interests, his arrival made the Sao Paulo press. Coming from the renowned, "noble" British traditional university, Oxford, as the press had it, to conduct research with an Amazonian tribe. *A Gazeta* interviewed signor Francis Huxley, in the company of Mr. Donald Darling, press attaché of the British Consulate. He is presented as an inquisitive spirit, the nephew of one of the most sagacious British writers of our time, Aldous Huxley, and son of the famed natural scientist, first Director General of UNESCO, Julian Huxley. The tone is clearly set. This young Huxley, belonged to the fourth generation of the intellectual family founded by T. H. Huxley (1825–1895), following others who had made their mark in biology, zoology, botany, horticulture, literature, art and exploration.

Given that 'Huxley' was such a household name, it is still something of a surprise that Francis Huxley made such headlines. His name, it is true, had already appeared in English newspapers after his expeditions to the Arctic and Gambia. He had studied the Tupinamba tribes of Brazil, for his anthropological B.Litt. at Oxford University, and before embarking on this journey, he had been cordially invited by the Brazilian government, aware of his Tupi literature research, to hear lectures in anthropology and sociology at São Paulo

University. "Why did you choose South America and specially the Tupi for your field of research?" one journalist asked. Huxley replied:

> To be honest, nowadays when anthropology in Europe is concerned, tribal peoples in Africa, Oceania and North America are favoured. This makes me tired, always to hear and read the same. That is why I have decided to research the natives of South America and chosen the Tupi, about whom the most was written so far.

He went on to say, in front of a sizeable gathering, that he did not regret his decision. Following his disappearance, weeks passed with no information. Fortunately, *O Globo* the third largest daily newspaper in Brazil would eventually report: "Surgiram da Mata!" – "they emerged from the forest!" Since his vanishing act had caused a veritable sensation, it was important for the press to report that this unsettling riddle was now solved. All three companions, Riberio, Boudin and Huxley stayed for six months in the region of Gurupi and in various villages of the Urubu tribes. They emerged richer for their experience, replete with copious research data and numerous colourful tribal artefacts. *O Globo* reported them safe and sound in Belem do Para, carrying a charming picture of a young, smart looking Huxley, adorned with a tie and, as was his usual habit, quite the English gentleman, sporting a tweed jacket.

In accord with the level of interest generated, Huxley and his fellow travellers into the unknown gave an evening of talks, spiced with music by Villa-Lobos and a showing of the film 'Uirapuru,' to an invited audience of the Institute of Anthropology of Pará and the North American Consulate. News of their return from the forest had attracted a sizeable and varied crowd. One journalist remarked that he found Huxley to be modest and slightly reserved when talking about his father and his uncle, though otherwise ably, and in an easy-going fashion, entertaining his listeners about his experiences with the natives. His comfortable ways with words would become a hallmark of his social presence and a feature of the narrative anthropology he was to introduce, which deftly navigated the rivers of his own life as they merged into the flowing tropical waters of the people he encountered in the rainforest.

Francis Huxley was a complex figure. This, no doubt is true of us all, as we necessarily confront the times and tides within which we move. As an exercise in biography, we hope our exploration of his life and work will have something to say about that general truth. We have no interest in fixing or identifying an essential 'Huxley' who will emerge as a constant figure in all periods of his life; rather, we wish to convey something of the journey – emotional, spiritual and intellectual – undertaken through a long and eventful life, and the various conflicts, personal, familial and epistemological, he sought to resolve along the way. We have therefore set out to write this in terms of two interlocking strands. The first of these comprises the 'facts of life' – detailing the Huxley family background, setting out the key relationships (familial, intellectual and romantic) – and institutions (educational, professional and vocational) through which his life was navigated. The second strand is chiefly concerned with the anthropological and psychotherapeutic dramas which he grappled with, both practically and as a writer intellectually. These are necessarily not entirely independent of one another.

To achieve an appropriate balance of wisdom and knowledge is difficult. One's heart and voice are seldom at peace. As members of the 'psy' professions – we will both be concerned with the means by which Huxley sustained (or failed to sustain) his well-being. Our efforts to understand the man must inevitably seek to map the external world he lived in – born as he was into the turbulent 1920s – with the inner worlds which developed in response to it. We must therefore contend with the forces and expectations which saturate, and continue to saturate, the social class landscape of the country in which he was raised.

We each have our own different relationship to this landscape, and so there is always more than one way to tell a story and there will be truths and partial truths that go untold or unheard as a result. Facts are always dependent upon a context for their life and understanding. We all enjoy a diverse number of lives – public, private, official and secret, approved and disapproved, fulfilled and unfulfilled. While acknowledging this, we can interrogate the record of Francis Huxley's life as we know it and provide an interpretive account of what propelled change or maintained stasis in the interlocking inner and outer worlds of the man – what truths were successfully reckoned with and which were not. Hermione Lee wrote that "a self that goes on changing is a self that goes on living."[3] With this in mind, we hope we will document the many changes in Huxley's life in a manner which will raise deep questions about the influences – conscious and unconscious – which not only shaped his life and how he sought to make sense of it, but which also course through the rivers of every person's life. This is, consequently, a biography which asks questions about the society Huxley lived in and whose influences still exact their share of misfortune. In entering the waters that flowed through the Huxley dynasty, we think of the present work, with its central examination of the intergenerational forces of family and class, as actively disturbing that river. We hope our readers will feel enlightened by what we offer.

Francis Huxley's life is unavoidably entwined with that of his ancestors. Often, through no fault of his own, he found himself ensnared in the trap that comes from being born into a famous family. What specific burdens did this entail and how widespread in the family where they? We like to think that his efforts to make sense of this intergenerational trap in part accounts for his narrative wit, as well as his honest and empathic approach to others – an aspect of his character which would lead to his attempted professional rapprochement between anthropology and psychotherapy and situate him at the heart of the 1960s counterculture, in the company of R. D. Laing.

Huxley was at his best when juggling with how human life has a cultural significance yet can never be wholly defined by it, nor its wholeness rendered entirely amenable to a conclusive narration, try as we might. The totality of life is as elusive as the final interpretation of a text. Francis remained aware of the shadows cast by our own body, both in the full light of its living and when the living processes themselves wind down and pass into the repositories of cultural memory. He, after all, grew up in the often-terrifying shadows of his forebears. The creative tension between the living and the dead animated much of his theoretical thinking and his relationships to loved ones and foes alike – and in his many love affairs the reverberations were striking. Francis was in some ways a master in the art of cultivating love but not in dealing with the slings and arrows of outrageous fortune which assailed those relationships.

Francis Huxley honed his storytelling skills through a graphic imagination, revealing just enough detail to wet a listener's appetite before exercising his seemingly inexhaustible powers of suggestion to bring closure to the dramatic narrative. The denouement of the tale would often bring the heart of the story into an iconographic familial focus – as his family was an endless source of the strange, the bizarre and the unconventional. His favourite maxims – "Beauty is truth and truth is beauty," was one; another "the Poet is no liar, for nothing he affirms" – signal to us that between the artistic and scientific poles set out by his illustrious family members he was a man more comfortable with the unpredictable and wayward truths of the arts than the sciences.

His humour carried him far from his more serious anthropological and practical work, writing his own idiosyncratic biography of Lewis Carroll – *The Raven and The Writing Desk* – which exemplified the operation of his own meticulous and playful intelligence as much as it illustrated the life and riddles of Charles L. Dodgson. In terms of writing style, elegance, sagacity, tonality and flow, he marched to his own tune – adhering to his own rulebook, that if one takes care of the sense, "the sounds will take care of themselves."[4] To his friends he was a witty and gifted master of storytelling, able to summon at the appropriate moment a refined dose of raucous laughter. But the laughs were punctuated by much sadness, and the weight of family silences and intergenerational mores were never far away.

When once, he asked his mother Juliette, why she did not let him know earlier about Aunt Margret, and her lesbian nature, she said: "Oh Francis, we do not talk about these things in our family. Please don't ask, you would not want to know the answer." Answers, both revealed and concealed, Huxley came to know, had their place in the human heart. We know now that Francis Huxley was hungry for knowledge, enjoyed the fun of knowing and was partial to gossip, for this is part of the emotional fabric which binds a community together. Let him have here, in this prelude, almost the last word: "If some of it now adds up to anything, this can only be coincidence, whatever we may like to mean by the word."[5]

Naturally we hope that the words which follow do add up to something – and give more than a flavour of a fascinating, fully lived, joyful and, on occasion, a painful and difficult life.

*Ron Roberts and Theodor Itten*
London and St. Gallen
March 2020

## Notes

1 *Folha Vespertina*: Headline: Misterio No Paradeiro do Cientista Huxley. Belem – Pará, 14 November 1951.
2 The Indian Protection Service.
3 Lee, H. (1996, p.11) *Virginia Woolf*. London. Vintage.
4 Huxley, F. (1976, p. 50) *The Raven and the Writing Desk*. London. Harper and Row.
5 Huxley, F. (1976, p.100); he goes on: "But, as the Archbishop said in his Sermon, 'Nothing is prejudged, and nothing is condemned, but upon such proof, as the nature of things requires, the testimony of others.'"

# Part I
# Introduction

# 1 Chronology and family tree

Can Wisdom be in a silver rod or Love in a golden bowl?

(William Blake)

1887: Julian Sorell Huxley (father) is born on 22 June in London.
1896: Marie Juliette Baillot (mother) is born on 6 December in Auvernier, Switzerland.
1909: Grandfather Leonard moves to Westbourne Square, London.
1912: Leonard marries a second time on 23 February, Ms. Rosalind Bruce.
1914: Julian and Noel Trevenen (born in 1889) are in the same rest home due to depression. Trevenen later committed suicide by hanging himself on a tree.
1915: Mademoiselle Juliette Baillot becomes Swiss governess to teach and be companion to Julian (1906–1989), daughter of Lady Ottoline Morrell (1873–1938).
1916: Juliette Baillot meets Julian Huxley at Garsington Manor.
1919: Juliette Baillot marries Julian Huxley, now a Fellow of New College.
1920: Anthony Julian Huxley, brother, is born on 20 December.
1923: Francis John Heathorn Huxley is born on 28 August, at Holywell, Oxford.
1925: Julian becomes Chair of Zoology at Kings College, London. Moves from Oxford to 31 Hillway, Holly Lodge Estate, Hampstead, home for seven years. Francis Prep schools at Byron House and learns to bicycle on lanes of Hampstead Heath. Francis' health also began to give serious trouble.
1927: Julian spents winter in Aigle, Chalet des Arolles at Diablerets, Swiss Alps, with parents, grandmother and brother, into 1928. Aldous, Maria and Cousin Matthew, D. H. Lawrence and Frida joined in.
1932: Julian has an affair, with Viola Ilma. Mother loses sleep and health and feels utterly lost. Leonard scolds his eldest to give his affair up, "or he did not wish to see him again."
1933: Francis at Frensham Heights School, Farnham, Surrey.
1934: Francis at Abinger Hill School, Abinger Lane, Dorking, Surrey.

4  *Introduction*

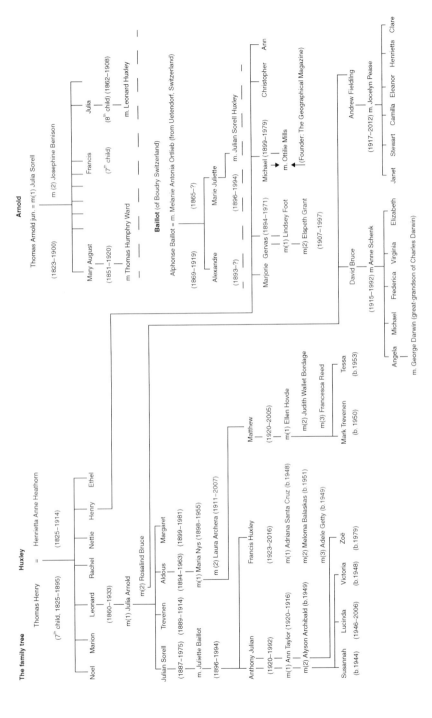

*Figure 1.1* Family tree.

1935: Julian is appointed secretary to the Zoological Society of London, till 1942. Family lives residentially in the Secretary House, Zoological Gardens.
1937: Autumn term: Goes to Gordonstoun School, Elgin, Scotland (till Spring 1942).
1938: Julian gets elected as a Fellow of the Royal Society.
1939: Anthony goes up to Trinity College Cambridge. Francis, at Gordonstoun, evacuated to Wales.
1942: Lives with parents at the Secretary House, Zoological Gardens. Friendship with Ferelyth Howard, takes up sculptures. Francis joins the Royal Navy, till July 1946.
1944: Becomes Assistant Navigating Officer on HMS *Ramilles*, on D-Day, 6 June, in the Channel to Normandy.
1945: August, first atomic bomb on Hiroshima. Huxley is on a warship preparing for invasion of Japan.
1946: Julian becomes the first Director General of UNESCO. Francis meets Claude Lévi-Strauss.
1947: Oxford student from July until 1951, Balliol College.
1948: Leads an Oxford University expedition of young scientists to Gambia. Receives 2nd Class Honours in Zoology. Becomes a member of the Anthropological Institute, which his great-grandfather, T. H. Huxley, co-founded and becomes an Emslie Horniman Scholar.
1950: Receives MSc. in Social Anthropology, Oxford, under Professor Meyer Fortes and E. E. Evans-Pritchard. In November, goes to Brazil to study Social Anthropology of Indian tribes – with grants from Brazilian Government, in cooperation with the British Council and from the Department of Scientific and Industrial Research – aiming to write his PhD.
1951: Conducts Brazilian fieldwork with the Ka'apor (Urubus), with Darcy Ribeiro, June till November.
1952: Returns in Spring to the UK for consultation with Professor Meyer Fortes, now in Cambridge University, and further studies. Goes back to Brazil in August.
1953: Second visit to Ka'apor, Urubus, in the Amazonian basin of Brazil, February till June, this time on his own.
1954: Becomes Curator of Ethnography, City of Liverpool Public Museum until 1955. Friendship with Sheila.
1956: *The Affable Savages*. Recieves Viking Found Grant to visit American Universities, till 1957.
1958: Conducts fieldwork in Weyburn Mental Hospital, Saskatchewan, Canada. Julian is knighted.
1959: Conducts fieldwork in Parapsychological Institute, New York. Fieldwork in Haiti, for nine months, till 1960. Writes the long essay *Charles Darwin – Life and Habit*.

1962: Meets Joan Wescott, fellow anthropologist and one-time secretary to R. D. Laing. Lives from now on in a flat at 18 Belsize Park Gardens, London NW3.
Translates *Africa Before the White Man* by Henri Labouret.
1963: Translates *The Origins of Life* by Jules Carles.
In October, becomes a Research Fellow in Social Anthropology, at St Catherine's College Oxford, till 1968. Plans to write *Anthropology and the Body*.
1964: Publishes *Peoples of the World*. Gets to know R. D. Laing.
1965: Organises a Royal Society Conference on Ritualisation for Behaviour in Animals and Man, together with Julian. R. D. Laing is invited by Julian to participate.
1966: Publishes *The Invisibles*. Julian has his last nervous breakdown. Consultation with R. D. Laing.
1967: On stage at the Dialectics of Liberation Conference. Laing moves to 65A Belsize Park Gardens, London NW3.
1968: Teaches at the Anti-University, 49 Rivington Street, London EC2. He appears as an invited guest on the prestigious Eamonn Andrews Show on ITV.
1969: Co-founds Survival International and active as a member of the Executive Board until 1990.
1970: Becomes a member of the Philadelphia Association, London.
1972: Becomes a member of the mission, "Tribes of the Amazon basin in Brazil 1972" sponsored by the Aborigines' Protection Society London and the Brazilian Government.
1973: Marries Adriana Paula Santa Cruz on 7 April, London.
Publishes *Tribes of the Amazon Basin in Brazil*.
1974: Publishes *The Way of the Sacred*. Becomes the Principal of Studies at the Philadelphia Association.
1975: Father Julian dies on 14 February.
1976: Divorces Adriana Santa Cruz on 17 September, London. Publishes *The Raven and the Writing Desk*. Marries Meloma Balaskas in November.
1977: Lives at 18b Wedderburn Road, London NW3, as a writer and private scholar.
1979: Publishes *The Dragon – Nature of Spirit, Spirit of Nature*.
1980: Separates from Meloma Balaskas-Huxley.
1981: Begins Friendship with Avice Simpson. Goes to Sheffield University Hospital by invitation of Professor Jenner, to study his wards.
1982: Leaves the Philadelphia Association London. Gives workshops in Switzerland on Mythology and Rites.
1983: 60th birthday, in London. Gives a talk at the Lewis Carroll Society.
1984: Meets Adele Getty in Happy Valley, at a conference: "The Way of the Warrior." Separates from Avice Simpson. Delivers the Prestigious Chichele Lecture, in All Souls, Oxford, on *Psychoanalysis and Anthropology*.

1986: In February, fire in his London flat, caused by a careless tenant. Divorces Meloma Huxley on 25 February. Juliette Huxley's *Leaves of the Tulip Tree* is published, which Francis Huxley substantially helped her write. She is 90 in December. Marries Adele Marie Getty on 10 November at Camden Register Office. Lives at Berkley Hills, Kensington until the 1990s.

1989: 23 August, R. D. Laing dies in St. Tropez. Writes: *Liberating Shaman of Kingsley Hall*. R. D. Laing Obituary, *The Guardian*, 25 August.

1990: Publishes *The Eye – Seer and the Seen*. Farewell talk at Laing memorial gathering, Piccadilly. 3 January.

1990: Lives in Santa Fee and environs in various places. In October, lectures at Conference in Korea on Shamanism.

1992: Brother Anthony Julian dies on 26 December. Starts to write *The Mutual Self*.

1993: Visits London and supports Mother after brother's death. Festschrift for his 70th Birthday: A Letter to Francis Huxley. Ed. T. Itten

1994: Lady Juliette Baillot-Huxley dies in her 98th year, 28 September in London.

1995: Sells family home, 31. Pond Street, Hampstead. Lives in a hamlet in Pojoaque valley, New Mexico.

1998: In autumn, separates from Adele Getty-Huxley. She moves back to California.

2000: 3rd R. D. Laing Conference in SOAS, London – Talk on "Laing and Shamanism."

2001: Publishes *Shamans Through Time – 500 Years on the Path to Knowledge*, edited with Jeremy Narby.

2002: Gives a workshop in Manaus, the capital and largest city of the Brazilian state of Amazonas.

2005: Moves to 1105 Wagnon Road, Sebastopol, California, 15 March. Lives in a small three-room cabin, in the middle of woodland, on the same patch as Adele and Michael Patrick Williams.

2007: Huxley is ill with cancer and has it treated with radiation and chemotherapy. Has an operation for cataract in one eye, whose first effect was to flood his vision with blue.

2012: Car accident. Gives up driving. Uncle Andrew Fielding Huxley (1917–2012), only six years his senior, dies.

2016: Ann Huxley, first wife of brother Anthony, dies on 2 January. Francis dies at home, 10:30 AM on 29 October, surrounded by closest friends, Adele, Michael and Cal.

# Part II

# Family life, ancestry and haunting

To understand Francis Huxley's interests in both the natural and political worlds, it is necessary, we argue, to trace these interests through the dense lineage of the family to which he belonged. This is no easy undertaking – and in intellectual biographies it is generally an aspect of a given story that goes untold. That is in measure due in no small part – not to any deficiency on the part of biographers, but simply because of the fact that it is rare to have available, so much information on the intergenerational familial context of knowledge. We hope therefore that this substantial part of the book will not only cast important light on what drove and shaped Francis' intellectual horizons, but will also raise important questions about the cultural situating of knowledge, how we value those that endeavour to produce it and how we conceive of the origins of knowledge.

We begin this task by considering the most immediate of the family contexts which surrounded Francis – that brought into being by his parents. Later we will enlarge the scope of our investigation to include the very great significance of Aldous Huxley, Francis' uncle, and the far reach of his great-grandfather T. H. Huxley – whose towering influence has persisted in every nook and cranny of intellectual investigation undertaken by members of the Huxley family. It is an influence which has also reached far beyond the intellectual sphere.

# 2 Parents

The twist of fate that leads to our existence in the world, we owe to our two parents. They in turn owe theirs to their parents, our grandparents – those four extend the ancestral line to our great-grandparents. Going back to four generations involves a branch on our tree of 32 persons. All of these can be considered together as a transgenerational unit, in which various genetic, physiological, emotional, behavioural and social factors of influence are distributed. Where in the world we are born, in what time and in what place in the family and community, all these shape our emergent survival strategies and customary modes of being and behaving in the world. What we can change in later life is not the red thread of the clan or tribe woven into us, but how we live this character we are perpetually in the throes of becoming, and give back to the world the music and language of our own unique rhythms, creations and love. Here we visit some examples from Francis' ancestral figures – a necessarily incomplete list, as is the case in any anthropological exploration.

**La Maman**

Lady Juliette Maria Baillot-Huxley, opened the account of her life with a quote from T. S. Eliot: "Each generation must translate for itself."[1] She was born on 6 December 1896, in the fishing village of Auvernier on Lake Neuchâtel in Switzerland. Her parents were Alphonse Baillot and Mélanie Antonia Ortlieb, the eldest daughter of a large family, whose father, Anton, was Maître-Ferblantier.[2] Anton Ortlieb's main professional achievement was his invention of a 'couleuse,' a container where the laundry is boiled. This invention, for a while at least, contributed to the success of Anton's family business. But as he hadn't bothered to apply for a patent, he gained "neither fortune nor recognition."[3] His early death from pneumonia left a heavy burden on his young wife. The eldest daughter, 16-year-old Mélanie (Francis' grandmother to be), was given the task of caring for her younger siblings. "Deprived of the enjoyment of her youthful years by the family's changed situation, my mother took her responsibility seriously and, according to her younger sister, became very strict with the small children."[4] Juliette's grandmother kept going, reliant on her Swiss faith that 'life continues, and we manage somehow.'

Tante Juliette, as she eventually became known, left home as early as she could to apprentice as a dressmaker at a prestigious Parisian house. After graduating she set up shop in London as a fashion designer. Whenever she returned to her elder sister Melanie's household, now set up in Neuchâtel, her daughter Juliette experienced 'la tante' as a glamorous person with charming élan vital. "I was named after her and received from her much loving kindness and understanding."[5] Juliette, in hindsight, felt her family of origin was rather prosaic, with little or nothing "to feed the veins of imagination or the hunger for understanding."[6]

Her father, Alphonse Baillot, as we have seen, orphaned at an early age, was brought up by his uncle Emil, a winegrower, who put Alphonse to work in an office of the notaire Baillot, a distant cousin. Following his then obligatory year in the Swiss Army, Alphonse found that his partner Henrioux had decamped with the securities entrusted to them. Instead of declaring bankruptcy, he assured his clients that he would pay back every cent. With the exception of the equivalent of 40 pounds owed to Tante Juliette, he eventually did. The 'Debt,' as it came to be called, plunged the young family into poverty. Alphonse found a job in the Compagnie des Tramways of Neuchatel, spending most evenings away from home. He turned moody, unsociable and occasionally violent – a source of fear in the lives of his children. The family ceased entertaining at home or having dinner guests. Mother Melanie, directed Juliette to an apprenticeship in the art of lace making, embroidery and handiwork. These artisanal abilities served Juliette well in later life, when she took up sculpture and refined her embroidery skills.

## Neuchâtel

Seeking to escape from poverty, the family moved to 31 Chemin Bel Air, 2000 Neuchâtel, a villa, close to the railway station. Susie Huxley remembers Neuchâtel from an early visit there.

> I was taken there aged four, to meet my "Great Grandmaman." I can remember the train journey … in the house there was a huge staircase. She gave me a big grey velvet stuffed elephant toy. I remember vividly, her garden which sloped down to a big railway cutting.[7]

At *Ecole Superieure des Jeunes Filles*,[8] the 18-year-old Juliette gained her baccalaureate. Alphonse had tried to prevent his daughter going there, but was overruled by his wife. There, the beautiful young Juliette met a young English student, "with whom she became affectionate."[9] In response, her concerned mother decided to send her romancing daughter to London, to stay with Tante Juliette, where her enjoyments were plenty and her brief romance was curtailed. As we will see later, Juliette employed an uncannily similar strategy, when her son, the 18-year-old Francis, fell in love with Ferelyth Howard, a young talented sculptor who was working for his parents at the London Zoo.

Mélanie set up a pension for young girls who came as language students. This new and hopeful beginning was dampened when another misfortune hit home. Papa Alphonse sank into dark moods, hid in bed for days and died suddenly, aged a mere 47. On the same day, war broke out (28 July 1914). With Alphonse gone, Mélanie sent Juliette back to London, with the onerous task of earning and paying back the outstanding part of 'The Debt,' still amounting 40 pounds, to Tante Juliette. Her best bet, to fulfil this task as quickly as possible, was to look for a job as a governess.

She left Neuchâtel as an 18-year-old, to be with her Tante Juliette in London, who helped her to find a job. Juliette was fortunate to come across an advert placed by Lady Ottoline Morrell seeking a governess. They met for an interview in the waiting room of Oxford railway station. The "unforgettable" Lady Ottoline, as Juliette saw her, offered her the job to be a companion to their daughter Julian, and so began the chain of events which would propel the shy Swiss girl, with a Calvinist upbringing, into an altogether different world – a world which would bring her into the orbit of Julian Huxley. The two years she stayed in the post were to turn around her life.

But to Juliette, as always there is something puzzling about why she had been anointed with the task of dealing with the debt. She would later mull this over with Francis. Why, Juliette wondered did her mother not allot this task to her brother Alexandre? After all he was older, earning a living and the debt had been incurred by the blind faith of Alphonse.

## Garsington

It was at Garsington Manor, the home of Lady Ottoline Morrell, that the half blind Aldous Huxley came to do manual work on the estate. His energetic elder brother, Julian, who already achieved a measure of professional recognition, came to visit him there. At Garsington, the nascent British art and academic world – to be immortalised as the Bloomsbury set – opened up to the young Swiss governess, as talk flowed freely around paintings, poetry, politics and the latest scientific and philosophical books, often written by these unusual visitors whom Juliette was permitted to meet, after duty was done. Political issues of the day were discussed as a matter of course, sometimes in the presence of ministers, as well as the many conscientious objectors who were doing their labour service on Morrell's estate. The leading lights there, Lady Morrell, Philip Morrell, Bertrand Russell, Virginia Woolf, Lytton Strachey, Roger Fry, Duncan Grant and assorted others, had all signed up to the pacifist cause.

Juliette Huxley presented her own enchanting version of life at Garsington in her memoirs.[10] Lady Ottoline (1873–1938), her employer, was experienced as a kind but dominant personality, a remarkable, middle-aged society dame, who brought Juliette completely under her spell. Green to the eccentricities on display, Juliette found life at Garsington a formidable challenge. She, we know now, showed courage, worked to improve her English, took up studying sculpting and carried out the duties of her employment, looking after and teaching daughter Julian, to Lady Ottoline's satisfaction. 'The Debt' was in the course of time paid back.

Mixing with the Huxley brothers, the Stephen sisters (Vanessa Bell and Virginia Woolf) and others, Juliette was witness to a time of sexual liberation, extending her own boundaries of tolerance to what "to her Swiss eyes first seemed indecorous in the behaviour of her Bloomsbury guests."[11] She responded to the libertarian ambience by becoming more daring herself. Sitting on the roof in Garsington, not uncommonly naked, Juliette vanquished her shyness and built lasting friendships with Aldous, Dorothy Brett, Marc Gertler, Bertrand Russell and D. H. Lawrence, even becoming comfortably accommodating with Lytton Strachey and Virginia Woolf. Of Mademoiselle Baillot, Lady Ottoline noted:

> She is a tall, slim, very pretty, shy, severe and composed Swiss girl, with plaits of fair hair done in two buns on her ear, she seemed almost absurdly young, but she herself seemed quite confident ... she came and was perfect ... she took part in all our life and with her lovely simplicity and intelligence was much liked by everybody. Juliette and I have always remained great friends.[12]

## Experiencing Juliette

All families are subject to their own home spun narratives as well as those constructed outside the bonds of family ties. The tales are all made more artful or curious in the telling. Of the many stories told about Juliette Huxley, two by the daughters of her oldest son Anthony are particularly informative. Susie Huxley recalls the stilted formalities that accompanied visits to their grandmother in Pond Street. Dutifully dressed up for the occasion by their mother:

> When we were small children we had to sit down, stiff back. We were supposed to speak French to Juliette. As soon as we could, we leave the table. We hated that procedure and would go to the kitchen, to sit with Alice. She told us the most amazing stories. Alice was a gem. She brought up Anthony and Francis, when they were small.[13]

Her sister Victoria similarly remembers:

> Grandmother was very strict, when we went to visit her and grandad for tea on a Sunday. Very often you had to be put in proper frocks and reminded to behave, my mother was very tense. I didn't realise then; you don't realise that when you're a small child. We had to sit up straight.

Victoria recalls a very different Juliette, once she had become an adult.

> There was a big change in the late 70s. I was living in London. I had a long-term relationship just broken. Granny Juliette was very supportive, and we really got to know each other. We had amazing discussions about men, sex and all sorts of things. She was incredibly supportive to me. We saw each other every fortnight. I would go there for dinner, or she would come to my flat. We got to know each other on that adult level. She told me a lot about her own marriage and various other things. She was certainly quite frank. "Susie," she asked me when I was turning up with different chaps, "are they really good in bed?" You would not expect most grannies to ask that, would you? When I had my first child, she was very supportive and loving. She helped me with payments and decorating the house.[14]

Once Julian was dead, in 1975,[15] Juliette began to tell Francis, her second son, of her misgivings about having married Julian, not the least of which was that she no longer appeared in charge of the major decisions that shaped her life. Francis, always spirited with numbers, would mention that his mother lived in five houses, all with the number 31 – two in Switzerland, two in London and one in Paris. Francis' own playful obsession with numerology may well have owed something to the patterns which recurred in his mother's life. Francis would ask: How was it that she was named after her mother's sister and Julian was named after his mother, that she came to be governess to Lady Ottoline's daughter, also called Julian? How was it that she has been called 'la petite anglaise' from an early age?

A story, which Francis told often and with relish, came from his childhood and concerned the 'gruesome' Castle of Valangin a good hour's walk to the north of Neuchâtel. This was a transgenerational "place of pilgrimage" for the Baillots. Melanie showed the children the dungeons and torture chambers which were still in place. This would send shudders down Juliette's spine, who would proceed to repeat this 'feast of frights' with her two sons, a repetition she was barely aware she was acting out. Francis found the castle and surroundings deceptively charming. She would treat her fright invigorated boy afterwards to a "luscious *cornets a la crème*."[16]

## The Arnolds

Francis Huxley kept a copy of Meriol Trevor's biography of his matrilineal ancestors, *The Arnolds – Thomas Arnold and His Family*,[17] in his well-stocked library. Familiar with this side of his ancestor's narrative, he would tell, with accompanying raucous laughter, the story of his great-grandfather Tom's 'quizzical madness' and 'ins and outs' with the Catholic church, invariably ending with "Just imagine."[18]

16  *Family life, ancestry and haunting*

Thomas Arnold, the Headmaster of Rugby School for 13 years (1828–1841), moulded the school in such a way that it would serve as a model for private education in the English system. It was he who introduced the prefect system, as well as organised sport into schools. He treated his school as a community, and this, according to Trevor, "was the secret of his success." He was described as gentle and dreamy, dark-haired and dark eyed, with some Cornish traits.

**Great-grandfather**

Thomas' third son, from his marriage to Mary Penrose, was Thomas (the younger; Francis' great-grandfather and younger brother of Matthew Arnold (1822–1888), the famed poet and critic, author of *Culture and Anarchy*). When Thomas the younger met Julia Sorell, she was 24 and he 26. By then, Sorell had already been twice engaged. She is described as possessing a passionate and wilful nature, great charm yet little intellectual power. Arnold seemed the least ambitious of men. Not by nature an activist, he was, however, an idealist with a gift for "shedding his cares both at home and on holiday." It was on one such holiday, visiting the Lake District, that he struck up a friendship with Wordsworth. Wordsworth's diligence and industry in nurturing his writing – he would practice every day – came to be much admired by both Julian and Francis. And this work ethic, one which dovetailed with both Arnold's and T. H. Huxley's, would become inscribed into family practice.

Thomas Arnold was 31, when he converted for the first time to Catholicism. On the occasion his wife hurled stones through the window of the chapel where he was inducted into his new faith. Her flashes of temper aside, Francis' great-grandmother, also radiated, her daughters and grandson Aldous testified, a goodness and love, when you were next to her. This occurrence of a fierce temper alongside a capacity for unbridled warmth was a combination which many would also note of Francis. Many a biographer of the Huxley family tree has commented upon the similar dispositions of various family members. To what extent these correspondences represents anything of real significance – in terms of either nature or nurture – is difficult to disentangle from the observed predilection of both commentators and family members to seek such correspondences, to say nothing of the recurring tendency in both the Arnold and Huxley lines for children to be given the same names as their forbears or the exponentially increasing possibilities for projective identification which such a complex system affords. Though this scenario has received little attention, it is not one that can be safely ignored.

Though Thomas had acquired a reputation as a man of "simplicity and industry," considerable consternation was aroused when, aged 42, he began to drift away from Catholicism. He moved to Birmingham, teaching at the Oratory School, there, but left after discovering his principles sat uneasy with the reigning ethos. He resigned and moved to Oxford in April 1865, returning to the Anglican fold. Criticised for this he responded that he had acted in good faith and not self-interest. It is true, each time he changed his allegiance to the Church, he lost out professionally. In becoming a Catholic he lost a school inspectorship in Tasmania and by leaving the Catholic Church and his connexion with John Henry Newman's educational projects, he had to build a new career at the age of 41. That was not the end of his travels on the religious merry-go-round however. In 1876, his 54th year, "he forfeited his chance of becoming Professor at Oxford by returning to Catholicism."[19] His frequent changes of religious heart caused havoc in his relationships and with his finances.

The preoccupation of Thomas Arnold with settling matters of religious faith forms an interesting counterpoint to T. H. Huxley's own challenges to ecclesiastical authority and the subsequent intellectual preoccupations of Julian, Aldous and Francis with the place of the sacred in human affairs. Was Thomas desperately in need of appreciation by whichever side he was on? Something of this uncertain 'toing and froing' between institutions can be found in the lives of many of the Huxleys – Julian with academia and UNESCO, Aldous with the literary establishment and Francis in his declared ambivalence to academia.

Thomas' wife Julia Sorell and her daughters eventually tired of the incessant instability. She and her daughters were fed up and embittered by the constant mooring and undocking from one religion and faith to another. It ended the marriage. Sadly enough, cancer was eventually to kill the 63-year-old Julia Arnold, in 1888, as it would kill her daughter, Francis' grandmother Julia.

## Julia Arnold – grandmother

Francis' grandmother, Julia Frances Arnold, the younger sister of Mary (later Mrs. Humphry Ward), the successful Victorian writer, was the seventh of Thomas Arnold's and Julia Sorell's eight children. She married Leonard Huxley in 1885. It was said that Lewis Carroll wrote "Sylvie and Bruno" four years later for the three Arnold sisters (Mary, Lucy, Julia). He also took photographs of Julia. Francis' grandmother was one of the first Oxford Home Students and later went to Somerville College, where she gained a first in English Literature. Leonard was at Balliol, as were the Arnolds. Not until Leonard had become a junior master at Charterhouse, Godalming, did they marry. Their first child, Julian Sorell Huxley, Francis' father was born there. The Arnolds influenced the intellectual life of our time principally through the Huxley grandsons, Julian and Aldous, none of whose lives could be said to have followed a strict inherited routine. This baton of a free-roaming intellectual spirit was in time passed on to Francis.

## Leonard Huxley – grandfather

Leonard, born in 1860, owed his name, given to him by his mother, to the fact that the first four letters formed an anagram of Noel. His father, T. H. Huxley, was an acquaintance of Matthew Arnold on the London School Board and together they would contemplate the whys and wherewithal of an education system which could work for the good of all. T. H.'s concern with betterment and improvement would be played out endlessly in the domestic sphere with profound consequences for Leonard, his soon wife to be – Julia Arnold – and all their future children. T. H. was a daunting presence in the lives of his children, for whom "nothing but the best would be tolerated."[20]

When Leonard subsequently announced his intention to marry Julia Arnold – Matthew's brother and "the daughter of fellow Balliol man Thomas Arnold" – it came as a further shock to T. H.'s dreams of steering his children's lives in his own desired direction. Leonard was considered "too young, too aimless" and though undeterred was made to promise a long engagement. Two years hence, and one week before the wedding, Leonard's parents evinced a discernible sense of disappointment, especially T. H. who, along with some of his Fabian friends, thought Leonard lacked ambition. Nevertheless, for Leonard, marrying Julia Arnold, a well-educated, and strong dynamic woman would lend wings to his future. T. H.'s grandson, Julian, entertained similar thoughts about his son Francis, before eventually acknowledging that Francis "turned out to be very able (though) – perhaps not so scientifically precise as his brother Anthony."[21] Leonard's brother Henry (1865–1946), opened up a medical practice. Henry would marry Sophy Stobart. Together they had five children, of whom Gervas (Aldous' favourite cousin) married Elspeth Grant, the feted author. Gervas' brother Michael founded the *Geographic Magazine*, where Francis, would later be welcome with his essays. This side story is illustrative of many things – the clannishness of the family, the overbearing attitudes to family success and the networks of opportunity that bridged various generations.

Leonard spent 17 years as a modestly paid Classics Master at Charterhouse school. He would achieve prominence later as a literary journalist and deputy editor of the Cornhill magazine and for his biography of his father, *Life and Letters of Thomas Henry Huxley*. It was published in 1900, having taken Leonard five years to complete, and was greeted in both New York and London with acclaim.

Once he had joined the *Cornhill*, the family moved to Prior's Fields, where his wife Julia Arnold Huxley would establish her school. The family would go on long summer holidays. In 1903, it was hiking in the Berner Oberland, while staying at the Hotel Rosenlaui, close to Meiringen, famed for the Reichenback waterfalls, the site of the legendary fictional encounter between Sherlock Holmes and Professor Moriarty.

Julian, Leonard's first born thought his father a kind man, full of boyish fun. Cousin Gervas, found Leonard silly, not the kind of father one looked up to, or turned to when one was in trouble. Francis had a similar take on his paternal grandfather, who he felt wasn't up to supporting and understanding his son Trevenen, whose suicide he thought might have been avoided.[22] Francis met Leonard, only once, saying of the occasion, "he was very kind to me and taught me the moves of chess."

After Julia Arnold Huxley's early death, her elder sister, Mary Ward cared for the four children (Julian, Trevenen, Aldous and Margaret). Her own son, Arnold Ward, was a fountain of sorrow, troubled with rising debts incurred from his addictive gambling. Mary Ward's role is significant in our tale, since she cared for Julian affectionately, and her care in turn cascaded down to Julian's sons, Anthony and Francis. She met T. H. Huxley and his wife Henrietta Anne Huxley on several occasions, describing him as without "a touch of bitterness" in his nature. Mary contributed to her brother-in-law Leonard's translation of Hausrath's New Testament. T. H. wrote her a 'vigorous' reply to her stance as a believer in Christian theism. She published this letter in her recollections. T. H., though an agnostic, was not without sympathy for Christian sentiment. Reflecting on this issue, in his own old age, Francis quoted his father's comments on Freud's view that,

> a father-complex acquired in infancy is the chief or sole reason for our personification of the forces of nature as a personal god ... My own case makes it very difficult for me to believe that this view is generally applicable, since although I experience a certain feeling of awe towards the uncomprehend idea of God, I never thought of God as personal. In addition, I have no grounds whatever for supposing that I ever had a father complex.[23]

Having quoted these remarks, Francis concluded:

> Julian's attempt to disprove Freud by proving him right is of exceptional interest, lamentable though it be: for besides pointing to Freud's blindness to the grandfather-complex, it sheds light on the workings of the family daimon.[24]

From T. H. onwards, all the Huxley clan were addicted to work, amply demonstrating the persisting influence and authority of the paterfamilias. It was expected of all the sons and daughters that they cultivate the ability to entertain themselves, be competitive at their schools and universities, and work perennially to sharpen their minds. After T. H. the hunger for social comparison would hang in the Huxley air, like desperation.

## The politics of the family: Julian, Juliette and sons

The intellectual worlds of Julian and Aldous were closely linked. Witness to their discussions, Juliette used to sit at the table – a spectator at what she would call a feast of knowledge. Julian was intent on educating his young wife, who at first had resisted his flirtations. His insistence that she marry him, sounded to her more like an order than a wish. Juliette's gut feeling was to say no, "however, Julian wouldn't take no for an answer."[25] Julian proudly presented his bride-to-be his first book, *The Individual in the Animal Kingdom* (1912) with the inscription: "To JB, to improve her mind."[26] When relaying this episode, Francis would raise his eyes to heaven and intone, "would you believe this cheek?"

A wedding photograph shows Juliette poised, beautiful and sad. The evening before the marriage in London, Juliette returned once more to Tante Juliette's house in town, from whose Baillot family house she was to be married. The big day itself was to set in motion 56 years of marriage. For Juliette that was more than enough. As a widow, she would confide to Francis, "if only she hadn't had to repay that last part of The Debt, she could have repaid Julian's father Leonard, who had thoughtfully, generously provided forty pounds for her to buy her trousseau."[27] Fate denied her the freedom to avoid stepping so young into wedlock. Their honeymoon is reported to have been an unhappy one. Part of it was spent at the Arnold family's Fox How holiday home, to enable Julian to observe the courtship behaviour of the Great Crested Grebe. He did so, lying on his back with his telescope fixed to his eye while his new bride sat forlornly, a hundred metres away, wrapped up in her own thoughts "lest she disturb the performance."[28] Their own sexual courtship was thus supplanted by that of the Grebe with the willing assistance of Julian's scientific egotism. Juliette, as she told her son, hid behind the rocks crying.

The marriage was beset with contradiction. Julian eventually 'won' Juliette over, and secured their home-base. This, however, seemed to provide the foundations not only for the furtherance of Julian's intellectual career, but for the pursuit of sexual infidelities also. Juliette remained fearful of being married and insecure. Somehow with perseverance, they were able – as she writes in her memoires – to find "in each other the response and warmth of our love ... deeper than words and so memorable that neither he nor I ever forgot its radiance."[29]

They settled in Oxford where Julian took up his fellowship at New College and became Senior Demonstrator in the Department of Zoology and Comparative Anatomy. It was still an unsettling time, with Julian's frequent comings and goings, while Juliette nursed her first born, Anthony. Their new home became a site for dinner parties, visits from Julian's colleagues and even tutorials given by Julian. Juliette celebrated her 26th birthday on vacation in Naples, picking up a silver charm to be hung over Francis' cradle. They visited Cumae – where the first ancient Greek colony on the mainland of Italy was founded. There, they hitched a lift back on an old cart on a very bumpy road. Francis recounts, "she was to tell me that she was then pregnant with me and feared I would abandon ship."[30] Something about this touched Francis deeply for he would come to call his most beloved dog 'Cumae,' honouring a bond forged between his unborn self and the Neapolitan village. His old friend Michael Williams saw the four-legged friend as the love of his life.[31]

Francis was born on 28 August 1923, at 8 Holywell Street Oxford, one minute's walk from New College. The initial happiness following Francis' birth did not endure. When Julian fainted in the lab, it heralded the beginning of a phase of deep depression. Juliette was, as a matter of course, affected, feeling a sense of guilt at having married him, and a further one of inferiority. Their difficulties were multiplied by being unable to trust and confide in one another, something neither had learned in their respective families of origin.

No longer able to flee into a romantic idealisation of marriage, they were forced to embrace the reality of their coupledom. In his free time Julian went singing with the Bach Choir, while Juliette gave the children all the love she had, supported by her mother. Her maternal instincts had to do battle with the so-called scientific principles of mothering espoused by the popular Dr. Truby King, whose dogmatic stance that babies should be fed on strict schedules, not on demand, was then influential. What King's popularity entailed, reinforced by the compliant media of the day, was that the natural bonding and trust between mother and child was to be subordinated to a crude market-oriented exercise of male domination. Of baby Francis, Juliette wrote "He was another marvel of delight, placid, content, hardly crying at all, with large grey-green eyes, and melting smile." For her, giving birth, first to Anthony and then Francis was she felt "perhaps the deepest experience a woman can have."[32]

As the house was big enough, the young Huxley family took in lodgers. Thus, Francis grew into a small friendly community surrounding the nuclear family, which provided some social recompense to the isolating mantra of the good Dr. King. In her interview with us, his second wife, Meloma Balaskas, remembered her first meeting with Juliette and provides a telling coda to the story of Dr. King and the damage he helped propagate.

> I was 26-years-old. Francis, 52. She is in her 80s. Being married I now have to meet her, and she thinks "who the hell?" We weren't really that close, but we had a connection through that. Francis didn't really have a strong connection with his family, with his father, with his brother. Julian, for Francis was a horrible old sick fart. His father died and I did the cooking. The day Francis' father died, I was driving a bit fast and a cat, like a spirit or something, came off and the cat was killed. When I got back to Francis, he told me that his father died hours ago, the time the cat died. One of those weird moments. He was so unconventional. Francis was so under nurtured in his childhood. Because of what Dr. King told his mum – never touch your children at all, unless you can touch them, when you feed them and change the nappies. He would later apologise publicly to the whole nation. Francis suffered. He was so terribly under nurtured.[33]

## Move to London

In 1925, Julian was appointed Professor of Zoology at King's College. For Juliette, it meant moving away from her 'fixed star,' Lady Ottoline, who continuously helped her former employee in times of trouble. House hunting brought them to the spacious abode of number 31 Hillway, in Highgate, North London. The family stayed there until 1932, enabling Francis the luxury of strolling up the hill to his prep school at Byron House. Juliette would take the boys to Hampstead Heath, where the brothers sailed their toy boats and learnt to cycle. It was at Hillway that Francis' health began to cause concern. Juliette notes that "he seemed to catch every illness," the list included measles, whooping cough and eye trouble, but worse was to come as he woke one morning to the signs of Bell's Palsy. Juliette's anxiety was compounded by the fact that Julian had neither the time nor the patience to play with his sons. Moments of reprieve were few but once in a while Juliette's mother would take Anthony and Francis to Bel-Air and there in their Swiss homeland open her heart to them in a wonderful and carefree manner. She found them both intelligent, adventurous and patient.

Juliette, overburdened and still unable to confide in Julian, was often anxious and stressed with the rota of her taxing responsibilities, especially dealing with Francis' health troubles, which Francis himself, from the outside at least, seemed to "bore ... with a strange patience and courage."[34] Julian on the other hand was typically impatient, and did not adapt well to fatherhood. A year into his Professorship at King's he was invited by H. G. Wells to collaborate with him and his son in writing *The Science of Life*. The lure of being part of such a writing adventure, proved too tempting to Julian. The financial stability afforded by the chair at King's was thrown to the wolves, as he resigned his position in favour of dedicating himself to freelance writing. He maintained his academic tries, however, as honorary lecturer as well as Fullerian Professor of Physiology at the Royal Institution. By the time he was appointed Secretary of the Zoological Society of London, in 1935, he had penned 14 books.

Writing with H. G. Wells, he shadowed his elders' dubious sexual morals by pursuing a young American girl, Viola Ilma to the USA. Captivated by his own self-belief, he swore to capture her "with my mind," and almost completely abandoned his family. Once Leonard got wind of the behaviour from his eldest, he intervened, telling Julian that if he did not immediately "cease all communication" with his lover, then "he did not wish to see him again." Despite this "Julian refused to accept such a condition, Juliette refused to intervene on his behalf, and Leonard was soon to die with the breach unhealed."[35] As the self-appointed Don Juan of the biological world, Julian followed up the liaison with Viola Ilma with an affair with the poet and novelist May Sarton. Sarton played along, flattered by the famous Huxley. Juliette's response to this madness of psyche and Eros, was an agonising cry: "Must I be made miserable so that you can be happy?"[36]

To all extents and purposes, Julian appeared more interested in the scorching erotic potential of young ladies, than in his sons, their talents or their development. His books, lectures and public position as a populariser of science were also of greater importance than the family. Summing up his father, for good and ill, Francis wrote:

Julian's character included a reticent if strangely noble element: he did not gossip in the way I understand the word; he was not given to profanity ... There was no malice in him, nor did he harbour resentment against those who did him in; and what Juliette found alarming, for her sake as well as his, was his lack of both insight and interest into the character and motives of people, himself included.[37]

## Double lovers

After Julian, May Sarton (1912–1995) would later also become lovers with Juliette. It was Francis who permitted Sarton's letters to Juliette to be published, writing a moving preface to the collection in which Sarton's final visit to his mother – then aged 97 – is described. The Huxley's 'ménage à trois' with Sarton was filled with dishonesty, clandestine meetings, cruelty, selfishness, narcissistic misery, pain and deception. Julian, 24 years her senior, was her father's age. His affairs with much younger women echoed through his son's life. Three times, Francis would marry women who were over 25 years younger than himself.

In 1937, when the 25-year-old May took up with Julian, Juliette was 41 and Francis 14. May was allowed to stay at their country apartment at Whipsnade Zoo. Through Juliette, she met for tea with T. S. Eliot, Samuel Koteliansky, Virginia Woolf and other grandees in the Huxley circle. When May first attempted to seduce Juliette, Juliette withdrew, granting her free reign to her husband. "Julian was not a good lover," Sarton remarked. "I always felt a bit like a nurse, rather than a mistress. He was neurotic, often ill."[38] As a lesbian, she desired Juliette more, yet despite her inner rage, still allowed Julian to exert his sexual demands on her. What she wanted with Julian was a more spiritual love, for the physical side of their relationship was,

> a repetition of the hell that Julian can create. He was having an affair with another woman. A relief, but terrible for Juliette, who didn't know. And terrible for Julian, this constantly seeking "intoxication and pleasure" instead of love and understanding.[39]

To ease his conscience, Julian suggested to Juliette that she embark on affairs on her own. She eventually had one with Alan Best, a then assistant director at the London Zoo. Juliette was more than likely aware of the propensity that her sons might follow the example set by their father. This, as we shall later see, had consequences. Despite this turmoil, Juliette was, according to Susie Huxley,

> wonderful with the children. She came out to visit us in Istanbul in the 1970s and ate and drank us under the table. She taught stories to our children and would sit for hours reading with and to them. She was a charming woman and mellowed as she got older. But if you think of being married to Julian, you have to have a certain amount of strength.[40]

From London, Julian and Juliette moved to Paris as Julian worked on setting up UNESCO. In the eyes of May Sarton, Juliette's accompanying elevation in high society, now made her even more of a sexual prey to be had. May would not rest until she could possess Juliette physically. Juliette – unaccustomed to a sexual relationship with another woman, and a degree of ambivalence due to May having been Julian's lover – felt unprepared for Sarton's desires. May, for her part, constantly required a muse – and frequently a new one, usually a woman – to keep her creative powers in full flow. Juliette, finding herself in a similar position to Julian before her, struggled to keep her emotions in check and their eventual love making a secret. She was aware of the dangers present in May's insistent narcissism and on occasions insincerity. After they became lovers in Paris, Sarton threatened to tell all to Julian. This horrified Juliette, for their pact was to keep their affair secret. "I really felt betrayed," Juliette wrote to May, and asked her to burn all her letters. May had told their mutual friend, Kot, about their affair, blind to the consequences. They both subsequently cut their ties with her. This infuriated May, and made her painfully aware, that as well as losing two valuable pillars of support, she remained outside the literary establishment.

After a 27-year hiatus, and only after Julian had died, Sarton once more contacted Juliette. Once Juliette had read May's letters to Julian she experienced "a posthumous shock." As for her own letters from May, she had most of them burnt. With Julian gone and the hurt of bitter betrayal mellowed by time, they renewed their correspondence. It is of interest that Juliette chose not to mention their relationship in her autobiography. Asked about this by May, she explained that having excised the requisite pages in which May featured, she could hardly put them back in. With this act of literary excision, she enacted revenge for past hurts. When May came to London once more, in October 1990, Juliette asked Francis not to leave the two alone, for "she frightens me." Francis heeded his mother's pleas.

## Nervous breakdowns

Prior to meeting Juliette Baillot, Julian had previously been unofficially engaged to a young woman, Kathleen Fordham. In 1912 Julian had been invited to set up the biology department in Rice University, in Houston. He returned from his first visit to Texas with ambiguous feelings for Kathleen. Francis provides Julian's account of what transpired when she came to visit him. "it was a painful scene; she took off her ring and thrust it at me, got up, kissed a photograph of me hanging on the wall, burst into tears and rushed out of the house."[41] In this aftermath Julian suffered a nervous collapse and entered the same rest home, where his brother, Trev, was dealing with his own turmoil.

Julian's emotional difficulties followed him throughout his life. In this respect he was not dissimilar to his grandfather, T. H. Huxley, whose black moods were well-known. In both their cases, 'the black dog'[42] as T. H. referred to it, these difficulties followed prolonged periods of intense work. Julian's dark moods weren't confined to periods of exhaustion and depression. He was also well-known for his inconsiderate behaviour and ill-temper. For example, when he and Juliette visited cousin Gervas, in 1955, Elspeth, Gervas' wife, found him "rude, vain and selfish."[43] Gervas, by then, was busy writing his first book, *Talking of Tea*, which was to hit the stands the following year, as was Francis' *Affable Savages*.

How family members contemplated the emotional troubles that attached themselves to family members is of interest. When Juliette chided Julian for his bad temper, she would remark that "you have a demon in you." He could have replied "I've known that since I was four years old" since that was how he saw it too. The attribution of a seemingly 'alien' force as responsible for the emotional instability, of course, does nothing to aid taking responsibility for dealing with it. This must be seen in context however. As a biologist Julian would have been only too aware of the dominating influence of biology in the scientific establishment's efforts to situate states of mental well-being within its domain.

Julian came to accept that he 'had' these nervous breakdowns, thrust upon him like an unwelcome visitor. His first breakdown was labelled as an instance of 'mild depression' for which he spent time in a nursing home. Three months after he married Juliette, in 1919, he had another. Juliette took him to Lausanne, Switzerland to see a doctor there, Roger Vittoz, who had written an influential book about nervous conditions. Julian wasn't thought very sick at the time, though at others he could swing from untouchable euphoria to sudden collapse. Vittoz, originally a GP, specialised in nervous conditions with reference to psychosomatic complaints. He first practiced the hypnosis he had learned with Dr. August Forel. This method was abandoned when Vittoz came to the view that it left the patient too dependent on the therapist. Vittoz wanted the patient to find their own autonomy, believing in the capacity of the soul to heal itself. Julian recovered and had no further breakdowns until 1944. Two more followed this, a prolonged and serious one from 1951 to 1952 and a final episode in 1966. He had a slight stroke in 1973 from which he only partially recovered. Francis related how, after this, he was never the same again and that in the writing of both volumes of his memoires, Juliette took a large hand.

## Independence

With the example set by his parents it is, perhaps, not surprising that Francis did not want any children. He rationalised this as not wanting to continue the family's madness. Like his great-grandfather, Francis did not deny Christian feelings, yet had little time for 'do-gooders' and missionaries of all creeds. In so far as he did not suffer fools gladly, he followed in the Huxley tradition. At the same time, he displayed a disposition fully in keeping with the Arnolds, travelling widely, knowing many a poem and classical dictums by heart, and being knowledgeable to a degree which is now uncommon.

Adele Getty, Francis' third wife, felt that the issues around Francis' father had a lot to do with "Julian being a walking contradiction."

> He (Julian) certainly influenced the world, yet never really showed up as a father. Juliette also had a very hard time with Julian. She had also talked endlessly about him. She said: "Every night I go to bed and Julian is on my pillow." Her biggest fear was when she died, he would be there on the other side. Julian wasn't mean or horrible. He had a lot of contradictions. As for Julian's ego and their honeymoon story. Juliette was wondering, why they were not in their room mating, because Julian was watching birds. These stories impacted upon Francis. Why didn't Juliette not go off or divorce Julian? Julian's affairs. Juliette once put the boys in the car and drove to the cliffs of Dover, to drive off them, but deciding against that. Francis would repeat the stories and the lack of Julian being a good father.[44]

Michael Schwab relayed a telling exchange between Francis and his father which Francis had shared. Francis had just presented Julian with a copy of his first book. "Perhaps you could read it and let me know what you think" Julian's response was "Aha." Two weeks later Julian gave the book back. He never read it or had anything to say about it.

## Brother Anthony

Anthony and Francis were not particularly close. When they were children, Anthony bullied Francis and only stopped when Francis eventually got the better of him. Francis, so two of his wives told us, really wanted to be closer. Anthony, though, rarely visited them, as his second wife, Alyson wouldn't have it. He lived on the other side of London. Anthony's eldest daughter, Susie, assesses the difference between the brothers as follows:

> Francis was a younger son, Anthony being the older brother, who worked and raised a family like a proper grown-up. In contrast there's Francis meandering around the world. Fascinating of course, and leading a wonderful life. I think that granny put up a lot in order to keep him. He was helping her with the biography, so there was a sort of trade-off.[45]

Like Francis, Anthony had his qualms about Julian. Victoria Huxley, Anthony's third daughter, when asked about this, said:

> Oh yes, as I said Julian would never stop talking. In his later years, somebody quite famous came to tea ... Someone quite learned. My grandfather wouldn't stop talking of his personal interests and achievements. This other man let my grandfather go on. The others were quiet. My father and Francis were furious afterwards.

Anthony Julian Huxley, horticulturist, botanist, writer and photographer, earned his reputation more with his pen than his spade. When not at boarding school much of his childhood, like Francis', was spent in the London Zoo. Come the Second World War, Francis joined the Royal Navy and Anthony the Royal Air Force (RAF). The same year that Francis' studies in anthropology got underway (1949) Anthony began a 22-year association with the mass-selling weekly *Amateur Gardening*. As of 1971 he became, like his father and uncle, a freelance writer. Professionally, Anthony brought the Huxley love of nature and a botanist's mind to the garden and immersed himself in the encyclopaedic world of plants. He wrote, co-wrote or compiled almost 40 books. Away from the professional side of life, Victoria Huxley enables us to fill in an important, more personal aspect of Anthony's story.

> My father and mother met in the RAF. They had to get married because of the pregnancy with Susan. Father and mother were both twenty-three years old. Just a month between them. Mother was the older one. When they went to see Juliette – no woman was good enough for her sons – she wanted to terminate the pregnancy and said it could be arranged. Julian intervened when he heard it. He said they should get married when in love. That's what happened.

And Victoria continued:

> Francis suffered the same faith when he wanted to marry Ferelyth. She was very controlling, my grandmother. She liked Adele, but I don't think she liked my father's second wife, Alyson. It ended very badly.[46]

These events are of considerable significance and we will return to them in due course when we come to discuss Francis' love life.

When Anthony died, Theodor came over to London, on Adele's wish, to stay with Francis and lend support. Unsurprisingly both he and his mother were in very low spirits. Victoria continues the narrative:

> It was a terrible time for us all. For Juliette it was awful. I had to organise my father's funeral. I was forty-four at the time. My father had power of attorney about my grandmother. Francis took over and wanted to move my grandmother near New Mexico. I had a huge row about this with him. I said, you couldn't even get her to the airport, she was so frail. Francis was very angry about this anyway. It was a very bad time between us. After granny died, he phoned me up, or he wrote to me, saying now she has died, we must patch it up, which we did.

But the difficulties for Victoria and the complications set in motion by Anthony's death extended well beyond the rift with Francis over what to do about Juliette.

> We got nothing from the sale of the Pond Street family house at all. Everything went to Alyson. My father had already cut us out of his will and when his and Alyson's daughter, Zoe, was born. He phoned me up one day and said, it was typical of him: "I want you to know, I cut you and your sister out of my will. I got married again. Now we've got a child, and everything is going to them." Because my father had died, it all went to Alyson.[47]

## Coda

To the outside world, the Huxley name is equated with erudition and correctness. It must not be forgotten that family members invariably find themselves asked to deal with the matrix of beliefs, expectations and values which have become 'synonymous' with their heritage. Susie gave an indication as to how this was still operative in her generation.

> The only time it really affected me; the Huxleys that is, was when they wanted to show me off. I got this long letter from Juliette asking me if I want to go and work on a farm in Ohio. Those hosts wanted to show me off because I am a Huxley, as Julian got me a job there.[48]

We ought not to underestimate the toll this cloud of expectations takes. What Francis did with his talents, and how he married the possibilities before him with the actualities of his family's past will, in large measure, be the subject of Chapter 4. First, we must turn to Aldous who, within the Huxley clan, exerted, possibly, the most significant influence on Francis.

## Notes

1. Huxley, J. (1986) *Leaves of the Tulip Tree*. London. John Murray.
2. Master Tinsmith, a title dating back to the age of guilds. The Master Tinsmith would obtain mandates, establish offers, manage employees, maintain contact with customers and was responsible for the overall processing of an order. At a stretch, one may discern echoes of the educational role this embodied in Francis' running of the General Study Programme of the Philadelphia Association in the 1970s.
3. Huxley, J. (1986, p.3).
4. Ibid., p.3.
5. Ibid., p.4.
6. Ibid., p.19.
7. Susie Huxley, Interview, 14 March 2018 in London.
8. Now, Lycée Jean Piaget.
9. Francis Huxley: *A Huxley Family Album*. Unpublished MS p.15. Francis Huxley Archive.
10. Huxley, J. (1986, pp.29–56).
11. *A Huxley Family Album*. p.16.

12 Morrell, O. (1975, p.34 and fn. 1) *Ottoline at Garsington. Memoirs of Lady Ottoline Morrell 1915–1918*. Edited R. G. Gathorne-Hardy. New York. A. A. Knopf. "I remember her as a singularly beautiful young woman."
13 Interview, 14 March 2018. London.
14 Interview, 15 March 2018. Oxford.
15 The very same year, Theodor met Francis for the first time in a lecture hall.
16 *A Huxley Family Album*, p.15.
17 Trevor, M. (1973) *The Arnolds – Thomas Arnold and His Family*. London. Bodley Head.
18 Personal communication to Theodor Itten.
19 Trever (1973, p.176).
20 See Clarke, R. (1968, p.130) *The Huxleys*. London. Heinemann.
21 Huxley, J. (1970, p.142). *Memories*. London. George Allen & Unwin.

> Francis, our second son, was born in 1923 at 8 Holywell. He too turned out to be very able – perhaps not so scientifically precise as Anthony, but with a more embracing imagination, which let him into out-of-the-way corners of human activity – investigating the vanishing rituals of South American Indians; Haitian voodoo; the effects on drugs on the human mind; psychiatry and the interactions of mind and body, and paranormal happenings like telepathy.

22 This will be discussed further in Chapter 4.
23 Huxley, J. (1927, pp.107–108) *Religion without Revelation*. London. Ernest Benn Ltd. This book is dedicated to the memory of his mother.
24 *A Huxley Family Album*, p.5.
25 Huxley, F. (1999, p.14) Foreword to "Dear Juliette." In. *Letters of May Sarton to Juliette Huxley*. Ed. Susan Sherman. New York. W. W. Norton.
26 Published in Huxley, F. (1999, p.14).
27 *A Huxley Family Album*, pp.17–18.
28 Having already published several papers on the "Courtship of Redshank and The Great Crested Grebe" (see Green, J.-P. [1978, p.62] Bibliography of Sir Julian Huxley. In *Julian Huxley – Scientist and World Citizen*, pp.53–184. UNESCO). His honeymoon research was published in November 1919, as "Some Points in the Sexual Habits of the Little Grebe, with a Note on the Occurrence of Vocal Duets in Birds." *British Birds*, 13 (6), pp.155–158. Only in 1968 did Julian Huxley publish his book on *The Courtship Habits of the Great Crested Grebe*, with a foreword by Desmond Morris. London. Cape Editions.
29 Huxley, J. (1986, p.74).
30 *A Huxley Family Album*, p.19.
31 Personal communication. Francis also called Cumae, the Duchess of Wagnon.
32 Huxley, J. (1986, pp.106–107).
33 Interviewed on 16 October 2018.
34 Huxley, J. (1986, p.110).
35 *A Huxley Family Album*, p.23.
36 Huxley, F. (1999, p.14).
37 *A Huxley Family Album*, pp.2–3.
38 Peters, M. (1997, p.112) *May Sarton – A Biography*. New York. Fawcett Columbine.
39 Ibid., p.125.

30  *Family life, ancestry and haunting*

40  Interview, 14 March 2018 in London.
41  *A Huxley Family Album*, p.12.
42  The expression, though it is often associated with Winston Churchill, has a much longer history. Samuel Johnson, for example, used it in a letter to James Boswell in 1779.
43  Nicholls, C. S. (2003, p.270) *Elisabeth Huxley, A Biography*. London. Harper Collins.
44  Adele Getty interviewed in April 2018 in Sebastopol.
45  Interviewed in March 2018.
46  Interviewed in March 2018 in Oxford.
47  Interviewed in March 2018 in Oxford.
48  Interviewed on 14 March 2018 in London.

# 3   Uncle Aldous

To understand Francis – as a Huxley – in a way beyond what we can clearly discern of him through his diverse writings and their relation to the collected works of his famed relatives, we need to understand his uncle – Aldous – whose influence was profound. We can say from the outset that Francis' relationship with Aldous shaped him in more distinct ways than his relationship with his own father. Francis felt a close reciprocal bond existed with this uncle. Noel Annan, the former military intelligence officer – later Lord Annan – author of the post-war classic *Our Age* which had considered the Huxley family to be prominent members of the intellectual aristocracy – lined up Aldous Huxley alongside Robert Graves, as a new breed of rebellious charges confronting pacifism, fascism and communism.

Aldous was the celebrated novelist, thought by many to have shone a guiding light on the unfolding tragedies of the 20th century. In his dystopian novel *Brave New World,* he anticipated the development of both test-tube fertilisation and the pharmacological manufacture of happiness to maintain social stability. Francis appreciated his uncle's prescient warnings of political tyranny and psychopathic destruction. During 1947, his father Julian and Aldous were feted in *LIFE* magazine as 'The Huxley Brothers' who, as Thomas' grandsons, extended the family fame. Aldous is introduced as a "mystic novelist," Julian the "atheistic head of UNESCO"[1] as if together, Janus-faced, they stared upon the mysteries of earthly existence. To single out, from the myriad complexity of facts surrounding the person of Aldous Huxley, the precise reach and extent of his influence upon the life of Francis is perhaps too great a task – but we can begin by highlighting those selected (and contextualised) aspects of Aldous' much commented upon life which we consider to have a bearing on Francis' own.

## Aldous Huxley – early life

Francis opened his book *The Way of the Sacred* in uncompromising terms. "The man who goes beyond appearances is a searcher after truth."[2] Since the days of T. H. Huxley it had become something of a family creed to deal with the world as it is given to us, to place trust in observation and to skirt the temptations of 'make-believe' and faith. His father Julian acquired an identity early on. He was seen, like his grandfather, as a budding scientist, whilst of Julian's brothers, Trevenen was cast as the humanist with Aldous somewhere in between – seen by others as aloof and critical. Julian, seeking to supersede his father Leonard's knowledge of birds, became obsessed with the naming and categorisation of nature. By all accounts he was something of a bully and Trevenen frequently bore the brunt of it.

Aldous' critical, sometimes blunt attitude was oft noted, together with a tendency to withdraw behind an enigmatic smile. His performance taken, even at a young age, as a demonstration that he was a superior being. Despite this he was well liked, considered funny and entertaining, and capable of accurately imitating others. When it came to his father, this could take the appearance of indifferent cruelty.

Aldous was 14 when his mother Julia died. She had been regarded as a charming and engaging teacher, with high intellectual standards and religious principles that transcended sectarianism. Francis writes that "she allowed her students more freedom than it is generally thought good for children, during the Victorian period."[3] Her laissez-faire attitude was firmly imprinted in the minds of her children. In his novel *Antic Hay* (1932), Aldous writes about Julia's beneficence, and wonders why goodness always seems to go hand-in-hand with fatal weakness.

On Julia's death, younger members of the family, especially Aldous, his sister Margaret and Trevenen, were farmed out to other family members – Aldous to his aunt, Mary Humphry Ward, then the grand novelist in the family. At this time Julian was gaining recognition for his scientific endeavours and Trevenen, now at Eaton, acquiring a reputation for amiability, brightness and a sensibility more attuned to people than science books. Soon afterwards Aldous was hit by a serious eye infection, *keratitis punktata,* diagnosed belatedly by his uncle, Dr. Henry Huxley, when by chance he was visiting his nephew. The late diagnosis meant a cure was not possible and Aldous suffered complete blindness for almost 18 months. Henry Huxley took charge of Aldous' medical problems, while his education was assisted by private tutors and the fraternal aid of his older brother. Trevenen read books to Aldous and helped him to learn Braille and play the piano. Taught how to use a typewriter, Aldous wrote his first novel which he shared only with Trevenen. One is struck by an identifiable parallel with Francis here, who as a child succumbed to Bell's Palsy. This too went unrecognised for a time and left Francis with a lifetime paralysis on the left side of his face and on his forehead. Further parallels in their lives are to be found. Aldous had three of his early poems published in *The Nation*, a UK-political weekly newspaper (later to merge with the *New Statesman*) which mistakenly attributed the copyright to Leonard. Something similarly untoward happened to Francis when his father Julian was given the copyright for the first paperback edition of *Affable Savages*. Both too passed their undergraduates lives at Balliol College, Oxford.

## Garsington Manor and Ottoline Morrell

When Aldous arrived at Ottoline Morrell's Garsington Manor in 1915, he was still a final-year student at Balliol. Regarded by all who met her as a phenomenal woman, of striking appearance and incessant warmth – particularly towards the disaffected artists and intellectuals who flocked to Garsington – Morrell designed her own outrageous line of clothes and, as the grand-society hostess, created a distinct and welcoming ambience for young writers, who like Aldous, were finding their feet in a perplexing world and needed a social and political bay in which to lay anchor. They repaid her hospitality not always as she would have liked. For all her ostensible popularity, Ottoline Morrell was often parodied by the writers in her brood; both D. H. Lawrence, in *Women in Love* and Aldous in *Chrome Yellow*, created an unflattering image of a frustrated, faintly ridiculous artist. Ottoline, for her part, found Lawrence, for all his poetic flair and communion with the divine infinite, "impatient" and "violent." One cannot help but wonder whether the divergence in their respective class backgrounds both inflamed Lawrence's behaviour and Ottoline's view of him. But the problematics of class were never addressed head on in the Bloomsbury circle. They would have other fish to fry. In a way, however, what was off the Bloomsbury menu would return to heat the intellectual and social climate within which Francis would himself later dine.

Lawrence deeply impressed Aldous on a number of fronts – his love of life, trust in the primacy of the instincts and his predilection for doing household chores, a habit unheard of in Aldous' social set. Aldous learnt of Lawrence's extraordinary method of writing novels. If something displeased him, he would be apt to rewrite the entire novel from scratch, rather than reworking and editing it – the primacy of the play of 'instinct' once again. Both Julian and Aldous found their future spouses in Ottoline's abode. In her eyes she had become a marriage bureau for the Huxleys. What we know now is that Francis' mother, Juliette, took a shine to Aldous well before Julian. Unfortunately for Juliette, Aldous courted Maria Nys, a Belgian refuge, five years his junior. After initially hesitating Maria duly consented. Perhaps for Juliette, being with Julian meant that she could, as sister-in-law, hope to remain in emotional proximity to Aldous.

The people Aldous met at Garsington (he eventually left in 1917 to teach at Eaton) were to become life-long friends of his and Juliette – T. H. Laurence, Bertrand Russell, Katherine Mansfield, Lytton Strachey, Clive Bell and Virginia Woolf. The enriching conversation and tensions among this assortment of dissenting novelists, philosophers, biographers, artists and poets both shaped and sharpened Aldous' imagination. Ottoline Morrell devoted a whole chapter to Aldous in her memoirs. She writes of him falling in love with Maria, having been scorned by the painter Dora Carrington, who "fluttered from one to another." As she did so "Maria sat still, silent and receptive, her pale magnolia face and beautiful dark eyes gazing out in a pathetic appeal ... That was the magnet that attracted Aldous."[4] On searing hot summer nights, a foursome of Juliette, Aldous, Julian and Dora conversed beneath the moonlight and slept on the roof of Garsington.

In due course, Aldous worked for the Air Board in London, living with Leonard's family and hoping to earn enough to foster a marriage proposal to Maria, whom, now residing in Napoli, he was missing. In 1919 they married in Belgium, settling in London a year later. Julian and Juliette were wed the same year, setting up home in Oxford. Aldous, more than Juliette, became close to the Bloomsbury Group, though it was not to last. J. G. Ballard considered his association with them a factor in his "decline." To him the Bloomsbury Group were "that bloodless set who haunt English letters like a coterie of haemophiliac royals."[5] Aldous survived because he had,

> far deeper roots in the Victorian age, with a rich mix of high-mindedness and a secure moral compass that we find baffling in our culture of soundbite philosophy.[6]

When Aldous' first novel, *Chrome Yellow* appeared in 1921, he modelled his characters on the people he encountered at Garsington – but "distorted, caricatured and mocked" them. Ottoline was hurt and horrified. She felt he not only dishonoured himself but implicated her in his cruel caricaturing. She, after all, had been the one to invite him into her home, giving him the once in a lifetime opportunity to meet these cultivated people. He had transposed conversations and arguments, by Bertrand Russell, Mark Gertler and others, with little attempt to disguise them. On learning of her hurt, Aldous reacted bewildered and defensively.

> I cannot understand how anyone could suppose that this little marionette performance of mine was the picture of the real *milieu* – it so obviously isn't ... I write something which seems to me immediately and obviously comprehensible for what it is. You, running on your parallel, read into it meaning I never so much dreamt of. Others on their parallels, find other meanings and contemptuous portraits of people unknown to you.[7]

## The unity of difference: Aldous and Francis

What Morrell had been subjected to under the cover of literary expression and artistic licence also came Francis' way – a disingenuous literary parallelism violating his nephew's honour and decency. Francis came to realise that this was how his uncle functioned when his literary imagination deserted him. Aldous' detachment meant that he was almost an outsider when it came to contending with the human condition. Francis, in contrast opted to immerse himself into the human mystery. The hidden symmetry between the two, however, was the manner in which they each pursued a kind of mythological quest to frame the relationship between human beings and the sacred.

This symmetry leads us to pause for a moment to consider the diverse emotional histories and circumstances which supply the present, and the extent to which we may glimpse the zig-zag lines of logic which bind them. To borrow a biological metaphor, Aldous and Francis together constitute a veiled form of convergent intellectual development – however manifestly different they appeared. Some of the more obscure writings which Francis produced suggest an awareness of the perverse logic which can underlie such 'twin' tracks of development. In the *Raven and the Writing Desk*, for example, Francis' explored the 'rules' of the game which shored up Lewis Carroll's venture down the 'rabbit hole.' Throughout, Francis iterates what he believes constitute the laws of Carroll's 'looking-glass world.' It is a game of 'Anglo-Saxon attitudes,' the first rule of which is that "you can come and go simultaneously as long as there are two of you."[8]

Perhaps Francis had a sense that he and his uncle were complementary beings in a Carrollian looking-glass world. A factor in this, no doubt, was that Francis resembled Aldous a good deal more than he did Julian, adorned as he was with blue eyes and fair longish hair which was usually swept back over his high forehead. One must not forget too, that the Arnold girls, Julia (Francis' Grandmother) and Mary Augusta, had themselves known Carroll when they were young girls – a fact of which Francis was aware. Thus, there were very real historical family ties that linked the Huxleys and Carroll. The effects of Carroll's strange life and his literary outpourings of strangeness can be considered as an echo, which over the years, reverberated through the conscious and unconscious lives of those families. In Aldous and Francis, we have two Huxleys weighed down with a vast family and literary heritage, passporting them to write, through the shadows of their inner inclinations. These come out of the page as indirect communications, expressing seemingly impenetrable truths, that must be read between the lines to make them bearable.

Perhaps these obscure threads are of a kind which conjoin people of different generations in ways they can hardly countenance – part of the unconscious fabric of the family hauntings we will later discuss. But for now, we wish to emphasise that hidden in the diverse writings of Aldous and Francis is an open secret, to be spotted not only about the relationship between them but of the path to redemption which each follows to be human. In other words, they followed not a religion without revelation as Julian did, but expressed a 'symmetrical bond' which requires revelation and they each sought it in the realms of the mysterious. The writings of R. D. Laing aside, these kinds of human entanglement are seldom discussed in the human sciences. Musings on the unity of opposites are, however, to be found in sacred and theological writings.

Aldous casually visited Julian in his biology lab, viewing Julian's experiments on the axolotl newt. By injecting the newt with thyroid, Julian caused it to shed its gills and become sexually mature ahead of time. The newspapers heralded Julian as the discoverer of the elixir of life and by such nonsense helped facilitate his career as a populariser of science. Aldous was always very interested in what Julian is doing and was proud of him but adopted a fairly ambiguous attitude towards science himself – alternating between utopian and dystopian misgivings. To be a Huxley, for both Aldous and Francis, meant taking a different stance towards the adoration of science that had originally propelled the Huxley name into the limelight.

**Doctoring the text**

Aldous turned to literature when the problems with his eyesight foreclosed the possibilities of a medical career. Charles Mason Holmes has argued that Aldous, under the shadow of the legacy from T. H. Huxley, remained fascinated with the workings of science. Because of this he strove to bring what he considered a scientific attitude to what he saw so that he became a "concerned observer of all the major problems facing the world." This motivated his approach to psychedelia and his beliefs that a technocratic elite was best placed to govern. Aldous' elevation of the scientific community to a level of wisdom beyond what was warranted, may be read as an effort to compensate for the absence of opportunity fate had bestowed upon him. The chances to practice this kind of science by proxy in the course of his writing were, however, infrequent.

> Most frequently, perhaps, he appears as a harried professional writer who, forced to write, sometimes avidly for money, had the next book in mind before the present one was finished; one, who struggled in some of his books to meet high literary standards.[9]

The environment which Aldous created for himself when writing, unfortunately, was not always conducive to others' well-being. Trev, his grandson, though sympathetic, recalls that Aldous could easily withdraw attention from those around him.

There are numerous analytic studies of Aldous Huxley's writing achievements, covering the length and breadth of the novels, essays and poems which he published. His success did not come easy. The years 1934–1935 were characterised by one commentator as the most "unhappy and unproductive" in his entire life.[10] In autumn 1935 he began a course of body-psychotherapy with the Australian F. M. Alexander, whose approach, the "Alexander-Technique," Aldous helped to advertise. Alexander got him back on track with self-empowerment exercises to hold his body up. Alexander was heavily influenced by the Maverick psychoanalyst Wilhelm Reich who had originally suggested that patterns of muscular and physical tension were the physical traces in the body of a person's history of conflict and distress. It was Reich we must thank for the term "sexual politics," a rich and dense phrase which has lost none of its power.

Juliette Huxley thought one of the problems Aldous faced as a writer was a constant struggle between expressing his ideas in fictional versus essayist form. Notwithstanding this, Aldous' reputation in his own lifetime was immense, and his exploration of writing, in both style and form – had, from an early age, an inspirational effect on Francis. It must be said, however, that in comparison to Aldous, Francis had a more judicious attitude towards the kinds of problems which can accrue from the misapplication or over-extension of scientific reasoning. Nevertheless, there were shared ventures and interests – not the least of which was parapsychology. In this domain they shared an acquaintance with Eileen Garret – whose purported gifts, have not withstood the scrutiny to which they have been subject. Francis notes that in 1955, both he and Aldous attended an International Symposium run by Garrett on the French Riviera – an attractive enough destination to probe the non-materiality of existence!

One of the next conferences (in 1959) – on *The Study of Precognition: Evidence and Methods* – saw Francis on the organisational committee. This one, held in New York, where Francis was spending increasing amounts of time, focused on the social psychological methodology in the study of precognition, and the history of research on spontaneous and experimental precognition. Francis was now in a position to introduce Aldous to his own array of professional contacts and proceeded to make his own scientific mark with a brilliant essay on Darwin – this was precisely the kind of essay – rich in its understanding and nuanced interpretation of one of science's leading figures – that would forever be beyond Aldous' ability to duplicate. At this time, fully immersed in Darwinian thought, Francis planned a film on Darwin with his sister-in-law, Ellen, a filmmaker of note.

## Telling tales

Biography, as Deirdre Bair has stated, is a form of critical enquiry, a means to interrogate our own cultural and intellectual history and throw an interpretive light into the shadowy recesses of our own society and our own ways of living. With this in mind, we may ask, how exactly did Aldous' life influence Francis and in what way did Francis weave his uncle's cultural, philosophical and intellectual lights into his own?

Francis had spent time with Aldous when he was four years old. Both Julian and Aldous had taken their wives and children for a winter's vacation in Switzerland. Back up was provided by Juliette's mother, Granny Baillot. D. H. Lawrence and Frieda von Richthofen joined them. Francis always felt it was a pity, that he couldn't remember anything about this event. However, he did recall visiting Aldous when he was living off Piccadilly, in Albany. His parents would visit and took their sons along. By the time he was 20 years of age, ready to join the Royal Navy, and to let his ideas of life meet the raw facts of experience, his uncle had become the most famous of all the Huxleys, toppling the notoriety even of his grandfather, Thomas Henry. Aldous was certainly a powerful presence in Francis' youth and continued to be so, even when Francis had established his own place in the family and the larger Huxley world. Considering Aldous and Francis together we note, a predilection for travel, to encounter diverse forms of human life and experience; a desire to filter these through both the heart and mind and to subsequently ask questions about ourselves as a species. The results did not always lead to an accumulation of wisdom. But the errors of the Huxleys are as instructive as their heralded successes.

In the course of his life Francis developed a reputation as a raconteur. His storytelling prowess, coupled with his closeness to Aldous led his parents to ask, after Aldous had died, whether he would take on the task of writing Aldous' biography. He declined, feeling this was beyond his capability, although by the mid-1980s he undertook to write a script for a biographical film of his uncle.

Compared to his tall, skinny, awkward, highly intellectual, rather remote and slightly cynical uncle, Francis was not content to just sit and absorb facts, ideas and the latest scientific news. Sometimes the conversations with his uncle were enforced monologues punctuated, and produced by Aldous' silence and shyness – the results of his near blindness. Aldous could absorb a good deal about the world in this fashion. Ottoline Morrell had noted that "Maria is his source of information about the majority of living people; indeed, she told me, that he had seen life through her eyes." But it is telling that Morrell's assessment of Maria's personality was not a generous one, for she found her perception and understanding of people's behaviour and experience, cheap and weary.[11]

Francis had recently published his first book *Affable Savages*, when he happened to be on a two-week stay with Aldous and Laura (after Maria died), at their home in Los Angeles – "a slightly mystifying time for both of us" he said.[12] Francis takes up the story – one of his all-time favourites.

> In 1956, he and Laura invited me to supper. I had just had my first book on the Brazilian Indians, *Affable Savages*, published and Laura provoked me to say, "So what are they like?" So, I started telling stories about these Indians. I dredged up the more grotesque and remarkable anecdotes that I could think of. Laura was delighted. Aldous kept on eating his lunch, and never said anything. I went away feeling that I had fallen into the adolescent forms of mania and had vastly disappointed my dear uncle Aldous, whom I really had wished to impress. I went away very cross with myself. Two or three days later I went to see Eileen Garrett, who told me that Aldous had been around telling all my stories and roaring with laughter as he told them.[13]

Francis' own laughter in telling this tale may well have been imbued with pain. His personal fieldnotes from Haiti provide some inkling of why that might have been.

Aldous, when he gets going, what marvellous stream of converse! And when he doesn't, how small he can make you feel, just by not talking. I feel pretty small in any case, even if he does talk; my style of talking is always trying to become something like his, so that I feel, when exposing him to it, that I am cheating in some undefinable but not very nice way.

This incident aside, Francis' experience in Brazil would later come to be appreciated by Aldous. In correspondence between Aldous and Humphrey Osmond, Aldous mentioned he was hoping to acquire some introductions from Francis on a forthcoming trip to Brazil and would be writing to him for assistance.

Francis, drawn to Aldous, knew that his father also admired his brother and was envious of Aldous' form of intelligence and fame. Francis hoped that Aldous could help him clarify his own intentions. On occasion Aldous would ask Francis which path he was going to take after his Amazonian fieldwork, but the outcome was seldom satisfactory. To have a true conversation with his uncle was difficult. Whenever Francis put out the bite, Aldous rarely took it. On the occasions when he did, it was a source of joy for Francis. If one knew the trick, to deluge Aldous with opinions and actualities, tales of beauty and luscious delights, then he would consider one worthy of attention. In the absence of any sensible reply, Francis was struck with a lingering sense of inadequacy. Knowing Aldous did not suffer fools gladly, he would nevertheless end up feeling foolish. Francis, later in his life, came to acquire a similar habit to Aldous. Francis' sense of inferiority set against his celebrated uncle is all the more tinged with sadness, when we learn how others, significant to Francis, saw the pair, comparatively speaking. Meloma Huxley, Francis' second wife, had this to say,

> Ronnie Laing told me, that he felt Francis was the more interesting and insightful person, had more to offer than Aldous Huxley.[14]

## First LSD session

Aldous subscribed to a 'perennial philosophy,' a perspective that sees the truth of the world's religions as being derived from a common metaphysical platform. He defined it himself as "the metaphysic that recognises a divine reality substantial to the world of things and lives and minds."[15] His exploration of these core sacred truths, in his book of the same name, marked out Huxley, long before the dawn of the swinging sixties, as a figure striving to build bridges between Eastern and Western thought. Aldous' perennialism, however, was concerned more with mystical experience than with any ultimate reality, as experience was for him, the only presumed means through which an ultimate reality could be known – a position Laing was to take much later when venturing into *The Politics of Experience*.

Aldous first experimented with mescaline in 1953, under the guidance of Dr. Humphry Osmond, in Los Angeles. He wrote up his account of his ensuing visionary experience in *The Doors of Perception*. The famed (and infamous) 1960s American rock band, The Doors, would subsequently help cement Aldous' place in counter-culture history by taking their name from the book.

The exchange of letters between Aldous and Humphry Osmond has now been fully published,[16] including, details of his LSD experience of 7 November 1956, as described in the exchange of letters between Osmond, Mathew Ellen and Francis Huxley. These are a valuable source for understanding Huxley's account of his experiences. Any discussion of his or others' experience of altered states of mind, however, brings us up against the inherent limitations of language. This is true whether we concerned with the accuracy with which someone is able to convey the insights, hunches, flights of fancy, physical, emotional, intellectual or social transformations accrued to them in the course of a chemically induced altered state or whether we are interested with the broader phenomenological characteristics of the experience which can be inferred from analysis and comparison of verbal or written accounts. As such Huxley's account can tell us much more than the episodic details of hallucinatory experience.

Osmond had trepidations about the experiment.

> Should I cut the dose in half? The setting could hardly have been better, Aldous seemed an ideal subject, Maria eminently sensible, and we had all taken to each other, which was very important for a good experience; but ...

He continues with the words Francis enjoyed presenting dramatically, "... I did not relish the possibility, however remote, of being the man who drove Aldous Huxley mad."[17] Aldous' pioneering drug adventure was certainly an act of bravery. In Dunaway's words,

> If necessity is the mother of invention, then psychological need must be the father of creative risk. In his pursuit of visions – those ever-elusive flashes of the celestial light he had documented in his biographies of visionaries – Huxley was prepared to take a drug which mimicked madness.[18]

In hindsight, Osmond reckoned his own fears were groundless. But the risks have been all too real for some. Even today, contemporary scientific opinion notes the notorious difficulty of predicting responses to psychedelics. Aldous read the possibilities afforded by psychedelics – a term which Osmond coined – in terms of their ability to improve the lot of our species. But his vision of hallucinatory enlightenment for political transformation – to make human beings as free as possible – was not one which he thought should be extended to the masses. He distrusted Timothy Leary's invocation to "turn on, tune in and drop out," fearful that any hard-won knowledge would be drowned out in an ocean of prattling irrelevance. His nightmare was one of a population narcotised by "undisguised trivialities."[19]

This domain of experimentation exerted a life-long fascination on Francis. In one letter Francis expressed his interest in the ritual aspects of communal drug experience and the correlates with shamanistic practices. In thanking Osmond, he writes:

> What a difference a few drops of LSD make! I know something now, of enormous importance, which is not the same as merely suspecting its existence. It is all puzzling.[20]

He would go on to work with Osmond in a mental hospital in Canada in the late 1950s, meeting Albert Hofmann on a number of occasions in Switzerland, as well as being employed by Eileen Garrett in a study of extraordinary experiences. Francis stayed free of the utopian longings which preoccupied Aldous, who, in his final novel *The Island*, envisaged the use of 'Moksha medicine' as the liberating medium for personal and social transformation. In a letter to Osmond, Aldous stated that he was "trying to imagine what could be done to create a good society, dedicated to eliciting all the latent powers and gifts of individuals."[21]

Aldous' distrust of Leary aside, neither he nor Francis really explored the potential negative ramifications of what they were experimenting with. Francis' perspective was more circumspect than Aldous' and his own experimentation rooted more in his anthropological knowledge. Neither a slave nor a strong public advocate of its use, he took LSD, in later life once a year, as an occasional ritual balm to "see where I am at, and bring myself back into order,"[22] following what he saw as the alchemists' dictum to 'make yourself a vessel.' For him, the self-knowledge gained from a judicious use of psychedelics had relevance to psychopharmacology, parapsychology and psychotherapy. It was never intended for use as a panacea to combat the ills of the world. In that sense the personal was not intended to be political!

## Aunt Margaret

Most families have issues in their history – the skeletons in the closet which are to be avoided, and not mentioned in front of children or in 'polite company' – strategies to avoid neurosis which usually go half way to producing it. Francis remembers asking Juliette, why he had not been told until he was 22, that he had an aunt. Juliette replied "we don't talk about these things." Margaret was the unmentionable aunt! Like Maria (Aldous' first wife), Margret was, in Juliette's words "on the other side."[23]

> "I only met Margaret in my middle thirties," Francis recalled. "She just did not fit into that form of high-powered intellectual conversation.

Margaret became a schoolmistress. Her expectations of following her mother and her father at Prior's Field, the family school, were cheated when the stepmother had given up her share of it to Mrs. Burton-Brown. She was very disappointed indeed. Then she started her own school. She had a female companion – a friend who died only a few years before her death. She was a very worthy educated woman. I have never heard a word from Aldous about her at all. My father never talked about her. In their minds she was a bore."[24]

Tellingly, Dunaway, one of Aldous' many biographers, described his younger sister as,

> in many ways the family's true rebel: the only member of her generation to enter teaching ... the only one to convert to Christianity; the only one who was gay.[25]

It is highly plausible that Margaret's sexuality is the reason her existence was relegated to the margins of the unmentionable. Given the available facts it is difficult to think of any other reason. In terms of honesty and authenticity, which Aldous in his written work aspired too, this bashful fact, shames those surviving Huxley brothers, not least as hypocrites, as both were married to bi-sexual women. Julian, Juliette, Aldous and Maria (as well as Laura later on) all enjoyed love affairs outside the marriage bed, sometimes even sharing their female lovers. One may almost consider this a continuation, well into the 20th century, of the hypocrisy of Victorian sexual mores. Amidst the libertarianism and proclamations of freedom espoused by the Bloomsbury set, it does not sit well.

## Transgenerational repetitions in the family

Juliette mentions early on in her autobiography, that Maria "did not fit into the pattern,"[26] without the 'pattern' itself being further clarified. After Maria, Aldous' first wife, there is Laura Archera, his second, who similarly did not conform to the orthodox geometry of relationships as Juliette configured them. Laura had a relationship with Virginia Pfeiffer, Ernest Hemingway's sister-in-law. According to Francis, Laura took advantage of Aldous' good nature,

> in every possible particular. I have my suspicions about Laura's grabbing. I think Aldous liked Laura because she had a darting, kingfisher mind ... She kept him well-stocked with small talk, as far as I could see, but I am told that he always liked gossip very much. He liked the company of pretty and beautiful woman, and he liked the company of large minds with obsessions.[27]

Trev,[28] her grandson, painted a similarly unflattering picture, both of Laura and the family reaction to her sexual orientation:

> My father never really acknowledges his mother was bi; he was outraged. When David Dunaway's book came out (1999) he wouldn't accept that his mother was bisexual. He felt outrageous about David's book, a pretty common reaction. I barely remember my grandmother. I remember her driving, when we were in California. We were driving along, and she drove in a white Cadillac convertible, some giant American car whipping us around. Laura is for me the ultra-evil. She was physically mistreating him. That's my opinion. Nothing good to say about her. She was not a nice lady.[29]

On the occasion of Juliette's 90th birthday, Trev and his girlfriend went for tea.

> I never spend that much time with Juliette, though she was quite an amazing woman, playful and quite remarkable. When I introduced myself to Juliette, her face colour was drained out, as she thought I, Trevenen was dead.

Here we see an echo of the tragic story of the first Trevenen (Aldous and Julian's brother). Sexual mores comprise but one of the many tangled psychological threads woven in and out of the lives of the Huxleys over the years. We see here once again this intergenerational entanglement as constituting a central theme in any exploration of what it means to be a Huxley – and necessarily a part of our story of the life of Francis Huxley.

One can conclude from the various biographies written of Aldous – some with original research, others recounting information second hand – that his coping skills were estimable, dealing not just with the early loss of his mother and brother, and his failing eyesight, but also the repercussions of his own tangled love life, not to mention that of his spouses. These would occasionally overlap. Amongst both his and his wife Maria's lovers was Sybille Bedford. Dubbed the "finest woman writer of the 20th century" and "prize chronicler of sensuous experience,"[30] she was later to become one of his own biographers. Francis spoke highly of her "confidential attitude to Aldous," in the course of delivering "as it were, the more public view of Aldous."[31]

When Aldous pursued an affair with Nancy Cunard – designated as being "unlike any other ... in its intensity,"[32] she, being romantically obsessed, "gave in, out of affection, exasperation; after a few days (she) discarded him."[33] Aldous was devastated, and took to hanging out in the "sort of smoky night club Nancy frequented."[34] Maria, far from impressed, confronted Aldous, delivering an ultimatum – to leave London the following day or stay without her. She spent the night packing, tossing things out the window of their Princess Garden flat, with an agitated Aldous "hovering round her all night. The next morning, they left via Victoria Station on the boat train to Italy."[35] The journey ended in Forte, where Aldous wrote *Antic Hay*, his tale of bohemian immorality and disenchantment; this was the same year Francis was born.

Aldous would go on to receive many women in his bedroom, which Maria no longer shared. The list would include Maria's sister, as well as Maria's own lovers which she shared with him. His older brother Julian was not to be left behind in such behaviour, and Francis' brother Anthony is known to have followed suit.[36] "It's a Huxley trait. I'm afraid in the man," said Susie Huxley. Francis himself, opted for serial monogamy, demonstrating that whatever legitimised this behaviour in the minds of other Huxley men, there was nothing helpless, uncontrollable or inevitable about it. His second wife, Meloma, remembers: "Arthur came around one-time." He asked Francis "Don't you want to have two wives?" Francis replied: "Arthur, I can barely keep my head above water with one. Why would I want two?"[37]

But there was one respect in which Francis did take after other Huxley men in his affairs with women. Like his grandfather Leonard, and Aldous with Laura, Francis married women who were at least 20 years younger than he was. Leonard, Aldous' father, was 52 years of age when he married Rosaline Bruce – 30 years his junior, four years after the death of his wife Julia. Although there is no direct evidence, his sons may well have felt a sense of betrayal. Certainly, this experience influenced Aldous' portrayal of marriage and his father in *Eyeless in Gaza* and in his other novels.

Laura, like Maria, would also later show her own appreciation of the allure of hard currency. Several in the family thought she took full advantage of Aldous' pleasantly generous nature. Francis, too, had his suspicions "about Laura's grabbing." On the other hand, Francis noticed that Aldous often met his obligations with money rather than emotions.

> Aldous had very little emotions to give to the world ... Maria, after all, was one of his great saviours in other senses: by the use of her intuition, by reading to him daily, by being his secretary-general, by looking after him in every particular.[38]

With the psychological acumen he cultivated, Francis saw these behaviours in the context of the psychological economy of sexuality, companionship, professional living and money, which was embedded in the Huxley family. With the Huxleys, issues with money were passed on intergenerationally as much as character, fame or intellect. Some of the twists and turns this could take are illustrated in the following tale. Aldous' father, Leonard, had been left £40,000 by his first wife (Julia Arnold). His second marriage, meant that under the terms of the will, any sums from the inheritance were to be made available to his children by his first marriage (Aldous, Julian, Trevenen and Margaret) only on fairly impersonal financial terms, whilst the money went to educate the two sons which he later had by Rosalind Bruce.[39] Whatever grudge Aldous might have harboured about this is unknown, but after Leonard's death in Spring 1933, Aldous, the now famously affluent writer, generously helped to pay for the education of his two half brothers, David and Andrew.

We asked Trev Huxley, about the sums which Aldous might have bequeathed to his only child, Trev's father, Matthew. He answered:

> No, Laura went for it. There was a provision in the will, that if you challenge it, you should get nothing. But my father should have challenged it ... Copyright law and in the US visionary rights are (also) something ... His last agent, Doris Halsy, was very sweet, but not a very good agent. There was a story (of) how ... DiCaprio was chatting her (Laura) up and there were friends and DiCaprio was interested in making a film of one of Aldous' books. One day I got the call ... from Universal Pictures. Can you sign the papers? ... I would sign off and Laura was ... fucking unbelievable, so it's very unpleasant. She would get really ugly really, really ugly. He didn't know what happened to all the copyrights. We still don't know, who owns some rights.[40]

On his 61st birthday, Aldous fell in love again. This time it was not with one of his many admirers, but his own daughter-in-law, Ellen Hovde, an accomplished documentary filmmaker, who had married Francis' cousin Matthew in 1950. The couple had two children, Trev and Tessa Huxley. Ellen was sympathetic to Aldous after Maria's death, and Aldous allowed himself to come extremely close to her. Trev Huxley tells how "she would record books on tape even when we were all together." She continued to do this until Aldous died. "She was," Trev said, "closer to Aldous than to my father."[41] In the summer of 1955, Francis was spending all his free time with Aldous and Ellen. This led to her becoming enamoured with Francis. "I married the wrong Huxley," she told her son![42] "This was a disaster in the family ... My father never spoke to Francis after that." When Francis would not marry her, Ellen was devastated. It is worth commenting that despite Francis' role in this tumultuous episode in the life of his parents, Trev's own relationship with Francis was quite sanguine.

> It was a relationship that was quite warm. In some ways, not intellectual. We'd talk about family members, and what went on, the crazy stuff. I was always interested in what he was doing. He was so in the middle. I did not sit there and read Francis books. I was interested in what he was doing ... wisdom of the heart rather than intellectual.[43]

Trev had come to accept that in the Huxley family few things went unexamined. His own tolerance and forbearance in the face of family difficulties is no doubt something he learnt from the numerous examples he had to draw on from around him.

## Fire

In May 1961, towards the end of Aldous' life, sparks, then flames, blew up in the Hollywood canyons. They eventually consumed his house. "The fire was horrifying," reports Ellen Hovde. "I remember writing to him that he must feel incredibly light, and he wrote back saying, yes, he did, that if you lose everything, the weight you've been carrying is gone."[44] Francis saw a darker side to what transpired. Behind the smoke and mirrors of the burned-out debris and the unresolved past ricocheting around Aldous, Laura, her lover Ginny and Aldous' deceased first wife Maria, lay something disavowed.

> I couldn't help but be stuck by the fact that when the fire came up, they both wandered around the house in Hollywood Heights which she's carpeted wall-to-wall with pure white, fleecy carpets. She says how she opened the drawers, closed them, looked at things and didn't do anything. Eventually she put Aldous into the car and drove down to Ginny's house and saved everything there – leaving behind those boxes full of Aldous' correspondence with all his friends and colleagues. It seems appalling, what was happening. She says it was too large to deal with.[45]

Maybe Aldous, Francis' wondered, was deeply embarrassed about saving as much as possible of his and Maria's archival belongings. Perhaps Laura was content to see it vanish in the flames. Either way, Aldous avoided looking any deeper. Francis has spoken that Aldous was not enamoured of Freudian speculation. He'd taken "against (him) in a big way." This is because "his sublimatory mechanism was so geared from an early age that he didn't want to see how it actually worked in himself,"[46] nor perhaps in others. Whilst Aldous was happy to open the doors of perception in one direction, he was just as happy to see them closed in another.

Asked about the fire which destroyed most of his grandmothers' writings, journals, letters and agendas, Trev Huxley noted the destruction wrought was not a simple matter of untamed natural forces.

> The tragedy of Aldous's house burnt down in a brushfire in California. I know the television trucks blocked the road to the fire for the fire engines. Truckloads of Maria's diaries were destroyed. Aldous took the manuscript of Eiland out with him. Everything else was burnt. All his correspondence everything … It is like losing your memory.

Francis must have felt that the fire which broke out in his own flat in London's Belsize Park some years later – one which turned a good part of his library to ashes, was a further resonance between Aldous' life and his own.

### "Oh, never mind, it's only a joke"

These were almost the last words spoken by Aldous Huxley. His final moments, before succumbing to the oral cancer that ended his life, were spent under the influence of LSD, a 100mm intramuscular injection, having been given, at his request, by his wife Laura. From being in great pain he passed into a more peaceful state. Francis' proposed film script, "Aldous" sets these moments against the backdrop of the Kennedy assassination, two very public lives ending on the same day – 22 November 1963. He was a child born in 1894 into an imposing family of scientific and literary ancestors. Francis could never entirely cast Aldous from his life, and his attempted biographical film script is indicative of this. It has moments of hilarity and is a testament to both his and Aldous' endeavour to make the contemporary world understood. Francis treated his uncle as a modern incarnation of the Renaissance man. He was someone who "spoke for the connections among science, mysticism, psychedelics, ethics, spiritualism and humanism."[47]

Aldous, like his brother Julian and grandfather T. H. Huxley, became noticed as public intellectuals, following a mostly liberal, if not libertarian faith in their ability to contribute knowledge and insight into human problems and to advocate for social reform. Their familial vision of human transformation, Julian would call 'self-directed evolution.' Julian's faith that the advance of human industrial civilisation could cure us of our collective ills was almost unbounded. Aldous and Francis in comparison had a profound common interest in human consciousness; its limits, extensions and transformations were to them personal and emotional projects as much as they were intellectual ones.

Aldous Huxley's intellectual endeavours in the public arena had, Francis would point out to his students, an ironic if not troubling counterpoint. Aldous was most anxious, Francis said, when he realised he was absolutely free to do as he pleased. He had earned this possibility through his own endeavours and the consequent enormous public recognition, adoration and reward which had come his way. Freedom is a highly problematic concept in the social and political commentary which emanated from Aldous. There remains a conflict between the idealism which he expressed and the de facto social contexts within which he expressed it. His views, enhanced by his own prestige, were always constrained by the force of circumstances and the conventions of class, as well as the conscious and unconscious habits into which these were imprinted. Nonetheless, Aldous, in his life and writings was a man who favoured sexual liberty and its expression. He carried this project forward in the midst of the post-war disillusionment of the 1920s, the decade in which Francis was born. The search for new "human potentialities" had, since the days of T. H. Huxley, become something of a family endeavour – one with roots in the Victorian era, an age when scientific activity existed, and was socially sanctioned, as an individualistic and leisurely pursuit. T. H. Huxley appropriated the future promise of Victorian science as a family mission to reduce social and political problems to scientific and educational ones. Getting the true measure of this family project – bequeathed as it was to Francis – was always going to be an impossible task.

## Notes

1 *LIFE*, 24 March 1947, pp.53–60.
2 Huxley, F. (1974, p.6) *The Way of the Sacred*. New York. Doubeday.
3 Huxley, F. (1988, p.3) A note from the screenwriters. FHA.
4 Morrell (1975, p.203).
5 Ballard, J. G. (2002) Prophet of Our Present. *The Guardian*, 13 April.
6 Ibid.
7 Ibid., p.216.
8 Huxley, F. (1976, p.35).
9 Holmes, C. M. (1970, p.x) *Aldous Huxley and the Way to Reality*. Westport. Greenwood Press.
10 Woodcock, G. (2007, p.158) *Dawn and the Darkest Hour – A Study of Aldous Huxley*. Montreal. Black Rose Books.
11 Morrell (1975, p.221).
12 Huxley, F. (1985, p.2) Interview with D. K. Dunaway.
13 Huxley, F. (1999, p.114). Aldous. In *Aldous Huxley Recollected*, by Dunaway, D. K., Preface pp.v–xiii, Alta Mira Press, Sage. Walnut Creek.
14 Meloma Huxley: Interview on 16 October 2018.
15 Huxley, A. (1945, p.vii) *The Perennial Philosophy*. New York. Harper 7 Brothers.
16 Bisbee, C., Bisbee, P., Dyck, E., Farrell, P., Sexton, J. and Spisak, J. W. (Eds.) (2018) *Psychedelic Prophets. The Letters of Aldous Huxley and Humphrey Osmond*. Montreal and Kingston. London. McGill-Queens University Press.
17 Osmond, H. (1965, pp.114–122) In *Aldous Huxley. A Memorial Volume*. Huxley, J. Ed. London. Chatto & Windus.
18 Dunaway, D. K. (1990) *Huxley in Hollywood*. London. Bloomsbury.
19 Kakutani, M. (2018, p.166). *The Death of Truth*. New York. Tim Duggan Books.
20 Bisbee et al. (2018, p.575).
21 See Horowitz, M. and Palmer, C. (Eds.) (1999, p.238) *Moksha. Aldous Huxley's Classic Writings on Psychedelics and the Visionary Experience*. Vermont. Park Street Press.
22 Personal communication to Theodor Itten, 2012.
23 Personal communication from Juliette Huxley to Theodor Itten in 1983.
24 Huxley, F. (1985, pp.9–12).
25 Dunaway (1990, p.386).
26 Huxley, J. (1986, p.43).
27 Dunaway (1990, p.18).
28 Mark Trevenen Huxley (Trev) interviewed on 26 April 2018 in Sebastopol.
29 Ibid. Trev further remarked about the denial. "Like my father's denial, vocal denial, if he knew his mother was bisexual he could have remembered that, if he would have, but he was so pissed off. I know he was wrong. Even when I was scared, but he did hear about it."

30 See Barrow, A. (2004) Sybille Bedford: Secret History. *Independent*, 23 May.
31 Huxley, F. (1985, p.22) Interview with David Dunaway.
32 Murray, N. (2003) *Aldous Huxley. An English Intellectual*. London. Abacus.
33 Ibid., p.147, quoting Bedford.
34 Ibid., p.147.
35 Thody (1973, p.15); Murray (2003, p.147). An episode which Maria would tell Sybille Bedford directly.
36 Suzi Huxley: "My father he was running three girlfriends at the time and married a girl from his office." Interview, 14 March 2018, London.
37 Meloma Huxley interviewed on 16 October 2018.
38 Huxley, F. (1985, p.25).
39 Thody (1973, pp.17–18).
40 Trevenen Huxley interviewed on 26 April 2018.
41 Ibid.
42 Trevenen Huxley was born in October 1951 and Tessa Huxley in October 1953. Mathew and Ellen divorced in 1961. Trev Huxley interviewed on 26 April 2018.
43 Ibid.
44 Dunaway, D. K. (1999, p.130) *Aldous Huxley Recollected*. New York. Carroll & Graf.
45 Huxley, F. (1985, p.20) Interview with David Dunaway.
46 Francis Huxley in Dunaway (1999, p.99).
47 Huxley, F. (1988) A note from the screenwriters. FHA.

# 4 Haunting

**The Huxleys: beginnings**

"I learnt a salutary lesson," Francis Huxley once remarked.

> When I was in preparatory school in England a boy asked me if I was the son of the famous Huxley, and I preened myself and said, 'Oh, yes.' The boy replied, 'What? Vic Huxley? The famous motorcyclist?' My face fell, and I realized after a time, that the name Huxley up in Cheshire is actually widely known. The best-known Huxleys at the time were Vic Huxley, and Huxley the fishmonger.[1]

The Huxleys, the illustrious family into which Francis was born, can be traced back to the 12th century, to the manor of Hodesleia in Cheshire. However, the noted dynasty with which its modern fame is associated begins with Thomas Henry Huxley (1825–1895) in the 19th century. Thomas Huxley was born in Ealing, London, the seventh child of George Huxley, an assistant school master and Rachel Withers, who Thomas was considered to resemble "very closely in physical appearance and temperament" – her temperament being one "of untiring energy and vivacity."[2] Rachel bore five daughters and three sons – testament itself to her vitality and strength. As a teenager, Thomas read passionately and though he received little formal education, profited from his father's acceptance of his passion for self-instruction. He exhibited an early knack for contemplating metaphysical problems, and by the time he was 16 had fled the family nest to London where he began a medical apprenticeship with his brother in law.

Attending Sydenham College for his preparatory studies for medicine, his dedication and diligence led to a prize for his work in Botany. Not coming from a well to do background, he was fortunate to win a free scholarship to enter Charring Cross Hospital as a medical student. One of his more famous mentors, Wharton Jones, a lecturer in physiology, encouraged him to publish his first work – on the microscopical structure of human hair. He completed his first MB at London University, aged 20, and subsequently found work in the Navy Medical Service as a resident MD at Haslar Hospital in the Portsmouth Harbour area. His talents and zeal for hard work were spotted by Sir John Richardson a naturalist, naval surgeon and arctic explorer. His devotion to his work earned him Richardson's recommendation as an assistant surgeon and naturalist aboard HMS *Rattlesnake*. It was a life-changing moment of good fortune which Huxley never forgot.

Thomas H. Huxley began his journey into professional fame aboard the *Rattlesnake*. His tasks, on a voyage of scientific and geographic exploration, alongside his doctoring duties, were to collect specimens and conduct whatever research he saw fit – this being chiefly to document the habits and development of the organisms he observed (and dissected). During the period of this voyage – between 1846–1850 – Huxley maintained a detailed journal and record of his activities. His zoological observations and conclusions were written up and sent back to England. Their publication in respected scientific journals earned him a growing reputation, leading to his election, at the early age of 25, to a Fellowship of the Royal Society. Huxley shared with Darwin not only the fact that they both embarked on lengthy sea voyages, but that the research which accrued from them formed the basis of many important theoretical reflections and innovations.

Once back from his voyage, in the course of which he fell in love with his future wife, Henrietta Anne Heathorn, his name grew in stature. He was awarded the Royal Medal of the Royal Society and elected onto its council. No doubt pleased with these accolades, he tried eagerly to turn them into bread and butter. All the professorial positions he applied for – in Aberdeen, Toronto and London – came to naught. Yet to marry Henrietta, because of his insufficient income, Huxley contemplated going out to her in Australia. He was saved from doing so by another moment of good fortune, receiving a surprise appointment to the School of Mines under the Geological Survey, where he was made a lecturer. His teaching methods, to which he brought his personal wisdom, experience from the field, humour and openness to learn new things, impressed pupils and colleagues alike. With a sigh of relief, we can imagine, he asked his fiancée over to London, and married her in 1855. This union formed the launch pad which would propel the family name into intellectual history. One of the reasons the name endures is undoubtedly Thomas Henry Huxley's association with Charles Darwin and the cultural turmoil which the latter's work instigated. Their first contact had occurred following his return to England from the Rattlesnake voyage – he had sent Darwin a technical report on some of his observations. Their first meeting occurred in 1853, at the Geological Society. It was the publication of Darwin's *Origins of Species* in 1859, however, that marked a turning point in Huxley's life.

Huxley's name achieved a prominence it had hitherto lacked following his famed exchange with Samuel Wilberforce, then Bishop of Oxford, at a meeting of the British Association. Wilberforce, heading the forces opposed to Darwin's ground breaking views on evolution, knew little science and relied on a speech which which was reported as being "eloquent, ignorant and persuasive."[3] Exact details of the meeting differ by account but common to all is that the combination of Huxley's humour and knowledge won the day. It is said that when Wilberforce had raised the question of whether, anyone were to be willing to trace his descent through an ape as his grandfather, would he be willing to trace his descent through an ape on the side of his grandmother?[4]

Huxley's purported response was that when it came to his ancestral preferences, his predilection was for his ancestor to be an ape rather than a bishop! Thus, did Huxley become in his own eyes 'Darwin's bulldog' and in Darwin's his "warmest & most important supporter."[5] His alliance with Darwin saw him "utter the greatest profanity since Copernicus moved the earth from the centre of the universe." Together they would "move man from the centre of creation."[6] Given the way in which the two men are locked together in this pivotal moment in the history of science, it is deeply ironic that Huxley's then view of science as "organised common sense" now stands in stark contrast to contemporary interpreters of Darwin who see the latter's work as "precisely *not* common sense."[7]

With his growing fame, Huxley was swift to put it to use in supporting the application and professionalisation of science. He established the first modern laboratory of biology in 1871, was involved in several Royal Commissions and lent his services to several universities. He was a passionate advocate that a general education in science should be available for all. He enjoyed penning popular science papers and pioneered science journalism. It has been said that "with Huxley the scientist was born." For while, "In Darwin we see an older ideal, the wealthy, self-financed gent whose home was his laboratory," with Huxley we see "twentieth-century corporate science in the making."[8]

Throughout his life Huxley remained tirelessly busy as a lecturer, committee man, writer, friend, provocateur of clergy, Darwin's populariser and paterfamilias. His lectures to working people brought him not only deep personal satisfaction but plaudits from the nascent Trade Unions. The predominant audience members for Huxley were the artisans and factory workers who enjoyed his evening lectures at Jermyn Street, School of Mines – later to become part of Imperial College London.

When, in the 1880s, workers' movements formed into trade unions, with their own colleges for further education and a new political party to represent their interests, T. H. Huxley was no longer seen just as a social reformer and moral authority regarding the disparities of social and economic life, but as one of the defenders of the foundation of industry and commerce. At one time, T. H. Huxley had been accepted by the workers as one of their own – due in no small part to the fact that,

> he was largely self-educated, and they knew it, he was the prophet of science and they shared his vision. He had no romantic illusion about the working classes.[9]

However, the trappings of success saw him morph into a structural conservative, who would denounce alternatives to the existing social order. As a result, the trade unions included him amongst those they saw as the "brutally selfish ruling classes."[10] This was undoubtedly as sad as it was unreal, certainly in terms of his financial means. Yet he reached the limit of being seen as a man of science defending his turf with wit and a vision of self-improvement through education and hard work. In the final analysis he,

> resided with increasing comfort in institutions devoted to imperial display, commercial advancement, and public instruction. From such positions, he could present himself as liberator of the people from the dogmas of priestcraft and the idleness of university dons, and as the gentle critic of the coarser practices of capitalism and imperialism.[11]

He was described by many as a tender and affectionate master of several scientific disciplines. For a while, he was the president of the Ethnological Society and effectively founded the Anthropological Institute in 1871, the oldest such society in the modern world. He was also among those who in 1880 petitioned Cambridge University to open its degree to women. He also wanted Oxford and Cambridge to open themselves up to the lower middle classes. Members of the succeeding generations, – his son, Leonard; his grandson, Julian, and his great-grandson, Francis – all went to Balliol College in Oxford. It was said of T. H. Huxley that,

> It is one of the marks of a master that his great wonders can fabricate a marvellous mythology, and a Huxley myth acquired in his own lifetime a great and almost autonomous power.[12]

It remains a remarkable fact that the Huxleys first came from nowhere. Four generations on, from the "enfant terrible,"[13] a man known to his students as the 'General' and to the press as 'Pope Huxley,'[14] the Huxleys reached the apex of their professions.

Huxley was a champion, not of power to the people but of power to the professionals. When Thomas Henry Huxley received an honorary Doctorate from Cambridge University in 1879, he had transposed himself from a lowly outsider to an indispensable "part of the new hegemony. The modernizing university had been willing to use him, now it was willing to honour him."[15] Huxley's pivotal role in the transformation of British intellectual life saw him take up arms against a knowledge-monopolising state-supported Church. In his mid-30s he was propagating rational explanations of life, and when aged 44 coined the first use of 'agnosticism' at a meeting of the Metaphysical Society in London.

At 58 years of age, Huxley became President of the Royal Society, overseeing the development of science from a position of power. His plate was now overfull with duties – Whitehall, Commissions, Fisheries, Schools – besides writing, lecturing, overseeing students in the lab and attending to family life. By the time he reached his 60th birthday, he was facing renewed episodes of

54  *Family life, ancestry and haunting*

depressed mood and was emotionally burnt out, leaving him unable to face the world.

Desmond summarises his two-volume biography of this first famous forebearer of Francis Huxley, by stating:

> *Huxley* is part of the new contextual history of science. This itself is a reaction to the old history of ideals, which displaced the person, made him or her a disembodied ghost, a flash of transcendent genius. Only by embedding Huxley can we appreciate his role in the vast transformation that staggered our great-grandfathers.[16]

Desmond then provides his own succinct picture of the context which gave birth to Huxley's fame and the emergence of a new non-conformist meritocratic ideal constructed around the cultural edifice of science.

> Huxley's radical teachers were waging a campaign of disobedience against the Anglican-run, power-grabbing College of Physicians. Huxley in the forties was among radical Methodists and rational dissenters – activists whose culture of resistance and scientific Calvinism had matured around the Lord's table ... young Huxley became heir to the dissenting resistance of cotton kings and medical activists.[17]

What successive members of the Huxley dynasty both endured and laboured to produce cannot be properly understood outside of this context.

**Inheritance and memory**

Our examination of the life and work of Francis Huxley permits us to extend the analysis of collective memory to the family – in this particular case to one of England's most fascinating and famous intellectual families, the Huxleys. The psychoanalyst Stephen Frosch has noted that "so much of one generation's life is spent managing the difficulties of the previous one,"[18] an apt summary as we shall see of the demands impressed upon successive members of the Huxley family. Much has been written about the Huxley 'dynasty,' from its inception as a social fact in Victorian Britain to the achievements of its preeminent stars; Thomas Henry (Darwin's bulldog), Julian Huxley (Director of UNESCO, Secretary of the Zoological Society of London), Andrew Huxley (Nobel Prize winner) and Aldous Huxley (novelist and essayist). Rather than a critical reflection on the pattern of success enjoyed by prominent family members it has too often been lazily assumed, that the reasons for it necessity lie in the realm of genetics.[19] The biographer of the Huxleys, Ronald Clarke, for example, erroneously claimed that an examination of the Huxley dynasty almost amounted to a "controlled experiment" of genetic inheritance[20] and frequently employed biological rhetoric in his scrutiny of the characters of family members. Similarly, the memoir of Julian Huxley, Francis' father, written by J. R. Baker[21] makes reference to him being affected by the genes "present in the chromosomes of his own body ... and those he shared with his relatives." Julian himself had written that his brother Aldous, "possessed some innate superiority."[22] Such rhetoric invoking the hidden force of ancestry has, of course, travelled down from the 19th century and was first put to work in the Huxley family by Francis' great-grandfather, T. H. Huxley, who had referred, in a letter to his sister, to the "place in society for which nature has fitted me."[23]

## Hauntings, dynasty and the burden of expectations

Here we wish to explore other possibilities amongst the myriad ways in which past life may permeate, saturate or even overwhelm the present – to view the Huxley family as a socially constituted site for family 'hauntings' in which the dead are never far away. In doing so we are concerned with how recurring patterns of intellectual thought have become embedded in, and promoted by, specific relationships which exist not only within the Huxley family system, but also between that family considered as a whole and the larger Western society which has conferred a specific set of meanings regarding what membership of the family entails. Of necessity, our reflections must call attention to the manner and extent to which intelligence is socially esteemed, valued and exploited in relation to the pantheon of other human traits and abilities, what the costs are of our present calculus and what wider functions are served by identifying a specific family as a repository of genius. Aldous Huxley's career as a screen writer in Hollywood, during the late 1930s and early 1940s, provides a telling example of how the social construction of genius was put into service by the powerful. In an interview with David King Dunaway, Jacob Zeitlin spoke candidly of this.

> By the time Aldous got here he had a great reputation as a travel writer and essayist. A lot of people had never read anything he wrote but cultivated him anyway because his name implied being right among the smart people ... they wanted him because he was Aldous Huxley ... It was the prestige they were after.[24]

Christopher Isherwood added that the studios "thought he gave them class."[25] Aldous thus became a piece of cultural property. One can but wonder whether, like the 'cruel optimism' of the 'American dream,' the purpose of such social construction is deceit – to fashion make-believe worlds in which we consent to others' socially defined superiority as a stage in the production of our own inferiority. This sets the ball rolling for the myth of meritocracy – that success awaits, dependent only on the application of genius or hard work.

The dictionary definition of dynasty – "a succession of people from the same family who play a prominent role in business, politics, or another field" is rather vague and suggests that of key importance is the bloodline

56  *Family life, ancestry and haunting*

or biological connection between individuals. The etymology of the word is more revealing. *Dynastie,* from late French in the 15th century, denotes a race or succession of sovereigns from the same line or family governing a country, while more directly, from the Greek, dynasteia refers to "power, lordship, sovereignty." The origins of the term thus lie in a feudal or monarchical system. What is relevant then, when we consider any dynasty, is a system of power and the relationship of family members to that power and the wider distribution of power which surrounds it. A large family tree, no matter how many able members people it, does not constitute a dynasty unless the family in question wields evident social and intellectual power.

Clues as to what membership of the family meant to Francis can be culled from his reflections on the Huxley family album, a photographic archive comprising 28 albums, spanning the years from 1908 to 1993, which had been bequeathed to him following the death of his mother, Juliette. One particular picture of his father, Julian sitting on the lap of his grandfather T. H. Huxley, prompts reflections on Julian's relationship with his grandfather. Francis' note in passing, that "genius, proverbially, has a way of skipping every other generation"[26] shows that he too had imbibed the myth that biology had implanted the workings of genius into the larger family network. Taken at face value, Francis would be aware that this aphorism implied that he had not been blessed with the intellectual abilities of his father and great-grandfather. Situated within a family network socially ordained as exceptional, and valuing intelligence as a supreme virtue, this

*Figure 4.1* Francis, Julian and Anthony 1952.

must have been painful and daunting. Francis' further thoughts in the document, echoed those of his mother, in suggesting Julian had inherited T. H.'s "black dog" alongside his "pugnacious genius," lend further weight to his acceptance of intelligence and personality traits as biologically inherited; this despite an acknowledgement of the influence of the Victorian work ethic, and Julian's propensity for overwork, with its concomitant tiredness, as sources of his repeated bouts of depression.

This emphasis on "the Gospel of hard work," alongside the myth of hereditary genius, was routinely instilled into family members. The example of his great-grandfather, Francis writes "was frequently held up" to his own grandfather (Leonard) as "an example to be followed"[27] with the refrain "Huxleys always get firsts" cascading down through the lives of the children and grandchildren in the course of their studies. Juliette, in her own evocative memoir, a nostalgic bitter-sweet hymn to her own rich life, described how this "heavy inheritance exacting its crusading achievements, and punishments"[28] rained down upon Julian. There was, she wrote,

> a compulsion imposed upon him by his family, to be worthy of both his grandfather T. H. H. and his Arnold parents, so that he was made to feel guilty if and when he failed. It was a terrible burden to put on a child and marked him throughout his life.[29]

For Trevenen, Julian's and Aldous' brother, who did not manage to live up to this maxim, the consequences were severe. The strain of gaining but a second-class degree in his finals contributed to his psychological collapse.[30] Francis tells us that 'Trev' had at this time also fallen in love with a woman working as a chambermaid in his step-mother's employ. Ronald Clark, the biographer put it differently: "Trev feared that he might have compromised one of his women friends" and "suffering from too much work and nerve strain, carrying other people's worries as well as his own"[31] he was led to take his own life. In Aldous' view, "Trev had the courage to face life with ideals – and his ideals were too much for him."[32] But were the 'ideals' really Trev's? The inculcated high expectations of academic success combined with the tensions which are invariably generated from inter-class relationships in a class-ridden society began their life beyond the boundaries of Trev's hopes, wishes and desires. Susie Huxley (Francis' niece) indicated that expectations to marry the right kind of person continued down the family line with Juliette policing her son's prospective partners.

> Our mother[33] wasn't approved of, as my mother got pregnant with me before my father and she were married. Juliette wanted her to have an abortion. She had dynastic pretensions. This was one of the things that drove her to, act as well, when the sculptress, Ferelyth Howard and Francis were getting close to getting married. Anthony went off to marry an unsuitable woman. Juliette said that "we are not having Francis to do the same."

Juliette's preoccupation with ensuring the 'good' family name and her strict and controlled vetting of her son's prospective partners had profound repercussions. Matthew, Aldous' son, felt he had been 'mauled' by his father, and burdened with this massive family legacy. For many a member of the family, the impression we have is of an immense weight of expectation and gravitas, always hanging over them. Trev Huxley (Mathew's son) continues:

> I'll tell you a terrible story about my father in the college. He was asked to write some articles and he first refused. But he had to do it. He said you can't publish my last name, because he couldn't write as well as his father. He was only eighteen years old. It was a big burden for him. People don't really know that much, as my father said to me. You know it's okay to use your last name, if you want. Most people can't get a book published. But it helped my father.

Juliette added to this picture in her interviews with David Dunaway. She felt it inordinately sad that Matthew had told her,

> he never published before Aldous died. He could not bear to; he was afraid. Oh, these fathers and sons – there's this book (*Farewell to Eden*, 1964), which is first class, which Aldous would have been immensely proud of![34]

The family celebration of relentless work and the demand for it was also felt keenly in Francis' life. Despite an extensive literary output encompassing several well-received books and numerous articles as well as being a co-founder of *Survival International* he was considered a touch lazy within family circles, in comparison to his older brother or his father. Francis felt it "was a bit of a curse to be the son of this famous man (Julian), who wrote over 60 books" while he "wrote only seven."[35] Rupert Sheldrake, who knew Francis well, thought that, although Francis derived a good part of his sense of self from being a part of this great family with its formidable intellectual tradition it was also a "a bit overwhelming and a kind of burden."[36] Though appreciating his father's intellectual and scientific achievements, Francis found him "arrogant and overbearing."[37] The impossibility of living up to what the family name demanded of one, may have contributed to what Rupert thought was a tendency in Francis to skirt round the edges of the intellectual challenges he pursued – as if he were afraid to truly look into the heart of the "central mystery" of existence.

Francis' niece, Victoria,[38] spoke candidly about how these family pressures were still operative in her generation, the 4th since T. H. Huxley.[39] Victoria's active refusal to "trade on the family name" engendered the wrath of her father (Anthony). He was furious, she said, when she applied to study English literature and language at London University. In his eyes, her subsequent degree "didn't count" because it was "not from Oxford." But the weight of the dead generations behind her, to use Marx's famous phrase, weighed like a nightmare in other, less predictable, ways. "You (were) made to be conscious of the family name" she said "and the expectations going along with it." These expectations demanded not just success, but success of a specific allotted kind. "While we were growing up" Victoria continued, "my mother had roles for all of us. Susie had to be the artistic one. My middle sister, the practical one. I was to be the brainy one, going to university." The result of all this was that Victoria sought to distance herself from "being a Huxley." In this she was not alone. "Henrietta (Andrew Huxley's daughter and Francis' cousin) changed her name, when she was a teenager. She could not stand the name, to be a Huxley." In Victoria's view "you could not escape it ... even if you wanted." By this she meant not only the manifest pressure to live up to the family name, but the dense network of significant relationships with influential and socially well-placed people which surrounded family members. Francis' mother, Juliette, was herself at the centre of the Bloomsbury circle and, despite then having married into the Huxley clan, also professed to finding it intimidating.

Seeking to remove oneself from the centre of dynastic drama as a ploy has much in common with the strategies employed by those who find fame in our celebrity-strewn world. A little-known study by Donna Rickwell and David Giles[40] on the phenomenology of fame provides further information on the pressures faced by those whose lives burn in the public flame of "symbolic immortality." They conducted Interviews with 15 adults who had at some stage in their lives attained celebrity status in the USA. The researchers noted repeated concerns expressed regarding one's mental health, along with mistrust, isolation, ambiguity and addiction to the status that comes with fame. Francis was acutely aware of the kind of difficulties which one encountered and like Victoria – though perhaps in a less forthright and unambiguous manner – also sought in some degree to remove himself from the circus which surrounded the family. As Rupert Sheldrake notes:

> He was very aware of that, being born into the intellectual and academic kind of world. And yet, being a kind of transgressive member of it, not having stayed in Oxford become a Don, leaving that kind of intellectual world behind, becoming a feral intellectual.

Francis would recount with a mixture of anger and amusement an occasion when he was invited to deliver a paper at an international conference in Japan. Curious, he enquired of the organisers why he had been asked to attend. "Because you are a Huxley," came the reply. Francis duly submitted his 'paper' – a scribbled note on a single page with a single word – 'Huxley.' As the name was all they were really interested in, that was all they got! "Naming is the first step in the process of liberation,"[41] Rebecca Solnit has written. Francis' repost is a delicious, ironic illustration of its truth.

The overarching narrative driving the Huxley story, cascading down the years and responsible for what has been called the "tradition of behaviour, which did not perish with the passing of the years" may well have also owed something to fear. T. H. Huxley had begun the 'dynasty' through his own relentless endeavours – although engendered by some fortunate connections and aid along the way. This desperation to succeed, it seemed, became, in the space of his adult life, frozen into the architecture of personal desires encouraged, nurtured, permitted and expected of all those bearing the family name. The dynamics of family life exhibit levels of complexity which do not stop here. The drive to emulate and recapitulate the fortunes of previous members of the family took other turns – to what degree these were conscious it is difficult to say. Julian had been named after his mother and her mother – both of whom were named Julia and his own wife, Francis' mother, was Juliette – the diminutive Julie. Whether he was expected to comport himself in ways reminiscent of his female progenitors is unclear but from a psychoanalytic perspective he may be considered to have simultaneously married his wife, his mother and grandmother – a ménage à quatre – a domestic and erotic trinity at home in the unconscious. Juliette herself pondered whether Julian was not seeking to find in her, his dead mother.

## Time and dynasty

There are grounds for believing that the propagation of this dynastic influence begins to wane beyond the third or fourth generation, the point at which the possibility of any direct lived experience with the original descendent yields to a communicated culturally shared narrative. Cultural theorist Jan Assman details this critical intergenerational period – one of between 3 and 4 generations or 80 to 100 years – as forming the temporal boundaries of what he calls communicative memory.[42] This intergenerational juncture marks the point at which someone has to contend with 'remembering' a socially relevant past more in terms of how it has been represented to them by others than by any direct knowledge of it themselves. T. H. Huxley died in 1895. Francis was born 28 years later, never having directly known him. If the waning social power of a dynasty matches this communicative cliff edge, then there is the distinct probability that Francis – as the son of Julian, and the great-grandson of T. H. Huxley – would be the family member uncomfortably situated to have felt its ramifications most acutely, experiencing a mismatch between cultural expectations of family members and the social and cultural possibilities still open as dynastic social power wanes. The generation of which Francis was a member may thus have been the first to be truly haunted by the ghost and legacy of T. H. Huxley.

The significance of this period of communicative memory has relevance way beyond the Huxleys. The wider political consequences of this are likely to be felt as memory and knowledge of the Second World War and its horrors will soon no longer reside in the lived experience of anyone. The approach of this experiential singularity may well have some role in the worldwide renaissance of far-right ideology, Holocaust denial and negative attitudes towards

European integration. Communicative memory within families has been relatively neglected in the psychological literature – though it is one place where it has been seriously examined. The Scottish psychiatrist R. D. Laing's studies of family dynamics makes explicit references to the conscious and unconscious messages and behaviours carried down family lines. Perhaps the wish to make sense of his place in the family was one factor in drawing Francis to friendship with Laing.

## Intellectual hauntings 1: fear, supremacy and eugenics

The huge expectations of success and the requirement to maintain social position which membership of the Huxley family engendered, cannot be neatly partitioned from the intellectual pursuits in which Francis and other family members were engaged.

The head of the Huxley dynasty, T. H. Huxley who had played a pivotal role in persuading the general public of the correctness of Darwin's theory of evolution, was not immune from the propensity to give a Darwinian slant to the organisational and political characteristics of society, influenced no doubt by Herbert Spencer, Darwin's contemporary who coined the phrase "survival of the fittest." In a misreading of Darwin's thesis that the struggle for survival occurred between Homo sapiens and their environment, Spencer argued that it was competition between individuals, groups or nations that drove social evolution in human societies and that biological theories could therefore explain what was observed in the social realm. T. H. Huxley, an enlightened man for his time, who believed in equal civil and political rights for people of all races and genders, nevertheless followed Spencer's lead, and subscribed to "social laws of gravitation." "No rational man" he thought,

> cognisant of the facts, believes that the average negro is the equal, still less the superior, of the average white man. And if this were true, it is simply incredible that, when all his disabilities are removed, and our prognathous relative has a fair field and no favor, as well as no oppressor, he will be able to compete successfully with his bigger-brained and smaller-jawed rival.[43]

It is difficult to read this today and not wince! We have already seen that belief in an innate biological superiority, outwardly recognisable through one's social heritage and family name, had been readily inculcated and absorbed into the world-view of family members.

Several of the Huxleys, who from T. H. onwards, were instrumental in popularising science and elevating its societal importance, have inevitably considered the social applications of these hereditarian ideas. Chief amongst these has always been eugenics – the state orchestrated improvement of the population through selected breeding. Francis' father, Julian, was a noted exponent and Aldous Huxley's writing also feature significant contributions to eugenic thought. Francis' own contributions to anthropology may also be better understood when they are compared and contrasted with these ideas of his father.

Thomas Henry Huxley, like his grandson Julian, had come to the view that rule by a technical elite was desirable. The social Darwinism of Spencer gathered adherents. For the patriarch,

> overpopulation was the serpent in the Socialist Eden. For a Darwinian, the unrepentantly high growth rate of the 1870s confirmed the Malthusian prediction. Peace and plenty in a socialist arcadia would only increase the number of births and start the struggle for resources all over again. Huxley had no faith that even a "despotic government" could control population by a eugenic program.[44]

Science was not neutral, as he used to think. The river of politics runs perennially through it, most clearly when its pronouncements enter the realm of population dynamics and the class structure. Science and knowledge in both T. H. and Julian Huxley's determination would liberate the masses. Julian is considered by some to be a crucial figure responsible for bridging the gap between the 'old eugenics' to a new 'reform eugenics' rooted in molecular biology.[45] His thought is premised on seeing humans as the leading edge of an evolutionary process which, transcending the purely biological, had now entered the domain of culture. Julian envisaged a programme of social planning which would position birth control, reproductive technology, euthanasia and social welfare within a biologically conceived framework. It is difficult not to see clear links between such "world-population-planning" and his own grandfather's championing of an educated society, policed and led by elites. Though identified as anti-racist and opposed to Nazi racial science, which he saw as pseudo-scientific, Julian's views were authoritarian and anything but egalitarian. He continued to espouse a form of racism, not dissimilar to his grandfather. This was presented, within what he considered to be a 'humanistic,' scientific, 'ethical' context – all the while supporting restrictive US immigration controls – designed in order to keep out supposed racial inferiors – and favouring the nurturance of a scientific-cultural elite.[46]

Rupert Sheldrake described his own experience, as a student at Cambridge University, of Julian's proselytising for the eugenic cause:

> When I was an undergraduate, I joined the Cambridge Humanistic Association, because I was converted to atheism as part of my scientific education ... After a few months I stopped going to the meetings, they basically were very boring ... I remember a lecture by Julian Huxley, who at that time was the president of the British Humanistic Association. He gave a lecture on the improvement of the human race though eugenics. That was the way forward. We needed to improve the genetic stock of the educated classes. We needed to have an upgrade of evolution. The

simplest way this could happen would be through sperm donations and artificial inseminations, the techniques were now available. We need great sperm donors. Then he described the ideal sperm donor. He had to be someone who came from a distinguished family, preferably a scientist who achieved distinction in public life, was somebody who was a leader of public affairs, somebody with proven intelligence, like being on the Brains Trust. It soon became clear that the ideal sperm donor was none other than Sir Julian Huxley himself.[47]

Julian's aspirations for a society predicated on eugenics were for many years shared by his brother Aldous, who in 1927 had argued that intelligence was a source of political power which, if harnessed appropriately, could underpin a truly 'rational' state apparatus. This would require the "creation and maintenance of a ruling aristocracy of mind"[48] in which the "naturally best men should be at the top" – these being "best fitted to govern."[49] "Only mental grown-ups should"[50] be allowed to vote, protested Aldous, simultaneously lambasting France where "certified idiots"[51] enjoyed the privilege. Extending these intellectual aristocratic ideals ought not, he thought, present any "insuperable difficulty."[52] In the same year he contemplated society "organised as a mental hierarchy."[53]

In *Brave New World*, written only four years later, Aldous took this vision to its logical conclusion, portraying a genetically engineered social class system. Shortly afterwards he would advocate compulsory sterilisation.

Aldous' lengthy flirtation with these beliefs was seemingly brought to an abrupt halt when he saw how they functioned in the real world when, in January 1933, Hitler became Chancellor of Germany. Had the British political establishment of the day swung their weight behind Aldous' favoured eugenics policies, the egalitarian post-war future would have been annulled.

In his eyes, to envision a socially organised aristocracy of the mind was a form of rebellion against a society organised, then as now, around the privileges of wealth and power – rebellion which would be in the hand of technocrats. In a "scientific civilisation society must be organised on a caste basis"[54] he argued. What Aldous had difficulty imagining – as so many still do – was a functioning society which was non-hierarchical. It is when contemplating such a scenario, and encountering the customary objections as to its alleged impossibility, that belief in the idea of social rank as biologically programmed into the human species comes to the fore. Aldous' views need, of course, to be seen in the context of their times. European democracy – for him a "blend of mob rule and irresponsible tyranny"[55] – appeared to be a failed project, with global disorder and economic chaos beckoning. Into the mist of intoxicating fear which this aroused, Aldous brought a range of ideas into which he had already been schooled – not just within his own family but within the social strata in which he moved and had been educated. That he performed a rapid volte-face and assumed a significant role within the antifascist movement does not wipe the slate clean.

Comparisons between the 1930s and our own troubled times are now made with alarming regularity. In the aftermath of economic and political disequilibrium instigated by the 2007/2008 financial crisis, European Social Democracy is again under siege from self-styled populist and neo-fascist political movements. In 2012, the British right-wing politician Jacob Rees-Mogg declared the choice for our age is between "the collective and constant mediocrity" and "freedom and great peaks of human endeavour."[56] Had this been said by either Julian or Aldous in their day, one would not have been surprised. Aldous Huxley's swing to the anti-fascist cause, as was the case with his brother Julian, challenged little in the ecosystem of ideas which connects our age with the age of the 20th century's most terrible wars.

When Aldous came to look back on his most famous novel more than a quarter of a century after its initial publication, he was still unable to recognise the problems and contradictions which came with his attachment to extolling intellectual elitism and supremacy. In *Brave New World Revisited*, he argued that the failures of Hitler's master race were in part because,

> The Nazis did not have time – and perhaps did not have the intelligence and the necessary knowledge – to brainwash and condition their lower leadership.[57]

In this appraisal, Aldous mentions neither the ravages of the Russian winter nor the crucial defeat of the German army at Stalingrad! Having proclaimed that the Nazis' own lack of intelligence may have cost them victory, Aldous proceeds to dig a bigger hole for himself.

> When he writes about such vast abstractions as Race History and Providence, Hitler is strictly unreadable. But when he writes about the German masses and the methods used for dominating and directing them, his style changes. Nonsense gives place to sense.[58]

Aldous denigration of Hitler's racial theorising did not, however, preclude him from making comments that would not have been out of place at a National Socialist rally. One year after the Nuremburg laws had been passed in Germany he wrote, "at the resent rate of decrease in the birth rate, the white race will be extinct in a few generations."[59] It gets little better when he elaborates upon what Hitler's supposed sense is comprised of. The dictator's view, that the masses are "incapable of abstract thinking and uninterested in any fact outside the circle of their immediate experience," and that their behaviour was "determined ... by 'feelings and unconscious drives,'"[60] for Aldous, contains "at least an element of truth." He adds, with respect to crowds, "Hitler was perfectly correct in his estimate of human nature."[61]

Fear of a herd mentality has been a recurring feature in discourse on crowd psychology since Gustav Le Bon's work in the late 19th century. As psychologists Fergus Neville and Stephen Reicher have noted, Le Bon, like Julian and Aldous Huxley, strongly identified with the social elite. It is a matter of irony that Aldous' views on the irrational, emotive nature of crowd behaviour properly belong to a school of thought, fundamentally Nietzschean in character, which was promulgated by the elites he himself identified with, and which they promoted in pursuit of their own class interests.

*Brave New World* will continue to be read as a dystopian novel, but in light of Aldous Huxley's affiliation with eugenics, elitism and state planning, one may consider the possibility that it is a good deal more complicated than that. David Bradshaw, his biographer, acknowledges that although *Brave New World* has been consistently interpreted as a milestone in English literature, condemnatory of genetic engineering, the view is a mistaken one. He observes that,

> At the time of the novel's publication ... Huxley did not regard the notion of a pyramidal caste system as abhorrent and he was, at the very least, equivocal in his attitude to the state use of eugenics.[62]

Aldous' stance, in conformity with a fear of the irrational mass, leads naturally to a justification for social control whether that is enacted physically, at the behest of the state, or through psychological means. In addition to the scenario of a cloned social hierarchy, the novel contains the dystopian thread of a populace kept in psychological and social stasis by pharmacological means. The dual 'nightmare' of planned breeding and mind manipulation which it portrays – though it differs from thought control via the propagation of what Chomsky would later refer to as 'necessary illusions'[63] – are nonetheless consequences which arise logically from the social identification and beliefs of Aldous Huxley himself.

To be fair to Aldous, his journeys in the hinterlands of Northern England in the early 1930s, revealed to him, as to Orwell, the ugly brutality of the English class system; that poverty was neither a crime nor the result of a character flaw. "I am ashamed" he wrote "of being a tourist from another world, sight-seeing in the alien Englands of manual labour and routine."[64] He was left with an enduring discomfort and a new found respect for working people.

Aldous placed himself firmly in the camp fighting for human freedom. He held this to be "supremely valuable," but it was an amorphous and ambiguous freedom which he defended and ultimately his commitment to elite thinking withstood the emotional challenge of his experience on the road. At the conclusion of *Brave New World Revisited*, written towards the end of his life, despite all his previous protestations against centralised political and economic power,[65] Aldous remarked that "there seems to be no good reason why a thoroughly scientific dictatorship should ever be overthrown."[66] Rightly fearful of the capacity of the powerful to utilise technology to shape the minds of the less powerful, he was unable to grasp the subtler means by which the forces of compliance were enacted closer to home.

Aldous' empathy for the less fortunate in society had its limits. "I had a great capacity for not being human"[67] he wrote. Francis described his beloved uncle in similar terms, as "an exceptionally intelligent tourist in the realm of feeling."[68] This can be sensed in his thinking on eugenics – and it suffused other aspects of his thought and conduct. Even while opening the "doors of perception" to rediscover "the perceptual innocence of childhood,"[69] Aldous could still insist that the keys to the door be kept from all but intellectual and philosophical heavyweights. Only they were blessed with the ability to extract the maximum benefit from their psychedelic excursions into the "unfathomable mystery of pure being."[70]

The same capacity for emotional detachment and self-aggrandisement was present in Julian. In making attributions about their good fortune, both saw no further than their own personal and cognitive makeup – which they and others in their social circles believed was their due inheritance. Contemporary psychologists have come to understand the proclivity for actors in powerful social groups to ascribe their successes to their own unique qualities as one of *cultural misattribution bias*.[71] This bias, which removes from consideration the privileges afforded by the groups to which they belong, has haunted the narrative of the extraordinariness of the Huxley dynasty.

Thomas Henry Huxley, whose journey through life occurred in the midst of the social transformations of the 19th century, was in a fortunate and crucial position – in the right place and at the right time. These transformations of intellectual, social, economic and political life came to shape the 20th century. They undoubtedly shaped the lives of all the Huxleys who would be born into it. Thomas Henry, Julian and Aldous Huxley were also the proximal familial influences in shaping the intellectual environment in which Francis developed.

## Intellectual hauntings 2: Francis Huxley and the human condition

Francis Huxley continued his great-grandfather's inestimable regard for teaching, combining erudition and entertainment in public adult education. What conjoins them is their interest in general knowledge, philosophy, scientific puzzles, cosmology anthropology, moral and religious thought, literature, poetry, paintings, music and ritual dance – and the desire to speculate on the sense and meaning of the great enigma of existence. The requisites were there, we might surmise, from his early days. He was intelligent, had wide interests in zoology and anthropology and was ready, in his own inimitable way, to play his part in this illustrious family. His fate as a member of the family was not something he could escape.

> When I arrived at Oxford just after the war, I remember walking down the Cornmarket on Saturday afternoon. The street was very crowded and a woman in her late 40s at a distance of about eight paces, suddenly stopped. As I came near, she put out her hands and said, "You're a Huxley" – to my horror! She had known my parents when they were living in Oxford,

in the early 20s. She had recognized me just by having known my father and presumably Aldous.[72]

He continues:

It was a slightly disagreeable moment in my life, to be so instantly recognisable. And also, alas, slightly flattering. There is this ghastly thing about being flattered by sharing a family name and being the pillion riser for large minds who zoom down the little ways of life. One sort of wades in there, thinking that everybody must acknowledge the force of genius.

In the midst of his proposed project on '*The Mutual Self*,'[73] Francis can be found ruminating on the network of family relationships and scholarly preoccupations which had preceded him. He summarised the intellectual heritage which Aldous brought as one derived not from the Huxleys but from the Arnolds, the side of his grandmother Julia's family. This was a family, Francis thought, "that concerned itself with literature, sweetness and light, and religion and morality,"[74] not so dissimilar, in fact, from the larger Huxley clan. This cursory list, however, omits other intersections of familial interest. Elsewhere Francis described his maternal grandfather, Thomas Arnold as a "natural mystic beset by rational doubts."[75]

The mystery of the world contested by the opposing claims of mysticism and rationality is one which pervades the thought of generations of Huxleys; Francis' particular contribution – the place of the sacred in human thought – will be examined later. Despite both T. H. Huxley and Julian working at the forefront of Evolutionary Biology, Francis was not the first of the Huxley family to sign up to a belief in the paranormal. His father Julian had many years earlier entertained the possibility that 'disembodied spirits' – explicable, of course, by science – may persist. Aldous, his uncle, also subscribed to an ultimate reality beyond the reaches of materialist science and like Francis was later to do, formed a friendship with the celebrated medium Eileen Garrett. For a while Aldous and his wife Maria ran a series of parapsychology experiments which took in anything from séances and hypnotism to levitating tables. Francis' sympathy towards the paranormal needs to be considered within this larger familial context and the roots of its fame in the Victorian era when both materialism and spiritualism vied for intellectual attention. The mutual tension and attraction between materialism and 'occultism' is one which echoes through early psychoanalytic thought and continues to draw blood in the present day.

Francis, like his predecessors, found no abiding solution to the conundrum of existence from either of these two frames of reference. His theoretical and practical endeavours, like theirs, concerned as they were with the place of human beings in the natural world, eventually turned to our political and cultural responsibilities in it. Just as Julian had stood at the helm of the

London Zoo and UNESCO, Francis would be instrumental in the founding of Survival International, dedicated to campaigning for the rights of tribal peoples. He also followed in the family footsteps, by moving freely between artistic and scientific modes of practice, in both thought and action – this having become something of a family creed. Perhaps more than his luminous relatives, however, Francis was moved to explore the limits of rationality. Consequently, his contributions, even while working in the same intellectual terrain as had other Huxleys, both reshaped the landscape and extended the boundaries of the known within it.

Francis' approach to the opposition between materialism and spiritualism, following Gödel,[76] was to stress the impossibility of reducing the world to a single axiomatic system, whatever its nature. His father Julian's advocacy for a humanistic science to replace religion was evangelical in its fervour. Aldous, for his part, had sought revelation without religion.[77] Faced with the dilemmas posed by this cognitive and familial duality, Francis emphasised the value of seeking understanding not only in material terms but in symbolic and even mythological ones. This was where Western thought could learn from those it studied in anthropological terms. Going beyond anything his father or great-grandfather had considered, he saw in Darwinism a failure to develop an aesthetic as well as an intellectual appreciation of nature, a neglect of "that feminine intuitive capacity of which Goethe, made such good use." For Darwin "nature was ... (but) male and full of machinery."[78] Francis here adopts a critique, not only in accord with contemporary feminist thought – which echoes Virginia Woolf's assertion that "science was not sexless"[79] – but sympathetic to Henri Bergson's insistence that evolution be appraised as a fluid creative continuity of the real.[80] Francis, like Bergson, thought that reducing the intelligibility of nature to issues of structural mechanics was profoundly mistaken. For both of them, questions of meaning and creativity were not only legitimate but paramount. To be cognisant of the dynamic creativity of life in the world meant extending one's intellectual and emotional being into relationship with the sublime. Francis saw that Darwin, once back in England, had turned his back on this, mutating into a repressed shadow of the exuberant soul that had sailed on the Beagle.

Francis read Darwin from a psychologically informed perspective and saw characteristics of the man still residing in the modern neo-Darwinian synthesis of evolutionary thought. Francis' propensity to read Darwin in this way may be considered in tandem with his wish to make sense of the psychological legacy bestowed on himself as a Huxley – the origins of the family's pre-eminence after all go back to his great-grandfather's confrontation with Darwin's master work. If Darwinian thought had been so influential in his own family was there not something to be gained by looking beyond its purely rational and evidential basis and examining the psychological conditions of its origins? Francis had a longstanding interest in the limitations of rationalism for understanding the human condition. His approach to this was fundamentally different to that taken by T. H., Julian or Aldous. In Francis' life and work can be found a genuine fascination with human beings who live outside the comfort zone of the everyday constructed world – whether constructed by common sense, scientific logic or Western norms. This, as we have seen, included those, who in our own and other cultures, pursued and claimed contact with a spirit world, but it also included those deemed 'mentally ill,' whose thoughts and actions were framed by our society as inextricably irrational. Francis may have been led to this by what he had observed in his own family – particularly the recurrent nervous breakdowns of his father. Julian's episodic psychological crises earned him a diagnosis of manic depression, but the label tells us little or nothing of what lay behind his problems nor of the difficulties beyond these episodes which his conduct and mood posed for his wife and sons.

One can almost see Juliette's difficulties with Julian immortalised in a photograph of the pair taken in Uganda in 1960, while Julian was UNESCO's adviser on wildlife conservation.[81] The picture contains three figures, Juliette, situated to the left, stands gazing into the distance on her right. Julian is to the right of the picture, with a supporting stick in hand, angled left foot forward and looking glumly towards the camera. Between them, almost directly adjacent to Juliette and with some distance between him and Julian, is a local African guide, standing tall, solemn and dignified, seemingly parachuted into the midst of a domestic dispute he can do nothing to resolve. The stamp of colonialism is not the only relational aspect frozen into the photo. It illustrates what Susan Sontag might have described as a "zone of misery"[82] – that it is not just the representative of a continent that stands between Julian and Juliette.

For Francis, when young, the more immediate difficulty may have been Julian's aloofness and distance towards his children. The Huxley obsession with work, success and recognition, no doubt, reminded Francis that when one lived in an environment in which one was loved only for what one did, psychological stability had to be reckoned with. What price the utopian improvement of humankind if it did not extend to one's own family? Aldous had written that "the treaties we make with fate are imposed on us; we have to accept their terms, almost unconditionally."[83] Francis might perhaps have begged to differ. The tension that hung in the domestic air led Francis to say that he did not want children, as he had no desire to perpetuate the madness which struck his family. He had a strong desire, however, to understand it and to avoid the fate of his father – an "expurgated version of a man,"[84] D. H. Lawrence had said of him to Juliette.

Francis' desire to comprehend people whom society has categorised as 'irrationally' 'other' is telling, reflective perhaps also of a wish to escape the bounds of a Huxleyan rationality imposed in a still imperially minded Britain on a family whose class position demanded emotional reservation, politeness and etiquette. That Francis entitled his study of the Ka'apor '*Affable Savages*' may be seen as a pointed rebuke and challenge to what was conceptualised as 'savage.' His explicit aim to accommodate himself to their world-view and allow them to reveal it in the pages of his book is the first hint that he is on a pathway that leads to the interior world of the other, and a world away from his upbringing. This journey would take him eventually into the company of R. D. Laing.

We now come full circle to a number of issues explored in this chapter. In the midst of the Dialectics of Liberation conference in 1968, Laing drew attention to the embeddedness of all levels of social organisation across time as well as space and its infrequent explicit recognition. This omission still haunts social science. There are important lessons to be drawn here about how we understand human beings – in this case Francis himself – pertaining both to the intergenerational limits on our perceptions of what makes us who we are and how we build enduring images of national, ethnic, cultural or family identity both within and outside of this limit – images which function as mythical warhorses, providing fantasies of direction and purpose to human collectivities. The story of Francis and R. D. Laing will be taken up elsewhere in this book.

## Notes

1 Francis Huxley interviewed on 10 July 1985, by David K. Dunaway, p.4 FHA.
2 Huxley, J. (1935, p.7) *T. H. Huxley's Diary of the Voyage of HMS Rattlesnake*. Edited from the unpublished MS. London. Chatto & Windus.
3 See Clarke (1968, p.58).
4 Ibid.
5 Desmond, A. (1994, p.267) *Huxley: From Devil's Advocate to Evolution's High Priest*. New York. Perseus Books.
6 Ibid., p.304.
7 Levine (2011, p.126).
8 Desmond, A. J. and Moore, J. R. (1992, p.xvi) *Darwin*. London. Penguin Books..
9 Bibby (1960, p.30).
10 White (2003, p.136).
11 Ibid., p.172.
12 Bibby (1960, p.234).
13 Desmond (1994, p.xvi).
14 Ibid., p.350.
15 Ibid., p.119.
16 Ibid., p.235.
17 Ibid., p.241.
18 Frosch (2013, p.119).
19 The underlying assumption, that high intelligence is carried from one generation to the next has been extensively researched. Studies pointing to IQ being highly heritable (that variation in population intelligence is highly related to variation in genetics) have routinely used the twin-study paradigm. This compares the IQs of identical twins to fraternal twins. The greater similarity in the IQs of identical twins has been interpreted as supporting the hereditarian thesis. The major problem with this is that identical twins share more similar environments than fraternal twins. The observed data as such can just as easily be taken to support an environmental thesis. In a critical review of this methodology, Andrew Coleman

([1987] *Facts, Fallacies and Frauds in Psychology*. London. Routledge) concluded that it was impossible to come to any firm conclusion.
20  See Clarke (1968, p.xiii).
21  Baker (1976, p.7).
22  See Clarke (1968, p.151).
23  Psychologists could, of course, consider this an example of the *Fundamental attribution error* – the tendency to attribute success to one's personal disposition rather than to external factors. At the time of this letter, T. H. Huxley was, on his own admission, a member of the establishment. The privileges of this membership were then socially bequeathed to all subsequent members of the family.
24  See Dunaway (1995, pp.37–45).
25  Ibid.
26  *A Huxley Family Album*, p.5.. Laura Huxley – Aldous' second wife repeats this discursive meme –also declaring that with Julian and Aldous "it sees as if the Huxley genes skipped a generation to assert their particular characteristics." See Dunaway (1995, p.6).
27  *A Huxley Family Album*, p.11.
28  Juliette Huxley (1986, p.70).
29  Ibid., p.141.
30  David King Dunaway (1995, p.3) 'explains' Trevenen's suicide as him being the "victim of an inherited family tendency to depression" thus blindly repeating the errors of biographers that behaviours in the Huxley clan are to be explained by biology, even in the presence of a good deal of plausible evidence to suggest otherwise. In addition to the noted family pressure to succeed, Trev's 'academic failure' and his relationship with the chambermaid; Naomi Haldane Mitchison, a friend of Aldous, when interviewed by David King Dunaway, remarked that both Aldous and Julian blamed their father for Trev having killed himself. It is also of interest that Julian's, Aldous' and Trevenen's sister Margaret has been somewhat omitted from the Huxley narrative. After Trev's suicide she largely broke off contact with her brothers. See Dunaway (1995, pp.9–11).
31  See Clarke (1968, p.163).
32  Ibid., p.164.
33  Susie is referring to her mother, Ann Taylor, who married Anthony Huxley, Francis' brother.
34  Huxley, J. (1985, p.7) interviewed by D. Dunaway on Aldous Huxley. 5 July. London. FHA, Tape 2.
35  Interview with Rupert Sheldrake.
36  Interview with Rupert Sheldrake.
37  Interview with Rupert Sheldrake.
38  Victoria is the third daughter of Anthony (Francis' brother) and Ann Huxley.
39  Interviewed in March 2018.
40  Rockwell, D. and Giles, D. C. (2009, pp.178–210) Being a Celebrity: A Phenomenology of Fame. *Journal of Phenomenological Psychology*, 40.
41  Solnit, R. (2018) *Call Them by True Names*. London. Granta Publications.
42  See Assman, J. (1998) *Moses the Egyptian. The Memory of Egypt in Western Monotheism*. London. Harvard University Press. See also László, J. (2003, pp.180–192) History, Identity and Narratives. In *Theories and Controversies in Social Psychology*. J. László and W. Wagner, Eds. Budapest. New Mandate. László provides a useful summary of Assman's key ideas. Frosch (2013, p.119) (see above

cit.) notes the section in the Bible (Exodus 20.5) where it speaks of the "iniquity of the fathers upon the children ..." referencing the time span as Assman's communicative memory – "... unto the third and fourth generation."
43 Huxley, T. H. (1865/2001, p.67) Emancipation. Black and White. In. *Collected Essays. Vol III Science and Education*. Nabu Press. See further discussion in Gould, S. J. (1997) *The Mismeasure of Man*. London. Penguin.
44 Desmond, A. (1997, p.193, quoting from his autobiography) *Huxley: Evolution's High Priest*. London. Michael Joseph..
45 See Weindling (2012, pp.480–499).
46 Huxley's opposition to Nazi racial science, his repudiation of race as a valid scientific construct and his authorship of the document 'We Europeans' in the 1930s has seen him favourably located as belonging in an avowedly anti-racist contingent. See, for example, Richards, G. (1997) *Race, Racism and Psychology. Toward a Reflexive History*. London. Routledge. His views on immigration have received less attention, perhaps, because this kind of racism has been a long-been-received wisdom in British political opinion. Though Huxley is rightly credited with replacing race with the more useable term 'ethnic group,' he continued to uphold a view that peoples could be differentiated on the basis of cultural superiority or inferiority and was supportive of Britain's imperial role.
47 Interviewed in March 2018.
48 Huxley, A. (1927, xviii).
49 Ibid., p.163.
50 Ibid., p.162.
51 Ibid.., p.163.
52 Ibid., p.159.
53 Cited in Bradshaw (1995, p.xiii).
54 Huxley, A. (1932) Science and Civilisation. BBC Programme, 13 January. Cited in Bradshaw (1995, pp.112–113)..
55 Huxley, A. (1920) *Athenaeum*, 10 December. Cited in Bradshaw (1995, p.11).
56 See Beckett, A. (2018) How to Explain Jacob Rees-Mogg? Start with his Father's Books. *The Guardian*, 9 November.
57 Huxley, A. (1959/2004, p.52).
58 Ibid., p.53.
59 Huxley, A. (1936, pp.84–88) How to Improve the World. *Nash's Pall Mall Magazine*, xcviii, December, cited in Bradshaw (1995, p.228).
60 Huxley, A. (1959/2004, p.54).
61 Huxley, A. (1959/2004, pp.58–59).
62 Bradshaw (1995, p.38).
63 See Chomsky, N. (1989) *Necessary Illusions. Thought Control in Democratic Societies*. Boston. South End Press.
64 Huxley, A. (1931, pp.50–52) Sight-seeing in Alien England. *Nash's Pall Mall Magazine*, lxxxvii, June. Cited in Bradshaw (1995, p.72).
65 See for example Deese (2015, p.17).
66 Huxley, A. (1959/2004, p.154).
67 Cited in Huxley, F. (1999) Preface to Dunaway (1995).
68 Huxley, F. (1995) 'Aldous.' Preface to Dunaway (1995).
69 Huxley, A. (1954/2004, p.12) *The Doors of Perception*. London. Vintage.
70 Ibid., p.18.

71 See Hegarty, P. (2019, pp.48–51) How Do We 'Other'? *The Psychologist*, May.
72 Francis Huxley interviewed on 10 July 1985, by David K. Dunaway (1999, p.3). FHA.
73 Huxley, F. (undated) A Proposal for The Mutual Self. FHA.
74 Ibid., p.11.
75 *A Huxley Family Album*, p.8.
76 Kurt Gödel proposed the incompleteness theorem. This states that no axiomatic system is capable of producing all known truths. An intriguing treatment of some of Gödel's ideas can be found in Hofstadter, D. (1980) *Gödel, Escher, Bach: An Eternal Golden Braid*. London, Penguin.
77 Deese (2015).
78 Francis Huxley (1959/1960, p.7) Charles Darwin – Life and Habit. *The American Scholar*, Autumn/Winter, pp.1–19.
79 Woolf, V. (1938) *Three Guineas*. London. Hogarth Press. Feminist critiques of science draw attention to gender inequalities in the institutions of science and, as well as highlighting issues in the methods, contents and values of pure and applied science, argue that scientific authority has been used to rationalise the masculine-dominated status quo. The latter has been a significant subject of debate in evolutionary psychology. See Crasnow, S. (2013, pp.413–423) Feminist Philosophy of Science: Values and Objectivity. *Philosophy Compass*, 8 (4); Rose, H. and Rose, S. (2001) *Alas Poor Darwin. Arguments against Evolutionary Psychology*. New York. Vintage.
80 Bergson, H. (2002) *Key Writings*. London. Bloomsbury.
81 The photograph appears in Juliette's biography (inserted at pp.152–153 and was also reproduced by the *Independent* newspaper for Juliette's obituary (30 September 1994).
82 Sontag, S. (2008, p.8) *On Photography*. London. Penguin Modern Classics.
83 Huxley, A. (1931, pp.16–19) Abroad in England. *Nash's Pall Mall Magazine*, lxxxvii, May. Cited in Bradshaw (1995, p.56).
84 *A Huxley Family Album*, p.20.

# Part III
# The facts of life

# 5   Gordonstoun

Every tale of a human life might be said to begin from an arbitrary point in time. One convention is to begin with the birth of the designated subject. To do this, however, belies the varied contexts – whether domestic, institutional, national, international and political, together with their respective histories – into which they are thrown. Where then to begin? In the tale of Francis Huxley, we begin with the first educational institution to shape his developing mind – Gordonstoun – and its own enigmatic encounters with the tides of chance and European circumstance.

## Education

Kurt Hahn (1886–1974) was born into a well-off industrial family, his parents living in a villa on the shore of Wannsee, the westernmost locality of Berlin – a place destined to enter the annals of dark human history as the site of the Wannsee Conference, presided over by the National Socialists Reinhard Heydrich and Adolf Eichmann and arranged to ensure the intergovernmental collaboration that would set the seal on the attempted extermination of European Jews. Kurt was the second of four sons. When his father died young, the 21-year-old Kurt inherited sufficient wealth to guarantee him a life, without the need for daily grind. His mother Charlotte kept an open house and literary saloon, with visitors of the likes of Arthur Rubinstein, Walther Rathenau and Lina und Raoul Richter. In two distinct periods he studied Psychology, Pedagogics, Philosophy and Classics at Christ Church College Oxford, possibly at the same time as Francis' father Julian Huxley was at Balliol College.

Hahn founded three large, well-known schools in his lifetime. Having been a fierce critic of Hitler and the Nazi movement, he was arrested within the Schloss Salem School, situated on the shores of Lake Konstanz, in March 1933 and spent five days in prison. He was set free, after the intercession of the British Prime Minister, Ramsay MacDonald and Berthold Early of Baden but was forced to leave Germany. He immigrated to Scotland, where he helped to found Gordonstoun School in 1934. It stands in 180 acres of woodland, within a stone's throw of sandstone cliffs and sandy beaches on the coast of the Moray Firth. Hahn's flight to the UK meant that he escaped the fate of other German Jews, whose lives ended in the Nazi death camps. Hahn founded Gordonstoun on the same principles as the Schloss Salem School – to counteract the corrupting influences of society and create, nurture and develop compassionate people, who could then take their appropriate place within the elite of a given society and contribute to its moral governance – *Plus est en Vous* – There is more in you (than you think). Hahn had once seen this line etched into the stone of a Belgian church. It became the Gordonstoun school motto.

Francis' grandmother Julia Francis Arnold-Huxley and his aunt Margaret Arnold-Huxley both founded primary schools in Surrey. By the time Francis came of age to start school, his father's younger sister was 30 years old and he might easily have been sent to her school. Instead he embarked on his formal education at Byron House Preparatory school, following his older brother Anthony there. Later he would attend the Surrey Hills Church of England Primary School and then Frensham Heights, an independent school and sixth form college, in Farnham, Surrey. For both, being apart from their upper middle-class intellectual parents was part and parcel of growing up in the 1920s and 1930s in England. Sparse documentation exists regarding Francis' primary schooling, but rather more can be said of his teenage years, when aged 14–19 (from 1937 to 1942) he was sent to Gordonstoun. His father Julian wrote,

> We liked Hahn's system of entrusting increased responsibility to boys and sending them on special assignments on land or sea: out of this grew the Outward-Bound movements which are now flourishing both in Britain and abroad.[1]

## Reflections on Gordonstoun

At Gordonstoun all the pupils had to practice housekeeping skills, making up their beds, mopping floors, cleaning their rooms and doing the dishes. Thus, despite being a costly enterprise as a private school, it was not an easy life. Some pupils readily experienced being bullied both physically and mentally, and therefore hated being there. W. H. Auden is quoted as having said, that every former English-boarding-school boy understands fascism, because he lived under such a regime. The writer and former pupil William Boyd likened his time there to "penal servitude."[2] He recalls the boarding school as being a dangerous place for junior pupils (9–15), until that is they reached a senior position, whence the cycle of bullying and intimidation would begin again from a newer loftier vantage point. If seniors detected a junior smoking, they would strip him, shave his pubic hair and have older boys anoint his genitals with toothpaste. Boyd was there at the same time as Prince Charles, who arrived in 1962. "I know Prince Charles had a miserable time" Boyd remarked. "It was a democratic school and he got no special treatment, so maybe that was the problem."

It is of interest that Queen Elizabeth, the Queen Mother (Philip's mother-in-law) had apparently warned her daughter and son-in-law, against sending Prince Charles to a boarding school in Scotland because she thought he would be miserable and lonely in the far north. She pleaded for Eton. Despite these instincts, Philip, now the Duke of Edinburgh, ruled that his eldest son would have to attend his beloved alma mater. The Queen Mother's apprehensions were well grounded with her grandson reporting his misgivings back to her and his mother. Though Prince Philip had loved Gordonstoun, Charles hated it. He considered his time there "a prison sentence," and referred to the school as "Colditz in kilts."[3] The 400 boys schooled there, regardless of size, age or weather conditions, wore shorts at all times. Each day began with a brisk run in the grounds followed by hot and cold showers and ended in pale-green dormitories with crude wooden beds, where the windows were kept open throughout the night.

Snobbish behaviour from privileged boys to members of the 'lower stratums' of society was the order of the day – as it still is – and issues of race and class were omnipresent. As in all such schools, talking to teachers only made things worse. On the surface, Boyd tells us, everything looked harmonious, equitable and happy. But in the underworld beneath this lurked a hothouse of Dantean intrigue and torture. The old-boy networks which still flourish in British society and indeed govern it, are formed here. It is an elite constituted by the five per cent of boys who went to these private schools. Gordonstoun has an explicit ideology against bullying, but that has not stopped the kind of behaviour which has haunted each generation there. Francis did complain later,[4] that he too had suffered there at the hands of others. The Gordonstoun system, wherein boys shared a dormitory with around six others no doubt afforded ample opportunities for conflict. There is more than a suggestion from interviews with those who knew Francis well that the one-upmanship, and the holier than thou attitude, which was bred in these groups of adolescent boys scarred Francis, who, like the other boys he boarded with, felt neglected by his parents – in Francis' case, particularly by his father. For all the blessing of a privileged education, it is accompanied, one sees, by the scars of emotional malnourishment. The political diarist Alan Clark described his time in private education – in his case Eton – as providing "an early introduction to human cruelty, treachery and physical hardship."[5]

## Francis Huxley at Gordonstoun

While at Gordonstoun, Francis studied French, History, Latin, English Language, English Literature, Maths and Physics. A year before Francis gained his General School Certificate,[6] a letter from Kurt Hahn to Julian (dated 20 June 1941[7]) paints an amusing picture of the alliance between the headmaster and Francis regarding the pains of religious education at the school.

Dear Huxley,

Your letter of May 25th has remained unanswered but I took action on it. For my sins, I go now to church, from which I had stayed away as repelled as Francis by Mr. Gray's meaningless sermons. In addition, there are now being held fortnightly school services, alternatively in the Anglican Church and in the Presbyterian Chapel, with no Mr. Gray or Dr. Jones officiating. I hope to make our school services as weekly event, sacrificing one of these services to a sermon by Mr. Gray once a term – by way of appeasement – so that Gray would only confront our boys three times a year.

In the meantime, I did not allow Francis, who has now for the second time functioned as acting Guardian, to absent himself from Mr. Gray's services. I told him:-

a) If I would demand from him after the service he should go up to Mr. Gray and say to him "You have warmed the cockles of my heart," I should understand if he rather died at the stake than did this. As it was, I only asked him, and for that matter myself, to sit through these services politely.

b) His, or my, staying away could only be interpreted as demonstration. I for my part believe that there was only one answer to the Anti-Christ and that was Christ. This was not the moment to demonstrate against the Church.

c) I promised him that I would reduce the occasions on which we had to listen to Mr. Gray to a minimum. This I have done.

I was grateful for your letter except that in consequence of this letter I have now to sit and listen to Mr. Gray myself.

Yours sincerely
K. Hahn

Hahn clearly thought highly of Francis. A postscript to the letter depicts him as a robust and charismatic individual. "He has had" Hahn wrote "a wonderful period of 'unfolding strength': in his work, as a citizen, and as an athlete. You must come and see him as Hamlet." On 23 June 1941, Julian Huxley, by then the author of *Religion without Revelation* (1927), wrote back:

Dear Hahn,

Many thanks for your letter.

I quite understand the position

and entirely agree with what you have done.

I am only sorry that you have suffered as a result.

Yours sincerely
Julian Huxley

## Gordonstoun 81

In this brief exchange we can get a flavour of the humanistic tone which both these men shared. That Hahn felt the need to obey the strictures of the Church of England's earthly representative, Mr. Gray, whoever he was, tells us something not only about the legal orthodoxy of religious instruction in British schools and the power over educational convention which the church then exercised, but of Hahn's assessment of the appropriate times for respect and rebellion. Hahn shared Francis' assessment of the preacher's wisdom and its dulling psychological import. Requiring his acting Guardian of the school, however, to show due propriety to Mr. Gray, while in the act of offering sympathy to the Huxleys' agnostic inclinations, informed Francis' father that the school master had a cool and discerning mind, in whose custody Francis would be well looked after. We are reminded of a story that Gregory Bateson would recount, about the inculcation of respect in Japan. 'The boy learns to respect their father, while the girl learns to *show respect to* their father.' Bateson liked the story, for it exemplified his notion of the difference that made the difference.

A photograph taken by Howard Coster[8] – remembered as the 'photographer of men' and for his innovative and dramatic use of lighting – gives us, the viewers, a slightly voyeuristic peek into a moment of Gordonstoun life – a

*Figure 5.1* Francis Huxley. Photographed by Howard Coster. Photograph reproduced with the kind permission of Gordonstoun School.

82  *The facts of life*

moment devoid of transgressive behaviour – in which a number of older boys are locked in what appears to be earnest discussion.

Francis is amongst them, with his back to us, seated to the right of the boy in the armchair. As in all such photographs which outlast the lives of those in them, we are invited to speculate and fantasise as to what the subject of their discussion was – what was happening immediately prior to the entrance of the photographer and what transpired when he left? We have no information regarding whose room the picture was taken in, though it may well have been one shared by all the boys. We do know that Francis was Vice-Guardian at the time (1941). The Gordonstoun archivist, Louise Avery, who kindly provided the photo, commented:

> Francis was one of the Colour Bearers in Wales (see the attached photograph – Francis has his back to us and looks to be sitting at a desk) and went on to become Guardian in Spring 1942. Colour Bearers were, and still are, roughly comparable to prefects in other schools. Hahn believed that the honour of bearing the school colours should be given to those who embodied the overall values of the school and gave responsible leadership to all other pupils, including the juniors.[9]

Louise also provided us with searchable copies of the *Gordonstoun Record*. Francis makes his first appearance in issue No. 3 in 1938 – being recorded in the August term list of the previous year. His examination results from the Oxford and Cambridge Schools Examination Board appear in the December 1938 edition. There F. J. H. Huxley is documented as having received three credits (a maximum of six was possible – performance in each subject was graded as fail, pass, credit or distinction). The previous summer he had visited, along with his mother, father and brother, his maternal grandmother in Neuchâtel. Then the troupe holidayed in the village of Ronco near Ascona, overlooking Lago Maggiore. These foreign excursions would have lifted his spirits in advance of the subsequent separation which Gordonstoun entailed.

Gordonstoun offered multiple opportunities to participate in sport. Besides rugby and cricket there was athletics, hockey, mountaineering, riding, sailing and birdwatching on offer. Indoor activities included acting (the Nativity Play, a Shakespeare Production), music, handicraft, as well as joining an assortment of societies, be it the Literary Group, Historical Society or Gordonstoun Society. The Gordonstoun Society was founded by a group of sixth formers, for literary, cultural and political discussion. At the second meeting, the discussion and talks focused on scientific knowledge and the decline of civilisation. It is noted that,

> F. Huxley made a good logical speech … but due perhaps to the re-incarnation of certain elements of the Junior Debating Society, the tendency in general was towards laboured abuse. So much time was thus

*Figure 5.2* Julian, Juliette, Anthony and Francis on holiday 1938.

employed that the proposer and opposer had to forgo their concluding speeches.

We learn that Francis took part in the St. John Society, an organisation within the school to study natural history which came into being in May 1938. The society was named after Charles St. John, an eminent naturalist, who lived and worked in Morayshire. The *Record* notes Francis' contribution amongst the society's varied outdoor activities.

> It was open to all boys and members of the staff ... In the summer term, with a membership of 30 boys, the Bird Section was the most active, going on expeditions on Saturday mornings and afternoons and on Tuesday evenings. Several week-end expeditions were made to the Cairngorms ... One evening Mr Marshall, the head forester at Nethybridge, kindly came over and gave us a talk on the birds of the Spey valley. In the Christmas term the organisation became more definite. With Mr Chapman as president, Murray was elected general secretary, and Parker treasurer. Huxley,

Bartholomew and Long became secretaries of the bird, meteorological and aviary sections respectively.[10]

The St. John Society, faced with problems of no allocated space of their own, was forced to hold their meetings in the Biology Laboratory. Nonetheless, with Francis there, they met almost every Tuesday evening to hear lectures on various subjects. These included one on a proposed expedition to Lapland, one on British ducks and one in which Francis "read a paper on *Camouflage in Nature*."[11] On a later occasion, members of the society were honoured by a visit from Francis' father, Julian, who, it is noted, "talked informally to several members of the Society." The same year of Julian's visit, the library, acknowledged with gratitude gifts of books from "Mrs Julian Huxley, Lady Eleanor Cole, Sir Alexander Lawrence, Captain Hendry, and many others."

## Expedition to Lapland

One of the highlights for Francis was joining the aforementioned Gordonstoun Lapland Expedition, which took place in Spring of 1939. Francis maintained a journal of this trip across Lapland, covering events from 4 to 27 April, diligently recording a variety of events. This was a first honing of his latent explorer's skills, which as an adult he would exploit in a uniquely fashionable manner, attested by the versatile nature of his fieldnotes from Gambia, the Amazon and Haiti.

Ten boys and two masters, Mr. Bickersteth and Mr. Chapman, left Gordonstoun on 4 April, travelling first to Aberdeen, then on to Newcastle, whereupon they boarded the '*Leda*,'[12] a vessel "no bigger than an ordinary cross channel boat" with the consequence that "she pitched and rolled horribly."[13] Many of those aboard, sailing experience from Gordonstoun's coast notwithstanding, suffered sea sickness. Francis complained about the unaired awful cabins which drove the boys to seek solace on the first-class promenade deck and by slinging their sleeping bags down between the rescue boats. His penchant for anecdotes and blunt communication is expressed in his encounter with some Spanish sailors who were also travelling on the vessel. These fellow travellers were due to join a merchant ship at Bergen, Norwegian. They "stank," he noted down – perhaps not surprising after a rough crossing.

The adventure across Lapland continued by a predetermined route which is not mapped out in Francis' journal. It ends somehow abruptly on 27 April. A fellow traveller provided further details, including a map, in an account published in the *Gordonstoun Record* No. 4. There was evident joy both in experiencing the polar light and in meeting a few native Laplanders – lappalainen. The map enables us to trace the journey from Lakselv in the North of Norway down to South Karasjok and on by Kautokeino to Karesuando. The records of this school expedition give us a fleeting glimpse of the transition from an ordinary, if privileged, school student to a fledgling explorer.

As Francis mentioned, they were largely reliant for their nightly accommodation and their physical recuperation upon Norwegian State huts, which were placed roughly 15 miles apart. Sometimes they had to make do with their arctic tents, cooking on mobile stoves which they hauled on their sledges – all of which, no doubt, was a significant and impressionable experience for the boys. It was, of course, the parents, who had had to open their purse to finance their offspring's adventure.

Back at Gordonstoun, in 1939, Prince Philip of Greece was elected Guardian, a post which Francis would fill three years later. The husband-to-be of the future monarch was a senior pupil to junior Francis. Unlike Francis, Philip did not have a functional family in England. Though Francis was embedded in a large family, he, like many of his generation from similar families, was forced to leave home at a tender age, to go to boarding school. The potential dangers and damages of boarding school are nowadays more commonly understood. In addition to the aforementioned abuse, a sense of abandonment, depression and emotional detachment are numbered amongst the risks.

Due to the Second World War, Gordonstoun school evacuated to Wales. In Report No. 5, we learn how the entire Gordonstoun community had been reassembled, and the daily school programme adapted to life in Wales. Francis was then a 'house helper' at Plas Dinam – a position of great responsibility akin to 'Head of House' in some other schools. This was a many-gabled, slate-roofed house, used by Lord Davies and his family. It is described affectionately as "long and rambling" and "though one's first emotion at seeing it is surprise, one gets really attracted to it as time passes." This house was in the village of Llandinam, which stands on the River Severn, on the Welsh Border.

## Amateur and family dramatics

The end of term saw the usual Nativity Play and carol singing, with Francis taking the role of one of the kings – a theatrical performance of Francis which, unlike others at Gordonstoun, passed without comment. Drama at Gordonstoun suffered, of course, from the war. This was to be expected, since times had led to the school becoming increasingly crowded and the lack of facilities for complicated productions made life difficult. The *Gordonstoun Record* minutes some notable "achievements" and though it could not be said that "facilities (had) improved" it was more positively affirmed that the "acting has not deteriorated." There were two main Gordonstoun drama institutions – in addition to the Nativity Play there was the 'summer Shakespeare.' The first Shakespeare performed in Wales was Hamlet produced in the village hall of Llandinam, in 1941. The Record notes its "astonishing success, largely due to Francis Huxley's extraordinary performance as Hamlet."[14] This was a night of some significance in the family.

Both Francis' parents had promised to be in the audience, for this would be Francis' final and most prominent theatrical role before leaving school with the General School Certificate. His mother Juliette takes up the story in her diary entrance of 20 November. Julian had gone to the States on a lecture tour, sponsored by the Rockefeller Association to generate support for the USA entering the war against Nazi Germany. Juliette had opposed the trip, as she thought the effort futile, despite both Clement Attlee and Anthony Eden, having expressed interest in the endeavour. Juliette tells us that Julian "spoke to Francis after great telephonic spasm in a few hurried words." He was going to the USA no matter what. With "German submarines swarming the seas like hungry sharks," Juliette felt a weight of "premonition and anxiety in her heart."

> The whole thing was fateful as a Greek play. I was deeply hurt, for all of us, and especially for Francis, who in four days' time was to play Hamlet at Gordonstoun. Julian was betraying the boy's expectation that his father would be there, watching a performance which Hahn, the headmaster, had been in the habit of preparing every two years for the school.[15]

The familial dispute shows Julian in a poor light, breaking his promises and betraying his son, who had seized his opportunity to portray, with considerable aplomb, the figure of Hamlet. Juliette stayed the weekend in Gordonstoun after the Saturday performance, strolling with her Hamlet under a clear starlit sky.

These are experiences which tore into Francis' heart. He had wanted to impress his famous father with his acting and emotional skills – but his desire for a token of recognition and esteem to reflect back from the eyes of the great man came to naught. Julian's behaviour, as on other occasions, appeared selfish and egoistical. A brief anecdote provides a further example of thoughtlessness. Julian gave Francis a copy of his *Memories II*, (1973)[16] with the following inscription: "For dear Francis with love, he dares know about Papa's later life." In this copy Francis wrote on the dedication page: "and nonsense on p.27. As JSH never even read Affable Savages."[17] The offending page in question (p.27) made one reference (of a total of three in the volume) to his son Francis, referring to "the brilliant social anthropologist Lévi-Strauss (who later gave valuable advice to our son Francis when he went on his anthropological expeditions to the Upper Amazon)." To this Francis inscribed in the margin: "Nonsense." Why? Because, Francis Huxley never went to the Upper Amazon. His fieldwork was conducted in the Amazon basin. A further reference to Francis illustrated Julian's efforts to present his relationship with his sons in a good light, describing them as "delightful and beloved companions, and we are lucky to see much of them."[18] It cut little ice with Francis.

After Gordonstoun Francis returned to his parents' London flat, ready to embark on the next phase in his life, and about to encounter, as we will shortly see, the preordained pains, sacrifices and liberties of love, all of which would serve up a white-water ride of angst and decisional conflict for the young man.

## Notes

1. Huxley, J. (1970, p.244).
2. See Brown, M. (2012) The Master Storyteller: William Boyd Interview. *The Telegraph*, 4 February.
3. See Keegan, N. (2017) Not Fit for a Prince? *The Sun*, 19 December.
4. Adele Getty interviewed on 10 April 2018.
5. Quoted in Kirby, A. (2005) Eton's Old Boy Network. *Independent*, 7 December.
6. This qualification was abolished in 1951 and replaced by the system of 'O' and 'A' levels.
7. At this time the original Scottish site of Gordonstoun had been temporally evacuated to be used as a barracks by the Army during the war. It was relocated to Plas Dinam in Montgomeryshire in Mid Wales.
8. Howard Coster, self-styled 'Photographer of Men.' (Stamped on reverse: Howard Coster, Felow of the Royal Society of Arts [F.R.S.A.], Lond.) Book by Terence Pepper (1985) Howard Coster's Celebrity Portraits.
9. Louise Avery, Gordonstoun Archivist/Library Assistant, Gordonstoun School, Elgin, Moray IV30 5RF. Wednesday, 8 May 2019 – Email.
10. No. 3 of the *Gordonstoun Record*, 1938, p.28.
11. No. 4 of the *Gordonstoun Record*, 1939, p.30.
12. "We were due to sail on the 'Vega' on the night of 5 April, but, owing to a succession of misfortunes, we literally 'missed the boat,' in *Gordonstoun Record*, No. 4, Easter 1939, pp.5–16.
13. A Journal of the Journey across Lapland, Spring 1939. p.6. FHA.
14. No. 6 Easter Term 1945. School News 1941–1944.

   This article is an attempt to bridge the gap between the present time and the last issue of the Record in April 1941. It is not easy to cover eleven terms in a single article, and sometimes the absence of notes and records may have led to omission and inaccuracy, for which the editors beg to apologise. The changes have been many and various, but the time covered lies entirely between our two evacuations, and thus contains no- such drastic change as the move to Wales in 1940 or the future return to Morayshire.

15. Ibid., pp.181–182.
16. Huxley, J. (1973) *Memories II*. London. George Allen & Unwin.
17. Ibid. FHA.
18. Ibid., p.89.

# 6   In the Royal Navy

Having successfully finished Gordonstoun, Francis, now residing in his parents' London Zoo flat, found himself in the midst of a burgeoning love affair with Ferelyth. His father was soon to resign his position as secretary of the Zoological Society, making it necessary to move home. The parents took possession of 31 Pond Street in Hampstead, what would be their final home. Having sailed during his boarding school days, and having been on the expedition to Lapland, our hunch is that when it came to serve in the forces in the great fight against fascism, Francis' prior experience made the Navy, rather than the Army, the natural choice. We have no direct information as to how he arrived at his decision. Yet as a 20-year-old playing with the idea of joining up, Ferelyth, being the elder, so the story goes, called him aside and asked him what he wanted to do. "Stay here in England with me or go into the Navy?" Francis: "Navy." Ferelyth "Sure, you want to do that, okay."[1]

He compiled what he called "Poems for a Sailor" – he had typed out up to 50, including ones from Shakespeare, Anne Richmond, John Done, G. M. Hopkins, Naomi Mitchison and his parents' lover, May Sarton. His motto was: "When he (the sailor) is on the ocean, to make him forget the monotonous motion, to help him remember, land and emotion."[2] With Ferelyth, he exchanged poems he had written separately or in love letters to her. Of their tryst more will be said later, when we come to narrating the various twists and turns in Francis' love life.

After an initial period of training, he was assigned as Assistant Navigating Officer (Lieutenant) to serve on the HMS *Ramillies,* a 'Revenge-class superdreadnought battleship,' launched in 1916. The training began with a trip "down the Clyde ... into the Irish Sea," followed by "a bout of sea-sickness from a mixture of apprehension and diesel fumes." In a letter to a friend many years later, Huxley recalls how

> we charged up and down at various knots, and then headed to Tobermory in Skye, where five or six of us from the same mess went ashore and investigated the whiskies and beer in the numerous pubs that stood on either side of the town's one road. The amount they could put away staggered me.[3]

## In the Royal Navy 89

A no-doubt fairly typical induction to life at sea! It is conceivable that when Francis joined the crew in 1942, he experienced the visit of Prime Minister Winston Churchill on the ship in 16 August in Hvalfjörður, Iceland. Churchill was returning from a conference in Newfoundland, Canada, after signing the Atlantic Charter with US President Franklin D. Roosevelt. Thereafter the *Ramillies* returned to Liverpool, for a lengthy refit before setting sail again in late November. The ship was torpedoed by a Japanese submarine in a battle in Diego Suarez, necessitating a return to Devonport for repairs, prior to returning to service in June 1943. She arrived in Kilindini in East Africa, where she re-joined the Eastern Fleet. By late August of that year, Captain Gervase Middleton had assumed command. He would subsequently feature in a legendary story Francis would often, and proudly, tell to gasping audiences. It is recounted in his mother Juliette's memoires and we will encounter it in all its glory shortly.

In January 1944, *Ramillies* was back in the dockyard in Portsmouth, and duly assigned to the Home Fleet. In the build up to Operation Dragoon (D-Day), *Ramillies* sailed to the Mediterranean, where forces were assembled for the imminent invasion of France. *Ramillies* was one of five battleships to support the Normandy landings. In August, Francis was en route to the south of St. Tropez, where the guns of Ramillies took out the heavy German-defence battery, supporting the invading infantry to move inland.

On D-Day, so the story goes, Francis was sitting in the wireless room, as radio operator of the ship.

> There he was in the Navy, doing this technical job, a scientist sort of thing. He was tuned in. The captain said, while they were waiting on board, let's listen to the BBC, listen to home sort of thing. Francis gets the radio working, the loudspeakers on the deck, the crew assembled: "This is London, we have the Brain Trust today, with us is Sir Julian Huxley." They listen to an episode of the Brains Trust on BBC radio. While they are actually bobbing up and down on the sea.[4]

Julian remembered it in a different light.

> Francis spent four years in the Navy and went all over the world. He was on HMS Ramillies during the Normandy landing, and as the great armada was gathering towards its epic beachhead, he was called by one of his shipmates to come and listen to "your pop's voice." A Brains' Trust session was being broadcast live from London![5]

The discrepancy in the accounts – the omission of the Captain's role in the episode and Francis' agency in actively tuning in – is perhaps incidental but in keeping with Julian's propensity to overlook anything which Francis did. Later, when he helped his mother to write her memoires, in the early 1980s we can safely assume that what we now read is Francis' account of a funny story taking place on D-Day on *Ramillies*. With Juliette's autobiography now back in frame, we can return to the tale of Captain Middleton which Juliette relates. It is a lengthy but highly amusing vignette concerning the life of the Ramillies.

> Francis, who had by now joined the Navy, was serving as Assistant Navigating Officer on HMS *Ramillies,* saw that half-dawn on the ship's radar, a twenty-mile stretch of sea, with the vast armada of battleships, destroyers, carriers, frigates – any craft able to carry troops or materials – each in its appointed lane, silently, steaming towards the Normandy coast; and above the sky swarming with planes, bombers, gliders, parachute-droppers, fighters. What I do not think history will never relate is the strange event which may, perhaps, have saved *Ramillies*. The 36,000-ton cruiser ... had travelled the Seven Seas between active service. On landing in New Zealand, the then Captain and crew had established a firm friendship with a Maori tribe. The Captain was presented on a formal occasion with a black and white reed skirt, knee length, which the Chief requested him to wear "whenever great danger threatened. The skirt will always protect the great ship." The skirt was traditionally kept in the current Captain's cabin and every sailor knew about it and, in the way of sailors all over the world, implicitly believed its magic. Now, if ever, the moment had come. German torpedoes from shore, bombs form defence batteries round Brest, every expected resistance, fiercely defending the coast. *Ramillies'* immense size was an easy target. Captain Middleton[6] emerged from his cabin wearing the magic skirt. The ship was unscathed except for a small scratch from a shell. I wonder at the sartorial courage of a Captain of the Old School, scrupulous to maintain the full dignity of his rank, walking the bridge in a grass skirt for the morale of his crew.[7]

Francis would be back in southern waters preparing for a planned invasion of Japan. Ramillies was finally released from the assault area on 29 August 1944, but Francis' time on board had unsurprisingly provoked worry throughout the family. Letters from Aldous to Julian in November 1942, acknowledge Francis "going to sea ... must be a very anxious-making thing for Juliette and you" and another to Frieda Lawrence writes "Francis is on a destroyer – which isn't a very healthy place to be."[8]

After the war ended, Francis was demobilised. He joined other ex-soldiers in a special intake at Oxford University in 1946, being accepted to Balliol College, the alma mater of his grandfather, father and uncle. We will conclude this brief detour into Francis' war record with a fast forward to Christmas 2015. On a visit to Francis, now living in Wagnon Road, Sebastopol, California, Anatol Itten (Theodor's son) asked him, as he was being shown pictures of his Navy Service, "Francis, did you ever kill anyone during the war?" Francis duly answered without any hesitation, "I hope so."

In the Royal Navy 91

*Figure 6.1* Francis Huxley (on the right) as a sub-lieutenant in the Navy, walking the streets of Hong Kong with two similarly uniformed friends 1944.

## Notes

1 Interview with Mel Balaskas Huxley, 16 October 2018.
2 Poems for a Sailor. 1942. FHA.
3 Letter to David Allen, 18 June 2003.
4 Interview with Rupert Sheldrake, 13 March 2018.
5 Huxley, J. (1970, p.250).
6 Admiral Gervase Boswell Middleton, CB, CBE (1893–1961) served in the Royal Navy during both world wars.
7 Huxley, J. (1986, pp.191–192).
8 Letter from Aldous to Frieda Lawrence 24 February 1944. From Aldous to Julian Huxley, 23 November 1942. In Smith, G. (Ed.) (1969) *Letters of Aldous Huxley*. London. Chatton & Windus.

# 7   Oxford

"Isn't fun to *know* things?"[1]

**First impressions**

On a warm sun-kissed day, we made our way to the porter's lodge ready to embark on a tour of Francis' old and illustrious college. John Jones, the emeritus archivist and Fellow of Balliol College, Oxford for over 30 years, a tutor of chemistry and still "pottering about this side," agreed to guide us through the lush historical grounds.[2] We had barely taken a few steps onto the well-groomed lawn at the entrance, when Jones explained that when Francis stood here for the first time in the autumn of 1946, the buildings would have looked rather different – black, in fact! An almost forgotten vestige of the age of coal. During the 1960s, they were scrubbed clean, as were many buildings in the UK at this time, to give them their now recognisably radiant creamy brown hue. He did not know Francis personally, though had heard of him. "I don't know who Francis Huxley's contemporaries were" he said "but 1946 was a bulge year, because a lot of people came back from the war."

The University of Oxford is described as a collegiate research university, the oldest in England, and in terms of longevity, bettered in Europe only by the University in Bologna – founded in 1088, eight years before teaching began in Oxford. As an elite institution favoured by the wealthy and the powerful for the education of their offspring, it has played a prominent role in the transmission of culture and power in British society.

When Francis came to Oxford, 'Sandy' Ogston was responsible for all the students in medicine and biological sciences and was the principal tutor. Oliver Smithies described him as a "a gentle but critical mind" who

> conveyed to his Oxford undergraduate students, of whom I was one, the need to keep in mind a simple question that is still relevant after half a century – "Is the conclusion sensible?"[3]

Jones knew Ogston in his later years. He was considered an impressive man. Two of his pupils in Balliol received Nobel prizes in Physiology or

Medicine: Baruch S. Blumberg (1976) and Oliver Smithies (2007). For one person to have taught two Nobel laureates is rare. When Francis arrived, Sandie Lindsay, who had been Master of Balliol since 1924, was still there. Sir David Lindsay Keir would take over in 1949.

## Balliol College

A community of scholars has existed on the College's present site since 1263, consequent to an act of penance by John Balliol (1249–1314) following a dispute between himself and the then Bishop of Durham. After Balliol's death, his widow, Dervorguilla of Galloway, established a permanent endowment and in 1282 enabled the College as we know it today to come into being with its own Statutes. This makes it the oldest college in Oxford.

Jones' book provides a wealth of detail for those keen to delve into Balliol's history, from its inception in the Middle Ages to its re-emergence in the mid-19th century as one of the dreaming spires' pre-eminent colleges. By the late 19th century, the friendship between Dr. Benjamin Jowett, Master of Balliol and T. H. Huxley would lay the foundation stones in the intellectual trail which would lead various members of the Huxley family to come knocking at Balliol's door. Until Francis arrived, Uncle Aldous was by far the best known of the clan, who, "crowned with the artificial roses of academic distinction,"[4] obtained what was still then demanded of a Huxley, a First-class degree. Francis, funnily enough, was the first to get a Second. His grandfather Leonard was the first of the family to enter the College. He was followed by his sons Julian and Aldous, then by his cousin Gervas, the son of Leonard's only brother Henry. The current archivist of Balliol, Anna Sanders, kindly answered our enquiry about Francis. "I can confirm" she wrote,

> that he was a student at Balliol College under AG "Sandy" Ogston 1946–1949 and earned a 2nd class BA. in Zoology from Oxford in 1949, taking a BSc. in Anthropology in 1950. There are no archives relating to Francis Huxley's life or work at Balliol College except for records confirming his attendance here as an undergraduate, and as far as I am aware his papers have not been deposited with any other archive either. St Catherine's College may have administrative records of his five years as a research fellow there (1963–68).[5]

So, Francis' record at Balliol and later at St Catherine's is somewhat on the thin side. But we can add just a touch to this. Jones told us:

> One thing we have almost no record of is the allocation of rooms. Where was his room? We don't know. A lot of people that year, 1946, had to live in town. The college has 230 rooms here on this site. Aldous Huxley lived all his time in town. I don't know about Francis. I know Julian Huxley lived here. I also knew him.

We do know, however, that in his undergraduate years Francis did live within Balliol's walls. His fellow student in anthropology, Audrey Butt Colson, explains:

> He did say when he first arrived in Balliol the porter took him to his rooms in the college and said to him: we are giving you the rooms your father had. This upset him quite a bit ... he wasn't the only one feeling the burden of having a famous father or mother in those days.[6]

When, as of 1949, he changed to read social anthropology as a postgraduate, he lived in various digs in the centre, including Wellington Square where the University's buildings are now. Audrey relates how on one occasion,

> he had forgotten his keys. To get into the house, as there was an iron railing in front of the house, he was climbing over them (to get to a window to open) when he was temporarily arrested by a policeman. He had a bit of problem with his big digs from time to time and all this came with very good humour.

Surveyed from a distance, Balliol history suggests a tolerant attitude and a diverse range of political opinion could be found there, albeit one not typical of Oxford in general. The air of liberal tolerance pervading Balliol might well have added to Francis' enjoyment of the place. But in addition to this, Balliol possesses a further peculiarity, compared to the other Oxford colleges. Here the domestic and academic facilities are completely intertwined.

Teaching of the science subjects, including zoology, Francis' major subject as an undergraduate, was delivered largely through seminars with the occasional lecture held at the relevant university department. Students were supposed to do both practical and fieldwork. During Francis' days at the university, student numbers would have been low – in Balliol there were usually only three or four students in the yearly intake. The other students he would have known in this quasi-monastic place would likely not have been studying science subjects. Then, almost everything under the sun was taught. Jones remembers that as an undergraduate:

> All students in the first year at least, had to have a small number of tutorials with a fellow, who was not in their subject ... I was assigned to a planning guy and had to write essays on town planning. I realised afterwards; the purpose of this system was simply to get people to know guys outside of their subject.

That system still operated in the 1960s and 1970s as a deliberate college policy. The predominant instrumental attitude to education that is now dominant on all UK campuses is our loss.

Francis would have climbed the stairs to the dining hall several times a day. In the hall, Jones reminds us that in 1946, food rationing still prevailed. For those with a healthy appetite it was tough luck and, worse still, students were still charged for a meal, even if they had decided to dine elsewhere. The hall itself has a simple and modest beauty, directing attention to the top table, reserved for dons and masters. The portraits of significant figures from the college's past line the walls, exuding the tangible strength and power of hierarchy, privilege and tradition.

Most of the senior figures who were around during Francis' period of residence at Balliol are now also immortalised on canvas. Francis would have known them all in flesh and blood, alive to their quirks, wisdom and follies. Amongst the portraits, there is one of Carol Clark (1940–2015), the first woman to be appointed to a fellowship at any Oxford college. A portrait of her, by Jean Lorch, hangs on the wall to the left, a touch higher than the others, drawing attention to this fact. There is other testimony to Balliol's distinct character amongst the Oxford colleges in evidence here. Spotting the majestic organ, situated opposite the high table in the dining hall, Jones had a story of how unusual this was. The instrument was put there by a Victorian Master. A minor scandal ensued, since he hit upon the idea of giving secular concerts on Sundays. "In Victorian England, the idea of a secular concert and even a singsong after dinner, was absolutely scandalous." Perhaps the scandalous ambience of Balliol was due preparation for what Francis would later encounter at home, or maybe it was his home life which prepared him for Balliol!

**Science mentors**

Since the teaching mood in Balliol College was one akin to an apprenticeship with a master, it is helpful, for our understanding of Francis' academic profile in ornithology and social anthropology, to have an eye on his more well-known teachers. From biographers of 'Sandy' Ogston, Francis' tutor, we know that he valued the art of making sense. Francis probably learned from Ogston a good deal of how modesty can prevail. Ogston was described as someone who became embarrassed by the importance others gave to his work – a mood alien to the contemporary academic! This was because, as Ogston would diffidently explain, the relevant idea "only took him a few moments to conceptualise."[7]

In the aftermath of war, many ex-service personnel had come to Oxford. Before returning to academia, Ogston himself had contributed to the war effort, seeking to apply his knowledge of chemical and physical processes so as to enable the deactivation of various poison gases which had been used in chemical warfare since the First World War. Ogston was far more than just a willing assistant in the military application of scientific knowledge. When he returned to academic life, he began what he oft described as a period of his life devoted to helping others fulfil their academic vocations. His tangible legacy is all about finding simple solutions to complex problems, but he envisioned science as few within his profession at the time – and few even now – were willing to imagine. "Science" he argued,

> is more than the search for truth, more than a challenging game, more than a profession. It is a life that a diversity of people lead together, in the closest proximity, a school for social living. We are members one of another.[8]

Such a sentiment, cognisant of the social responsibility and social nature of scientific work, would not only be out of place, but positively unwelcome in the harsh competitive environment of the modern corporate university. But it is a sentiment which had a far-reaching influence and touched many of those whom Ogston taught.

Besides Ogston, Francis had Peter Brian Medawar as a teacher for the first two years of his zoology studies. Medawar was for many years considered one of the most enlightened public faces of science and was described by Richard Dawkins as the "wittiest of all science writers."[9] After his stint at Oxford, Medawar became Professor of Zoology at the University of Birmingham from 1947 till 1951, subsequently moving to the University of London where he became Director of the National Institute for Medical Research. It was in this post that Medawar wrote to Alan Bullock of St Catherine's College in 1963, providing an outstanding testimonial for Francis' application for a research fellowship.[10]

> Medical Research Council        28. March 1963
> Dear Bullock,
> I've just learned quite by chance that Francis Huxley is a candidate for a Fellowship in the College.
> I must tell you that I think he is absolutely first rate (he was my pupil at Oxford and I've kept in touch since). He is immensely learned but also brilliantly imaginative – and his thinking has a hard centre. I trust his judgement on many subjects more than I do his father's! He is also a very likeable man indeed, who would be good value in the S.C.R.[11] I feel that (unless indeed you have other candidates of superlative quality) he would be a great catch for the College.
>
> Yours ever
> Peter Medawar

That Medawar, a Nobel Prize winner and astute philosopher of science, should trust Francis' judgement in this way (he wrote this when Francis was 41 years old), and more so than Francis' father Julian, speaks volumes for the young Huxley. Perhaps he recognised in Francis an appreciation for the art of science. Medawar, renowned for his critical analysis of induction,[12] lamented scientists' poor grasp of methodology. He meant by this, their

98  *The facts of life*

under-appreciation of the different types of experimentation and the distinct roles they play in the pathways to scientific discovery. He cultivated a distinctly humanistic outlook towards scientific understanding and championed the art of observation in tandem with intuition and imaginative exploration. In his view, how a student approached observation could lead not only to new insights into the natural world but to a deeper understanding of oneself.

In seeking to demystify scientific method and have it treated as a specific form of human endeavour, Medawar passed on to Francis a sort of methodological common sense. As Medawar put it, science must be treated as more of an art than

> a dialogue between fact and fancy … We should think of it rather as a logically articulated structure of justifiable beliefs about nature.[13]

For Francis, an aspiring scientist (natural and human) this was a significant and innovative perspective.

> It begins as a story about a Possible World – a story which we invent and criticize and modify as we go along, so that it ends by being, as nearly as we can make it, a story about real life.[14]

We will witness, in this and later chapters, how this storytelling prowess is evident in how Francis approached exploration and observation and sought to convey information.

### Ornithologist on expedition

Francis was in the group of young scientists who made up the Oxford University expedition which visited 'Jan Mayen.' The Norwegian name translates as Devil's Island. "It has no equal in the Arctic" Huxley wrote,

> either for the great numbers of birds it supports, or for its disagreeable climate … Since Jan Mayen is the only land in the North Atlantic between Iceland and Spitsbergen, great numbers of the truly oceanic seabirds gather there for the breeding season.[15]

This stark mountainous island, 300 miles North-East of Iceland in the Greenland Sea, is a series of extinct volcanoes. The leader of the exploration club was the Australian A. J. Marshall, who had come to Oxford as a DPhil Student, eventually becoming Professor of Zoology.[16] In August 1947, Marshall, the geologist R. C. Bostrom and Francis spoke on the BBC Home Service[17] about their findings, impressions and experiences of the expedition. The journey to the island had begun from Newcastle on 9 July. One week later, the 12 strong expedition (from Merton, Magdalen, Balliol and New College, Oxford), with fellow scientists from Glasgow University and a Gaumount British film crew, set sail on a Norwegian sealer, the Polarbjørn,[18] from the harbour of Aalesund. When finally, after three days sailing, they emerged out of the thick fog, they were greeted by the majestic site of the ice capped mountains rising 2,500 metres directly from the sea. As they inched closer to the island, they were greeted by the sight of thousands of birds, nesting on the cliffs amongst the overgrown mosses and yellow lichens and below the cliffs, swarming in the sea, around the bow of the Polarbjørn.

In order to make the most of the time they could spend on the island, Marshall decided, that botanist and entomologists would work together, as would the geologists, whose tasks comprised collecting rocks, surveying the retreating glaciers and mapmaking – continuing the earlier efforts of the Imperial College Expedition of 1938. Huxley and his colleagues discerned that,

> to find out where a particular species of bird was nesting, we had only to look for a certain kind of cliff: for though the island is wholly volcanic, the actual structure of the cliffs varies a good deal, and the birds differ in their choice of nesting sites.[19]

They were faced with the conundrum of why the adult kittiwakes and glaucous gulls, during the breeding season, do nothing but eat, dawdle and sleep when they might be nesting. Were they not broody? The answer, Huxley's team found, was somewhat mundane. Aside the obvious explanation, concerning the physiological condition of a bird and its behaviour within a given environmental context, their main conclusion was that there were simply not enough suitable nesting sites.

We are fortunate to have these documents of the young ornithologist Huxley. They show him as a well-versed scientist, studying animal behaviour in its natural habitat, which is, according to him, "always complicated by interpretation."[20] His reflections on their approach to observational work evidence the influence of his mentor Peter Medawar.

On the 24 August, after six weeks on the island, the expedition was picked up by the Polarbjørn, returning from Greenland to take them back to Norway. Francis, the former Navy officer had been enriched with the experience of how nature, animal habitat and human observation of the aforesaid, could produce startling insights. Marshall praised him for his observation of one bird, found "in large numbers where the books said they should not be during that particular season."[21] Within a year, Francis would be selected as leader of a further Oxford University expedition. Besides his knowledge, his ability to listen and appreciate what others knew, his quizzical liveliness and sense of humour would be tremendous assets when it came to overcoming any difficulties in the way of an expedition.

## Gambia expedition 1948

Together with five other men from Oxford and three from Cambridge University, Francis set sail from Liverpool on 6 July aboard *The Tarkwa*, heading for Bathurst, now known as the City of Banjul in Gambia, which they duly reached on 14 July. They planned to travel and survey in Gambia for seven weeks. Besides himself in the role of leader and ornithologist, he had recruited two zoologists, one soil chemist, two geographers, a surveyor, a botanist and an entomologist. Few places had been subject to such interdisciplinary investigation, giving the expedition a very modern slant in its scientific approach. In Bathurst they garnered further supplies, which they had not brought from the UK. In what seemed an extravagance to the 25-year-old Huxley and a mark of former colonial times, they recruited 14 Africans to join and look after them in one way or another. In addition, they had two washer women, two interpreters and two cooks, to spare them the chores of domestic labour and provide them with more time to undertake the work which was their priority. They took their ship 120 miles upriver to the busy export centre, of Kuntaur. Here, where the Gambia ceases to be navigable for ocean-going ships, Huxley decided to set up their headquarters, the plan being to continue exploration in smaller interdisciplinary groups, as had been the practice in his previous expeditions.

It became clear to the group that Gambia with its dependence on groundnuts as a cash crop, brought numerous traders from the neighbouring countries of Senegal and Guinea Bissau to the river, a special biological habitat unfortunately of malaria, bilharzia and tsetse fly. In assessing the situation of the African farmers – and their ability to protect their crop in a swamp ecology – their habitat was undoubtedly a factor in why the country

*Figure 7.1* Francis Huxley. Gambia expedition 1949.

had, at that time, one of the highest rates of disease on the continent. In the Kuntaur district, Huxley found stone circles, seeing these as a sign of continuity with the past, which were used in rituals to create a feeling of belonging for the people there. He observed how they were used with veneration as altars to pay due respect to earth-spirits. Further enquiries with his African informant revealed them as burial places, shelters of times long gone. Excavations were undertaken, though their age was difficult to determine. Francis' own estimate, as good as anyone's at the time, dated them to the 11th century. His reflections here read in hindsight as the first stirrings of the future social anthropologist.

The research tasks for Huxley's team, in the districts they planned to survey, were to look into the daily lives of the local peasantry and their social–agricultural attitudes in relation to their cultivated environment. What is the condition of the soil and crops growing therein? How come rice-growing was a woman's job? In what way can the local community subsist and feed itself, considering the country's need to increase food production for export? They sought to bring their findings into a collective summary drawn onto a land-utilisation map. This they produced with consummate care. Huxley published a non-specialist article of their work in *The Geographical Magazine* in 1949. The magazine had in fact been founded by Francis' uncle, Michael, 14 years earlier. Correspondence from Michael to Francis survives demonstrating Michael's enthusiasm for the expedition and its value for "modern geographical exploration."[22]

Together with the other two geographers E. Gordon and J. Pook, the expedition carried out a comprehensive land survey covering 12 square miles. Besides Francis' general article, there are a number of other publications from team members on the record.[23] Huxley told the story and relayed their sad conclusions regarding the misfortunes of Gambian agriculture, the inefficient economy and the broader ecological situation, in a lecture to the Royal Geographical Society. In the audience was Uncle Michael, who wrote to him, a week later:

> I enjoyed hearing your talk last week and did my best to reinforce the family claque ... if only we could get some more lively pictures of people in relation to the environment where you were operating, I see no reason why we should abandon the idea of publishing an article about this aspect of the Expedition's work.[24]

Thanks to Michael's connection to the Colonial Office about further printable photographs, and the Royal Geographical Society allowing Michael Huxley to have a special copy of the land-utilisation map, to be made and coloured accordingly for reproduction, Francis' article, was in due course written. In it he provides the above details of the expedition, its methods and findings which he situates in the context of the history of the then colonial protectorate. He notes not only how it first came to appear on maps as a distinct territory, marked out as it was with ruler and compass, but the accompanying unpleasant side of European trade, which in the 18th century came with the usual mixture of "guns, liquor, axes, cloth, which all helped to aggravate the political situation."[25]

To that awful litany, we could add illnesses, venereal diseases and corruption. Francis the ornithologist learned how the ricebirds raid the cereal once it is ripe, managing together with the baboons, which in 1948 equalled the human population, to destroy "nearly half of the total groundnut crop of the country." They left Gambia after seven weeks with a hope, that the dire state of socio-agricultural affairs revealed by their fieldwork could be improved by developing more rice-growing fields supported by irrigation and the building of small dykes holding the water in the fields, with marshes and swamps developed to gain more land. Their balanced assessment of what politics and administration can do was appreciated by the British Governor, Sir Andrew Wright.

With the ample material Francis brought back to Oxford he was ready for his final undergraduate year. The Honorary Secretary of the Seabird Group, W. R. P. Bourn egged on by David Snow, a celebrated English ornithologist, wrote to Huxley in October 1952, asking him for the material on seabirds collected by the Gambia expedition, and enquired what he intended to do with it. He wished to incorporate Francis' collection and use it to "attempt to define the distribution of different species and review the systematics and breeding data of the residents."[26]

## After ornithology comes anthropology

Francis was now in a position, to cast his net wider beyond zoology and the philosophy of science, towards social anthropology. After graduating with an Upper Second, he left Balliol and enrolled in the one-year diploma course in the Oxford Institute of Anthropology, living in various digs in town. As a student of Edward Evans-Pritchard (1902–1973), he picked up several tips for fieldwork. Evans-Pritchard was an experienced anthropologist, having conducted extensive fieldwork in Africa with the Azande and the Nuer. "The anthropologist," he wrote,

> must live as far as possible in their village and camps, where he is, again as far as possible, physically and morally part of their community. This is not merely a matter of physical proximity. There is also a psychological side to it. By living among the natives as far as he can like one of themselves the anthropologist puts himself on a level with them. Unlike the administrator and missionary, he has no authority and status to maintain, and unlike them he has a neutral position.[27]

Evans-Pritchard has been characterised as the personification of the best of Oxford-style scholarship and raconteuring. Huxley took his advice to heart.

To his reportage, he added a narrative approach, giving the local people their own intimate voice in his writing. As a student of Evans-Pritchard and Meyer Fortes, the latter his true mentor, Huxley was in a favourable position. To their wisdom he threw in Lévi-Strauss' innocence and wonder. The social anthropologist, Mary Douglas, thought Evans-Pritchard's strength lay in his fieldwork, "his weakness in schematic ordering." This, she held, came from his "personal scepticism about the possibility of objective knowledge and thence from an unusual sophistication on epistemological matters."[28] Explaining the situation in 1949, she said.

> At that time, there was no undergraduate degree in this subject. There was a 1-year diploma course with an exam at the end. Then followed the writing of a B.Litt. thesis (normally using just written records, usually taking one year). All being well, the DPhil. course followed, entailing a long period in one's chosen field of research. Diploma students normally were graduates and had a degree in some other subject and frequently came in from other universities, often from abroad. Because Francis already had a degree from Oxford Biology Dept., he did not take the diploma course, but went straight on to the B.Litt. year.[29]

People who joined the department thus came with degrees in various subjects. Francis, already in Oxford, had completed his science degree, Colson arriving from Exeter, had obtained hers in history at London University as an external student. Francis, as an Emslie Horniman Scholar, seemed a perfect fit into the Oxford system. Audrey, describes how Francis,

> didn't take a diploma course unlike us nine students in our year. This included a history of anthropology across the board, we all were taking three papers out of six or seven options. Francis didn't take the one-year diploma. The reason was, we understood, this is not official, he didn't take the diploma because he already had an Oxford degree. All of us others came from other universities. He attended the lectures, of course, anything he wanted to attend. He was really writing up his second stage of the course, (the) B.Litt., which was then converted to an M.A.[30]

For this work he received his MA in 1950. The students usually gave a copy of their thesis to the social anthropology library and the main Bodleian Library in Oxford. Meyer Fortes, then Reader in Sociology, was Francis' tutor in social anthropology and thesis supervisor. When Fortes transferred to Cambridge in 1950 to become 'William Wyse Professor of Social Anthropology' at Cambridge, Francis too went there for a time, especially when he returned from his first field trip to the Ka'apor in the Amazon basin of Brazil in 1952.

It is worth recalling that social anthropology at that time in Oxford, was largely dominated by Evans-Pritchard – E-P, as he was generally known.[31] Evans-Pritchard was an Africanist as were most of his Oxford colleagues.

Fortes, Francis' chief mentor for his fieldwork was convinced, like others of his time, that the so-called primitive or tribal societies were "different from what he called 'civilized societies.' They were small-scale and not very differentiated internally, and they sustained themselves in a state of equilibrium."[32] Fortes' cultural preconceptions as we know have not stood the test of time, but he offered something else, another more sustainable view which influenced Francis profoundly. Adam Kuper argues, that at this time, at Francis' alma mater in the late 1940s, "every professor had to have a theory." Fortes' initial published fieldwork on the Tallensi people of Northern Ghana was considered modest. He was, however, psychoanalytically inclined, interested in individuals' experiences and their place in a man or woman's destiny.

> Generalized ethnographic descriptions have one serious defect. They do not enable us to see how ritual or belief is actually used by men and woman to regulate their lives.[33]

Francis, among others, heeded Fortes' cautionary words. In his future research he would pay due attention to the contexts of personal history and social relationships, their embeddedness in the rites and religious ideas enacted and the corresponding mythology which went with them.

## Why anthropology?

Francis never ceased thinking about the nature of anthropology. His fieldnotes are replete with ruminations on the subject. Social anthropology would become his final academic destination. In this he veered towards analysing the mythology, rituals and social structure of a tribe, in his case the Ka'apor, rather than getting bogged down in a 'material approach' where the focus is upon objects and their properties and the ways in which material artefacts are key to understanding a culture and its social relations. Francis chose instead to depict, describe and show the mundane lives of members of the tribe, in order to show them as both the subjects and the object of an anthropological study. In later reflections he would come to distance himself, from what he considered was *de rigeur* in the 'hey-days of this profession' when he joined it. This was when

> (in the days after the Second World War), its members were employed to advise and educate the military; and continued into the early sixties when the international scene invited social engineering on a large scale.[34]

In addition to Evans-Pritchard and Fortes, Edmund Leach exerted a further influence on Francis in his student days. Leach, was already a feted PhD lecturer at the London School of Economics, when Francis encountered his work.

Later as Professor of Anthropology in Cambridge, Leach would venture close to Lévi-Strauss' structural anthropology in his theoretical reflections. When applying for a research fellowship at St Catherine's, Francis expressed a wish to make use of "this French school" for the way in which it "examines social forms by using methods derived from linguistics, and ... (Its) interest ... in the topological relations to be found in mythology and kinship systems."[35]

Leach's engagement with French structuralism led to a popularisation of narrative anthropology, which Huxley co-pioneered. This sought to engage with what is personally experienced in the field, as a participant observer in a given society, and to bring it into a cosmological, mythological context – avoiding, where possible, any problems with metaphysics – by steadfastly applying the results of the fieldworker's analysis to the function of the society of the tribe and simultaneously the behaviour of the individual composing it.

Having been raised in the English functional school of social anthropology, Leach and Huxley created a merger between this and structuralism. It is an open secret that one's position in the social-class hierarchy and one's cultural background was an important aspect of the functional operation of British anthropology. In writing "Glimpses of the unmentionable in the history of British Social Anthropology,"[36] written towards the end of his life, Leach influenced, in part, how we have approached the present work. "Of one thing I am quite certain" he unequivocally stated:

> Unless we pay much closer attention than has been customary to the personal background of the authors of anthropological works, we shall miss out on most of what these texts are capable of telling us about the history of anthropology.[37]

"British academics are still far too sensitive about such matters,"[38] he argued. What somewhat irked Leach, was not so much the "overwhelming dominance and academic prestige of Oxford and Cambridge" but the "conservatism and social arrogance of those who were effectively in control of these two great institutions"[39] during the early part of the 20th century. The Huxley family was included as prime members of that powerful interconnected "intellectual aristocracy." Francis, as an undergraduate and graduate student in Oxford, certainly profited from this network, as a matter of course.

When Stanley J. Tambia came to discuss and write the life of Edmund Leach, he made another important point.

> He would maintain that creative thinking was possible only if you were prepared to take risks. Inconsistency did not worry him because he thought it was consistent with Hegelian dialectical mode of thought. His impulsion was to "experiment," "probe" and push at the margins.[40]

## The facts of life

This is what Francis Huxley undoubtedly endeavoured to do too, though largely outside of the confines of academia, away from the security, fame and institutional power to define debate, and yet unconstrained by the bureaucratic infringement of one's freedom to explore phenomenon exactly as one wishes.

## Notes

1 "My father Julian was an enthusiast for anything he had learnt. He used to quote Bertrand Russel's remarks: Isn't it fun to *know* things!" quite frequently. Francis Huxley (1999, p.77) Interview with David Dunaway in Dunaway (1999).
2 On 12 March 2018.
3 Obituary – *The Independent*, 9 July 1996.
4 Smith, G. (Ed.) (1969, p.112) *Letters of Aldous Huxley*. London. Chatto & Windus.
5 Anna Sander, Archivist and Curator of Manuscripts, Balliol College, Oxford. Email to authors on 18 January 2018.
6 Audrey Butt Colson, interviewed in May 2018.
7 Smithies, O. (1996) Obituary: A. G. Ogston. *The Independent*, 9 July.
8 From a 1970-lecture to the Australian Biochemical Society.
9 Dawkins, R. (Ed.) (2008, p.179) *The Oxford Book of Modern Science Writing*. Oxford. Oxford University Press.
10 Staff file, St Catherine's College Oxford.
11 Senior Common Room.
12 Medawar, P. (1969/2008) *Induction and Intuition in Scientific Thought*. London. Routledge.
13 Ibid., p.59.
14 Ibid., p.59.
15 Huxley, F. (1947, p.117) Birds of Jan Mayen – Nesting and Breeding Habits.
16 A brief scientific account of the expedition is given in 'Oxford University Expedition to Jan Mayen, 1947.' *Polar Record*, 5 (35–36), p.199.
17 Later to be renamed as BBC Radio 4.
18 The name means Polar Bear.
19 BBC Home Service (1948) Rocks and Birds of Jan Mayen. Transcript: p.5.
20 Huxley, F. (1947, p.117).
21 Marshall, A. J. (1947, p.5) *Study of Wild Life on Jan Mayen. Oxford Goes Exploring*. Oxford University.
22 Michael Huxley, letter to Francis Huxley, 14 July 1949, FHA. He was discussing the forthcoming publication of Francis' article on Gambia, in *The Geographical Magazine*.
23 A Land Use Map of Kuntaur in the Gambia by E. Gordon and J. R. Clarke's (1953, pp.299–315) The Hippopotamus in Gambia, West Africa. *Journal of Mammalogy*, 34 (3) (August).
24 Michael Huxley, letter to Francis Huxley, 25 January 1949. Written on the stationary of his Geographical Magazine. It took Francis till early July, to reply to Michael, that he would actually write this article. FHA.
25 Huxley, F. (1949/1950, p.271) Exploration in Gambia. *Geographical Magazine*, XXII (6).

26 Dr. W. R. P. Bourne, 18 October 1952, letter to Francis Huxley, Balliol College, from St. Bartholomews Hospital, London. FHA.
27 Evans-Pritchard (1951, pp.78–79).
28 Douglas (1980, p.121).
29 Audrey Butt Colson interviewed in May 2018.
30 Huxley, F. (1949) The Social Mechanism of a South American Tribe. An account of marriage, war and exchange among the Tupi-Guarani of Brazil, with comparisons drawn from South American Tribes. Thesis presented for the degree of Bachelor of Science at the University of Oxford. p.108. FHA.
31 Later to become the world-famous Professor Sir Edward Evans-Pritchard. See also Evans-Pritchard (1951).
32 Kuper (2016, p.135).
33 Fortes (1983, pp.9–10).
34 Huxley, F. (1992, p.5) World Culture. *International Synergy Journal*, Santa Fe, 6 (2), pp.5–10.
35 Francis Huxley (1963) One-page short Biography, for the application to St Catherine's Research Fellowship. FHA.
36 Leach (1984).
37 Ibid., p.22.
38 Ibid., p.3.
39 Ibid., p.22.
40 Thambiah (2002, p.67).

# 8  Love and history

Francis had relationships "with so many women," his niece, Victoria remarked, "and most were half his age." Once Francis had reached his late 40s, this was undoubtedly true, though not before. His correspondence from Brazil shows that he had a good many female friends in the home country. After he took his own digs in Oxford during his postgraduate year, he acquired the reputation of an outstanding host, cultivated in the arts of cooking and conversation. Thus, we take it, he was coming into his own as a man, preparing for a life ahead on the rocky shores of Eros, if not civilisation.

Here we will consider some of the major intimate relationships in Francis' life which we found noteworthy. These necessarily include his three marriages, beginning with Adriana Santa Cruz, when he was 48 years of age, by the standards of the day rather late for a marriage. All of these affairs of the heart occurred in a distinct context, within the shifting emotional and geographical boundaries in which Francis led his life. What we have been able to assemble, though far from exhaustive, tells us something singularly important about Francis Huxley the man, the places of the heart visited by him and how these relate to the rest of his life.

### Ferelyth – first love

Ferelyth, Gaelic for 'water-fairy,' grew up with her older sister Jean MacGibbon, the later novelist, in Golders Green, neighbouring Hampstead Heath. Her mother was a concert pianist and her father a merchant. During the First World War her Great-Uncle, Ernst Howard and Aunt Sophy, put on charade parties in their spacious St. John's Wood home. Ernst Howard entertained a number of writers, painters and musicians there. May Sinclair, the poet and novelist was there and "Julian Huxley played God under an umbrella. That was early on and he meant nothing to me. But his father, Leonard Huxley, did."[1]

Ferelyth Howard (1916–2005) was Francis' first great love. She studied sculpture under John Skeaping at the Central School of Arts, London and subsequently joined his 'Zoo class,' going on to draw and sculpt animals for most of her artistic life. Her sister Jean, in her personal memoir wrote,

Had it not been for my sister I should have been inclined to discount my version of what went on. But Ferelyth, born when I was three and a half, seems to have known at once that, between the three of us, she had been dropped into a queer kettle of fish. This gave her much unhappiness; but it kept her saner in the long run. Recognition of the truth, however painful, is the foundation of sanity.[2]

On leaving school, the 18-year-old Ferelyth went to Vienna. She learnt to play the cello, distancing herself from her mother's affections for the grand piano. She became an adventurous and compassionate traveller and sculptured and forged her own innovative tools at the Central School of Arts, and Crafts, where "she wrested from copper rod a life-size gibbon monkey that hung there in the staircase well." David Buckman, who included Ferelyth in his dictionary of "Artists in Britain since 1945,"[3] subsequently wrote her obituary in *The Independent*:

> In the summer of 1939 she went on a student exchange visit to America, but just before her return the Second World War started and officially, she became an alien, unable to travel home ... After Pearl Harbour, she was permitted to return to England. She worked in Air Ministry camouflage, then joined the WRNS ... While in camouflage she returned to the Central School, the back of which she found damaged after bombing, with her Antelope (one of her most noted sculptures) looking out into open space. By now she was friendly with Julian Huxley, Secretary of the Zoological Society, who arranged for the Antelope to lodge at Whipsnade Zoo, where it was fixed on a plinth beside the restaurant. It was only when Fellows of the Zoological Society decided that it was not suitable that it was retrieved by its maker, eventually finding its way into a private collection.[4]

Francis met his first love, then, at the flats which his parents occupied – courtesy of his father's employment as Secretary of the Zoological Society of London and Whipsnade Zoo. Julian was employed there from 1935 to 1942, and together with Juliette was running the show. Francis came home from Gordonstoun, as a 19-year-old, primed to enter adult life. Ferelyth was already a vivacious 26-year-old artist, working with live animals as models for her sculptures and running odd errands for the Huxley household. We know that their families were acquainted and it is likely that this opened the path for Ferelyth to become friendly with Francis' parents and in turn to initiate their second son into the arts of love. In her book on sculpture she would later write,

> The starting point here is for the individual to need to share experience by his own way of "doing and making" things, for it is only through the arts that man can bridge the gap of separateness.[5]

110  *The facts of life*

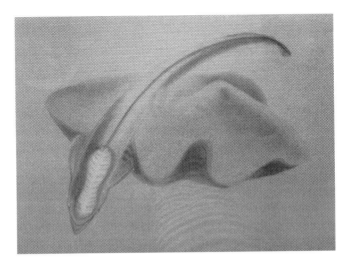

*Figure 8.1* Painting given to Francis by Ferelyth Howard.

Ferelyth presented Francis with a painting which, until his dying day, he would keep over his fire place, wherever it was that he set up home. She also made a drawing for him, to hold dear when he was at Gordonstoun.

Her love, was intensively romantic. In one of her letters she addressed him as: "Hallo Old Star." In another she wrote,

> I think of you all the time, conscious always of your absence, fighting always against the queer vacuum inside me, wondering fearfully if you are unhappy or uncomfortable – and me so uselessly unable to help. Tell me as soon as you can, if you are still allowed little parcels, even very little parcels, please, or I shall send them whether they reach you or not! God Bless you my dearest, your own Ferelyth[6]

Both Francis' nieces, we interviewed, Victoria and Susie, have told us how Juliette did not want a 'repetition' with Francis and his first girlfriend, "the sculptor woman" as they called her, being unable to recall Ferelyth's name. Their own father, Anthony and their mother, Ann Taylor, had married young in 1943, due to Ann's pregnancy with Susie. While Ferelyth was doing her sculptures in Regents Park Zoo, Juliette became increasingly aware of what for her were 'danger' signs. As Susie put it:

> You can't have two disgracing sons coming up in the family. We rescued that sculpture (Ferelyth's) which was lying in the garden. It is made from a piece of driftwood. Juliette also made driftwood sculptures from an ebony log from the wreck of a Spanish armada, which washed up on the

shores of Wales, the ebony being used as a ballast for the ship. Francis and Anthony found this piece of ebony on the beach.

Juliette's, "very controlling" behaviour, as Victoria saw it, won out. During the Second World War, Francis joined the Royal Navy while Ferelyth, was in the Women's Royal Naval Service. Ferelyth "married our cousin, Bill Wills, a bomber pilot," her sister Jean recounts. "Together they became proficient gliders. She could come out very strong on anything she felt deeply about."[7]

When their love was blooming, it had been an exciting, creative, passionate and joyful time, for both of them. For Francis, this search for the elusive butterfly of love had been a formative and important experience. Some of his early poems, inspired by his affections for Ferelyth, he kept in a folder, together with Christmas cards and drawings from this time. There remains, in addition, a postcard in Francis' hand, to his old flame:

"For every flower of happiness and felicity in the bright years, with all my heart. Francis."[8]

We heard from sources close to Ferelyth, that she relished telling stories of how she drew the animals whilst she was living in Regents Park. It seems to have been a happy and exciting time for her also. Francis visited her and her family once while he was an Oxford graduate shortly before he went to Brazil.

Margaret McMullen, an acquaintance of Ferelyth in her later years wrote to us.

> I can see how Ferelyth and Francis would be drawn to each other, both much interested in birds, beasts and the natural world. I only met her sometime in the late 1990s when she was already losing her sight and no longer able to drive. She always invited me in to show me her work, which I greatly liked and admired. The conversations we had during our journeys when she reminisced about her school days at Weybridge were of another age and to which she refers, without naming the school, when she writes of her love of the natural world in her notes. These tales were told with humour as well as nostalgia.[9]

## Oxford onwards

In Francis' 'Oxford Journals,' he writes a good deal about Liz; going out for meals, trips to the cinema, walks and talks are all noted down. As was his habit then, no dates are given, though as he mentions meeting Meyer Fortes (sometimes just MF) and E-P (Evans-Pritchard) it is clear that these date from his time as a postgraduate in 1949/1950. When he discovered a book on the history of hell, he found himself instead wanting a history of heresies, for

> sexual morality is governed not by the will of God but by other people's frustrated denies. Laws of sexual morality thus fence in and do not lead

out. As long as they are regarded as final in themselves they are therefore unhealthy.[10]

A suggestion of his lingering dissatisfaction with his parents' mores and how they crushed his affair with Ferelyth perhaps? From his time in Brazil, there is correspondence from Val Mitchison. He received his mail there, care of the Indian Protection Service (Servicio de Protecao aos Indios). "Darling Francis," she writes from her home in the Temple, London "It's an extraordinary feeling to be no longer an undergraduate; very nice but still odd." She goes on to tell her beau, who, of their fellow students, had already decided to get married, who were still longing to be bridesmaids, and who was newly in love with who; this besides the more practical "frightfully complicated" business of finding work. There is the expressed fear that Francis is retreating into the jungle beyond reach. "When if ever you hope to come back? Dearest Francis do look after yourself as much as you can and come back soon, in the meantime very much love, Val."[11]

When he returned to London in the autumn of 1953, he wrote to his father,

> As I think you know, I had to give up my candidacy for the British Museum keepership but I've got another museum job on the line now, I think, at Liverpool … it will be the same kind of work, listing their S. and Central American collections, but only for a year and I can take my time over it.[12]

His option to go for a St. John's research fellowship "doesn't look at all hot," he wrote in the same letter, since not being a John's man (coming from Balliol) he was told, one must be so much better than anyone else. So, Liverpool it was to be.

## Liverpool to New York

Francis was an Assistant Curator of Ethnography, at the City of Liverpool Public Museum, as it was then called, from March 1954 through the major part of 1955, during which time he lived at 5 Percy Street in the Liverpool 8 district. Delving into the archives of the museum, Marion Servat-Fredericq, Assistant Curator for the Ethnology Department at World Museum in Liverpool, unearthed the following:

> In 1954 Francis Huxley was appointed to the Ethnology department to catalogue the Central and South American material at the museum. He left in September 1955 to go to America, having completed a basic catalogue and mounted a small American exhibition at Sudley House. I found a handwritten piece of paper which mentions him … Beasley seems to be mentioned in it, which might suggest Huxley worked on some of the Harry Geoffrey Beasley collection.[13]

*Love and history* 113

Francis thus left a smaller imprint in the city than the Fab Four, though we have some correspondence indicating he was "enjoying the work."[14] The ecstasy of work, however, was tempered by life outside; "A dull fortnight here in Liverpool with nothing much doing," he wrote to his mother, after seven months in the fine seaside air, "I have just unpacked a horrible lot of horrible old Peruvian clothes out of graves – poo, they do smell. And such dirt!"[15] Once in a while, he would take a few afternoons off to write up his Brazilian material for a book planned with the publisher Rupert Hard-Davis, someone he experienced as encouraging. Whilst in the city, however, we know he built at least one significant relationship, becoming close with someone identified from the letters only as Sheila (possibly born in 1932). We know very little about their time in the town, though we do have an envelope from a Sheila Brandick from when she was living in Saskatoon, Canada, who we believe is the same person. We also have a letter to Sheila dated the 19 March 1956, a time when Francis was residing in Riverside Drive in New York. In this he writes:

> Dearest Sheila, ... I wish you were here to walk round them (the Met. and the Frick museums); I enjoy your knowledge and your eye for things. And not just to walk round the museums, either – it would be fun if you were here in general, just as Sheila, to see the sights, and spend the dollars, and drink iced water.

Sheila had had the idea to give Rudolf Wittkower's book on Bernini to Aldous and Laura Archera as a wedding present, pre-empting Aldous' own expressed intention to buy a copy for himself. Francis recorded Aldous' delighted reaction after unwrapping their gift.[16]

As we know, Francis did not return to Liverpool. It was "beginning to bore" him, as was his "beastly book."[17] He would spend the next three years in New York, and in Saskatchewan and Haiti, conducting fieldwork. Michael Schwab, a long-time friend, who Francis had invited to stay with him after his third wife Adele had left Santa Fe and Michael's own marriage had crumbled, added a significant postscript to the tale of Francis' liaison with Sheila. We told him that we had found two photos of Sheila besides his computer screen in his study at Wagnon Road (in Sonoma County, Northern California) where he lived at the end of his life. Michael recalled

> While we were living together in 2000–3, he is remembering ... as if it was the first time he realised, what an opportunity he missed with Sheila, his young arrogance, impatience, lack of realisation what was happening, and when he came to America, he had a photo of her. He made it into a silhouette. He had copies of it all over the house in Santa Fe. It seems to come through that experience, all his regrets of his life. He was inconsolable for days.[18]

Finding Sheila's address in Canada, in Francis' little book, with the same picture he had on his desk, we assume he wrote to her on occasion and she back to him. Maybe there was more than just this correspondence after the fact. The mental hospital in which Francis worked in 1959 and Sheila's home 'Green Gables' in Saskatoon were not that distant – around 140 km – perhaps a couple of hours by car – by North American standards, well within reach.

## Ellen Huxley

We may recall from earlier in this book, Ellen Hovde's statement, made at the beginning of November 1956, when she and Francis took LSD together with Matthew and Humphry Osmond, at the Huxley's Sanford Rd. house in Woodbridge. As we have seen, she declared that she had "married the wrong Huxley." The following weekend, Julian and Juliette were visiting Ellen, Matthew and Francis in Woodbridge. Elle wrote to Osmond on Tuesday 12 November:

> We told them all we could; they were extremely interested. But they were obviously nonplussed by Francis and me, and I do believe felt quite shut out – as who would not when in the middle of an ordinary conversation a single would make us roar with laughter. I am sure Juliette thought we were living together ... as indeed we were.[19]

Francis temporarily left to go to Chicago, calling her immediately after settling into the International House to hear her soothing enamoured voice. Ellen, the daughter of a professor, grew up in Pittsburgh, Pennsylvania, studied theatre at the Carnegie Mellon Institute, went to Norway as a graduate and in due course returned to New York. It was there she met her husband to be, Francis' cousin, Matthew Huxley, then working at the Elmer Roper polling agency. They married in 1949 and had two children, Trevenan and Tessa. In 1955, months after Maria Huxley's death in the February of that year, Aldous spent the summer with Ellen and Matthew in Connecticut. Aldous, her father-in-law, would remain emotionally close to Ellen up until his death in 1963.

Ellen, as we have seen, was a renowned film director, founding her own production company 'Middlemarch Films' with Muffie Meyer in New York. Together, they produced more than 100 films and videos, to both national and international acclaim; favourable reviews came from *The New York Times*, *Time* and *Newsweek* as well as an Academy Award nomination and honours from the Directors Guild of America. Ellen's love for Francis led them, in 1957, to plan a film on Darwin for the National Educational Television, though the project never came to fruition. It fell through, Francis told his father, because:

> the producers weren't really interested in what we wanted to do, and we weren't interested in what they wanted to do, nor could we get any

guarantee that either of us would be able to work on the series if they took it on: so we just abandoned it.

Once Ellen's affair with Francis burst out into the open, Matthew never spoke to him again. The affair certainly ended her marriage. Trev, Mathew's son, told us he didn't know too much about it, as

> no one wanted to talk about it ... my father moved out of the house. I never saw them fight. Clare White, my father's cousin by marriage ... when I was 19 years old asked her about it, she said, "yes Francis ... your mother liked Francis a bit too much."

Trev and Francis never took this up in conversation. Trev's sister held it against Francis, to his dying day. Trev, somewhat down to earth, concluded,

> To me it was not my business. My mother never sat down and talked to me about it, neither did my father. That was the end of Francis and my father. My father never spoke to Francis after that, as this truly was a disaster in the family.

In January 1959, Francis gave his take on the breakdown of Mathew and Ellen's marriage in a letter to his parents.

> Ellen and Mathew, as I think Ellen has told you, are separating: It is not surprising, but remains painful in the extreme. They have really disliked each other for a long time. They themselves are both relieved and anguished at the same time, in some terribly ambiguous fashion; they have also been in a minor storm of ill-health. Altogether little has been happy: I have left the house some time since, I am staying with a film-making friend of mine at the moment ... and am about to get myself a place elsewhere ... What I write appals me, it comes out so fusty-musty and shapeless.

This was followed a couple of months later with a further, longer exposition in which he sought not only to contain the anxieties of his parents, but also to frame the drama in terms of the intergenerational legacy of the Huxley clan – a "force" as Francis depicts it which shapes, constrains and otherwise influences the moves and motives open to family members. In a letter home he writes:

> No, I shall certainly not come back to England now: what should I do that for? It doesn't help me one bit, and at the moment I am selfish enough to think of that first. Whether I really wrote such a disturbing letter or not, I don't remember: but I feel you have taken more out of it than I put in. What I mean was that there were too many Huxleys in the situation as it

was, and that it was not just a situation involving Ellen and Mathew and me, but involving the shadows of all our parents and the way we react to them. This, I hope, is obvious: it is obvious of course in any such situation. What is difficult, and what I was writing about, was to distinguish these shadow forces, whqich have been too active for my liking, from what I really want to do. My great weakness is to allow other people's emotions to blackmail me into doing what they want me to do: and while it may be perfectly right for me to do that thing, yet I have to do it for myself or its not worth anything ...

So please don't be so involved. No one is likely to explode or throw himself under a car, or do anything foolish: and while this is obviously a very Huxley situation, involving as it does two sides of the family with their distinct characters and lack of character, if you follow me, it's easier to deal with the less is forced to be.

This is the earliest correspondence which we are aware of, to hint at the scale of the psychological drama all the Huxleys are embroiled in, whether they like it or not. As Francis here indicates, he likes it not one bit – and hence construes it as a force which acts in the shadows, not directly in awareness. We have already argued that Francis' wish to make sense of his place in the family was a factor in drawing him to Laing. It is equally likely that some of Laing's reasoning about 'the politics of the family' drew directly on his knowledge of the perturbations in the lines of communication in the Huxley family system.

"It was a passionate love affair," Trev continued,

my mother was crushed when Francis did not marry her. Francis was more like having a good affair. My mother was very beautiful and brilliant when young. It was a bad situation with a silver lining. The affair was in the 50s. I was seven. They connected about the LSD trip. I don't know how long it went. I don't know how it all came to the surface or what happened. My sister Tessa, resented Francis being involved in my father and Ellen parting.

When Francis came back from Haiti in 1959 with malaria, he took to bed upstairs in Ellen's and Matthew's home.

Sometimes my mum would go up and he was shaking under stacks of blankets. This was my first experience with someone having a serious disease. I think he was really sick. That was in Brooklyn Heights, before my parents broke up. My dad and mum talked about him. I knew it was very serious. Francis suffered a lot.

In his long letters to Ellen from Port au Prince, Haiti, he regaled her with stories of his ritual voodoo adventures, and pondered why people become anthropologists. "As for myself, I have nothing much to say. I live in a pleasant enough hotel on the main open space in town." He goes on to ask Ellen how spring is in New York, asking her to write to him. Later in the year he would complain of "becoming fractious." While in Port au Prince, his troubled thoughts escaped on a letter to another close female friend.

> Dearest Catherine, ... I suppose I always understood you, sometimes without wanting to; and now that I am beginning to understand myself, I understand you better. By which I mean that I can feel myself going in and out of your words, as it were, with the confidence you speak of that you can go in and out of mine ... I wish there was something to be thankful for in the unhappiness I am concerned in, but I don't see it. I feel depressed here in Haiti too, which is unfortunate, though to hear from you has nourished my spirits.

He goes on to say that Matthew has sent him an unpleasant telegram – though he refrains from revealing its contents. He does, however, remark on what Juliette has told him, that Aldous is understanding regarding what is happening between the two of them, and confesses to feeling helpless about Matthew, "as most people do." The subjective truth of their relationship, he muses, is that "the negative has been powerful." Notwithstanding all their difficulties, Francis was able to accept that a certain creative impulse had come from it, one which enabled him to see the effect of family ghosts, in the full light of day – "now that I see how I make them." In an evident low mood, lamenting his unused potentialities, Francis went on "I mind too, horribly, being thirty-six and nothing done, nothing resolved, that is, into myself, as it should have been by now. And all the wasted time and unused efforts."

The response from Ellen was almost immediate.

> Francis?:!;........! I know you will not marry me, even that I am perhaps the last woman on earth you would marry. What to do? Fight for new stakes? Yes. Hope for something? I hope not. Love you? Yes, always. Be lonely? I am very lonely ... but not desperate.

Seeking to anchor her emotional turmoil in thoughts of surer safer times she wrote,

> We two were able of tremendous happiness and discovery and growth together. I remember our first LSD session ... you looked at me and your face cleared, and your eyes cleared and you smiled the most beautiful smile, as if to say do not be frightened because I, really I, am here.

For both of them, she goes on, despite the terrible ruckus falling in love has caused in their respective relationships, there were always, to begin with, "rare occasions when we could look at each other with reassurance and say, yes, it is safe to know me." Despite what must have been intense pressure within the broader Huxley family to keep the lid on the affair, and with its consequences spinning fatefully out of control, they both refused to quit one another. She rubs this into Francis in a most loving way.

> The part I must now swallow, of course, is the most difficult ... to get over the conviction that to "know" me is to love me. You see, lots of people have loved me, and some still do, but nobody has ever known me before, and I am baffled because I had always felt that this would be the highest form of love and the one which would fuse all others into the glorious white light of the universe ... which we would contain.

Ellen was seeking some kind of answer from Francis, but her question is an unanswerable and universal cry from the heart – to be loved and recognised when the heart is in residence in its most painful existential place. Francis responded, not by reference to his own morality and intentions which he felt could be easily bettered, but by grasping for a spiritual rope to hang on to.

> Ellen Ellen Ellen. Thank you for all your letters, and your constant Ellen-ness. Your dream is one of the most telling. If you can find your way through that darkness, what can't you do? I lost myself in it for a long time ... The way of the Tao is one's own way. When you understand the term Buddha you know the meaning of Buddhism.

This realisation helped to sustain their bond. Francis and Ellen not only made love but a life-long friendship. When Francis wrote his 11-page report about their first LSD-night experience, Ellen replied, with what can presently stand here as her finale, that she found his writing utterly fascinating and awe-inspiring. "Don't ever again let me hear you complain of not knowing as much as other Huxleys, and I think Aldous will be jealous but in the nicest possible way."

## Joan

Huxley met the social anthropologist Joan Wescott around 1962, when she was working as a secretary to R. D. Laing. Joan Mildred Arato was born into a family which can be traced back to the Piedmont and Tuscany regions of Italy. She married Roger W. Wescott in February 1959, in Mason, Michigan. Just over nine years later, in October 1968, while in London, she divorced him. There are pictures of Joan and Francis joyously travelling and hiking in the Pyrenees a year before. For a while they were inseparable.

Francis and Joan's relationship was, by all accounts, experimental, passionate, intense and conflictual. Being eight years Huxley's junior and a fellow anthropologist, she did not easily have to succumb to Huxley's wants or experience. In Joan's terms they were close to being equals. In terms of the ability to argue, impress, enchant, inspire and hurt one another deeply, they were also on a par.

Their volatile relationship formed a pivotal part of Huxley's mid-40s. In their correspondence, which we have some access to, they incessantly challenge one another, raising, amongst other issues, the intrusion of gender prejudice into their intimate lives. They each seemed to possess an aching desire to see the other as they truly are. There are welcome outside comments, from the likes of both Francis' mother, Juliette and R. D. Laing. We understand that some of the empirical data for Laing's celebrated book, *Knots* (published in 1971), depicted as the protagonists Jack and Jill, are, in fact, based on Joan and Francis' entangled love life. Being both anthropologists added an extra layer of complexity to the story, as they each sought to unravel the mythology of the other. Paul Zeal, psychoanalyst and one-time friend of Francis, said of their relationship,

> I think if there was some sort of "in therapy partner" for Francis, it was Joan Wescott. I'm not quite sure. Though Francis wrote down a lot of knots, which became part of Laing's book "Knots," that therapeutic type of enquiry, if you were living in the PA network at that time, there was therapy going on all the time. In a certain sense, everything was therapy.[20]

In 1962, Wescott published her research with the Eshu-Elegba and the Yoruba peoples, in the Kingdom of Dahomey, West-Africa. She gave a signed copy to Francis "with best regards, Joan." Her field experience between 1955 and 1957s saw her grapple with the sculpture and myths of Eshu-Elegba, the Yoruba trickster, something which endeared her even more to Francis, who was fascinated by shamans. In the course of her work, Wescott had surveyed public and private collections of Yoruba art in Germany and Switzerland, abstracted from a much fuller record which includes photographs of the more interesting or representative specimens.

In her paper on *The Symbolism and Ritual Context of the Yoruba Laba Shango*[21] (also published in 1962), Wescott tells us, how as an ethnographer, she often had to face the difficulty of interpreting symbols and symbolic acts existing within a specific tribe's culture. The art was not to jump too quickly to sanctioning an all-encompassing first explanation. Patience was the order of the day. She learnt to decipher, depict and explain discursively, just as Francis did, what the people she observed, intuitively perceived and responded to.

The workable interpretation, for Westcott, lies waiting to be discovered, nested in the whole experience of ambiguity, self-reflection and self-understanding (necessarily involving her relationship with Francis – in the paper she had explicitly thanked Leopold Stein, her psychoanalyst, for his help) extending outwards to society, culture, history and geography. It is hard not to find parallel strands of thought flowering in the Situationist movement's artistic and spiritual concerns with psychogeography which emerged in the 1950s.

Over the years, Francis and Joan cultivated what can easily be described as a tempestuous marriage – an affair which bridged the wild waters between the heart and the mind. There is in their correspondence and their work a dialogical storytelling between the two. Their conversations narrate a shared fondness to not only reveal their prejudices beyond the bounds of a traditional female–male relationship, but to insist – sometimes subtly, sometimes not – on challenging the other. Their letters and annotated cards, bear intimate witness to their joys, be they sexual, emotional or reasoned delight. With both protagonists being learned in the arts of deception, trickery and the workings of the unconscious as well as both accepting paranormal phenomenon within the domain of the real – the wealth of possible charges, counter-charges, sticking points and undecidable gambits, to say nothing of theoretically possible entanglements is extremely rich. Laing was wise to note that much could be learnt from what went on between them.

Westcott was always an avid communicator, both in words and silences and pictorially in the many postcards which she sent. Francis was definitely appreciative of the images which Joan dispatched from Italy, Spain, Turkey or even the English interior – certainly at that time a neglected side of the anthropological quest. When the Anti-University of London was going strong in 1968, Brian Evans remembers how Francis was teaching there, the audience captivated by his presence and delivery. Amongst them were folks from his Oxford days,

> Anthropologists and people who obviously held him in high regard as an anthropologist. He was supremely good as a raconteur. He also came with anthropologist Joan Wescott. She threw in her own stories and the like. They were an extraordinary double act.[22]

Donald J. Cosentino, Emeritus Professor, UCLA African Studies Centre, referred to both of them in his 1987 article: "Who Is That Fellow in the Many-Colored Cap? Transformations of Eshu in Old and New World Mythologies."[23] Equally at home in both their fields, Cosentino, praised Huxley as a brilliant observer for his treatment of the Ghede's loa in Haitian lore and Wescott for her 1962 study on the Sculpture of Eshu-Elegba. They were in Cosentino's eyes a formidable intellectual pairing.

In a later talk which Francis gave on "the body and the play within the play," he considered the content and context of embodied love and their professional relationship with it as tied to a fundamental anthropological concern,

> that of understanding how the social power incarnated by the symbolic mode allows a tradition to perpetuate itself. The body is then not just a vehicle for meaning but the instrumentation of the symbolic awareness per se.[24]

This distinction between having a body and being a body is intrinsic to the experience of love. Contemplation of our own bodily nature in relation to the loved other is suggestive insofar as when we physically touch the other person's skin, as lovers, we also touch her or his soul – a term saturated with meaning, out of favour in contemporary scientifically oriented psychology but which might be usefully reappropriated from anthropology.

Joan and Francis hoped both for a curative resolution of where they were each 'stuck' in their primary scenario – a desire that they could be transformed through their relationship, that love could realise its ever-present potential to heal. Professionally they knew that

> one of the difficulties facing the anthropologist is, of course, that symbolic action is a rite is a collective and generalised affair and not just the singular expression of an individual.

And yet Francis understood that "the rules of drama, through which body symbolism and cosmic imagery are eventually harmonised" stipulate that "the animism of the one find(s) its consummation in the logic of the other." A mirrored dance between the inner and the outer, reality and the symbolic order. They thereby persisted in applying the conceptual repertoire of their discipline as an instrument of understanding when describing to each other what their experience felt like. Joan and Francis were both, in their own ways, compassionately skilled in iconographic sense making. Just about the time Francis would meet his match, he wrote:

> The art, in the end, is to use these effects in order to create meaning, for meaning is the only real governor of the innumerable contradictions we consist of. To find meaning we have to know the worst as well as the best. In the end it is more dangerous to pretend that all is safe, and that we have nothing inside ourselves, which is startling, extraordinary or even dangerous, than really to see it in spite of our fears.

This for him was key to the notion of living authentically. Having been initiated into each other's intimate world, they could simultaneously inhabit two different vantage points, one personal, the other a theoretical step higher. What they saw and subsequently spoke about, was not always in extremis. As often as they came close to being a secure and powerful couple, they could find themselves tipped over into a crisis, the bond between them fractured and the seemingly well-organised North London cosmos they inhabited threatened with annihilation. The customary limits of everyday human life offered no exemptions for them. Structure, form and function could all give way to tears.

The anthropology of their existence together was never isolated from their more 'external,' conventional anthropological leanings – which as we have suggested included the weird, the wonderful, the strange, the uncanny and the paranormal – the invisible world beyond pure reason, of magic, mystery and possible mayhem. Together they invited the Brazilian Shaman Lourival de Freitas, alias 'Nero' when possessed, to England in July 1968. They staged healing sessions with a group of people in Brighton and London, both primed to take notes and observe what transpired. The strange world of the paranormal, in psychological terms, however, is never far from the estranged world of human emotions – sometimes a panacea for it, sometimes a refuge from it, sometimes a denial of it.

In a longish letter to Huxley, Rosalind Haywood, parapsychologist and one-time president of the Society for Psychical Research (SPR) attempted to give Francis, still caught up in the complexities of life with Joan, the helpful but forthright advice, he sought from her. She writes:

> about (Joan) whom I can be quite blunt as I've never met her. I feel torn between wanting to hit her over the head for being a nuisance to you – though I hope at times, a pleasure – and a feeling of fellow-woman sympathy on account of her beating father, Mafia genes and so on. BUT – I have a feeling that this emotional blackmail mustn't go on either for her sake or yours. I quite see that you can't say that, or your guilt complex would immediately engulf you, but perhaps I can speculate about it? ... I mean, on thinking it over, surely an anthropologist ought to see that it was the most natural thing in the world for an ordinary woman to splutter, when angry with her husband ... At 37 it's time she learnt to be constructive ... Anyway, the fact was that in pretty well all you said, you were worrying about her and she was worrying about herself ... I am into Joan it is merely through affection for you and that probably if she were with me and painted a PATHETIC picture of her sorrows, I would fling maternal arms around her and say "There, there, ducky." But this saying is not always the tonic people need.

Heywood's sympathies were clearly not with Westcott. "Sometimes" she continues towards the end of this letter, people need to be told: "Well, so what? Get along and do something and don't moan."

Joan went to see Laing occasionally, as late as the early 1980s. By then she was in a suicidal frame of mind. Laing said to Francis that he hadn't known what to say to her, but then just blurted out: "You still look like a good fuck." Not Laing at his most sensitive, but this actually picked her up and led Joan to say something pleasing about her former lover – that she "found not a shred of impatience in Francis."

When in March 1981, Theodor met Joan for the one and only time at Francis' flat, a while after they had split up, Francis bluntly declared that Joan was about to take her last drink and die. Francis mentioned that Joan had never finished her PhD, which still bugged her. But then neither had he finished his. What unfolded in front of him was raw and intense.

JOAN: "Oh, I could kill you. Do you see that you are so vital and have experience of so much of the good life, that I never had, and cling to it, ha ha ha. But we drink some of your blood."

FRANCIS: "You only want my brains."
JOAN: "No, you fool. I want your hearts."

This invocation of Joan's hidden injuries in the realms of class and privilege stung. Not long afterward, Francis was markedly upset and angry that Joan should continue to reproach him for issues which had been trenchant when they were together.

Francis:

> Your note on the door was not letting me in and then you weren't welcoming me. I was left to be on my own in the garden. You don't have to bring it up again, because I have my clarity and foolishness, that I should have just fucked off and gone on. Oh, the wasted time and mistakes.

Francis proceeded to raise his voice, commanding full attention in his living room.

JOAN: "You had brought it up, Francis."
FRANCIS: "You come over to me and interrupt me."
JOAN: "You brought me into the open again, while I was slowly dying. The other day you told me the first time about your tears, you shed in front of the stone garden table. It's the unshed tears between us that bothers me. I only saw you cry little while you sat in front of my fireplace and then talked of that bad time of the morning when you wanted everything to stop. Then your mother came and picked you up to go with your father to the senile place."
FRANCIS: "Yes. And that's when he cried the first time in front of me, asking me to get him out of there and to get his mother to fetch him, the great living British biologist. So, I left him. During the night mother asked the assistant to calm him down. They gave him an extraordinary sleeping pill, the reaction of which was that we sat for a moment around him with tea, when he lied back, breathing and then began the death breathing. He came up again, jolly in the afternoon, then in the evening put to bed, got a glass of wine, drank a sip, gulped and then passed off. Ha ha ha."

"That's not funny," says Joan. "Oh yes," said Francis.

There are some strange coincidences in their relationship. Joan, in her final days was living in a trailer at 11999 Coleman Valley Rd. Occidental, California, 9 miles from where Francis was then living. This very important woman in Francis Huxley's life died on his 66th birthday. Francis only learnt about this via Deborah Joos who had been in a caretaker group offering palliative services, and had been chosen to look after Joan. She is certain that Francis never forgot Joan, nor she him. Deborah showed us a precious gift Francis had given her. He and Joan used to sculpture together. It is a little sculpture that looks both like a tear and a fish. Francis kept it throughout his life. It is a poignant reminder of the ties that bind people together in life, of their unfailing persistence. Having been told the story of Joan's final days, Francis wanted to see where she lived and where her grave was. Deborah and her husband Jacques took him out there.

The sad story underlying Joan's early death – she was 58 – was that back in 1978 her London flat had been fumigated with lindane, a substance for eradicating beetles. It has been banned since 2009, under the Stockholm Convention on Persistent Organic Pollutants as a known carcinogen. Joan traced her illness – thus a case of environmental poisoning – to this. Deborah's husband assumed that in some way the failure of her relationship with Francis had also contributed to her early death.

Deborah and Joan had had long conversations about love and men.

> He wanted more from Joan than she was willing to give him. She said that to us. I think when he went with young women, they were more adoring. He was more intelligent. He didn't want stupidity. I think, with Joan he got a very intelligent woman, an equal anthropological thinker, a colleague.

Deborah continues,

> She was not yielding to him. She knew what she wanted. She was head-strong, she was determined, she wasn't going to be put down by anybody. The younger women in Francis' life after Joan yielded to him, as man of authority. Joan had probably as much authority as he then, her persona, her own life. The other ones, they were still forming.

We asked her if Joan ever mentioned Francis when she knew she was dying?

> There were no regrets that they didn't marry or have children, as there was nothing about the housewife in her. After Francis she never had a deep relationship with another man again.

Liberally distributed in Francis' cabin, in Wagnon Road, were a variety of fetishes which he had personally hand-crafted.[25] They reminded Deborah of West-Africa. It is not fanciful to wonder whether Joan, as a West-Africanist sculpture specialist had influenced Francis in these arts. Deborah remembers Francis being reticent to reveal more about what lay behind his creations.

> (he) didn't dare answer my probing about the meaning of sculptures. He was very modest, had a great sense of humour, and would deflect praise. He had his British cool.

In the conclusion of our interview with her, Deborah described the core of Joan as she experienced her. She was a very intense, very beautiful woman, I enjoyed being with and I noticed she was able to live through her last days as a victim of cancer with equanimity. She was very brave.

It's perhaps too easy, when exploring the emotional debris of Francis and Joan's relationship, to underestimate how important a person she was in his life. With her, the challenge of an equal relationship in terms of age, intellect and professional standing had been met. Francis was ready to marry. His reverence, respect, imaginative and romantic compassion had got him to a place where he was ready to commit to a partner, juxtaposing the requirements of love and companionship, with the recognised, internalised psychological theatre of gender and social identity.

## Adriana – first marriage

The bare facts: Marriage with Adrianna Paula Santa Cruz on 7 April 1973, in Hampstead, London. Divorced on 3 November 1976, Hampstead Registry Office. Adrianna is the daughter of Victor Santa Cruz, the accredited Chilean Ambassador to the UK from October 1959 until 1970 when President Allende was ousted by a US-backed military coup. The Ambassador was honoured with the Royal Victorian Order by the Queen in 1965. With his wife Dona Adriana, they had two sons and two daughters, Lucia and Adriana. Lucia was at one time in Cambridge as a research assistant to the then Master of Trinity, Lord Butler, and, aged 19, was introduced to Prince Charles at a dinner party organised at the Master's Lodge.

Michael Schwab, who used to meet Francis with his wife Inka in the 1970s, met Adriana once. He remembers her as,

> a very passionate woman who challenged Francis a lot and they fought a lot. I can't give you much more than that. It was a brief encounter. He told me afterwards how difficult it was, it didn't last too long. She was younger and very beautiful, energetic and passionate and she was enchanted by his mind and he by her body and passion.

Victoria Huxley remembered her, as a "fantastic and exotic bird of paradise. Half his age, however." Her sister Susie mentioned the cover story in the family, concocted possibly to please Juliette, that it was a marriage of convenience, to allow Adriana to stay in England. Victoria certainly didn't fall for this.

> Not at all. No, they had had a great time and didn't last for a long time because Francis didn't have a lot of money. She came from a privileged rich background. I should think, living with him, in a sort of not very pecunious Hampstead flat, you would assume ... I don't know what she was doing. She always wore designer clothes, very beautiful she was,

always presented as such. I only saw her when I went to Pond Street and she and Francis were there as well.

Asked about Francis and Adriana meeting Prince Charles and Lucia, she can't say, but thinks it possible. Robin Hanbury-Tenison invited Francis and Adriana down to his hill farm on Bodmin Moor in Cornwall. They knew each other well, being co-founders of Survival International and having been jointly on an eight-month journey to survey the tribes of the Amazon basin in Brazil in late summer of 1972. He remembers meeting Adriana on three occasions.

> Francis was very charming. I remember him and she was here. We had more a social relationship less than an intellectual or practical one. He did come down to stay with us in Cornwall a couple of times. He brought that Chilean girl, Adriana Santa Cruz with him ... They would have been here during this heyday. The 13th – 16th May 1971, he came with René Fuerst and Adriana, and again on 28th May to 1st June 1971, again with Adriana. Maybe he came down to give some help with his advice. The first secretary of the Brazilian embassy and his wife came to stay as well. When we were going to do the first Survey of the Indians in Brazil it was all nicely set up. Teddy Goldsmith came as well. That's when we started again. 30th of March to 4th April 1972, Francis came, and he was still with Adriana.

René Fuerst, a fellow traveller in 1972, remembers Adriana.

> Robin Hanbury-Tenison invited us from Survival International, for a party out in their Manor, a spacious Georgian farmhouse on the edge of Bodmin Moor. It's a beautiful estate. Adriana, Francis and I went there by train. When we arrived at the small station we stepped out and there was a Bentley with Hanbury-Tenison coming to pick us up. Huxley, me and Adriana, had three lovely days there.

Our attempts to find further news of Adriana unfortunately met with little success. We contacted her sister in Chile, by now a Member of the Board of the Universidad Adolfo Ibañez, who kindly wrote back to us:

> I regret I can be of very little help in your endeavour. I had very little contact with Francis Huxley. We coincided in England for a very short time as my parents left London in 1970 and I did in 1973. I think I only met him once. My sister was very young when she married. I may be completely wrong, but I feel it is a time of her life she would not like to remember or talk about.

In a further communication she added

*Love and history* 127

*Figure 8.2* Adrianna Santa Cruz 1971.

I regret to say that sadly I do not keep in touch with my sister Adriana. I know she lives in Belgium, but I do not have her exact whereabouts. I am sorry I am not able to help you further.

When Adriana and Francis split up, the love and passion had turned decidedly sour. Michael Williams remembers Francis telling him how it finally ended in a station on the London Underground. Francis had returned to his flat in Belsize Park Gardens, which he had been sharing with Adriana. He asked her to leave, as the split, according to him, was final. She refused and proceeded to threw stuff around, whereupon Francis upped and left himself. He walked to his home tube station, Belsize Park, a torrent of anger coursing through his veins. Just as he was about to enter the carriage of the train, Adriana caught up with him and tried to push herself through the still open door. Passions promptly erupted and engulfed them both. He blocked her path, not wanting their loud argument to continue in the carriage and then tried to push her out. Adriana, however, would not relent, and continued to try and fight her way in. With his verbal outrage yielding diminishing returns – Adriana simply took no notice – Francis finally punched her, the shock of which made Adriana stagger back from the outbound bound train. This left Francis doubly ashamed, both at this atrocious act and at having vented his anger in so exposed a public place. How sad for him, not to be seen in his own suffering by Adriana, how sad for her, that her relationship with her husband ended in assault on the London Underground. Love derailed on the Northern

Line – where prior to onset of the digital age, the train indicators had for many a year suggested the subterranean passage of time flowed at a different rate. On that evening the temporal anomaly had a ring of truth to it. Little wonder that Adrianna might wish not to remember it.

"It must be noted" Francis would later write, "that the water in which revenge is drowned comes from tears."[26]

## Meloma – second wife

The facts of life regarding Francis' second marriage, to Meloma Balaskas, record that it began in November 1976. Less than four years later, the two separated and were finally divorced in February 1986. Meloma Balaskas was born in South Africa in 1951, making her 28 years Francis' junior. She had come to London to join her brother and a close girlfriend she knew from Johannesburg. Once there, she entered psychotherapy with John Heaton, from the Philadelphia Association, and looked after her niece, Keira, as well as Laing's and other people's children. Victoria Huxley described her as a very sensible woman.

> First, she was a girlfriend of Francis. She was from South Africa and here (for residence) she ... needs a permit. Francis said that he would marry her to stay in the country. It would just be a marriage of convenience, as far as he was concerned. My grandmother was outraged. I remember that my grandmother was thinking to advertise, for a man to marry Mel.[27]

In a long interview, Mel recounted how she met Francis for the first time in Belsize Park.

> He passed, and someone said this was Francis Huxley. I saw this guy as quite unusual and very English. His walk and the way he held himself.[28]

Her brother Arthur was hosting some talks in his new spacious flat and it was there she first met Francis.

> I was on one side of the room and he was opposite me in the room ... he looked across at me and the first thing he looked at was my feet. You know in England the feet are mostly in shoes, and I was barefoot. He looked at my feet and with real interest in my eyes too. My whole body was tingling. I was about 25, (must have been in 1974) ... he was 52, he was double my years. Love at first sight for me. Because this was the first realisation that he was an anthropologist. According to Laing, one of the very few who really treated native peoples, ethically, as real people, without any condescending attitude.

*Love and history* 129

The year in which she had been born, Mel noted, was one in which Francis had been in the Brazilian Amazon. When they first met, she was living in the house with her elder brother. Francis would come around.

> My brother couldn't quite believe me, that this elder man came to see me. By the time Arthur and I had to leave this short term leased house, Francis and I had established a love relationship. He came to help me find a flat. It was my first home completely on my own. I painted the floors and walls; Francis would bring me beautiful paintings and food. He knew I needed to be independent and have my own space. This was a precious time for me also ... Francis and I spent time on the weekends together, ending up in his or my place. Being in his circle of friends, some of them are more intellectual friends, who tried to ignore me because they would have all this discussion. Once Francis was saying to them, "look, we stand on our heads without words; there she stands on her head.[29] Just leave her alone."

So, when did marriage appear on the cards?

> I had my Visa which had not been cleared completely. Every year for another year. When I came back from a visit to Amsterdam in 1976, I heard the news that my cousin had died. It was when the Soweto things (were) going on. I came back to South Africa. It was a very emotional time. I ran out of time for renewal. When back in London, the immigration officer stopped me at the airport and wouldn't let me into the country, even though I had already been in England for six years.

At the time, Francis was away for the weekend. Mel told the customs officer that she actually had an English boyfriend, whereupon they said: "Then you have to get married," an exchange which in today's xenophobic encrusted climate would be less likely than a meteorite strike on the high street.

To her joy, a wedding was arranged. It seemed to her, to be the opening to an exciting life in which they planned to have children. Whilst Francis was, as she put it, "very protective" towards her, Mel also felt he was a great influence on her development.

> One-time, they went to Oxford together. Francis used to be a don in anthropology at Oxford. We went there to have lunch. Imagine wild me marching with him into the dining hall right up to the high table. His colleagues who organised this who were there with their wives too, were all in their 40s and 50s. Here comes this man with me in her 20s, walking passed all the silent and standing students. Up to the stage to sit down. There was a blessing in Latin. We had this gourmet meal. I'm sitting on the big table. I asked, if all the students were eating what we were? They were laughing. Oh, don't get mad. I found it quite strange feeling that they were quite envious, Francis, coming along with his young wife.

*Figure 8.3* Francis with Mel Huxley 1975.

> I felt I grew up with Francis. I also grew up to trust my own taste. We were making masks with papier-mâché. I was surrounded by beautiful objects from all over the world. I began to wear incredible ethnic clothing and robes with embroidery. I felt very feminine and very soft.

She went to Indian-classical-dance classes, took up Aikido and singing lessons with Professor George Cunelli. Ronnie Laing, prolific amateur pianist that he was, knew him and referred several people from his friendship circle to him. Her personal development in Francis' circle seemed to proceed at a breakneck pace.

> Francis really wanted me to be able to read more. The books surrounded us, and we listened to music. He wanted to teach me more of that. I was open. A lot of it. I mean just the differences, the different age and anything. I needed to get out there into the world on my own. I needed my own adventure. Within the marriage I found a safe and warm like place, to be able to stick my head out.

Mel confessed that she didn't "like to go out of (her) comfort zone that much." Suddenly, however, what had initially signalled safety came to be experienced as restricting.

> The marriage just came to a point, one winter's day, I just could not move any more. I felt like completely stuck. With Francis, Ronnie and other guys, we met and sort of did a circle to clarify what was up. No hard feelings. They realised it wasn't working any more. They called an intervention. What did we like about each other? We both like butter and cream. That says it all really. Thus, we came to the end of our journey together. When we separated. I hadn't realised the degree to which I was relying on him.

After the separation they remained friends. Mel, still feeling insecure, went to him and sought his advice. When Francis later married Adele, his third wife, Mel was invited to their wedding. On the occasion Francis thanked her publicly for

> preparing him for her, so to speak, to opening in him a trust, that showed him the power of love. It was very nice to have this appreciation in the open at the wedding.

She remembers Francis, for all his 'Englishness' – which she thought could easily put off non-native people – as someone who fundamentally had a heart of gold. She remained enamoured of his storytelling and how she used to happily lie in his arms and listen to his past adventures. Despite the fun and the surrounding fame in Laing's entourage, there was a melancholy resignation that not only could they not always get the unconditional love they yearned for, but that perhaps something from their time together had passed through her hands, that the "wild and precious life" was beyond capture. It could only be lived and then pass away.

> Younger people have a certain kind of beauty. I know I have sort of kind of tribal kind of thing. It's more my Greek roots and barefoot that attracted him. I felt beautiful with him and addressed beautifully. I felt appreciated on a level I haven't received since.

132  *The facts of life*

**Adele – marriage into California**

Francis Huxley married Adele Getty on 10 November 1986 at Camden Registry Office. They separated in 1998 and were divorced in 2006. In her two long interviews,[30] Adele discussed the course of her relationship with Francis, from the moment of their falling in love, through falling out of love and on to settling into the pattern of a quasi-'daughter–father' relationship, a reflection of Adele being 26 years younger, but one which nonetheless maintained a clear sense of mutual love. Victoria Huxley remembers Adele fondly. "I'm very grateful for her. She'd been marvellous to Francis."[31]

Adele first encountered Francis when she

> was about to teach a class at Sonoma State University, called *Ritual*. I wasn't sure which text to use for this class. My chairperson suggested that I use "The Way of the Sacred" by Francis Huxley. I asked him who is Francis Huxley. He replied: The anthropologist of the family.

Two years later (now 1979), she started working for the Ojai foundation with anthropologist Joan Halifax. Her first chance to meet Francis in person fell flat, as Joan had broken her arm resulting in all of the seminars having to be cancelled. Adele was looking forward to meeting the author of *The Way of the Sacred* – "one dream I had, instructed me to do this," she said. It was one of the core books for the class she was teaching.

> It was kind of crazy for me. I didn't want to do it, but my committee said you really ought to do this. I didn't know anything about rituals. The committee helped me to draw up a curriculum. I ended up teaching this for several years."

Finally, in the summer of 1984, the Ojai foundation put on a month-long retreat, entitled 'The Way of the Warrior' where all the participants come together and stay for the duration. Adele says:

> We ended up being a group of about hundred people on the land during that month. The number of people on the faculty who were invited, stayed the full month, including Francis, R. D. Laing, Rupert Sheldrake, Jill Purce, Francis Varela, John Lilly, including various native Indians. Francis was the first teacher to arrive. My job was to be a liaison with the teachers who came. I felt very comfortable with him and he of course was very flattered that I'd read *The Way of the Sacred*.
> At that time MDMA was a legally sold substance, and we used it … in couple therapy being used all over the United States. I asked Francis and Rupert pretty immediately if they had this experience, or if they were interested in it. They said "yes" and wanted to as soon as possible and "we will wait for Jill to arrive." We took MDMA together and that was the

beginning of a deep bonding and hearing family stories from each. That ended up being our ongoing friendship with Rupert, Jill and the kids.

Thus, her relationship with Francis and falling in love with him occurred in highly unusual circumstances. Both were at that time still with other partners. Francis with Avice Simpson, and Adele with Sonny. After the Way of the Warrior month was over, they travelled together to Mexico with a team of the Ojai foundation and then once back in California were faced with the decision as to whether to stay together or not.

Francis was travelling on to Vancouver, to give a workshop with psychotherapist Andrew Feldmar, and invited Adele to come along. He then decided that he would accompany Adele in going back to Point Reyes where she lived with Sonny, take MDMA together and tell Sonny what had happened.

> He said: oh, you were lovers at the conference? Because there was an old lover of mine among the teachers. Yes, I said. Sonny: "who?" This is very unusual. I was 34 and Francis was 61. This was a very unlikely relationship. We sat there for a second. Sonny: "Francis?" Sonny's an amazing guy who supported me emotionally as I made the transition.

A month or two later she would travel to London. Francis had by then already returned and confessed to Avice that he was in love with another woman. Being with Francis, for Adele, was an amazing opportunity to raise her education through a relationship.

> I respected him and was totally amazed and intrigued by his super polymath's intelligence, which was really great for me. We found that we loved many kinds of common or same areas, my work of rituals with Native Americans ... I can say that it really developed me in a way that was wonderful.

Back in London, Adele began making her entry into Francis' social world.

> Then I found myself totally falling in love with Juliette. I gave Francis, before he went back to London, a piece I wore, depicting the Goddess Isis. A glass wax casting of Isis and he gave me a Tibetan Milan Sun disc. When Francis went to his mother to say, "bon jour, je suis de retour," Juliette picked up the medallion, weighting it in her hands, and asked: "Where did you get this, you met a woman did you?" "Yes, I did," was the plain answer, and Francis asked her for a favour: "Don't ask me any more questions."

To his amazement, Juliette heeded his request. Adele remembers going to Pond Street for the first time and her future mother-in-law opening the door.

"Darling," she said, embracing Adele, and then warmly welcomed her into the family. In the ensuing days, weeks and years, Adele would spend a lot of time with Juliette whenever the couple were in London. "She was part of my ongoing education," Adele said.

It was in the early period of their relationship (January 1986) that Francis' top-floor flat in Hampstead's Wedderburn Road suffered a serious fire which caused a lot of damage. Adele and Francis arrived to find many of his beloved books lying in the front garden, covered by fresh snow, the firefighters having thrown them out of the window in the course of combatting the blaze. It was not just the loss of so much of his intellectual history that was devastating for Francis. They had only just redecorated their home prior to the destruction. It was standing in Wedderburn Rd, in front of the ruins that Francis proposed. He and Adele decanted temporarily to Juliette's, then for a while with another couple, in a shared house in Point Reyes, California.

It was in Point Reyes that they celebrated their bonding with a ceremony on Sunday, 10 May 1986. Both his former lovers, Ellen and Meloma came. In a letter to Juliette about one week later, Francis described to Juliette how marvellous the event had been, wishing she could have been there.

> Adele was so beautiful and I love her so much. She had the diamond earrings on, and a gold sun-mirror hanging round her neck, and a dress which is a little North African, and a little Greek, and a little Amazonian, of roughly woven soft cream white cotton trousers.[32]

By the middle of the night, the ritual celebration was over. Francis, ever the social and cultural anthropologist, cemented the bonding ritual by constructing a Moebius strip, "nicely doodled with coloured pencil and, of course words." Meeting on a little island in the middle of a pond, where on the one side stood the women and on the other the men, the two invoked the presence of the Buddhist Goddess Guanyin, the all-seeing Goddess of Mercy alive to the cries of the world.

As the Point Reyes ceremony was not legally binding, they returned to London for a civil wedding in order to obtain the appropriate legal recognition and to make Juliette happy. Rupert and Jill were witnesses. Back in California, they moved to Berkeley Hills for a couple of years, then to San Francisco. The constant journeying back and forth to London – as Juliette was becoming increasingly frail – was a difficult and, as Adele described it, disruptive time, more so than expected, for both of them.

In October 1987, aged 64, Francis finally passed his driving test, which merited a mention in a letter to Juliette. Francis' new-found driving status came in handy, as Adele was often busy conducting workshops and writing her book on the Goddess.[33] Eventually they moved to Santa Fe, where Francis had previously undertaken some anthropological work. They already knew a couple of people there and were soon joined by their friends from Point Reyes, Pauline and Robert. In 1997, they eventually built a home, in a small community in Pojoaque, 16 miles to the north. Both thought this was where they would put down roots and settle. Adele, who loved designing, planned and organised the contractors.

> It was designed to be a writer's house. A formal library was in a very large room. Francis had a separate studio. It was made for us to spend the rest of our lives in there. In reality it lasted two years but felt like only a minute. By 2000 I was gone.

Whilst in Santa Fe, Francis was content. The surrounding nature was important to him, giving him opportunities for daily exploration and observation of plants, birds and other animal life. As a zoologist, a seasoned anthropologist and someone with important connection to Aldous Huxley, the Santa Fe community welcomed them warmly. There were plenty of dinner parties and merriment, and yet, overshadowing his and Adele's joie de vivre, was Francis' continuous head-neck pains which he suffered. Adele recalls:

> Santa Fe was very good for his joints and he found the climate very agreeable. But there were days when he collapsed into bed. Really suffering consequential depression. He did not ask for painkillers, for his mind might be affected.

To Francis, a foggy mind was worse than pain. Injections to the bone relieved the pain but the side effects sent him to bed exhausted for days. Adele saw it as a "tragic part of his life." Indeed, these physical ailments undoubtedly interrupted and in some ways curtailed his writing. Reflecting on these difficulties prompted Adele to think about their beginnings once more and how she had envisaged things playing out with a much older man:

> It probably took us six or seven years to ever say anything mean to one another. When I gone-in with Francis, that changed my life. I was totally rational about this much older man in England. Everything that was going to happen as a result of different countries. First, he seemed very old to me, age 61. I thought if I get 10 years with this person, I will be totally happy. He's so extraordinary. I just wanted to take this opportunity to be with him. I'm all into this relationship. That's how I felt. The last couple of years there was stress around Juliette. There was stress around building the house.

There eventually came the further stress of ending their marriage and the thorny question of finances. Francis had money from the Wedderburn Road flat, Adele's parents and on occasion Juliette also helped, enabling them to survive, put bread on the table and do the necessary travelling to and from the UK. Francis also took to selling some of the Huxley things he inherited.

Despite the presence of these beneficial trophies from the family, Francis remained scarred by the emotional legacy of his father. Adele reached the point where she could take no more:

> I got really angry with him. Told him that it was really time he dropped it. It didn't seem that this is gonna be a solution, and you're 75 and he's been dead for 20 years. The issue round his father was a lot to do with Julian being a walking contradiction. Unfortunately, Francis could not do for himself what he managed for Juliette.

For Adele, there were three specific incidents which were pivotal to bringing the curtain down on their marriage.

> We were with friends. The first time he told me to "shut the fuck up," I was shocked. The second time in another instance, he told me "fucking shut up," I couldn't believe it. He never talked to me like that before. I told him on the second occasion: "If you ever do that to me again, I will leave you. That's not acceptable." The third time happened when we were having dinner with just another couple to which we were already close. Francis loved chocolate. I woke up one night in bed. I had this overwhelming smell of chocolate. As I woke up, I realised I had an entire chocolate bar melted on my chest and he had been eating the better part and laughed. It was funny to both of us. I was telling this story to Robert and Paulin because they knew he loved eating chocolate in bed. He and I have laughed about it. What happened I was telling the story and he told me to "fucking shut up."

What deeper reasons underlay Francis' aggressive outbursts is unknown, his battle with constant pain may have been one factor but we cannot be sure. When they drove home, Adele turned to him and said "That's it!" Extremely angry she wondered whether he was intentionally sabotaging their relationship.

In due course Huxley returned to London, ending 1999 there, finishing his book on *Shamans through Time* while for several months being the house guest of Jill, Rupert Sheldrake and their sons Merlin and Cosmo. Adele stayed put in Pojoaque, until Francis returned, then packed up and left for Sebastopol. Initially she didn't want a divorce, letting Francis, by that time 77, stay in her house.

The pact they made was that Adele could continue to love Francis, no longer as her husband, but as an elder, allowing her to pursue her own life in a new direction – which she did – she and her subsequent partner Michael having him on their land in Wagnon Road to his dying day. The transformation of the relationship from a much younger wife to a daughter figure was really a gift from the 'daughter' to her father. Francis thus moved, in 2005, from Santa Fe, which he had loved for the climate and the people to Northern

California. Adele had said to him "I hope you're still around in 2012" to which Francis replied "No way will I have to be around for 2012."

As it was, Francis was. He celebrated his 90th birthday in the back garden, in between the two cabins on the land. Adele ended up several years older than Francis had been when they first met, something unimaginable in the beginning. During the interview with Adele, we asked her "of Francis' past relationships, which did he see as his most important ones, which did he treasure the most? Adele was quite clear in her answer.

> Both Ferelyth and Sheila. Mel he was fond of. Everybody was less critical than Joan. That was a real love hate relationship. Francis had no bad feelings about any of his ex-wives, and never wished any former partners ill will.

We wonder whether Francis sometimes regretted having left London for good in order for the relationship to work. Adele could not live in London, "just in terms of the weather," even so she enjoyed the intellectual and cultural company she found herself in as Francis Huxley's wife. Santa Fe, in turn, was heaven for Francis, for the weather eased his rheumatic sufferings and he enjoyed being surrounded by native culture and D. H. and Frida Laurence's Ranch at Lobo Mountain near San Cristobal, where Uncle Aldous used to hang out. He also found inspiration taking visitors to Bandelier National Monument, under an hour's drive away. In his library was *The Delight Makers,* the story of Adolf F. Bandelier's eight-year ethnological fieldwork and archaeological study among the Pueblo Indian of New Mexico. Francis knew the intimacies of native life and how extraordinary Bandelier's success had been in accessing the inner heart of the Indians.

In 2012, Theodor asked Francis how long we could still count on him being around. He replied, "until I know the meaning of life!" In another year, while he suffered the side effects of radiation therapy, and shuffling around his cabin had become even more agonising, he muttered; "I am tired from doing nothing and just walking round my cabin." Theodor asked again. "I thought you were my friend." Francis replied with a mighty laugh. Since he now had difficulties hearing, with or without hearing aids, Theodor took the opportunity to ask him one last time, "Have you found out the meaning of life?" Francis responded with laughter. "Yes, a long time ago. It's women," he said.

## Notes

1 MacGibbon, J. (1984, pp.21–22) *I Meant to Marry Him – A Personal Memoir.* London: Victor Gollancz.
2 Ibid., p.12. A charming coincidence is that her husband, the publisher James MacGibbon, and his publishing house MacGibbon & Kee, merged with Francis' first publisher Rupert Hart-Davis in 1972, which was acquired in 1963 by its parent group, Granada Publishing.

## The facts of life

3 Buckman, D. (1998) *The Dictionary of Artists in Britain Since 1945*. Bristol. Art Dictionaries.
4 Buckman, D. (2005) Ferelyth Wills – Sculptor of Animals in Wood. Obituary. *The Independent*. Thursday, 6 October. David Buckman kindly suggested contacting Bedales school, where Bill Wills, who she married, was teaching, in order to get in contact with Jackie, Ferelyth's youngest daughter, and the local newspapers in Hampshire. For this we are very grateful.
5 Wills, F. and Wills, B. (1975, p.7) *Sculpture in Wood*. London. David & Charles.
6 Letter send from Barton on Sea, Friday night. No date. FHA
7 MacGibbon (1984, p.157).
8 The card has no address, date or postmark and is of a painting 'The Annunciation' in the National Gallery, Washington D.C. Archive, FHA.
9 Margaret MacMullan replied to an email placed by Theodor in the local free paper, the Chichester Post, for information on Ferelyth Wills. She writes "I met her in her last years when she and her husband lived in Emsworth and from whence I gave her lifts to our mutual Old Scholars' Association Reunions near Godalming." Email, 2 July 2018.
10 Oxford Journals 1951–1952. FHA.
11 Letter from Val Mitchison to Francis Huxley. 2 August 1951. FHA.
12 Letter to Julian Huxley, undated, probably end of 1953. JHP.
13 Email: Montag, 8 July 2019. Marion Servat-Fredericq, Liverpool.
14 Letter to A. Digby, from the Acting Director, Keeper of Ethnology, British Museum, 30 June 1954.
15 Letter to Juliette Huxley, 1 October 1954. JHP.
16 Francis Huxley's letter to Sheila, from New York, 19 March 1956.
17 Letter to Dearest Mummy and Father, 4 April 1955. JHP.
18 Interview with Michael Schwab, July 2019.
19 Bisbee, et al. (2018, p.575) Appendix 2: LSD experience of 7 November 1956; letters between Humphry Osmond and Matthew, Ellen and Francis Huxley..
20 Paul Zeal interviewed in March 2018, London.
21 Wescott, J. A. and Morton-Williams, P. (1962, pp.23–37). The Symbolism and Ritual Context of the Yoruba Laba Shango. *Journal of the Royal Anthropological Institute of Great Britain and Ireland*, 92 (1), (January–June). See also Wescott, J. A. (1957, pp.133–135) Yoruba Collections in Germany and Switzerland. *Man*, 57 (September); Wescott, J. A. (1963, pp.9–15) Tradition and the Yoruba Artist. *Athene*, II (1); Wescott, J. A. (1964, pp.545–547). Review of: Nigerian Images by William Fagg, Herbert List; African Mud Sculpture by Ulli Beier; Primitive Art by Leonhard Adam; Coptic Sculpture by John Beckwith. *Journal of the Royal Society of Arts*, 112 (5095) (June).
22 Interviewed in March 2018.
23 Cosentino, D. (1987, pp.261–275) Who Is That Fellow in the Many-Colored Cap? Transformations of Eshu in Old and New World Mythologies. *Journal of American Folklore*, 100 (397) (July–September).
24 Huxley, F. (1975, pp.29–38) The Body and the Play within the Play. In *The Anthropology of the Body*. Ed. J. Blacking. London. Academic Press.
25 In this sense intended here, fetishes are inanimate objects worshipped for their purported magical powers or because they are thought to be inhabited by a spirit.
26 Huxley, F. (1976, p.101).
27 Victoria Huxley Interview on 15 March 2018, Oxford.

28 Mel Balaskas Huxley. Taped interview received from Johannesburg on 16 October 2018.
29 A reference to Mel being an accomplished yoga practitioner.
30 Adele Getty interviewed on 10 and 16 April 2018, Sebastopol.
31 Victoria Huxley interview 15 March 2018, Oxford.
32 Francis Huxley letter to Juliette Huxley, 14 May 1986. JHP.
33 Getty (1990).

# Part IV
# Social anthropology
In search of the world

# 9 Anthropology and its challenges

Beyond family holidays in Switzerland and the school expedition to Lapland, Francis Huxley's first serious act of practical and intellectual exploration beyond the shores of the UK took him, in 1948, to the Gambia – then still a British colony – as leader of the Oxford University Exploration Club. The expedition, financed from *The Geographical Magazine* Trust fund, was charged with several tasks, as part of a broad remit to assess the country's interlinked economic and environmental challenges. Though this was not an anthropological expedition, it had much in common with one – involving a necessity to familiarise oneself with local customs, beliefs and practices in tandem with developing an appreciation of the ecology, geography, history and lifestyles of the region's people. In his account of the group's work, Francis makes a passing reference to his first cross-cultural encounter with dragon mythology; the ninki-nanka (dragon devil) a legendary beast in West-African folklore, his informants assured him inhabited the Kuntaur riverine forest. The fabled creature which it is death to see and death to be seen by has "no solid proof of its existence" and is therefore "all the more deeply feared."[1]

We see in the procession of experiences from boarding school, family holidays, school expeditions and finally the Gambia expedition, Francis' psychological preparation for the arduous personal trials which is necessary for an anthropological fieldworker to overcome – separation and isolation from one's usual personal, cultural and ecological habitat for an extended period, facing unpredictable and unknown challenges on a daily basis, a potentially quite different diet, added to which are the difficulties of communicating and operating in a different linguistic habitat. Rebecca Solnit wrote of "getting lost" in the "unfamiliar," a readiness to "be greeted by what you have never seen before."[2] In later life Francis would draw comparisons between this preparation and the training analysis for a psychoanalyst. In our conversations with the anthropologist Adam Kuper, he spoke at length about this issue of adaptation.[3]

> I've got several things to say. There is often a problem with young people going to the field, Some, as the colonialists used to say, "go native." In

144  *Social anthropology*

> the field you can become enchanted and absorbed, you might even find a local partner. Perhaps, when they study a cult, young fieldworkers get converted. If this happens you lose objectivity and analytical distance.

Francis Huxley – on his first trip out to Brazil to live and work with the Ka'apor was a relatively young man of 27–28 years old. As we know, he flourished – Kuper was quite aware here of the social-class dimensions behind why that was – and to the psychological preparation provided by Huxley's upbringing adding a further element.

> Now the question about the way in which fieldwork changes people. This depends where you are coming from. For Bateson and Huxley, coming from the English intellectual bourgeoisie, the experience of fieldwork could be liberating, it let them get away from the rather rigid way they had to behave as English gentlemen.

To contextualise Francis' accomplished adaptation to fieldwork, Kuper makes clear that the risks can be varied and serious. The experience of entering the field for the first time is not just a confrontation of sorts with an 'other' but a confrontation with aspects of oneself. In contemporary terms, psychologists might frame this under the rubric of an 'openness to experience' in all its untamed manifestations, a capacity to suspend one's customary cultural judgements and throw oneself into a new pattern of experience, the summative effect of which may well lead to a depatterning of what has gone before. As Kuper noted, this "could be traumatic."

> Some people who went out into the field had psychological breakdowns. Rivers had a student, John Layard, who had a homosexual crush on him. When Rivers left him alone on a South Pacific Island, he had a breakdown. When he came back to England, Rivers was, for a while, his therapist. Layard later became a Jungian therapist.

As Kuper made clear, the risks do not end with the possibilities of becoming psychologically overwhelmed. Perhaps a critical factor in shaping one's responses to anthropological 'immersion' lies in the prior expectations of the other that one brings to the situation – how much one expects to find in common with the people encountered. That Huxley explicitly set out to portray the Indians, whose company he kept, as subjects in their own right is a pointer as to why he adapted as well as he did. Questions of perceived and actual similarity, both psychological and cultural, are brought to life under the long shadow of the history and politics of relationships between diverse groups of human beings. In contemplating this, it was of great interest to us that Kuper, drawing on his own experience in South Africa, expressed the view that to him "fieldwork was a political act."

The ample coverage of Francis' research with the Ka'apor in the Brazilian press, points to several other aspects. The various articles are testament not only to the inherent concern which the host nation directs to foreign visitors to its indigenous peoples – something which has intensified as the environment and indigenous and tribal people's rights have climbed up the political agenda – but also, on Francis' side, to the necessity to respect local officialdom and smooth diplomatic channels where possible. His famed-family membership no doubt helped in this respect, more than one newspaper story made reference to his celebrated uncle and father, while describing Francis himself as extremely curious and wise.[4] As we mentioned in the preface, his presence in the country and his 'disappearance' in the largest rainforest on Earth were also irresistible and spectacular events for the press to feast on.

On his own admission, when he set off for Brazil in November 1950, Huxley was keenly aware that "he had never seen the inside of a tropical jungle" and knew "nothing of the practical difficulties of anthropological field work there."[5] Few others were any better prepared, this after all was a mere five years after the Villas Boas brothers had set off on the trailblazing Roncador-Xingu expedition, the first Brazilian state venture, which would open up the forested interior.[6] Francis was in debt to Darcy Ribiero for organising the practical details of the journey – which included a ten-day boat trip up the Gurupi river – and for initially accompanying him to several villages from which he acquired the confidence that he had "a fairly good idea of how to treat both the Indians and the jungle."[7] That still left the not inconsiderable task of mastering Portuguese. For Francis, fluent in French, this was readily achievable and to his own satisfaction, he attained a familiarity with the language which was "good." In a letter to Meyer Fortes he relates how his mealtimes were preoccupied with the task.[8] The local language, spoken by the Ka'apor, however, presented a more formidable challenge. In a letter to Rupert Hart Davis, in May 1953, he confessed that he couldn't "speak Tupi well" and "can't help losing some of the flavour" when he was hearing an Indian tell a story. This meant he was sometimes "still in need of an interpreter."[9]

These challenges of personal adaptation should be seen as just the beginning of the hurdles the anthropologist must confront. Once out in the field and on the return home there were an array of thorny ethical and political matters to attend to. In his inaugural lecture as William Wyse Professor at Cambridge (1953), Meyer Fortes, Francis' major mentor, described anthropology as

> indispensable for coming to decisions about our own political and ethical values, and for understanding the climate of our time. It is the duty of anthropology to proclaim this truth and to continue dispassionately to investigate the biological and social qualities of human groups without regard for race privilege.[10]

146  *Social anthropology*

The prevailing ideas about race when Huxley first ventured out into the Brazilian jungle would be largely cast aside as he ignored the evolutionism which still exerted a powerful influence in anthropology and set about showing the Indians there as human subjects in their own right.

## Notes

1  Huxley, F. (1949/1950, pp.270–277).
2  Solnit, R. (2006, pp.22–23) *A Field Guide to Getting Lost*. London. Canongate.
3  Interviewed in January 2019.
4  Estudando od indios brasilieros. *Gazetta*, Sao Paulo, 1 March 1951.
5  Huxley, F. (1956, p.11) *Affable Savages*. Viking Press, reissued (1995) Salem. Sheffield.
6  See Hemmings, J. (2019) *People of the Rainforest*. London. Hurst & Company.
7  Huxley, *Affable Savages*, p.12.
8  Letter to Meyer Fortes, 2 May 1951.
9  Correspondence with Rupert Hart-Davis, 1st May 1953 a/c Serviço de Proteçao aos Indios. Brazil. Tupi is one of the four main language groups of Brazilian Indians.
10  Drucker-Brown, S. (1983, p.15) 'Obituary.' *RAIN*, 56.

# 10  The Ka'apor

Francis' exploits with the Ka'apor helped nurse narrative anthropology into existence. This was, in no small part, due to his disciplined approach to work. He was diligent, not only in his prior preparation – financial planning, language learning, digesting available knowledge of the Indians – but also once in the field, constantly writing and reflecting on what he was hearing and observing. He strove with each new experience to understand humanity as it appeared before him, always on the look-out for the bigger picture. It was not that this was all assured. His correspondence with Meyer Fortes before venturing into the "great unknown" betrays his anxieties about what lay ahead. Once in the field, "now all alone in ... the village of Kwata, ten hours march" from the SPI post, he confessed to getting on "more or less alright" whilst possessed of the irksome feeling that "somebody's hiding something," a natural enough response in a strange new environment. By the time he emerged from the jungle nursing "conjunctivitis," "worms and something peculiar that's swelling up my lymphatics" as well as "missing friends"[1] he was already immersed in a perpetual questioning of his own experience and culture. "I'd never bothered before to think about what it meant to be English," he wrote on his way home. Language, he had come to think, gives one the "illusion of familiarity," that one understands the surface truths of events when, in fact, deeper knowledge lies hidden beneath it. This questioning of deceptive familiar truths was to become a hallmark of his work. His numerous letters from the field and on his way home evidence an incessant questioning of English, Brazilian and Indian culture and the search for a bigger cloth into which they can all be woven. He noted, after his return from being 'lost in the jungle,' how the Brazilian press were almost indignant that he had not "even suffered one bellicose gesture from the savages." They were intent he surmised on "turning everything into either blood or water."[2]

The effect of his ruminations on his own discipline was slow burning, but what of the effect on himself? By all accounts his two trips into the Brazilian jungle exerted a profound effect upon him. This reached beyond any lessons pertaining to professional objectivity and detachment and took in the joys which his friendship with the Indians had given him, and the feelings of connectedness that were forged with nature under the canopy. These things are evident in much of the writing of *Affable Savages*. The following extract captures something of the benign beauty that haunted Francis for the rest of his life.

> The moon came up. It was a lovely night, without a wind, the tree-trunks at the edge of the clearing standing out remarkably white; and a lively noise of frogs down by the stream … We drank some more sweet manioc soup, rolled ourselves large cigars and tawari bark and then Antonio-hu and I lay down at either end of my hammock, head to foot … I asked him about the stars. He told me about the Milky Way, which he called the Tapir's Path: the souls of dead tapirs walk along it, eating "fruit souls and leaf souls," as he said. There was Grandfather Many Things, or the Pleiades, each of which was really a man dressed in his feather ornaments. Antonio-hu pointed to the east – "When Grandfather Many Things shows itself there," he said in his deep grating voice, "it's summer." He lifted his pointing finger to the Zenith: "There, the rains start! When Grandfather Many Things is there, we know it's time to plant." His finger pointed slowly to the western horizon: "The rains are over."

How could such a memory not endure? Bettina Blume – who with her husband would buy Francis' parents' house in London's Pond St. from him in 1995 – was one of many people we interviewed who spoke fondly of Francis and remembered how he would tell her "stories of his life and the research with Brazilian tribes." Bettina bought the house from Francis when he was a sprightly 72 years. Tales of his earlier Brazilian self flowed from his fond storehouse of memories and charmed her immensely.

Francis' initial forays into the field, and his reflections on the nature of the encounters there, set in motion a preoccupation with issues – of human subsistence and civilisation, cultural and economic change in an increasingly interconnected world, and the nature and construction of our relations with the natural world. His time with the Ka'apor would also leave a moral imprint on him; a sensibility that their lives and those of other Indians demand recognition and acknowledgement, of sorts, from the side of the world that we inhabit. The inseparability of everything he encountered in the jungle would lead Francis to a perennial theoretical interest in the problems of anthropology and eventually to his practical involvement with Survival International.

In the hundreds of letters which Francis wrote from the field on his various travels, no subject crops up more often than his musings on the nature of anthropology – its aims, methods, nature and relationship to science and scientific method. He was consistently sceptical of an overly scientific approach, feeling that it cuts us off from a mythological tradition. It can even be surmised that after Kant, any suggestion that we can fundamentally know the world beyond our senses must perforce be reliant on myth.

His fieldnotes suggest Huxley might have countered this view by arguing that what distinguishes a mythology from science is its capacity to personify

*The Ka'apor* 149

*Figure 10.1* Darcy Riberio and Francis with the Ka'apor 1951.

the world, so that within the bounds of its consecrated symbols one finds one's allotted place in the greater scheme of things. But is it not also true that in industrial societies one locates one's place and meaning in the world by reference to these scientific 'myths' – and that it is precisely because we do and that the nature of these myths is *impersonal* that many humans feel adrift in an ultimately meaningless world? In one sense then, Huxley's contention seems to be that mythology is a function of how we *feel* about ourselves as human beings – in a symbolic order of our making. Lévi-Strauss was adamant that without exception, all human beings live in societies ordered by language, technology, arts, empirical knowledge, religious imaginings and within a given social and political organisation. The crucial distinction then – if we are to make one – between our own industrial societies and those of indigenous or tribal peoples, concerns our frameworks for making common meaning. Francis lamented how his own efforts to embrace a way of thinking distinct from the Western cultural heritage, he has been heir to, have been handicapped by his immediate background.

> I'm sorry for myself, that my particular family has been so evolutionarily, humanistically minded that it has stopped thinking in that ancient way which gives one a great deal of support. You know, it's all been from the top of the head, not from inside of the heart. And one needs both.[3]

In Francis' own rationale for pursuing anthropology, he sought to align the symbolic order with the material, with no absolute reduction of one to the other. What is striking, however, in a good deal of his work is his expressed interest, from the earliest days of fieldwork, in understanding other cultures through their psychological dimensions. The "frame of mind"[4] behind a story held more importance than its literal truth. This stance led him in a number of different directions – first, to an interest in psychedelia and the irrational modes of thought one can find in forms of madness; secondly, to whether anthropological data suggest the existence of psychic powers[5] and finally, to insightful work on the interconnected webs of myth and fable in world culture. We'll now turn specifically to his interests in psychedelia and the paranormal.

## Notes

1 Letter to Bill from SS San Velino, undated.
2 Letter to parents, undated.
3 Huxley, F. (1977) *Embryos and Ancestors*. Unpublished Manuscript. Evening event organised by the Philadelphia Association.
4 Huxley, F. (1952, pp.35–47) The Affaire Guajaja. *World Review*. August.
5 Francis Huxley with Ted Baston and Carmen Blacker (1974, pp.298–301) Discussion. Where the Map is the Territory. *Theoria to Theory*, 8.

# 11 Saskatchewan

Francis' preoccupation with myth grew directly from his fieldwork. His explorations of unusual states of mind and their potential was also born of experience but was also certainly influenced by his Uncle Aldous' experimentation with psychedelic agents. Francis embarked on these chemically assisted inner journeys with considerable zest, egged on by Ellen Hovde to try mescaline and LSD. She, her husband Matthew and Francis were all enthusiastic explorers. Ellen, taking the lead, expressed a longing that the trips would take her "to the source that one knows and trusts."[1] This was in late Spring, 1956. The three of them were living at Maplewood Rd, in New Haven, Francis having decided to spend at least a year in North America. His base to begin with was New York but he found himself travelling to Los Angeles, Philadelphia and Chicago, attending various congresses and even finding time for a swift visit to Mexico, to research the miraculous virgin of Guadalupe, a figure which Aldous, four years earlier, had noted "consistently turned up in my visions."[2] Eventually, Francis went to Saskatchewan, Canada, where he would approach psychiatry from the vantage point of an anthropologist, something his colleague Gregory Bateson would also do in the Veterans Hospital in Los Angeles. Francis' position, however, departed from Bateson's, eschewing a medicalising aetiology in favour of a grounded ethnology.

Ellen's plan was to have Humphry Osmond in their cottage to conduct a four-way experiment. "If Dr. Osmond comes, I'll be there like a rocket," Francis wrote to Ellen. The date for this first LSD experience was set at Wednesday, 7 November 1956, at Sanford Rd, Woodbridge. Ellen wisely cautioned Humphry (with whom she now was on first-name terms) that

> Huxley *children* are highly strung characters with complex problems (so are their relations). Knowing as little about LSD as I do, I would hate to cause earthquakes without the possibility of a clean-up campaign.[3]

Ellen's caution is intriguing, given what we now know about the commotion this trip caused in their triangular relations. Osmond wished for Ellen, Matthew and Francis to make notes while on LSD and for him to subsequently write up their group experience. These documents, some of which are now publicly available, shed light on the perception of reality as it appears to persons under the influence of LSD. Hofmann, the discoverer of this substance, told Huxley during a conference in Switzerland, that it is the base, not the acid (as it came to be called), which is the potent chemical component driving the hallucinatory effects.

One of Huxley's abiding skills was in intuiting information from the appearance of things, to abstract the so-called hidden realities from appearances. The LSD experience was for him, then, not only an opportunity to dive head-first into the swirling ocean of life, but also a first-rate means of practising anthropology. In a mocking, though telling remark, he suggested that anthropology was also for him, at some level, a vehicle for contending with family issues.

> After my first field work in Brazil with a tribe of more or less ex-cannibals (I found cannibals very interesting for family reasons: there are many ways to eat people) I worked for a year in a mental hospital in Canada.[4]

It is important to keep in mind at this juncture that Francis was kin in a family where melancholia and 'bipolar' psychological fluctuations were well rooted. His experience of a damaged father, who had been treated in various mental hospitals and whose excesses had caused his mother great distress, most probably led Francis, as a social anthropologist and increasingly a mythologist, to an inviting, albeit uneasy, position. Would LSD open the door to understanding the psychological theatre in which his own family were players, and what kind of spiritual awakening was possible under its influence? He mentions cannibalism as the Huxley family mythos almost as a matter of fact. One might surmise from this, that he knew the familial context in which the LSD was imbibed was going to stir things up and potentially devour someone. This it did.

At a cognitive level, one can read this incident as Huxley loosening up his own mental framework, but perhaps he was also intentionally setting in train a social and sexual reconfiguration to bring that understanding about and with it to challenge the status quo. Mind-altering substances, whether mescaline, LSD or psilocybin, heighten disjunctions between what is seen and felt, and our unconscious knowledge, thereby enabling us to make fresh sense of what we have to deal with. When a Zen master goes to sleep, they sleep. When they wake up, they are awake. The in-between is dreamland, the psychological landscape which LSD accesses in its own unique way. Reality is always mediated through our senses – we build a socially consensual world on the basis of our assumed common perception of that reality. But the commonness is more assumed than actual – and what do we do when that sense of commonality is fractured? Whom do we trust when accounts vary – a seasoned anthropologist, a psychiatrist, a psychologist, psychotherapist, priest, reverend, shaman, artist or politician? When there are no objective guidelines, what then – the inner voice, a reliance on intuition? In the resort to psychedelics, we find the first rumblings of the slogan that was to become a by-word of the 1960s – 'the personal is political,' that what is inside is also outside – and vice versa. Expression of this sentiment would reach its cultural apotheosis in the lyrics to one of the Beatles' songs on the White Album. In *Everybody's Got Something to Hide Except for Me and My Monkey*, John Lennon sings

> Your inside is out when your outside is in Your outside is in when your inside is out …

Francis' meanderings around this point in time were somewhat haphazard. When Aldous wrote to his brother Julian on 23 June 1956, he said:

> We are expecting Francis from hour to hour; but, like God, he moves in a mysterious way. The last we heard of him was from Chicago, to the effect that he would probably be in Southern California about the twentieth. Since then, only silence. But no doubt he will suddenly manifest himself one fine morning.[5]

Francis' first experience of LSD opened up not just the pandora's box of family relations but a long-standing interest in medical anthropology. This led to a fascination with how disturbances of the spirit, are manifest and treated in various cultures. His interest during the late 1950s was to compare what went on in an old and cramped mental hospital, Wyburn, in Saskatchewan, with the treatment of the so-called mentally ill people on the island of Haiti. Wyburn, in his eyes, was "one of the most appalling bits of education" he'd had.[6] For people like Huxley, Irving Goffman, R. D. Laing and Thomas Szasz, the 1950s were formative years for confronting, first-hand, the depths of inhumanity meted out to people in the name of care. As an anthropologist he had to learn the basics of psychiatric jargon, in order to guess what the diagnostic labels were supposed to denote. We are none the wiser today.

## A bricolage of LSD

Besides the father, was the son, who, like his uncle, journeyed to the inner citadels of the self by staring into the LSD saturated sky, charged with intense changes of emotion, perception and thought. Under its influence, the illusion presented by the normative social and cultural prospectus that it could nurture a life free of alienation, was now seen as highly suspect. LSD opens up our capacity to perceive the world differently – to question the assumed dogmas and customs which govern everyday life. With the standard filters removed, a different light is cast on the world we inhabit and on who inhabits it. The dullness of habitual perception may be superseded by a poetic and musical dreamworld, flooding the senses. Aldous and Francis talked with Julian, about their experiences with mescaline and LSD. When Julian was offered some, he declined. As we know, Julian had his share of nervous breakdowns and no doubt felt his psychic constitution insufficiently robust to experiment with compounds that might remove him from his scientific and philosophical comfort zone.

Whenever Osmond came to London, and if by chance Francis and Aldous happened to be in town, a lively and vivid discussion was guaranteed. They embraced a collective faith in the transforming potential of LSD. Six days after his first experiment and back in Chicago, rooming at the International House, Francis wrote to Osmond:

> *My dear Humphry,*
>
> *When I left Newhaven and arrived in Chicago, I got just the feeling you did, and so telephoned Ellen since I don't know where you are to hear her voice and to talk with one of us.*
>
> *It is all very strange, and though I have a continued temptation to rationalise our experience into familiar terms, I remember how St Francis answered a monk who wanted to know whether a little latitude wasn't allowed in interpreting the Rules – "No," he said, "you must obey them literally, literally, literally, without gloss, without loss, without gloss." And now that I'm trying to write out an account of that night, I find that I'm always thinking, in the end, of basic religious truths, and that nothing less will serve. This is extraordinarily exciting, as well as embarrassing, because religion, after all, is full of four-letter words – even the original unspeakable name itself. I myself am more grateful to you and the others that I can say. That one night was a complete life in which I saw the beginning and the end of things – and, more important really, saw that we are one another in some indescribable manner, as you say in your letter. The only way to make sense of this is to hold it as being literally true, I'm certain. It is a mouthful that will take us all some chewing.*
>
> *I've got most of my memory of it down on paper, but it reads tame and dodgy and flabby. I know this doesn't really matter much, but still; it would be nice to be able to speak out the original freshness of it all.*
>
> *I'm amazed, as I write, at the complexity of the experience, and how the accidents, so to speak, were as important to it as the purpose of the group. This is why I, for one, think that if you had had "better" safeguards that night, we would not have learnt what we did.*
>
> *It is amazing how the group helps itself it really does construct a telos or purpose, if given time and of course love. What would have happened had there been no love the night? I do not like to think. And do you know why you began to repeat "together, together?" It turned out to be, I think, the unique and necessary word for us.*
>
> *It will be interesting to make some ritual to protect the group from becoming separated – or just staying separated – from becoming frightened and wild. And if you are to use LSD to explore the mind further, we will have to use such books as the Tibetan Book of the Dead or the Egyptian or the*

*Aztec one – one which in fact leads the soul on its journey through the other world. (I think certain phases of LSD experience must be very like being "dead" as the Tibetans understand it.) And then, of course, there is a great master of shamanistic experience to be used somehow. Not to mention John Custance and Beers and what they have to say of Wisdom, Madness and Folly. Ah, what fascinating work is to be done!*

*I will let you have what I have written as soon as I type it clean – there's rather a lot of it, since I needed to write it all down for my own benefit. What a difference a drop of LSD makes! I know something now, of enormous importance, which is not at all the same as merely suspecting its existence. It is all miraculously puzzling. Ever, Francis*[7]

Quoting this letter, in full, permits us to see why Huxley's life started to shift. Wisdom Madness and Folly, something he experienced hitherto in the Huxley tribe, was the name of the boat he would now sail to new and hopefully more enlightened shores. So what did he experience and how did he describe it in his longish report of 23 November 1956? Osmond, their guide on this first trip had written to Uncle Aldous "*To fathom Hell or soar angelic, take a pinch of psychedelic.*"[8] Had it then been hell or heaven which was encountered?

Fortunately, since 2018, this report has been in the public domain, as has Ellen's.[9] Hers is prosaic, listing elegantly the precise time and sequence of events, apt for the meticulous film director she was. It is a welcome accessory to Francis' more anthropological reportage. They began at 7.15 PM. By 8.00 PM, Francis, despite turning himself upside down in his chair, appeared to Ellen, quite normal in this position. She felt there was plenty of time:

> no need to hurry, no need to worry – a real sense of luxury come over me …surely the feeling of having got "within" time, is one of the greatest of luxuries.

Eyelids closed, she saw a pale-blue-pastel kaleidoscope with black spots and a scalloped one which was apparently much at one with what Francis saw. They put on music from Guillaume Du Fay and even listened to Aldous talking on an LP record, *"Time must have a Stop."* This was disquieting for Francis,

> for Aldous' voice and what he says creates an almost irresistible centre of attraction. The feeling of being private evaporates. When he gets up to walk around, it is a reassuring experience, for thought I may not be "me" anymore I still have a body that obeys me.[10]

Being a group of four, he describes the phenomena of understanding each other by a kind of telepathy, a joint intimate awareness of each other's presence. An unspoken joke gets all of them laughing, giving way to an animistic flowing connectedness with the objects around them, which, when touched, feel part and parcel of them too. When Francis looked at Ellen, he felt, "how fortunate that one of us is a woman." The sense of being woken up by LSD, brokered the question as to what exactly had lain dormant. Old issues buried within Francis' subconscious came to the fore. "I remember having been forced to eat things, forced to be good which something horrible was done to me, at various other times, long forgotten but now vividly immediate."

Francis' thought then moved to an awareness that LSD is a much bigger puzzle than psychoanalysis. His vision then opened up into an immense eternal emptiness – this, a Buddhist aim of arduous practice, was in no way menacing for him. With the forced sugar-taking, an abrupt arrival back into 'drab reality' ensued, with the four facing the realisation together, that they had failed in their attempt to change the world. But that is not strictly true, for their world had changed. When Ellen and Francis interlocked their fingers to become a new couple among the Huxleys, something had happened, which they were reticent to talk freely about.

A love affair with Ellen was the comforting music Francis was dreaming about for the first time in his life, "pure music without tune," he wrote. A tail-piece of his report that fell short of the publication, is worth quoting here, for Ellen and he were not the only ones to own up to love as the answer. Humphry Osmond,

> while I was being fed with sugar and niacin, talked considerably about himself (I learned two years later): about how he doesn't love Jane at all, and about the reason for Mathew not liking him – this being that Humphry fell in love with Maria. Humphrey continued till Mathew shut him up almost forcibly.[11]

A dance of luscious longings, thus permeated the air of the pharmacologically charged reality. "Francis and I danced, and flowers grew in the air," Ellen wrote, while Matthew, jigged into a cuckold voyeur, desperately fought to hold on to his scientific anchor. This merely compounded the emotional chasm between him and Ellen, who by now hated him for not giving in to joy –

> he seemed to sit on the rim of the world, and we others in the bottom of the cup. Why didn't he laugh? Francis and I lay on the floor, hand in hand, our noses pressed into the sheepskin rug – this is pure joy.[12]

For Mathew the unfolding reality, nested in a perceived unreality, contributed to sobering a mind betrayed. How are we to make sense of him getting a metronome down? Osmond thought it absurd, to which Ellen and Francis laughed. Francis: "and yet ... the music and the metronome." "Yes" Ellen said. Matthew remained silent, as did Ellen. She felt "love is the only thing which will rescue any of us." This being even more certain to her than being "totally responsible for the universe," which Francis felt they must rebuild. They existed inevitably in a changed personal universe, never quite the same again, as Aldous was fond of remarking after his own initiation with LSD.

This ritual of healing through the circulation and celebration of love is far from being unique to LSD. Echoes of the same can be found in the poetry of William Shakespeare:

> *Take all my love, my love, yea take them all:*
> *What hast though more than though hadst before?*
> *No love, my love, that though mayst true love call;*
> *mine was thine before thou hadst this more.*[13]

In contrast to the sense of fullness which grew from initial emptiness and engulfed Ellen and Francis, was a corresponding stasis of emptiness in Matthew.

Nearly two years later, in August, 1958, Francis would again take LSD with Ellen, Matthew and Fritz. Why Matthew agreed after the trials of the first experience is anybody's guess. The pursuit of comprehending the totality, structure and mystery of lived experience continued unabated. "What we call god is the meeting of selves and essences and their existence," Francis noted in his two-page philosophical script, elaborating on his LSD-fuelled insights. He went on:

> At the bottom, existence, in the middle, the laws by which existence co-exists; at the top, the creative outcome and the transcendent unity of existence. Science deals with the middle; theology is divided in its efforts, dealing now with the bottom, now with the top. Both presumably are one and the same thing. But matter is the more extraordinary mystery, which we can never know about till we are it.[14]

Francis at this time was 35 years old. The understanding he developed under LSD became a road map of sorts to freedom. He would continue to exercise his mind and to play with these perspectives deep into his middle ages, culminating 15 years later in his book, *The Way of the Sacred*. The psyche, Francis argued, "given the right conditions, has its own natural telos towards completion, and that it can deal with itself adequately." Huxley thus conceived of the mind as a self-organising goal-oriented system, perpetually in a state of becoming. The art of living required getting the right conditions, and the condition right, to support the knower in the knowing of his or her elusive self as it leaps off the cliff edge of every moment.

Francis meanwhile seized this opportunity to ask Osmond, if he could find him some research area or hospital, like Wyburn, where he could participate as a social anthropologist. Osmond, well placed in his work and by now in the Huxley network – for he was corresponding with Aldous and Julian too – promised to do his best and find Francis a suitable placement. "What I would like you to do" he said,

158  *Social anthropology*

is to treat a mental hospital like Mayan tribesman and draw out the customs and beliefs of us natives from the same sympathetic detachment which you use for the scarlet ponchoed horsemen.[15]

The result was that Francis eventually ended up in Osmond's Wyburn team. It was Aldous who reported to Julian on 12 December 1957:

> Francis, I gather is now in New York with Matthew and Ellen. As I understand it, he is making a study of environment in relation to mental patients – with a view to the designing of a more satisfactory kind of mental hospital.

### Spaced-out in Saskatchewan[16]

Osmond wrote to Aldous in April 1957.[17]

> About Francis Huxley. I'm hopeful Commonwealth will give us monies for an architectural anthropological study of psychiatric wards, that I may possibly be able to interest Francis in coming up at least for a while.

It took time to get things sorted. Francis, eager to take another step into the art of soul-searching under the heavenly influence of LSD, now also had one foot planted on the career-laden tracks of mother earth. Osmond's hope was that Francis' expertise could provide an anthropological perspective, on how a large hospital such as Weyburn, ticks. Osmond also enlisted people with other areas of expertise, including the architect Kiyoshi Izumi and the psychologist Robert Sommer, intending to develop a social psychology of architecture, with specific reference to how a safe and asylum giving environment could be built. This vision – to demedicalise the constructed environment – would still be considered radical if proposed today. Just how radical the aims were can be garnered from Carson Bisbee and colleagues' introduction to how the psychedelic prophets went about their plans to reshape healing environments:

> These men produced a trenchant critique of modern psychiatry and its overreliance on institutions to segregate people with mental disorders from mainstream society. In the Osmond family home, Francis Huxley, Izumi and his wife, Amy, and Humphrey and Jane Osmond took LSD in 1957 with the express purpose of interrogating special reasoning and considering mental hospital designs.[18]

LSD thus quickly advanced from a tool for heightening and changing perception in the inward exploration of the mind, to one employed for the specific purpose of cultivating creative beneficial applications in the world. Social anthropology's direction, which Francis brought into the discussion, was that all social relations depend upon common and communally held space, where time is equally shared – and it is these which make healing rituals possible. During his year in Weyburn, Francis is a frequent presence in Osmond's letters to Aldous.

> Francis is at work on our long stay wards is very alert, intelligent and amiable. He meets regularly with our gifted Japanese Canadian architect Kyo Izumi and they both seem to be seeing things from slightly different viewpoints.[19]

Aldous, in turn, then passes on the news to his brother Julian:

> I hear of Francis from time to time (though not from him) through Humphry Osmond. He seems to be doing two things – an anthropological study of the asylum and a special study, in conjunction with an architect and the resident psychiatrists and psychologists, to determine what kind of buildings are most suitable for mentally ill patients.[20]

Come June 1958, Francis was labouring away in Wyburn, aiding and abetting others in the team to recognise the complexity of the problems they faced. There was so much to do, Osmond wrote to Aldous. The lack of appropriate models for understanding mental health and social wellness, Osmond kept arguing, "led to a questioning of psychiatry's authority in medicine and society."

Francis' Wyburn sojourn certainly disabused him of the merits of orthodox psychiatry, but he, and no doubt others of the Huxley clan, would have been pleasantly nonplussed by the psychologist Robert Sommer, who conducted a simple experiment in Weyburn. What is good for so-called healthy people, might also be good for those with troubled souls. In 1958, Summer sought to determine the relationship between letter writing and the length of hospitalisation. The experimental design was simple:

> The names were secured of all patients in a mental hospital who received or sent letters during a given one-week period. There was a highly significant relationship between length of hospitalization and receiving and sending letters. The longer a patient remained in the hospital, the less likely he was to receive or send letters. Women were found to receive and send proportionately more letters than men. Patients who received letters were 10 times more likely to send letters than patients who did not receive letters. The probabilities of receiving and sending letters and receiving visitors were estimated for various durations of hospitalization. It was found that after one year in the hospital, there is a drastic reduction in sending letters, receiving letters, and receiving visitors.[21]

Insofar as we have hundreds of letters by Francis, Aldous, Juliette, Julian and others to each other within the family and long correspondences, like the one between Humphry Osmond and Aldous Huxley, we can safely attest, with Sommer, that receiving and sending letters sustains well-being!

Besides the English psychiatrist Humphry Osmond, his Canadian equal, southern-Saskatchewan-born Abram Hoffer[22] formed the core of a team conducting meaningful research in other areas than LSD and mental health – this included testing high doses of vitamins B and C in combination with targeted nutritional interventions. Hoffer, the biochemist and psychiatrist, is still best remembered for his discovery of the hallucinogenic properties of LSD, as well as his 'adrenochrome hypothesis' of schizophrenia.[23] Hoffer was hired by the Department of Public Health a year before Osmond came to Saskatchewan, to establish a provincial research programme in psychiatry. Like others in the team, he was critical of psychiatry. He aspired to a more rigorous understanding of biochemistry and human physiology to practice what he called "nutritional psychiatry." Hoffer, Osmond and their colleagues also employed LSD in their treatment of people with alcohol dependence. Using patient reports, Hoffer concluded that it was their numinous psychedelic experience, which helped them to give up self-medicating with booze. Dyke (2010) concluded her overview of the work at Wyburn, by noting that Osmond, Hoffer, Sommer and others all shared a common wisdom that the facility functions as a therapeutic environment. The reforms put in place from 1957 onwards, the time Francis was among them, the so-called Izumi-Osmond-Sommer design was unfortunately

> never fully realized, their in-depth discussion about the role of the mental institution in modern society tapped into the broader international trends: namely, modernism, anti-psychiatry, and deinstitutionalisation. Their concerns about the new mental hospital began before anti-psychiatry had blossomed into a recognisable movement.[24]

The institutional backlash against this challenge to psychiatric hegemony has been long and fierce and shows no signs of abating.

After his year as an anthropologist in the hospital, Huxley left, enriched in a way, but with a bad experience and utterly dissatisfied with how people were treated. He endured a further decade of this dissatisfaction until he involved himself with The Philadelphia Association in London and become friends with the Scottish psychoanalyst R. D. Laing. Bitten by curiosity, he began to wonder if people, who were not subject to these systems of diagnostic labelling and were not enclosed in rituals of degradation, fared better and more humanely. He was contemplating what Bateson had referred to as a 'double bind' – one of false doctrine and pitiable treatments, wrapped up in a straightjacket of lies, which one could not contest without providing further 'evidence' that one was due the 'treatment.' He wrote to Ellen, feeling "uneasy" about Osmond who had been deluging him with letters,

> What is in him? I think he's in that state where he's just discovered a truth, as much a truth about himself as it is about the world ... Well

as long as he doesn't go into overdrive and vanish from human eyes in the next year, it'll be all right. But just imagine if he didn't have the position he holds, in the hospital. It's really cruel how people who see their personal problems numinously playing about them and play with them in turn, are at once shut up in a hospital and aren't allowed to practise themselves and the stages of their troubles upon other people similarly affected, as shamans do – who manage to keep themselves and others more or less sane.[25]

Huxley goes beyond expressing a concern for Osmond to suggesting that shamanic practice is a means for normalising and accepting human disturbance through ritual. That it is, in fact, a means not of marginalising the disturbed but of bringing them into the common human fold, dissolving the borders between sanity and madness and between social ostracism and social acceptance.

## Lysergic acid divorce

With Aldous having provided his own account of the doors of perception in 1954, Francis was encouraged to write up his own often blissful experiences of life in the pharmacological utopia. Aldous' final sentence in *The Doors of Perception* concerns the reality of a person who returns back through the open door.

> He will be wiser but less cocksure, happier but less self-satisfied, humbler in acknowledging his ignorance yet better equipped to understand the relationship of words to things, of systematic reasoning to the unfathomable Mystery which it tries, forever vainly, to comprehend.[26]

Francis wrote up his second experience, reporting that on Monday, 4 August 1958, at around 9.00 pm, rather later than intended, they all took 100mg of LSD. The participants were Matthew, Ellen and Fritz. After an hour Francis started to feel alterations in the depth and roundedness of his vision.

> I also saw my mind as a thing for reproducing images ... I tried to imagine Sheila: what I saw (that was after the putting in order) was a series of transparent circular curlicues in a pure girlishness.

When he finally went to bed at eight in the morning, he saw images of little blue-petalled flowers, with yellow centres. He let himself loose, by about 11.00 or 12.00 AM.

> I began to enter the enormous world of no mind, unwillingly and timidly. This is the moment when panic begins: when "emptiness" appears as loneliness, and there is too much of it and no way out for the ever of the moment.

Having had his baptism nine months before, this second time of taking LSD did not take him by surprise.

> I sat in the armchair by the fire, and for the first time regained that experience of being able to feel others as part of my own psychic space: of including them and their actions in my substance.

Francis was now able to compare this second experience with the first, where there was "no centre anywhere and 'I' did not exist as such." On this occasion he experienced the destruction of barriers without losing a sense of his own existence. He experienced simultaneously having and not having a centre.

> I think, I was arranged as in a circle around an empty space, the otherness of the world being now within myself but still other. The first time, I existed more as a point or solid, even though I was nothing – that I, I was an awareness without self-contact. This time, I retained self-contact by forming the nothing into a circle.

In the course of the event there were fractious encounters between Matthew and Ellen and between Matthew and Francis. Subsequent reflection laid bare some of the tortured dynamics which reverberated through the relationship network of the Huxleys. Matthew broke into a conversation Francis was having with Ellen and told him "to stop and not talk like Aldous." Francis comments how, in his cousin's life, 'Aldous' is "his great stumbling block: he refuses to make it part of himself." Francis had his volume of Robert Graves' poetry to hand which they took turns in reading from. Some worked, others caused friction. Matthew went upstairs, refusing the group's pleas to come down again. Fritz did, however, succeed in motivating him to briefly sit in front of the fire again. Matthew proceeded to bluntly state that

> Ellen obviously couldn't live with him and she replied, yes she could, to the end – he replied perhaps she could endure him, but that wasn't the same. She said, I would have to think very carefully before I could answer that, which was at once a threat and an invitation: a laying down of a line.

After that, Francis, as was his saving grace, left them to their own devices and made Fritz and himself a cup of tea. On his return to the fireplace, Matthew confronted him with a question.

> Had he been mad for the last five years, and only now realising it, or had he become mad in the last few hours. And if so, should he get professional advice. What is wrong with him, in the sense that he couldn't understand a word of what Ellen and I talked about, were interested in.

Francis insisted he understood. The following day, after further thought, it struck him that his cousin reminded him more and more of Julian – factual in conversation and organising tasks, and insensitively polite and courteous to others. They no longer trusted each other.

One can also read this as a reflection on how Francis had internalised his father, as a kind of self-pitying patron and corrector of other's faults. In that mode it can also be read as a judgement on both himself and his father. At sunrise we find Ellen and Francis on the veranda, holding hands and eventually slowly releasing them. "Between our hands then, she said, a lotus grew and flowered." It was still remaining when their hands no longer touched.

Osmond, now back in New York, reported to Aldous in April 1959, that he had seen both Matthew and Ellen. His letter underscores the decline in their relationship with a suggestion that Francis had some responsibility for this. "I had the curious feeling" he wrote

> that they were living in very different worlds whose boundaries could only be crossed by an active and concerted effort of love. I don't think that the chances of that effort being made are good in recent years neither Matthew nor Ellen seem to have been together alone long enough to develop mutuality of feeling. One of the awful side issues of the mobile age of leisure is that few have any time for serious matters. Francis has not helped particularly, though I don't think it is fair to blame him. His strong views on emancipation of women have, I think obscured the real problem which is not how might things be arranged in an ideal state of affairs, but how to cope with the here and now which is not ideal.[27]

By the time Aldous wrote to his son Matthew, in the February of the following year, Ellen and Matthew had made their marriage break definitive.

## On stage for LSD

Of the issues explored at the Weyburn hospital, one had been whether LSD could be envisaged as a 'model psychosis.' Francis presented his report of two LSD experiences with Osmond to the research committee in August 1957.[28] Paramount in his findings was that the subject who has taken LSD knows, despite all the hostility he or she might feel in the course of the experience, that it will wane when the trip is over. Though similar in form and content, the person suffering paranoid delusions in a real psychosis has no such comforting assurance of recovery. This crucial distinction, Huxley hoped "will lend useful directions to further investigation of … psychosis." Any and all differences in the processes of recovery from both chemically induced and actual psychoses – including changes in the sense of time and space and the re-integration of the self-concept – could be studied. These experiments continue to pose profound moral and ethical questions regarding the treatment of human suffering and the exploration of the human psyche. Should we allow, let alone, prioritise psychopharmacological agents to influence the access to and management of painful emotions within a suffering person? And if so – what 'rules of engagement' are appropriate? Are we open to using psychedelic drugs in a safe and supportive environment in a manner similar to the rituals of native humans in which the experiences are married to a lived cosmology? Just how effective can these be in helping to recover 'normal' integrative thought processes and emotional well-being following a psychotic episode – itself a likely sequela of earlier trauma?

Over the years, Francis was invited to many conferences to elaborate on his experiences with LSD and on having guided many people from different professional backgrounds through their first LSD journey. One of the most prestigious of these took place in Switzerland in January 1970.[29] Chaired by Arthur Koestler, the congress featured Albert Hofmann, Rudolf Gelpke, Daniel X. Freedmann, Humphry Osmond and, among others, Francis Huxley. Huxley spoke on experiments with hallucinogenics, again extolling the importance of ritual in any undertaking with them. He also spoke at length about Aldous, arguing that in his view LSD has a great influence on the holding patterns and postures of human beings. He provided copious anecdotal details of Aldous to support his case. The picture of Aldous standing up straight, five hours into his first mescaline journey, on the hills of Los Angeles, enjoying the view, showed Francis something he had never seen before, namely Aldous holding himself up like a man, no longer embarrassed by his height, radiating his full strength.[30]

In a discussion with the psychologist Max Lüscher,[31] chaired by Arthur Koestler, the two were asked whether they favoured the prohibition of cannabis and LSD. Francis took the view that drug use is a religious affair, and daringly suggested that "one has to pass over to the church the use of cannabis."[32] To him, Western society was estranged from both the world and the gods. "What we experience now is a religious cult without a tradition," he argued. Instead of giving psychiatrists a licence to dish out LSD, Huxley suggested that churches hold rituals where hashish and LSD could be consumed, where people could dance and sing, rather than furtively indulging their psychedelic preferences in socially ordained seclusion. Francis was unequivocal that taking LSD and cannabis aided him as an anthropologist, furnishing insights into other peoples, whether native or so-called civilised, which he otherwise would not have gained. In his mind, if psychiatrists really wanted to make a difference to people who seek out their help, they could do worse than to experience hallucinations for themselves.[33]

Francis' interest in LSD led him to explore its possible connections with extra-sensory perception (ESP) and mediumship – but efforts to turn this into manageable data met with little success.

In a letter to his parents, he mentions sending off his long exquisitely honed essay on Charles Darwin, which he had previously discussed with Julian. He reflects somewhat wistfully on his time in North America now that he was about to travel to Haiti; "I am sorry in many ways that I came to America: I would have done much better to have got a proper job." Much may be wrapped up in that pithy sentence. A sense that the excursions into mediumship had not yielded what he had hoped, that, adventurous and daring as he is, that he feels he is drifting? Huxley was always struggling to discover who he was and what the nature of the world was in which he was doing that struggling. Haiti would provide more questions than answers.

## Notes

1. Ellen in a letter to Dr. Humphrey Osmond. 7 May 1956. Bisbee et al. (2018, p.555).
2. Smith (Ed.) (1969, p.643).
3. Bisbee et al. (2018, p.570).
4. Huxley, F. (2007, p.26) Shamans through Time: Tricksters, Healers, Voodoo Priests and Anthropologist (with J. Narby and J. Mohawk) In *Visionary Plant Consciousness: The Shamanic Teachings of the Plant World*. Ed. J. P. Harpignies. Rochester. Park Street Press. pp.24–38.
5. Smith (1969, p.796).
6. Huxley, F. (2007, p.26).
7. Bisbee et al. (2018, pp.555–611) Appendix 2; letters between Humphry Osmond and Matthew, Ellen and Francis Huxley.
8. Osmond to Aldous; Smith (1969, p.795 fn.).
9. Ellen Huxley, letter and report to Humphrey Osmond, 24 November 1956. Bisbee et al. (2018, pp.602–608) Appendix 2.
10. Huxley, F., in Bisbee et al. (2018, p.586,) Appendix 2.
11. Francis Huxley, report draft, November 1956, p.11. FHA.
12. Huxley, E., in Bisbee et al. (2018, p.605) Appendix 2.
13. Sonnets: 40 Shakespeare in Love (1999, p.54) *The Love Poetry of W. Shakespeare*. London. Faber & Faber.
14. Typed report, 4 August 1958, LSD session, two pages. p.2 FHA.
15. Osmond, H. Letter to Francis Huxley. Bisbee, et al. (2018, p.608).
16. With our salute to Professor, Dyck, E. (2010, pp.640–666) Spaced-Out in Saskatchewan. Modernism, Anti-Psychiatry, and Deinstitutionalization, 1950–1968. *Bulletin of the History of Medicine*, 84 (4).
17. Bisbee, et al. (2018, p.325).
18. Ibid., Introduction lxii.
19. Ibid., p.368, 31 January 1958.
20. Smith (1969, p.846), 15 February 1957.
21. Sommer, R. (1958, pp.514–517) Letter-writing in a Mental Hospital. *American Journal of Psychiatry*. December, 115 (6).
22. Born 1917 – Died 2009.
23. The claim was that adrenochrome was a neurotoxic substance that may induce schizophrenia-like symptoms. It was speculated that the disorder might be cured by megadoses of vitamin C and niacin which would reduce levels of adrenochrome in the brain.
24. Dyck (2010, p.665).
25. Francis Huxley, in a letter to Ellen Huxley, from Santa Fe, 17 August. No year given. It could be 1957.
26. Huxley, A (1977, p.64) *The Doors of Perception. Heaven and Hell*. St. Albans. Triad/Panther Books.

27 Bisbee et al. (2018, p.412).
28 Report to the Committee on Model Psychosis. 1957. Ms. 13 pages. FHA.
29 This took place at Gottlieb Duttweiler-Institut (GDI) in Rüschlikon/Switzerland. All sessions were taped, and where need be translated into German. Edited and published by GDI 1971, Vol. 3: *Rauschmittel und Süchtigkeit*.
30 Huxley, F. (1971, p.91). Experimente mit Halluzinogenen. In *Rauschmittel und Süchtigkeit*. Herbert Lang, Bern. pp.89–94.
31 Born like Francis in 1923, and died also aged 93 years. Max Lüscher, was Professor in Basel and Berlin, Philosoph and Psychiatrist creating the Lüscher-Colour-Diagnostic test.
32 Huxley, F. (1971, p.134) Anthropologe und Psychologe im Kreuzverkehr – Francis Huxley und Max Lüscher. In *Rauschmittel und Süchtigkeit*, Herbert Lang, Bern. pp.133–139.
33 Huxley, F. (1967b, p.157) Stop / Go with LSD – Behind every work of art lies the human body. *Geographical Magazine*, 40 (17–18).

# 12  Haiti fieldwork

In his first letter home, from Port-au-Prince, on the Monday before Easter, Huxley tells his parents of the few days he'd spent with Eileen Garrett in Miami, in a house teaming with rich congresswomen. He was impressed neither with the wealth on display, nor the climate and Palm Beach environment. "It was rather appalling, living among such money: it costs 100,000 dollars a year alone just to water the lawn," he wrote. Having previously earned the trust of Eileen Garrett, in the course of his work on mediumship, she was now ready to tell him a

> considerable lot about herself and the way she works. What on earth are auras, I wonder? I think they must be a kind of synaesthetic phenomenon into which the medium translates impressions of many kinds, whatever they may be "in themselves." Abe Hoffer, who is the biochemist from Saskatchewan, was visiting at the same time, and he, of course, being a logical minded scientist, wants to build an aura metre.

We can just about hear Francis' laughter. Borrowing from what he learnt from the scientist and philosopher Peter Medawar, he had a rich discussion with Abe Hoffer. Hoffer's rationalist line was that what can be perceived can be measured, whilst Francis argued, what needed to be measured was not outside but inside Eileen. After all, he concluded,

> the Parapsychological foundation which she is head of, has for its ultimate purpose the explanation of Eileen Garrett to herself: an admirable venture, even though people sometimes get a little bewildered by the tactics she employs.[1]

Garrett undoubtedly helped Huxley considerably. He was first put up in The Excelsior (thanks to Garrett opening her purse for him) a pleasant enough hotel, with lots of interesting visitors flowing in and out – Haitians, Cubans and other foreigners like himself. He wrote a grateful letter thanking her for hosting him at Palm Beach and giving him this current opportunity, both on a personal and professional level.

The obvious difficulty here was that Garrett was Huxley's benefactor. How impartial could he really be when it came to scrutinising her claims? His attempt to approach mediumship through an anthropological lens has considerable merit – not to say novelty and ingenuity, but its potential shortcomings in not seriously questioning whether these people had any genuine paranormal abilities in the first place – whether they believed they had or not – is a problem. As we shall see later – in Garrett's case there is very good reason to question it. What is really needed here is not just an anthropology of supernatural belief, but an accompanying anthropology of disbelief. Two sides of the same coin.

The existence or not of a paranormal realm can be considered part of a much larger question – one which has taxed Western philosophy for generations – regarding the relationship between "the soul, the spirit, the body the society and the environment."[2] Ted Bastin, in an intriguing interchange with Francis and Carmen Blacker referred to the "religious intuition of the kinship between our bodies and the external world around us (which) ... many philosophies have reduced to systems of correspondences."[3] Francis responded, that he saw the cosmos as represented/conceived/perceived as a total approximation of these relations, one which was expressed

> by traditional songs, by rites and by stories: it is figured in images, built into the forms of temples and houses, and endows number and geometric forms with meaning. It is in fact, symbolic, which means that it is a kind of universal explanation.[4]

He goes on to say that one may learn "a great deal from how a cosmos is described by a traditional society," of how humans can create a likeness to the outside world in the experience of their own body. It is in what follows that one may discern the genesis of the problem – a very subtle one at that, it must be said – which anthropologists make when looking for evidence for paranormal phenomenon in the practices and experiences of those living in other societies. Huxley continues,

> I would say it is the clue to the development of consciousness as culture. One of its main features is the classification of experience to different realms ... The second main feature is that it describes in figurative language how something in one class of experience can be translated or transformed into another.

The problem which arises here, is that anthropology, historically conceived and practiced as a branch of Western epistemology, is locked into a totalising discourse – one which seeks to enclose all classes of *other* (and others') experience within a unitary framework. What is fascinating about this, is that the avowed cosmologies of the 'other' as discussed above are not so constrained – they may be diversely present in a system of meaning, embracing song, rites, stories, images and architecture. Thus, a shaman's cognitive-symbolic operations – the ritual symbolism – performed in a dissociated state in the course of ritual practice come to be mistaken (by others) for operations on the external world. In his fieldnotes, clearly torn between two distinct ways of thinking, he also wondered about how "consciousness works when organised as a cosmos." At the same time, Francis could also bring great perspicacity to thoughts on the paranormal. On the question of life after death, he thought there was a very specific problem rarely attended to. It was not that the question of survival was "inane and without meaning" but that the "questioner is wanting continuity of himself, and he asks this question in this way because he cannot find it in his daily life."[5]

By the time he got to Haiti he was fully immersed in this line of thought. He had also self-consciously worked on improving his anthropological fieldwork skills.

> After my first fieldwork in Brazil, I came back and started leafing through my field notes, and I was horrified to discover that I had written down the meaning of what I had been told by the shamans, but not their exact phrases. I hadn't captured the lilt of their phrases, the poetics of their language. I realized that I hadn't been actually listening to the words that were spoken, so I spent nearly eight months learning how to remember *words* rather than meanings, and this proved to be one of the most mind-clearing things I've done in my life.[6]

He thus learned to listen to the words that were uttered by a shaman or healer, and held them accurately in memory prior to any subsequent description. Francis' approach to fieldnotes was significantly different in another way from his time with the Ka'apor. Largely dispensing with notebooks, he communicated a good deal of the experiences and impressions which constituted his anthropological material to friends and loved ones in letters. In his assessment of the political corruption, exploitation of the peasants, the power of a large, corrupt, secret police-force, he made no bones about how detested and depressed he was with the ethical and moral insult one had to stomach. When he went to see Maya Deren – who had conducted prior fieldwork in Haiti,[7] she asked him why he wanted to go to Haiti at all. Ostensibly it was to answer the question of whether voodoo had anything of its own to offer in the treatment of madness. The plausibility of the proposition was anchored in his belief that dissociation provided a common psychological thread to both voodoo and the distress its practice might seek to alleviate. Nowadays, dissociation is often considered as a response to trauma, one which allows a person to distance themselves from experiences which threaten to overwhelm them.

To get there, he first settled down to learn some creole and set about the few introductions he had, necessary for any anthropologist in a new field. Strolling around the picturesque town of Port au Prince with its wooden houses and fretted gables, the odours of mango, dried fish and bougainvillea, he was reminded of Brazil. Now proper work was to begin, once again.

> In Haiti I learned a number of notable things during my stay. One was that the type of mental perturbation that overcomes shamans and voodooist is very similar. The insights come out the same way. The only thing that distinguishes a possession cult from a shamanic one is that among the shamans, it's the shaman who gets enlivened by the spirit, while in a passion cult many in the congregation go through a process of dissociation and trance.

Together with his guide and friend Gerard la-Guerre, whom he fortuitously met, Francis continued to be aware of the socio-cultural conventions being acted out. He came to Haiti to build mental and experimental bridges between his experience in Weyburn, the possibilities of LSD as a healing agent and the alternative healing arts which he was encountering in Western Europe, most certainly in England of the 1960s. He recaptures this bridging drama as follows:

> In Haiti they diagnose your disorder according to which *loa* (i.e., spirit/god) is either tasking over what it should not or is out of place in you and trying to get back into balance. They have a very large pantheon of such *loa*. In order to heal, a voodoo priest will help guide patients into a state of possession in which they can manifest that spirit which is creating the disturbance, to show its face in public so that its issues can be resolved or it can express what it wanted to express through this person. These pantheons come from West Africa, from Angola, from the Congo even from Ethiopia. A diagnosis could be: "aha, you're suffering from a misunderstanding from Sobo, that thunderous spirit who deafens you with ringing in your ears and spots before your eyes." There is a whole ritual activity by which you summon this spirit, and you sleep on the magical point of this spirit, after a somewhat arduous initiation, it comes and takes you over and a process of healing can begin. After that you have to go and renew your contact with this spirit periodically because if you don't, you are back at square one.[8]

As a folk religion, voodoo functions to maintain community spirits and, through the 'mambo' (priestess), to protect members belonging to any given temple (houmfor), by his or her ability to call upon the pantheon of Gods (the Loa). The path to being a mambo is a long, arduous, secret and costly one. Herbs and their effects have to be learned by aspirants, as well as songs, and a considerable degree of theatricality employed to nonplus the audience and hold their attention to the fact that a possession needs to take place to alter his or her state of mind. The act of a loa taking possession of the mambo bears comparison with the old Christian peasant saying: 'Which devil rides you?' Huxley saw in the voodoo ceremony the importance of the act of recognition – of being seen again or anew – the glue which holds any social grouping or society together.

In the course of his stay, with the help of his friends and companions, Gerard LaGuerre and Sal, Huxley met at various locations on the isle, the voodoo priestesses Dieudonne, Idem and Josephine. As an experienced LSD taker and guide, he was able to discern the role of suggestibility in much of what he witnessed. Both magic rituals and LSD taking are heavily influenced by the environment in which they occur. A sanctified environment can help to create the harmony required for the suggestibility engendered by visual, musical, tactile and poetic forms to flow into one's innermost self and dissolve the pre-existent boundaries there. Momentarily the 'self' becomes 'all'.

By October he had found himself a house in Jacmel, from where he wrote to Ellen.[9] He reported feeling dismal and disappointed, and having partaken in many rituals, sometimes as a participant observer, at other times actively dancing and merging himself into the collective congregation, he was troubled by what he had seen. He describes the sense of disenchantment found in Haiti, vividly in his book, *The Invisibles*.[10] There was just nothing tangible on offer, nothing concrete beyond deception, petty rivalry and ritual, holding the crucible of magic together. While the principal research aim had revolved around the healing potential of voodoo ritual, it made way for a more nuanced sociological undertaking – of approaching the folklore and mythology that underpins the Haitian way of life, tempered by knowledge of Haiti's "terrifying inheritance from the days of slavery."[11] The nine months he spent there became an expedition through smoke and mirrors.

There were also more down to earth practical issues to contend with. Dieudonne, a mambo, and one of the subjects who took LSD under his guidance[12] had apparently also fallen "violently in love"[13] with him, making Francis seek a cure for her infatuation in his dreams. In the letter to Ellen he relates how mad women or men are cured in Haiti – a key occupation of his visit.

> It takes a madman to cure a madman, which is carried out often whenever a voudou priest cures a madman because he himself has often been mad, and his cure was the sign of his entry into the voudou profession. Or how madman being bathed in the same water, which has its traditional roots in the way you can treat madness here – usually with madman's urine, to be sure, but occasionally with their bathwater too.[14]

At times, it was all a bit much, and in another letter to one of his female friends, Lola, a fellow anthropologist, he wrote how he had been attacked by flattery, flirtation, whispers, confidences, shoulder-crying, demands for money and boasts, leaving him "exhausted."

172  *Social anthropology*

He left there, "happy that I did not have to live with its problems"[15] though not without some pleasure and gratitude for the friendship and hospitality which he had received – the persisting 'little virtues' in human affairs. What Francis was able to accomplish there, was to humanise, what to Western eyes had been coded as the work of the Devil. But his time in Haiti was less gratifying than the days, weeks and months he had passed under the canopy of the Amazon, the people more ground down by the socio-economic inequities of daily life. Life in the emerald forest was, for him, always a more attractive proposition than navigating the socio-economic and symbolic dust clouds of modern slavery. Still, what emerges from his Haitian experience and its failed quest for tangible evidence of a two-way street linking the earthly "chain of existence" to the invisible realm, is a very fundamental question for anthropology. How does one suspend belief in one's own ideas when they are being relied upon to gather and organise data?

In the wake of this, he mentions looking forward to going to France for a parapsychology conference and then to England, where he has not set foot for three and a half years. Following these he will return to Haiti, sadly missing the July pilgrimages to a miraculous virgin on the hills, "near a voudouist waterfall where interesting things happen." What concerns him now is, where to live next, once he has met his own current research demands and those of Garrett. Lola, then engaged in fieldwork in Mexico, is asked by Huxley "What is one doing all this for?" He, for one, has not managed to get to the bottom of the shame and prudery in Haiti. What works for the sane and what works for the insane? Trance possession states are commonplace, he found, with no clear dividing line between the healers and those seeking to be healed. Francis now attempted to collect his thoughts – pondering the shrouded symbolism at work under LSD, magic, possession and ESP in contrast with the Chinese Taoist fables oriented to the betterment of one's self. But, all in all, Haiti was an interesting experience. Feeling overwhelmed both physically and mentally, he decided it was time to take a step back from the imponderable weight of these issues. He returned, we might say "fittingly" with a serious liver-fluke infection, the symptoms of which – fever, nausea, a swollen liver, severe abdominal pain, jaundice and anaemia – are seriously debilitating. Aldous, concerned about his nephew, "so gifted and so crippled" as he put it, wrote to Osmond from the Palace Hotel in Gstaad Switzerland:

> I might go back to England for a bit in which case I look forward seeing you. When you're there, incidentally, do try to do something for Francis. He is in a bad way, psychologically, can't work, can't commit himself to a job or to marriage or even to a love affair.[16]

The Haitian episode had been educational. Francis was by now determined not to be side-lined as a freethinking and insightful anthropologist. Never one to be complicit with colonial projects, whatever country lay behind the sin, the experience had nonetheless made him uncomfortable. He wrote to his father from Haiti: "It is always difficult in this country to know whether one is liked because of oneself or because one is a blanc, who has money."[17] The step back would be a step in a different direction – back to academic life as Research Fellow in Social Anthropology at St Catherine's College Oxford.

**Notes**

1. Huxley, F. Letter Home, 23 March 1959. FHA.
2. Ibid., p.300.
3. Ibid.
4. Ibid., pp.300–301.
5. Huxley, F. (1961, p.175) Marginal Lands of the Mind. In *The Humanist Frame* (pp.169–179). Ed. J. Huxley. London. George Allen & Unwin.
6. Huxley, F. (2007, p.29).
7. Deren, M. (1975) *The Voodoo Gods*. St. Albans. Paladin.
8. Huxley, F. (2007, p.28).
9. Letter to Ellen, 7 October 1959. FHA.
10. Huxley, F. (1966) *The Invisibles*. London. Rupert Hart-Davies.
11. Huxley, F., *The Invisibles*, p.231.
12. A typed report about her taking 50 gamma LSD, 17 August 1959. Ten pages in French, and duly translated into English. MS FHA.
13. Letter to Catherine, 25 August 1959, FHA.

    "I hope, it is just my person as a Blanc who has money and prestige. Her husband looks on it in a stony and vicious fashion, she flirts with me. You reader might nod, and say: Here we go again, remembering Ellen and Francis and Matthew." See also p.112 *The Invisibles*.

14. Letter to Ellen, 7 October 1959. Francis uses different spellings for voodoo, in his letters. FHA.
15. Huxley, F., *The Invisibles*, p.231.
16. 4 August 1961. Bisbee et al. (2018, p.491).
17. Letter home to Parents, August 1959. FHA.

# 13  St Catherine's Oxford

The 1960s can be remembered for many things, both good and ill and highly contested. What is beyond question is that those years opened up the imagination of an entire generation. With regard to the accepted mores of the day, everything was up for grabs. The bounties of experience which Francis Huxley had, by this time, already summoned to his granary were plentiful. With his contributions to contemporary understanding of native peoples, he offered to his readers and listeners their imaginings, their dream worlds and a new-found respect for the cultural relevance of others. If we wish to make sense of this period as a time of renewal, that is not to be underestimated. His own reflections on the tumultuous changes of the counter-cultural heyday were sober.

> What hides behind appearance is not only self-consciousness but mystery, and these two together provoke a man into thought. Science, our present method in gaining knowledge, has done much to dispel mystery, superstition, and also the sense of the sacred, though it has done so by increasing self-consciousness in curious ways.[1]

This denotes more than a degree of scepticism towards the dreams of scientific reason. In his profound study on Darwin, Huxley had focused on how a habit, acquired in youth and early adulthood, a phase he himself was now leaving behind, could relate to a specific person's subsequent mind-set, and the ideas and imaginations brought forth by it. The habit of mind which Darwin, a friend of his great-grandfather, had cultivated was to regard "species as collections of animated structures and habits continually acted upon by Natural Selection."[2] Francis had tried to discern something more fluid in Darwin's thought. For him mental habits always developed in a context and according to that context could either free up or stultify one's prospects for growth. From his studies of the psychological dramas both inside and outside mental institutions, which were designed to affect a person's internal focus, he had concluded that a person's private internal rites, known since Freud's day as neuroses and complexes, can potentially be freed when embedded in a socio-cultural ritual which situates an individual's life within a relevant cosmology.

In the spring of 1963, he wrote to the warden of the new St Catherine's College in Oxford, hoping to secure the position of Research Fellow in Social Anthropology.

> I am now at work on a study of the non-respectable fringe of ritual practice in Britain, such as fortune telling and other mantic arts, new religious and psychological cults, and unorthodox medical practices. These activities are curiously widespread, and they deserve attention because their existence indicates that established religious, psychological and medical practice often fail to provide the kind of services many people require.[3]

The application was successful and would get him back to serious work, almost three years after he had left Haiti. He would be back on his Oxford University home turf, for a three-year tenure, with an option for a further two years. His pleasure in being awarded the fellowship was considerable.

In the intervening time since Haiti, perhaps his first serious stint at becoming a freelance author, he had sought to make ends meet by translating two books from French into English,[4] writing reviews and essays, as well as appearing on BBC radio on several occasions, presenting material which would see the full light of day in his books *Peoples of the World* and *The Invisibles*. His article *Haiti Chérie* also made it on to the front cover of *The Geographical Magazine*.[5] Until he fully recovered from the ills which he brought back from the Caribbean, he had stayed first with Ellen in New York and thereafter at Pond Street in London. With his late 30s and early 40s, earmarked by a continuing desire to make a mark, he hoped that the chance to earn a steady income and to have an academic base at Oxford University would give him the platform he needed to move forward.

Academically he was hoping, in due course, to earn a place in the mainstream. Rival mentions him in a footnote[6] in connection to Audrey Butt Colson, who had started lecturing the same year as Huxley's *Affable Savages* was published. Francis was hoping that in the near future something more permanent than the research fellowship would turn up. It didn't turn out that way. There is no mention of him in the official *History of Anthropology at Oxford* by Rivière. His foray into the establishment circles of anthropology ended here. From the side-lines, he nevertheless managed to aid a few future professors of social or medical anthropology on their way. When Rivière published his book on *Marriage Among the Trio, A Principle of Social Organisation*, he remarked:

> The basis of this monograph is my doctoral thesis presented at Oxford in 1965. Some of the changes which have been made are as a result of comments made by my examiners, Dr. Edmund Leach and Mr. Francis Huxley. I'm

grateful to them for their suggestions, but there are certain points which they queried which remain unaltered; I disagreed with their assessments of these points at the time, and continue to do so, so the fault is mine not theirs.[7]

Rivière would go on to reference *Affable Savages*, on a number of occasions. When we asked Professor Stephen Hugh-Jones about France's chance, in later life, to be an academic at university level, he said:

> Francis wouldn't have had a snowball's chance in hell in a department ... (he) was slightly a black sheep ... I wasn't nearly (as) over the wall as Francis ... I find a lot of academics are conservative narrowminded and think they are the centre of the world. I think Francis felt this much more radically than I did ... there was an element of Francis as a naughty boy.[8]

It was an opinion shared by Rivière, who, of course, knows Hugh-Jones quite well. In conversation with the authors, he said: "In fact, the job I got in Oxford, he got turned down for. I know he applied for the job and he did not get it."[9] Rivière continued:

> I think he would have driven colleagues absolutely mad. He wouldn't have been a departmental person in the small department ... You have to do all sorts of things, meetings, give tutorials et cetera et cetera. He would have given it up quite shortly. You needed to have a lot of anthropological publications as well, in journals. Actually, a research fellowship, especially for him, would have been really where he should have been. He is somebody who can just sit and get on with things, not in fact in a department where you have to do all the things. It was perfect to do things like the research fellowship at St. Catherine's.

Rivière viewed Francis' research habits as being at odds with the prevailing ethos. Once done with a field of inquiry or a theme, Huxley would move on to the next challenge.

> South American Indians were being done. Voodoo was done, and then the next, that's my impression. There were great intellectual sparks coming out, but there was no permanent fire, in fact.

One of these sparks was a book project Francis worked on whilst at St Catherine's – *The Body and Mind in Anthropology* which included an analysis of mythology and its functions. It was intended as a historical and comparative study, "largely completed, on a tribe in the 16th century," similar to the Ka'apor. During the first three years of his tenure, Francis would give a series of lectures with the intention to work them into future chapters. He also published a number of technical papers on his fieldwork in Brazil and Haiti, which can be found in his bibliography. Rivière noted: "This is an interesting topic which a lot of people (have) turned to in more recent years. Francis is the sort of person, who's been there, ahead of everybody else. (Laughter)"[10]

## The research fellow

In those days, the anthropology community in Oxford was, by all accounts, very sociable. When the Friday afternoon departmental seminars ended at 6pm, most participants packed their bags and sauntered off to the pub. Evans-Pritchard and the other Africanists were keen on drinking – Francis, along with Audrey Butt Colson, not so. Francis once humorously remarked that, his professor, Evans-Pritchard was basically living on "liquid food."

The social forces at work within the community needed attention. As was his life-long habit, once settled into the daily routine at St Catherine's (Catz as it is known locally), there was fun to be had, organising parties, and entertaining guests with playful rituals. Rivière remembers how he once had lots of little hot-air balloons, which had candles in them. Lit within those little balloons, they floated away over the college's grounds. Lots of people said his window boxes almost entirely were planted with cannabis. (Laughter).[11]

Butt Colson, now a lecturer in the Department of Ethnology and Prehistory at the Pitt Rivers Museum[12] saw him from time to time. The department head and curator of the Pitt Rivers Museum, was a West-Africanist, Bernard Fagg. Teaching at different locations, Francis and Audrey would meet weekly for the Friday seminars in social anthropology. At the time Oxford anthropology was beset by what has been described as a 'big feud' between ethnology and social anthropology. Under Evans-Pritchard and Meyer Fortes, social anthropologists were at loggerheads with the ethnologists. "There were objections to our teaching there ... so we were not all popular," Butt Colson remembers. Francis was attached to social anthropology. When he began his three-year fellowship, he came "into my room in ethnology and warned me: 'They set out to destroy you.' I was laughing. I was under a different system. We had our own department."

Her post entitled her to lecture on social anthropological topics of her choosing, mostly Latin American ethnology with geography mixed in, and social ecology which, as far as Butt Colson recalls, was one of the most popular set of lectures in the whole of university at that time.

> I was laughing, but I was thanking Francis very much, as it was very generous of him to come over and warn me. We felt wonderfully independent. All members of the university have the right to attend any lecture course they wish, so social anthropology students could attend my lectures if they wanted to, despite the problems between the Institute of Social Anthropology and ourselves in Ethnology.[13]

Francis was now quite content to be where he was, pursuing his own interests and activities, happy to depend on "the workings of imagination, to make good whatever deficiencies in 'real' knowledge"[14] the methods might contain. In his role he was free to travel the length and breadth of the British Isles to inquire into unorthodox religious, medical and psychological practices. His wanderings would bring him to the Harley Street door of a maverick Scottish psychiatrist, with whom he would become life-long friends, and set his eyes fortuitously on his great love of the 1960s, fellow anthropologist Joan Wescott. It is fair to say, that getting to know Joan and Ronald David Laing, boosted the aims and endeavours in which Huxley delighted in. His research fellowship was a success, and was renewed for two more years. In a letter, dated 18 February 1966, congratulating Francis, the chair of the Research Committee, Alan Bullock, wrote:

> My only point in writing this letter, apart from expressing my personal pleasure that we shall have you here for a further two years, is that the Research Committee would be glad if you would not take on too many more commitments in the way of supervision. I know it is a difficult situation for you, in a Department which is hard pressed to find supervisors, but it might be useful to you in refusing work which you would rather not take on if you could tell the Department that the College is being a bit sticky.[15]

While at the college Francis had thrown himself into a range of activities. Besides mentoring students, conducting research and writing, he helped his father organise a major two-day conference on Ritualisation. He was liked by colleagues – Evans-Pritchard describing his former student and now colleague as a "modest and extremely pleasant person."[16] Francis was grateful for the academic opportunities, which gave him a solid Oxford home-base and a measure of scholarly independence. Additional pleasures could be had on the other side of the fence; he still had his London flat, and a growing circle of friends from varied quarters in life.

When he came to the end of the five years at St Catherine's, Peter Rivière was subsequently appointed there, as a South American specialist. Butt Colson continues:

> Our Head of Department (Ethnology & Prehistory) was Mr Bernard Fagg who was also "Curator" of the Pitt Rivers Museum which was a part of our Department). He was a West Africanist. The post vacant at the time was not tied to any particular area of research and I think Fagg was thinking of the prestige associated with the name Huxley. Fagg was thinking of Francis to be a possible candidate, and he was thinking to invite Francis, to give a talk to all the undergraduates and all the people in social anthropology. We all turned up to this meeting and Francis spoke. He unfortunately, was at his most provocative and spoke a lot about female menstruation and rare habits in various societies, and went into very considerable details which, perhaps in our days people wouldn't turn

their head if you would say that, but they did then and my heart sank, thinking and knowing our new curator is not going to appreciate that. He was there, and he didn't ... I was so disappointed because I thought he would make a wonderful colleague ... So unfortunate, we didn't know what he was talking about, it was a very embarrassing lecture ... so the opportunity was lost.

Francis had this kind of quirky humour, which sometimes others in the established anthropological set up found a bit overpowering. Along with this humour was his hard headedness, if they wanted a Huxley, they had to take him as he was. The reality was that there were few lectureships in social anthropology on offer at the time, especially for Latin Americanists.

One can wonder whether he purposefully marginalised himself or consciously decided that the path he took permitted him sanity in a world gone haywire. He had once sat in the back of a taxi in Sao Paulo, asking his driver, what to do with the now empty can of cola he had. "Throw it out of the window, we are under polluted," the driver said. Traditional moral values, as he saw them, seemed to have no place there, except as a joke. He would later speak of the disparate forces within himself, as a system of relationships of opposition and complementarity. In that respect Francis was not alone. In the battle raging within himself, it cannot be said that he neglected the possibilities afforded by his own conscious subjectivity for pleasurable recreation, even while he was engaged in researching the spiritual forces which permeate the world.

Peter Rivière, now Professor Emeritus in social anthropology at Oxford, spoke to us about how he experienced Huxley, as a fellow researcher in Oxford. He began by saying:

> He was around much at the time, when he was a research fellow. He was always extremely good company. He had an interesting sort of career before that. I remember *The Invisibles* coming out, that fitted the pattern, so to speak, of his interests in mystical phenomena and suchlike. I looked at *Affable Savages* very carefully, as it was the area I worked in full. It's extremely good by modern standards, a bit unfortunate that he calls them Urubu, I'm afraid. You know, it's called "vultures," in Brazilian. The real name is Ka'apor. Also using the word savages. It's now totally unacceptable these days. It was terribly well received. Not simply in academia. It was a popular book. Very interesting material in that, worth keeping.[17]

## Outer limits

After Huxley left Oxford, their paths occasionally crossed. Rivière knew about the report of the Brazilian tribes, which Francis in the main had written with John Hemming and valued the work done in surveying numerous tribes and how they were living and coping. Rivière met Francis, once, when the latter was teaching at what the former dubbed an 'adamant alternative university' – the Anti-University of London. How did he see Huxley's relevance today? His judgement pointed to a harsh truth both in Francis' predicament and approach.

> California was a perfect place for him in many ways. His stuff is so disparaged in certain ways, putting together a work, you know, discussing my work is relatively easily, because in fact, there are not that many furrows being ploughed. His is a ploughed field, which starts in the middle, then goes in every direction.

There is a plaintive fact here, that Francis, knowledgeable as he was of it, was averse to the kind of unexciting systematic enquiry one can often find in the sciences. His bent would be to land 'helicopter-like' when entering a new field and then proceed to explore in every direction. This 'generate-and-test' strategy can be encountered in the sciences – it can even be said to be the 'strategy' that nature herself favours in natural selection – but rarely, if at all, does it work in an already established field. Francis was aware of this. It can even be found satirised in his *Raven and the Writing Desk,* where under Rule 9 one finds, "The description of a circle does not explain the point it is drawn from."[18]

During his five-year research period in psychological, bodily and spiritual healing practices found on the British Isles, he continued his connection with Eileen Garret and cultivated an extensive correspondence and a warm personal relationship with parapsychologist Rosalind Heywood. As in Haiti, Francis used letter writing as a means for making fieldnotes, diligently keeping carbon copies of his postings. With Heywood, he exchanged professional views on ESP, and shared their common experiences of seances both had attended, with Francis also feeding her various curiosities from his wide readings. We can witness here an energising relationship of kindred spirits, even though Rosalind was 28 years his senior. Energy, Francis told her, in human beings, is stored in the form of images and this imaginal repository constitutes a life force which, if it cannot be contained, is likely to manifest itself within an individual in a parallel world of hallucination. He is here alluding to the capacity of images to contain what sometimes language cannot and where what is being encoded in an imaginal form carries devastating consequences for the stability of psychic life. This fits well with a trauma model of psychological disturbance, but such a perspective was not well understood at the time. And, so Francis, argues, perhaps this perturbation in 'psychic energy' moves to other peoples' minds, then 'imagined' in them as ESP, which after all,

> is based on the human faculty for being infinitely suggestible: the question is how far this suggestibility can go.[19]

There is a certain logic at work here which is not unreasonable. We must also remember that there has long been a close association between psychoanalytic thinking and speculation about the paranormal – both being rooted in the seemingly immaterial. Freud was a significant part of this current of thought, and from 1911 onwards was a corresponding member of the Society for Psychical Research, remaining a member until his death.

In the midst of this fanciful speculation, it is easy to overlook the import of what Huxley's research was saying. While at Oxford, he was laying down the groundwork for his work on the *Body and Mind in Anthropology* – the original site of his research interest. The fringe activities in our societies – both now and then (50 to 60 years ago), whatever else they are, constitute a bedrock of common activity and confer an identity and sense of belonging for those who seek them out as well as practice them. Huxley's report provides an erudite summing up of what is at stake.

> There seem to be ways in which the confusions of the body are allowed to speak for themselves in terms of certain kinds of imaginary, sometimes primitive, sometimes complicated and pseudo-rational. Given a theory with verbal thought, images and the sensations of the self come together in curiously constant ways, it is not difficult to decipher the process by which fringe activities owe their success ... and the sociological reasons for this.[20]

The gist of his research conclusion is that the symbols and rites used in ESP, Voodoo and alternative healing activities, can be understood as transcriptions of the physical sensations experienced during dissociation. Gregory Bateson's epilogue to his 1958-work, *Naven*, his cultural study of people in New Guinea, contains a brief summary on what he takes to be inherently problematic when dealing with such phenomena. There is always present, a certain "formal difficulty" which

> must in the end always limit the scientific understanding of change and must at the same time limit the possibility of planned change ... Certain mysteries are for formal reason impenetrable, and here is the vast darkness of the subject.[21]

From our own contemporary perspective, we may reflect on the uncomfortable fact that the mystical imaginings of a society can gain a wider traction when the images at play capture a widespread dissatisfaction with the social order and speak to a disunity and distrust in the policing of that order. The invisible forces which populate the spirit realm – which in Haiti gave rise to Voodoo – may all too easily come to stand in for the unseen, or distal, political forces that operate below the horizons of awareness.[22] It is all too easy to fan the flames which these can light.

182  *Social anthropology*

When a world, be it personal or social, is out of kilter, ensuring the common welfare is part and parcel of our social, emotional and imaginative responsibility. Healing on the fringe might then be seen as just "the art of living with the skill to be alone without being lonely and making room and inner space for other human beings."[23] Huxley's message is that what transpires on the fringes of society is of relevance to us all.

### Huxley and psycho-anthropology

Audrey Butt Colson kept up her acquaintance with Francis after his fellowship at St Catherine's ended. On one occasion she went to see him in his roomy artefact-adorned flat in Belsize Park Gardens and agreed to take some LSD under his guidance. Audrey describes what happened:

> I should say now, we all got the impression that Francis was much nearer to his uncle Aldous in all of this, than he was to his father. Francis had already experimented with LSD. He had his writing qualities and interests in all sorts of experiments. As a good anthropologist I've been in the field, of course I wouldn't mind trying LSD. I spent the best part of a morning and afternoon with him in the flat. He gave me these tablets and then started to experiment. We experimented looking in the book of colours. Different coloured pictures as a set. I couldn't stand the colours of the red bus. That was running around in London was a bluey red. I became attached to the orangey red. He played music and asked me to see what colours I was attaching to the music that was playing. I always remembered in Beethoven I saw brown. Francis said "Bit of Mr Brown" composer laughter). Fascinating experience and we were both of us terribly happy. We were laughing and enjoying ourselves and doing those experiments … When I got back to my studies and Pitts museum, now the Department of Ethnology, which had to be redecorated, I remember I chose the rather blatant orange colour for the cushions and for my chair and the curtains. The head of our department didn't like the colours, I'm afraid. I am tracing this back to those LSD tablets and Francis. That is an experience associated to him, which I treasure very much.

This episode showcases Francis' ability as a guide for his fellow explorer of the mind. That role and how it worked was pertinent to his anthropological studies of mediumship. In the draft for his proposed '*Body and Anthropology*' book, he discussed this. "Some mediums" he observed,

> who can't provide information about sickness, character or personal problems, or the dead do another thing (we find a lot of this in Haiti): they do what amounts to a series of pronouncements on the ritual behaviour you should follow. These are couched usually in the form of getting to know your spiritual guide. This tends to be the woolliest of all, because

(being) completely immersed in the occult; they don't really, as far as one can see, take on what a person is in his or her real life.[24]

Huxley, who detested dogma, thought that the research into unorthodox therapies might yield valuable insights into the workings of therapeutic relationships and be of potential benefit to the more official varieties, not least in understanding better the matching process which occurred between therapist and 'patient' where the ministrations of the therapist were unique to each person seen. The ramifications for psychotherapy are obvious. Sadly, although he had written seven chapters, the book was never finished.

Butt Colson remembers how Francis generously invited her to his parents' home in Pond Street, to meet his guest for supper, Alain Gheerbrant,[25] who was a member of an Expedition to the sources of the Orinoco-Amazon (1948–1950) where they had met the Yanomami, at that time virtually unknown. This art of connecting disparate experienced people and creating new structures of relationship, was typical of Francis, and Audrey, like others we spoke with, recognised this. She concluded; "We were very fond of Francis. He was a great person and people often didn't appreciate him."

As the 1960s drew to a close, Huxley decided to finally put pen to paper and write his book on *The Sacred*, as it was initially called. Wolfgang Foges, managing director of Aldus books, invited him to send in a sample chapter. When, a month later, it had not materialised, Foges' secretary, Frame Smith, mentioned it in a letter to Julian. "I telephoned Francis. He has not got his chapter ready, so we will keep on chasing him!"[26] A letter dated 2 May 1972 from Frame Smith to Juliette Huxley gives an update on the progress.

> Francis has finished his text, as you know, and is helping us very much on the picture research. I am trying to help Adriana with the projected book, and she has told me of the exciting possibility of Francis and her going on a splendid journey in the autumn. But I believe it is still not settled.

This was a project which Francis did eventually complete, and in which he put to good use the material he had gathered in the course of his research at St Catherine's. How native peoples and western peoples think of themselves and the world around them in terms of health and illness would feature prominently in it.

## With the BBC

In the 1960s, Francis made frequent appearances on BBC radio and television, as well as on the Canadian Broadcasting Service. He had a soothing and modulated voice, one well-suited to radio. In 1967, he recorded on the Sunshine label, his story for "children and grownups" *Esmeralda Fufluns*, a delightful surreal fairy-tale of a dragon with a more than Dionysian iteration.[27] The *Sunday Times* were fulsome in their praise for both Huxley and his accompanying guitarist Julian Hayter.

"Huxley invented" Esmeralda "to please a sick friend," the *Sunday Times* revealed. "It is not like anything I've ever heard before," Pat Williams, the producer and a storyteller herself, confided, "except perhaps Lewis Carroll." In the tale, Dr. Happy makes jokes and tells Esmeralda his own list of pastimes. Our hunch is that Francis was comforting Joan Westcott with this fanciful play. Some of the vocabulary and thematic aspects of the ode (e.g. criticism of intellectuals), as well as the emotional content, circumscribing as it does feelings of anger, loneliness and happiness, exemplify the adult content, as does the conclusion. "And that was how they played dragons, and the amber-coloured bees like the game so much, they changed habits and buzzed in each other's ears: If you sting for your supper, you'll go to bed honey! Which they did."[28] The sexual politics of the fable and the symbolism at play we'll leave to others.

Other involvement with the BBC was of a decidedly more serious nature. On 19 October 1960, he conversed with his former fellow student, Audrey Butt Colson; Christoph von Furer-Haimendorf, the first anthropologist to

*Figure 13.1* Joan Westcott 1967.

be allowed into Nepal and Stewart Wavell who brought back stories from the Semai Senoi aborigines in Malaysia. Their conversation focused on shamans, the medicine-men and woman who are responsible not only for healing in native societies, but who also, through storytelling and the leading of ritual dance, exert a profound influence on the mental health of their communities.

The question of whether the jungle has an 'evil face' was debated on the BBC Home Service, in April of the following year. The synopsis for the programme read as follows.

> In conversation together, five travellers to the world's principal jungles share their experiences, make comparisons, and shatter a few popular illusions. The speakers are from South America, Africa, Burma, and Malaya. Richard Owen, Gerald Durrell, Francis Huxley, John Hanbury-Tenison.

The following month, we could hear him on the Woman's Hour (15 May 1961), discussing native peoples' beliefs and customs he had encountered and recorded in the field. He spoke further on these in the BBC Television programme entitled 'How Should We Face Death?' His illustrious company for this programme included one Dr. L. Colebrook, FRS, A general physician doing clinical research on pain, Bishop Anthony Bloom and J. P. Corbett, Professor of Philosophy, a self-proclaimed atheist. The discussion covered euthanasia, attitudes to death and taboos around death, where Francis added the anthropological perspective.

In another broadcast, '*The Travellers*'[29] he joined Mary Douglas in considering cross-cultural approaches to body symbolism[30] and how the manifestation of witchcraft and sorcery is experienced by social anthropologists. There was a further appearance with Butt Colson in a programme entitled 'Casting out Devils' in which trance states were debated, and then in August 1965, in an hour-long programme devoted to the Indians of the Amazon Rain Forest, he shared air-time with his, by now, friend Nicholas Guppy, author of Wat-Wai.

Come 1969 and Huxley's services were again called upon by the BBC. In the programme notes for the 'Noble Savage' put out by the corporation, we can see both the exalted company Huxley was keeping, and with regards to the language employed "I am as free as nature first made man,"[31] some of the colonial imprint that the BBC was finding hard to shed.

> Since the great European discoveries began 500 years ago, the primitive peoples of the world have found themselves in collision with the white man. Tonight's documentary tells the romantic and then tragic tale of this collision in South America and Australia, with the camera penetrating deep into the jungles of the Amazon and Arnhem land, with Claude Levi-Strauss, Francis Huxley, David Attenborough and Jean Liedloff.

A further appearance for Huxley followed on the Eamonn Andrews Show – a pioneering UK-chat-show which aired on the BBC from 1964 to 1969. Psychologist Brian Evans elaborates:

> (It was) a big thing to be invited on the Eamonn Andrews show. This was the "in place" to be in at that time. When Francis appeared there, he told so many funny stories about voodoo and all the stuff, he took the show over. When he did, Andrews realised, that he was good TV and he let him talk and talk and talk to entertain. The same happened also at the Anti-University.[32]

After this succession of TV appearances, Huxley's life moved on to decidedly practical matters. His subsequent endeavours saw him involved in the founding of Survival International and, in picking up the invitation of R. D. Laing to join, he became a principal figure in The Philadelphia Association (PA), Laing's alternative mission for addressing mental suffering.

**Notes**

1 Huxley, F. (1974, p.278) *The Way of the Sacred*. London. Aldus Books.
2 Francis Huxley 1963 – Brief account of original work. SCC.
3 Ibid.
4 Huxley, F. (1962) *Africa Before the White Man*; Huxley, F. (1963) *The Origins of Life*.
5 Huxley, F. (1963) Haiti Chérie. *Geographical Magazine*, 36 (2), pp.69–83.
6 Rival, L. M. and Whitehead, N. L. (Ed.) (2001, p.18, fn. 8) *Beyond the Visible and the Material. The Amerindianization of Society in the Work of Peter Rivière*. Oxford. Oxford University Press.
7 Rivière, P. (1969, p.12) *Marriage Among the Trio: A Principle of Social Organisation*. Oxford. Clarendon Press.
8 Stephen Hugh-Jones interviewed in July 2018.
9 Interview with Peter Rivière, March 2019.
10 Ibid.
11 Ibid.
12 Audrey Butt Colson interviewed in March 2018.
13 Ibid.
14 Report on two years' work as a Research Fellow in Social Anthropology. p.1. FHA.
15 Letter to F. J. H. Huxley, St. Catherine's College. SCC.
16 Handwritten letter from Professor Evans-Pritchard to the Master of Catz, 28 March 1963. SCC.
17 Peter Rivière interviewed in March 2019. Rivière also recalled fond memories of Lévi-Strauss, the grand doyen of social anthropology. He says:

> I got on rather well with him. I found him really very easy to get on, in fact. I will always be a bit astounded about the first time I met him. I went out to Paris, to sit on the jury for someone's doctorate. Lévi-Strauss was on the jury. He spent the whole time rather prominently, picking up a pocket watch, take it out, look at it carefully and then shoving it back into the pocket. After about

half an hour of doing that, I felt that he said, it could be wound up, that interview (laughter). A bit like Lewis Carroll's rabbit.
18. Huxley, F. (1976, p.46).
19. Francis Huxley's letter to Rosalind Heywood. Undated, possibly 1969. p.13. FHA.
20. Huxley, F. (1968) Report on two years' work as Research Fellow in Social Anthropology. SCC; see also: Huxley, F. (1966) *The Body and the Mind*. R. D. Laing Collection, Special Collections Department, University of Glasgow Library, MS Laing L 226; Huxley, F. (1966, pp.423–427) The Ritual of Voodoo and the Symbolism of the Body. Philosophical Transactions of RS London, 251 (772); Huxley, F. (1975, pp.29–38) The Body and the Play within the Play. In *The Anthropology of the Body*. Ed. J. Blacking. London. Academic Press.
21. Bateson (1980, p.302).
22. See Smail, D. (2005) *Power, Interest and Psychology*. Ross-on-Wye. PCCS Books, for an interesting discussion of the role of proximal and distal forces in our understanding of the causes of psychological distress.
23. Huxley, F. (1992, p.10) World Culture. *International Synergy Journal*, Santa Fe, 6 (2), pp.5–10
24. Chapter 1. The Spiritualists. p.4. FHA.
25. He travelled through the basin of both rivers for two years and wrote of his travels in L'Expédition Orénoque-Amazone (1952). He is considered the first Westerner who had peaceful contact with the Yanomami Indians.
26. Letter from Miss Frame Smith, Aldus book, to Sir Julian Huxley, 18 August 1969. JSH.
27. www.youtube.com/watch?v=Cz66C1dL1yE. Reviewed in the *Sunday Times*, 10 December 1967.
28. Huxley, F. (1967, p.6) *Esmeralda Fufluns*: Script. FHA.
29. *The Travellers*, BBC Home Service Basic, 20 December 1963, 19.30.
30. Douglas, M. (1975, pp.84, 88.) *Implicit Meanings*. London: Routledge & Kegan Paul. When Mary Douglas' edited volume on *Witchcraft Confessions and Accusations* was republished in 2004, Francis was thanked for chairing discussions and being a stimulus, even so he did not write a chapter for this book at the time of its original publication (1970), being fully absorbed in writing *The Way of the Sacred*. See Douglas, M. (Ed.) (2004, p.xii) *Witchcraft Confessions and Accusations*. London. Routledge.
31. The World about Us, BBC Two England, 28 September 1969, 19.25.
32. Brian Evans interviewed in London on 13 March 2018. Huxley joked about appearing on the show during one of his Anti-University classes.

# 14 Survival International
## Anthropology and social justice

The attention Huxley devoted to the problems of anthropology, though manifestly often theoretical, narratively driven and immersed in the workings of the cultural–symbolic order, went well beyond these and ultimately found their greatest application in a concern for the well-being of tribal and indigenous peoples.

In 1969, Francis Huxley, John Hemmings, Robin Hanbury-Tenison and Nicholas Guppy came together to found Survival International – quickly renamed from its initial title, the Primitive People's Fund. The impetus for their action had been an article in the *Sunday Times* magazine on 23 February of that year by Norman Lewis[1] who had been sent by the paper to investigate the role of commercial interests in the massacre of Indians, this following publication of a report by the Brazilian Figueirido Commission. A couple of weeks later, a letter by Nicholas Guppy, the environmentalist, together with Huxley and Audrey Colson was published, calling for an organisation for tribal peoples to be set up.

Hanbury-Tenison takes up the story.

> The first I must have been consciously aware was when Francis Huxley and Nicolas Guppy and Audrey Colson wrote that letter to the *Sunday Times*. Then he came, and we all made contact and they all came to my flat in Westbourne Terrace, London. That's where it all began. I think he was rather a grown-up and serious … When he first arrived, he was rather quiet, shy but a forceful academic. Nicholas was very much noisier and with Francis we had an anthropologist. First time round we all talked about ourselves and our experiences. You can imagine when Francis spoke about his experiences with the Urubu. He was never an organisational man. He never played any part in the committee work or structure of the setting up. I'm a rather bossy person. I said something must be done, and everybody nodded wisely and said yes, something must be done, not just talk. I had a bee in my bonnet. Anything works. There is one person who is responsible. We wrote to various people to get some money. Teddy Goldsmith and I employed a young man, Robert

Allen, then found an office. We had to do all the boring stuff to get a charitable status.[2]

Huxley provided the anthropological, intellectual bedrock for the undertaking and played a necessary part in reminding the others of the necessity to avoid "romantic ideas of the natives" a la Rousseau. Privately he viewed the anthropologist as being in some way "a mutilated man: in a curious revolt against his own society," such that "he travels to others to see if they have what is missing in his own."[3] With this in mind he was determined that Survival International must not carry the imprint of this romanticism. His contributions to Survival board meetings have been characterised as "sparse," occasionally "quirky" but always "charming" and "incisive," while former colleagues from the organisation see his general contributions as having helped to "open up people's understanding of the complexity and depth of people's spiritual lives."[4] More mundanely, but no less important, he furnished a set of illustrious contacts to support and lend weight to the project, including his father Julian, although he was less involved in the treadmill of legal paper work and bureaucracy necessary for it to succeed. To Hanbury-Tenison it had seemed initially unlikely

> that you can start an international organisation on our idea, that took quite a long time until everything was set and until we made anything happen. We were a talking shop in the beginning, but it got the good start with these contacts, especially the Huxley contacts were very useful ones. I only remember the one meeting with Julian. He was extremely friendly, agreed, probably for Francis. He was cordial and said yes. Then I wrote to him about Claudio and Orlando Villas Boas. We got his blessing.

Villas Boas was a key figure to have on board. He and his brothers, Orlando and Leonardo, had by this time acquired a hard-earned reputation for exploring, contacting, learning about and defending the interests of tribal peoples in Amazonia. Their contribution to the political struggles of the Indians and their considerable skills in bringing tribal peoples together cannot be overestimated.[5] Claudio amongst them was highly experienced in dealing with the kinds of political hurdles they would need to surmount in order to operate effectively in Brazil.

Not long afterwards, one of the founders, Hanbury-Tenison, was invited by the Brazilian government to assess the possibilities for coordinating aid to various Indian groups. Ten weeks of travel, covering eight areas of Brazil, led to various proposals to extend the bounds of national parks and to vastly increase aid. Come 1972, and two of the other founding members – John Hemmings and Francis Huxley – were involved in an Aboriginal Protection Society mission, invited by the Brazilian Ambassador in London, visiting 27 tribes throughout the Amazon basin to check on what actions had been taken in response to the Hanbury-Tenison report. The other two members were Edwin Brooks, a geographer and former Labour MP, and the ethnologist René Fuerst. It proved to be the only time, before or since, that foreigners were given access to all the indigenous peoples of Brazil and provided with Brazilian Air Force (FAB) planes and other transport to reach the remote territories.

Huxley became friends with both René Fuerst and John Hemmings in the course of the mission's two-month long journey. Fuerst found Francis to be straightforward, "simple," someone with whom he "could have fun"[6] and found him to be an "exquisite observer." "Francis and I understood each other perfectly." He told us. "Indians respected him as he respected them ... I can only praise him." Brooks was the least impressive member of the outfit. John Hemmings saw him as rather "ridiculous," someone who "didn't know anything about Brazil" and owed his presence on the team more to political considerations than any academic or experiential weight he carried. The final published report,[7] effectively written by Hemmings and Huxley, was happy to allay accusations that the Brazilian government of the day was "practising or conniving at the physical extermination of its Indian population."[8] It did however highlight the "very real and pressing dangers facing the Indians of Brazil" due to an "ignorance and prejudice which readily ally themselves with the ruthlessness of interests whose cupidity is content to see pledges broken and even the small Indian Reserves violated rather than lose a chance of gain."[9] In addition it provided a stark warning of the dangers of missionary work, noting many of the criticisms levelled against them are "well-founded," not least in their potential to disrupt existing patterns of social organisation without providing an "adequate substitute."[10] On the question of religion, the concluding comments display Francis' abiding interests in both shamanism and psychological well-being.

> While this report is not the place to discuss the nature of Indian religions their psychiatric aspect should not be ignored as a necessary safeguard of mental health.[11]

With that said, on the final page of the report, the authors drew attention to the overarching context of international finance capital to the Indian's plight.

> The real predators of the Indian may well be in New York, London or Frankfurt, rather than among the poor *caboclos* trying to find a new life in the interior.[12]

Within three years of the report's publication, however things took a turn for the worse. Relations with the Military Government turned sour and Fuerst, one of the report's authors, had to leave Brazil as persona non grata.

Survival International is not a lone organisation in the struggle to defend the land and rights of indigenous peoples – but it is now acknowledged as a leading global defender of those rights and has without doubt sharpened

*Figure 14.1* Francis Huxley with Karaya children, Santa Isabel, Aragonia River 1972. Courtesy John Hemming.

what the writer Toni Morrison referred to as our moral imagination. It has also indirectly spawned a number of other organisations – the Forest People's programme being but one. It is not only active in the field working with indigenous people but embraces a significant wider educational remit. Kate Hoberstone, who currently works for the organisation, summarised these aspects as follows, while also imparting something of Survival's international structure;

> A huge part of our work is to educate the general public, to deconstruct a lot of myths that surround tribal people. The idea that they are backward, the idea that they would be like us if they were given the option, the idea that they are primitive, the idea that they are violent. That they live short life's blighted by unnecessary disease. A lot of our educational work will focus around deconstructing those myths, promoting the idea that actually, as I said, they are full contemporary societies, they also have things to teach us as it were … We create material, booklets and leaflets. We do talk universities, not just with students, we talk with and try and influence decision-makers … We see (ourselves) as a single organisation, that incidentally is working in (several) countries. We disseminate the same material. The same message is just that they are in those different languages and tailoring the way we broadcast our message to the particular language areas. We are very

different in that respect, to organisations like Oxfam or Amnesty, which actually can operate quite differently and run different campaigns in different countries. Our campaigns are the same in all the countries. We are one organisation really.

This message, that tribal peoples are a feature of the modern world, that modernity embraces a far bigger field than industrialisation is an idea that would have been close to Huxley's heart. It would be a mistake however to think that Survival International has enjoyed uncritical and unequivocal support amongst the anthropology community. Adam Kuper,[13] for example, has expressed scepticism as to whether lurking behind Survival's name there still lingers an unwarranted romanticism and "anachronistic anthropology" that sees indigenous people as 'primitive' and closer to nature, that "the rhetoric of the indigenous-peoples movement rests on widely accepted premises that are nevertheless open to serious challenge, not least from anthropologists."[14]

In commentaries to Kuper's article, other anthropologists drew attention both to indigenous people's capacity and predilection to define themselves in ways which escape accusations of essentialism and for the necessity to address the consequences of the "misguided, misplaced, or blatantly racist policies of the past"[15] or indeed the present.

In the course of speaking to us about some of the changes Survival International has undergone over time, Kate Hobberstone spoke directly to some of Kuper's concerns.

> On the communication side of things, we definitely changed how we operate in terms of how we carry out our field trips. In (terms of) the fundamental message we remain extremely consistent ... I can't speak to the end of the 60s, from what Stephen tells me, we still have contact with dozens, I could say hundreds of communities. It is still very much about what do they want? How do they want their voice to be broadcast? It's not us saying, we think you should this or that. It is us going and asking them: What's your greatest problem? What can we do to help you articulate that? Its Survival being the platform to broadcast their voices. In that sense no, our methods have not changed. But on the communication side of things, yes, necessarily, they have changed.[16]

As the organisation was founded, and has grown around efforts to support indigenous people to gain *more* control over their lives, a general objection to the actions of NGOs, do not strike home. But importantly, critiques of Survival and other similar organisations offer no viable alternative for how to structurally and organisationally combat the very real injustices being perpetrated across the planet. Lévi-Strauss was vehemently opposed to applying the kind of measurement yardstick which places human societal development at various points on a linear scale – the underpinning of all schemas which pit so-called primitive peoples against modern urban industrialised humans.

In large modern societies doing without agriculture is a luxury we can no longer afford: we have tens or hundreds of millions of mouths to feed. If our ancestors dispensed with farming, as they still could have done, humanity's evolution would have been different. When compared to the size of our population, that of hunter gathers appears derisory. But can we claim that the fantastic growth of the population over the entire expanse of the earth has represented progress? All the diverse forms of productive activity over the millennia constitute choices. Each offers advantages but we must pay the price, consenting to endure the damaging effects.[17]

Anthropology is always politics of a kind, as is any kind of research conducted with and about human beings. The unjust allocation and distribution of power is an ever-present reality with consequences which affect all aspects of human behaviour and social organisation and how we understand these. Francis Huxley's life and work brought together the twin strands of anthropological and psychological thought which were concerned not only with the natural varieties of human experience and the social and cultural systems which fostered and nurtured them but, conversely, with the politics of social and political systems which sought to interfere and destroy these realms. Where Huxley married his unconventional style of academic and research work with political activism, the behavioural and human sciences, under the pressure of the neoliberal cauldron, have largely turned their back on any practical reckoning with power. A reckoning with power is what defines the organisation he helped set up. It remains an organisation committed to advancing knowledge with justice. Reflexivity lies at the heart of this enterprise.

## Notes

1  Norman Lewis (1969) Genocide. *Sunday Times Magazine*, 23 February. More background of this can be found in Chapter 9 of John Hemmings (2003).
2  Interview with Robin Hanbury-Tenison in January 2018.
3  Huxley, F. (1962, pp.150–156) Which May Never Have Existed. Review of Claude Lévi-Strauss, *Tristes Tropiques, Kenyon Review*, XXIV (1), Winter.
4  Interviews: Marcus Colchester in August 2019, Stefan Hugh-Jones in July 2018.
5  For a history of the Villas Boas brothers work in Amazonia see Hemmings (2019).
6  Fuerst is alluding to occasional visits to local brothels in between flights around the country. Hemmings describes how on one occasion,

> Francis, Edwin and I came back in the middle of the night. We returned the boat we pinched. But René wouldn't, he was still lying there in his hammock, on the other side. So, the next morning our plane will come. The sun was up, we had to go over and try and get René. He was lying there in the hammock stark naked. The prostitutes were rather shocked by this, he got them to give him a chicken. He was eating this chicken, naked in his hammock (laughing) and he said: "This is paradise. I don't want to leave here."

7  Brooks, E., Fuerst, R., Hemming, J. and Huxley, F. (1972) *Tribes of the Amazon Basin. Report for the Aborigines Protection Society*. London and Tonbridge. Charles Knight.

8 Ibid., p.103.
9 Ibid., p.146.
10 Ibid., p.143.
11 Ibid., p.145.
12 Ibid., p.150.
13 See Kuper (2003, pp.389–402).
14 Ibid., p.390.
15 Plaice, E. (2003, p.397). Commentary on Adam Kuper.
16 Stephen Corry has been the Director-General of Survival International since 1984. His own book *Tribal Peoples for Tomorrow's World* (2011; London. Freeman Press) provides a useful introduction to the challenges facing tribal and indigenous peoples and the political and conceptual minefield which surrounds them.
17 Lévi-Strauss, C. (2016, p.36) *We Are All Cannibals and Other Essays*. New York. Columbia University Press.

# 15 Cosmology and the sacred

## The world of appearances

The fruitful partnership between ourselves and the world is built upon the sensory information we receive. The world of appearances, given to us through our sensory apparatus, is all we have to go on. Philosophers describe this as the phenomenal world – to distinguish it from the noumenal world – that which is held to exist *in itself*, and which lies beyond the reach of our senses, fundamentally unknowable. If one is to find a recurrent thread in the total body of work which Francis Huxley left behind, it undoubtedly concerns the human desire to relate to and reach beyond the everyday world of appearances into this hidden realm – a realm which all human cultures, throughout recorded history, have sought to commune with. For Huxley, our insatiable quest to grasp the meaning of human existence in relation to this 'invisible' world is what defines the search for truth. How human cultures the world over address and relate to it preoccupied him throughout his life.

Huxley's quest, while also reaching beyond the sensory world, diverged from the favoured anthropological stance of the day, one associated with the celebrated French anthropologist Claude Lévi-Strauss. Lévi-Strauss' *structuralism* – a reaction to the perceived bias towards phenomenology in French philosophy and the apparent disdain for matters scientific which accompanied it in the years following the Second War[1] – sought to provide a mathematical basis for the discipline. Influenced by developments in linguistics, Lévi-Strauss focused on kinship systems – the system of relationships existing between different family units[2] (e.g. father–son, mother–daughter, uncle–nephew, etc.) – and endeavoured to unearth its hidden rules.

Rather than an expressed interest in discovering fundamental anthropological laws of nature which could be expressed in mathematical form, Huxley turned to the study of meaning and the iconography of the sacred – seeking in his own way to deal with the problem which Lévi-Strauss had referred to as reconciling the problem of metaphysics with the problem of human behaviour.[3] In a letter to his parents[4] he wrote,

196  *Social anthropology*

> To me the real interest in anthropology is not in the theoretical working out of social systems, of systems of economics and agriculture and kinship and ritual – these lead to the worst kinds of determinism and into that kind of dead social mechanism which the book *Religion and the Rise of Capitalism*[5] exemplified – but in the spiritual correspondences the acceptance of these systems leads to.

He saw the beliefs and systems of meanings which different people subscribed to as being intimately related to how the societies they lived in were organised. "Things" he said, "only have meaning when they are organised." Huxley was here effectively challenging crude Marxist interpretations which contend that social and economic conditions alone determine the nature and contents of human consciousness. Reversing the thrust of these, he argued that how societies were organised could be better understood not by postulating sets of underlying rules but by considering how different forms of social organisations were related to the implicit meanings which the social systems in question carried. This position implies that neither the form of social relations nor the meanings in the society were ontologically prior. In addition, for Huxley it was "spiritual forces [that] give rise to the social systems they organise." In these brief remarks he is suggesting that we must understand the cosmology of a given society (the set of prevailing beliefs about the nature, origin and existence of the world) and its form of social organisation as inseparable – that context and content are inextricably interwoven. This obviously has considerable implications for how we understand our own strongly hierarchical societies.

Huxley's interest in meaning, however, did not mean that he turned his back on the objectivity which science prizes. Some years later, in *The Way of the Sacred*[6] he wrote,

> We must conclude that sacred matters are also objective ones. We are not here concerned with the objective materialism of science ... and certainly not with the sentimentalities of religion that look to subjective feelings as their hallmark. The sacred is objective in the sense that it is what men traditionally strive toward, besides being the home of that perplexing object known as the Wholly Other. It allows one to introduce into human affairs – the absolute being.

This is a notably different take on objectivity than one customarily encounters in a scientific education. Here Huxley points to the common strivings of both scientific and theological thoughts to provide ultimate explanations for worldly existence. It is a position which sits comfortably with the German philosopher Immanuel Kant's strictures on the limits of human knowledge. Kant interrogated the question of what it was possible to know and what could be known about the presumed ultimate nature of reality. He proposed that concepts such as space, time and causality arose from cognitive structures which already existed in the mind prior to any specific experience. These *a priori* concepts he suggested were the foundation stones for all our perception and knowledge. Given this, Kant was clear that the formulation of causal chains of reasoning to explain the changing nature of the world before us must ultimately encounter a dead end. This 'limit to pure reason' makes itself known when we arrive at the end of this hypothetical causal chain and confront the inexplicable mystery of being situated at the site of the prime cause.

## The sacred world

The sacred, for Huxley, similarly confronts us with an indefinable absolute given – and rather than becoming lost in an infinite regress of cause and effect which leads to an ultimate postulated cause for which no reason can be given, we can choose instead to confront the "plain fact of experience."[7] These plain facts of experience in culture after culture postulate a sacred world, a domain where incorporeal intelligent entities roam – accessible within the realm of human experience but invisible and not amenable to objective observation. This willing interest in how humans in different settings play, imagine, mythologise and ritualise what is fundamentally unknowable helps explain what at first sight may seem paradoxical. While Francis had a notable respect for the sacred, it was somewhat inconsistent, in so far as he displayed a scornful attitude to the Abrahamic religions. Rupert Sheldrake[8] attributed this in part to an underlying respect for scientific convention that had run through the Huxley family for generations and in part to the fashionable anti-religious sensibility among the English intelligentsia of the day. Rupert felt that Francis, though intrigued, never fully engaged with the mystery that lay at the heart of conceptions of the sacred. What can be added to this is that Huxley's fascination with the sacred occupies a space which the philosopher and cultural critic Svetlana Boym was keen to explore – the imaginative space of wonder and astonishment which evades both scientific reductionism and religious devotion – it is a space which solves the conundrum Nietzsche posed – one which permits us to affirm the life-enhancing power of art, the "exalting and intensifying temperament acquired through religion,"[9] that is to stand squarely in the face of the mysterious without succumbing to the sentimentalities and presuppositions of religious or metaphysical need. It is one which requires an openness to unexpected experience,[10] tolerates uncertainty and ambiguity and revels in what Boym called profane illumination. Perhaps the capacity to inhabit this liminal psychological zone, suspending at once both belief and disbelief towards unfolding culturally situated experiences (whether one is immersed in novel cultural settings or within one's own native borders), is perhaps the sine qua non of the anthropologist.

At this point it is worth remarking that while Huxley lacked common cause with Lévi-Strauss' mathematical dreams for anthropology, there was one important line of thought on which they both agreed. Lévi-Strauss[11] had argued that human beings no matter where in the world or what culture they lived in possessed common mental structures which were the ultimate basis for the various forms of social organisation which existed in the world. This was part of his thesis that the so-called savage mind was actually no different to that of the average person in the West. Mythic thought and scientific thought were really not that different. Both employ metaphor and analogy in complex ways and address deep problems of knowledge.

## Myths, motifs, meaning and method

Outside of Huxley's encounters with the Ka'apor[12] in the Amazon jungle of Brazil and the Voodoo practitioners of Haiti, he had a passion for tracing the genealogy of sacred symbolism, as in his companion works *The Dragon*[13] and *The Eye*.[14] These texts offer us no profound ultimate explanation for the genesis and intricate cross-cultural ties which are to be found between enduring symbols, but they do enable us to grasp the immense scope as well as commonality of the symbols, motifs, myths, fairy-tales and ritual practices which in culture after culture narrate the spiritual dramas of human existence and their close ties to the natural world. While Huxley's knowledge of such myths was prodigious, he resisted the evolutionist gambit – favoured by some functionalist anthropologists – which not only seeks to provide an over-riding explanation for their ubiquity and ultimate origin, but also proffers a ranking of the world's societies on a scale of social progression.[15] In practice, evolutionist thought has an ignoble history as a bi-product of social Darwinism and racial pseudoscience.

Reassessing Huxley's contribution to anthropology in 2010, Pascal Diebe[16] described it as "a revisited functionalism," conversant with the "imponderables of an authentic life." Functionalism in anthropology is associated with the work of Malinowski and Radcliffe-Brown in the early 20th century. As a school of thought this sought to apply an organic analogy to the different parts of a society and their inter-relationships.[17] As a functionalist, Huxley's views are probably more akin to those of Radcliffe-Brown who viewed society through the prism of the emerging discipline of cybernetics – a system of relationships maintained through mutual synchronous feedback.

Huxley attributed great importance in such an overall system, to the existent sacred/spiritual beliefs and practices. He was seen by his friends and colleagues as a "prime raconteur[18]" – at home with the rich, dense texture of the world's myths. Perhaps it is enough to say then that his take on anthropology had much in common with the mythology he studied – owing much to the human propensity for storytelling and the need to make narrative sense of fundamental ontological and existential mysteries. Any self-respecting list of these would include the origin and creation of the world, humanity and the myriad life forms which share their existence with us, as well as the inescapable facts of love, sex, conception, birth and death, the unrelenting reality of change and the potential transformations of inanimate and animate matter.[19] Myths, the grand story of any culture, are now widely recognised to have a purpose beyond their manifest content; they situate the meaning of a single life within a larger context; they may remind us that the world is strange and purposeful, continually in flux and not entirely amenable to logic and rationality. Perhaps these aspects of myth are the truths we encountered when we first entered the world. And to these early truths we may add that myth reminds us that time progressed before our own (individual and collective) existence began.

Francis' work came after the Second World War in which he had served, and perhaps its radical nature, initially unappreciated, should be seen in the context of a world which was changing fast. Indeed, despite its pioneering nature – both in its eschewal of the prevailing ethnocentrism of the time, inserting his own subjectivity into the narrative and opening a space for the Ka'apor to speak for themselves and explicate their own world (rather than it being seen as the job of a foreign anthropologist) – departing from the traditional and somewhat dry conventions of academic writing, Huxley's work remains 'off the beaten track.' Jeremy Narby[20] who worked with Francis on *Shamans through Time* described Francis as having "stepped outside of the whole game ... looking at it with distance and amusement." Rupert Sheldrake saw him as a "transgressive ... feral intellectual" operating beyond the usual confines of academia. The chronicle of his time with the Ka'apor, *Affable Savages*,[21] was initially dismissed by some in mainstream anthropology as not a serious work. Meyer Fortes, one of the most renowned anthropologists of the 20th century, even used it as a warning to other young anthropologists against working in Amazonia. "Look what happened to Francis Huxley" he would say.[22]

Adam Kupers' otherwise excellent survey of British anthropology[23] found no place for Huxley's work. Kuper attributes his own unfamiliarity with Huxley and Huxley's marginal status in anthropology to be due in part to the fact that his work in Amazonia was atypical in British and Australian anthropology which favoured those who worked in the former colonial hunting grounds of Africa or the South Pacific respectively.[24] Given the affinities between Huxley's approach, the art of estrangement and the off-road place which his work inhabits in contemporary anthropology, it might be fitting to consider him within the roll call of what Boym articulates as practitioners of the 'off-modern.' Boym's theorising of the off-modern[25] encourages one to imagine counterfactual realities – bound by the possible twists and turns which history did not take. She argued that we understand our own realities better when we can extend our attention to give dignity to the defeated, marginalised or postponed narratives of human history. In this sense Huxley's work can function as an interrogation of the actual development of anthropology as well as the wider values in the society which nurture it. In the mid-1950s the intellectual community, let alone society at large, was reluctant to hear what native people had to say for themselves.

Like many social anthropologists from the mid-20th century onwards, Huxley was apt to reflect on the aims, purposes and methods of his profession. In one of his letters to his parents,[26] his thoughts on his field are shown to anticipate the methodological, stylistic and ethical sensibilities of modern social science. Anthropology, he mused, must be an "appreciation (of) the people it describes" and when done appropriately permit the anthropologists to reveal themselves in the course of their exposition.

## Psychoanalysis, myth and etymology

Huxley's approach – following that of Meyer Fortes, who he considered his mentor – was also profoundly psychological, indeed psychoanalytic.[27] His approach to the sacred followed this line. As remarked earlier, he did not seek to explicitly explain the interconnected web of myths and symbolism which he documented. He remained wary of reducing anthropology to the psyche.[28] However, his privately recorded sympathy with C. G. Jung's notion of the collective unconscious does suggest that he probably attributed some role to the Swiss psychiatrist's posited collective mental storehouse to account for the recurring nature and widespread presence of many of the themes and images which abound in mythical tales. That endorsement of Jung aside, he was severely critical of Jung's failure, not only to take the social context on board[29] but also to make clear the link between the forms of energy which he was describing as constitutive of the activities of the collective unconscious and the preponderance of static images which Jung regularly used in his work on unconscious symbolism.

Freud argued that dreams were "the royal road to a knowledge of the unconscious mind,"[30] while Nietzsche insisted that they were the source of all metaphysical speculation.[31] These epigrams aside, Joseph Griffin[32] provided a detailed empirical argument that the biological and psychological function of dreams is to deactivate patterns of emotionally arousing stimuli that remain problematic at sleep onset. In a similar vein, Antti Revonsuo[33] has proposed that dreams are naturally biased towards simulating ancestral threats with the dream process having evolved to provide a virtual world within which we can rehearse how we deal with threatening stimuli. Citing supporting evidence from normative dream content, children's dreams, recurrent dreams, nightmares, post-traumatic dreams and the dreams of hunter-gatherers (Yir Yoront, an aboriginal society in Australia, and Mehinaku Indians in Central Brazil), he believes dream content is more consistent with the original evolutionary environment of the human species than the present one. We do after all exhibit phobic reactions to snakes and spiders much more readily than to guns. This does not mean of course that dreams may not still serve useful social functions. Huxley[34] in fact cites the example of the Naskapi of Labrador whose dreams play a central role in the process of divining where they should go hunting. If Revonsuo is correct, we can expect the repertoire of motifs and images which are salient in the cultural imagination of a given group and which feature strongly in their myths and ritualised behaviour to reflect significant threats in the group's history. As Jung would have it – dreams help us find our way in a world filled with danger.

Huxley's own predilection for mixing etymology with imagery hints at a further possibility – one which is by no means incompatible with neurobiological speculation and which Lévi-Strauss with his interest in structural linguistics may too have favoured. This third possibility envisages the lexicon of a given language (encompassing both the form in which it currently exists and its historical antecedents), as comprising a dynamic repository of representational possibilities.[35] In contemporary parlance, the sum total of our language may thus be considered as a form of social and collective memory. Let's consider a few examples in order to clarify this notion before we expand on its potential relevance for understanding Huxley's treatment of sacred myths.

Found everywhere in world mythology, the dragon embodies a taboo aesthetic – that violence can be beautiful[36] – a suitable reason in itself for enquiring into its enduring significance. Huxley begins his essay by noting that the dragon, including its serpent form, functions as a fundamental "animating principle[37]" – *the genius loci* of every place[38] – bound to every variety of natural location (rivers, mountains, seas, bridges), object (bridges, buildings) and person (men, women, children). The noun *genius* stems from the Latin *gignere* – to beget. The original meaning of a 'spirit attendant on a person,' by the 16th century had come to mean a 'person's customary disposition.' By the mid-17th century it had evolved to its present day meaning of 'exceptional natural ability.' Our disposition is of course what drives us, and we can discern in the ancient and modern meanings, echoes of Freud's notion of Eros, the life instinct. What drives us is hence a dragon – our own personal 'daemon' or benign guiding spirit as the Greeks referred to it. From this we have derived the modern vernacular form of 'demon' – now personified and externalised as an autonomous malign force from the spirit world.

Dragons – as Huxley noted – appear in many guises (e.g. serpents, stags, bulls, horse, mermaids, storms[39]). They are customarily transformative, "dangerous,"[40] "hot-blooded[41]" and "notoriously promiscuous[42]" – which concurs with the hypothesis we have just discussed concerning threat simulation. In sacred iconography and mythology, guiding spirits, dragons and sexuality are found in close semantic proximity.[43] Huxley writes of the legendary dragon-like monster, the Tarasque which is depicted in a Celtic monument as "sporting a large erection," while another version of the monster appears in Spanish folklore as preying on children. Huxley also notes that the "deer is figured as the foreparts of the dragon in the Old World" with its horns "emblems of virility[44]" – an influence upon our modern expression of 'feeling horny.' Furthermore, the fire-breathing dragon Huxley[45] tells us is

> associated with what the Greeks called the *genius* of a man – the ancestral principle embodied in the head, brain, spinal marrow and penis. The Greeks believed that when a man died his genius took the form

of a bearded serpent ... They worshipped the serpent in the shape of a phallic herm.

Lest it be thought, all these dragons are male, we can keep in mind that the first dragon is held to be "One made of two genders"[46] so that it can mate with itself and give birth to the myriad forms of life. "The real form of a dragon" Huxley remarked "can be a goddess."[47] In an explicitly female incarnation, as mermaids, famed for their beauty and wisdom they "drown men in the course of their seductions."[48] Sex is thus never far away from what 'drives' our behaviour or what terminates it. Freud recognised that the duality of sex/conception and death represent two ends of a continuum – signalling both the beginning and end of life and the entry and exit points from the mystery of consciousness. They are unsurprisingly linked in our symbolic life, and accordingly in myth, dragons are harbingers of death as well as sexual union. Huxley tells us of the Bayart, a "dragon-horse," which is the "horse of death that bears the souls of the dead to the Other World,[49]" a motif that frequently appears in horror films, the source of many a disturbed night's sleep. The word "nightmare" itself derives from the old-English "mare," a mythological demon or goblin which is said to bring torment through frightening dreams. Mare is of course also the female of a horse.

We see in these few examples how the contemporary lexicon harks back to mythical thought and retains a link with the social memory of earlier meanings. As such we may consider these older meanings as the linguistic (structured) unconscious of modern thought.

Huxley argues that dragons "haunt our imagination" because they are "the outer aspect of an inner knowledge."[50] The inner knowledge in question, is clearly behavioural – violent, fear-inducing, creative and sexual in nature – perhaps one reason why the impulses behind such behaviour, often regarded as difficult to manage or control, reappear in myth in a variety of guises as a host of benign and malign autonomous agencies, a theme I will now consider when discussing Haitian voodoo.

## *The Invisibles*

*The Invisibles*, Huxley's account of his fieldwork in Haiti was published in 1966. It had had a long gestation; his stay of nine months having been undertaken between 1959 and 1960, immediately after a period working in a mental hospital in Canada. As we have indicated, the ostensible purpose for the trip was to investigate whether "voodoo had its own way of dealing with insanity."[51]

Huxley's various publications[52] and fieldnotes[53] recount the Haiti trip in a rich, revealing and thought-provoking tale in which his ability to establish a rapport with the locals is much in evidence. Nowhere, however, is any evidence evinced that the numerous events and encounters described owe anything to a world beyond the senses – a fact which Huxley acknowledged when writing about Anthropology and ESP in an edited collection on *Science and ESP*.[54] Huxley's notes describe "Voodoo dances turn(ing) into a kind of fourth rate cabaret show"; he notes the "great theatrical element" with "a lot of (it) ... play acting on a high level." Occasionally, it is "comic and awful." It is not that Huxley is unsympathetic to the Haitians – he is, on the contrary, generous with regard for their forbearance in the face of extreme economic hardship, endemic corruption and the post-colonial aftershocks of occupation and slavery.[55] In fact, it is these details which provide richer insights into the nature and meaning of Voodoo than its proclaimed reality as a manifestation and manipulation of spiritual forces. In its function as a family ancestor cult, the practitioners of Voodoo are in fact revealed to have much in common with what spurred Eileen Garrett to pursue her own career communing with the deceased.

There are ample reasons for considering Garrett's dissociative ability to stem from an upbringing characterised by herself, as alienating, isolating and abusive.[56] Such factors are now widely believed to constitute risks for dissociation and psychological disorder,[57] with dissociation itself viewed as a defensive strategy employed in the face of a frightening and hostile environment. Huxley meanwhile notes that,

> For many enslaved Africans such spiritual traditions and practices provided a vital means of mental and emotional resistance to bitter hardship. Indeed, although their beliefs and rituals may not have freed them, Africans seemed to be successfully frightening their captors.

He further observes that it is the peasant class, which encompasses the majority of Haitians, who in the main practice Voodoo. The psychological and material legacies of past injustice – an evident self-loathing, widespread distrust, poverty and desperation for money – Huxley observed had created a "Haitian psychology ... based on fear and the urge to destroy." He describes supernatural fears and credulity as being instilled early into children alongside unrealistic social and moral standards. This concoction of adversities, he wrote, "has the effect of cutting off their bodies from their minds."

Huxley is at his most perspicacious when examining the symbolism of the body in Voodoo practices. Just as we have considered language as a disembodied form of collective memory, so too may we contemplate the rituals and practices of Voodoo as a collective mnemonic system for keeping alive and maintaining an unbroken bond with deceased relatives. When we examine the pantheon of spirit entities[58] in Voodoo (Baron Samedi, the cemetery God, king of the zombies, patron of love, black magic and healing; another erotically charged cemetery spirit – the Guédé; the Grand Bois[59] [great tree], the loupgarou [literally a werewolf, but denotes a woman who turns into a vampire and sucks children's blood] and the loa – are just a few of the disagreeable characters on parade) and the manner in which they become manifest, we can appreciate how, in this society, the body, through the appearance of specific needs, moods, emotions and behaviours, symbolically 'encodes' an otherwise invisible past in a society, where literacy levels are low. In support of this, Huxley presents a detailed account[60] of how individual loa, "ritually defined," may represent a specific behavioural and postural set, whose primary locus may be situated in the head, belly or neck, for example. Huxley's view that "memory itself is attached to posture and action"[61] is reminiscent of Wilhelm's Reich's conception of muscular armour.[62] Reich's position, influential in psychotherapy and in, for example, the Alexander Technique, was that configurations of muscular tension, rigid body postures and patterns of autonomic activity may hold in place/maintain specific distressing memories. Huxley appears in fact to be suggesting that Voodoo rituals are cultural vehicles for re-enacting bodily memories of past tensions and conflicts, both individual and collective. He was alive to the close connection between bodily sensations and the cosmology within which they are interpreted. Some human groups, he noted,

> – and I think us also, for we forget how really primitive our sensations about illness can be – consider that there is something about illness which makes them feel they are not alone in their bodies.[63]

Rituals are also expressions of social convention, belief and social power – and it is therefore through the literal 'incorporation' of symbolic representations important to group identity and memory that a given tradition may perpetuate itself. As such, ritual is a living cultural museum.[64] To fear and destruction therefore, Huxley adds a need for collective remembrance to the proposed mix of Haitian psychology. This warrants further thought and examination in other contexts, not least our own European one.

### Shamanism and the paranormal

Huxley's psychoanalytic 'deconstruction' of Voodoo ritual might easily be read as an empirical treatise in support of Feuerbach's maxim that "theology is anthropology."[65] What is perhaps surprising is that Huxley's failure to garner any convincing first-hand evidence of paranormal feats did nothing to dissuade him from belief in the paranormal. "Facts, metaphysics and the sensational all play their part,"[66] he believed. His own attitude, gleaned from his written works, is best described as ambivalent and inconsistent. He readily admits, for example, that "proof" of ESP is "tricky;" that "the pronouncements of diviners are [usually] based on information previously gathered by ordinary methods"[67] and "may be neither exact nor true"[68] and that the anthropological evidence, is contradictory, the most convincing of which is usually encountered third hand. In more measured moments, he reflected upon the psychological (fear, hope) and social conditions (material poverty and hardship) that coalesce with metaphysical belief systems and magical practices, noting as he did that "the revolt of the [Haitian] slaves ... was hatched and bred in voodoo."[69]

Despite these reservations, he confesses[70] to believing in ESP and admits to "getting a reputation as a hand-reader."[71] Nowhere, however, does he tell us what the actual basis of this belief is, nor does he review any compelling evidence.[72] One is led to surmise that the ubiquity of the belief was a persuasive factor. "Wherever one finds divination practiced," he observed, "one finds a belief in the possibility of ESP."[73] A comment of his, in a letter to Eileen Garret, hints at a further intriguing possibility:

> I suddenly realized, when I was talking to you, a fact so obvious that it's almost invisible – namely that ESP, which is a form of communication cannot do without meaning, and does not manifest itself except by means of intelligence. *It is at the other end of the spectrum from science*, which always tries to convert intelligence and purpose into matter; to make ESP show itself strongly one must provide human purpose for it to flow into and not try to explain purposes away (italics added).

One possibility is that Huxley's belief in the paranormal is in fact grounded, like many before him, in a reaction to the kind of militant 19th-century materialism which members of his family tree were at the forefront of promoting.[74] Huxley, as we have said, certainly acknowledged the mysterious. At the same time, he maintained faith in a hidden order to the world – an order, that escapes the explanatory power of materialist reduction, and which one might relate to through intellectual and artistic endeavour, through ritual, and through the use of psychedelics. The latter are activities which produce dissociated states of mind, and they recur frequently in accounts of shamanic practices. The Shaman is the gatekeeper and guide to this hidden realm and possesses the ability to harness the benevolent and malevolent forces which reside in it.

Together with Jeremy Narby, Huxley collated an extensive reader[75] on Shamanism. The project and an "intellectual friendship"[76] grew out of a personal correspondence which they had begun subsequent to Narby's reading of *The Way of the Sacred* and Huxley's reading of Narby's *The Cosmic Serpent*. One learns from the material in the book that Huxley was far from alone in anthropological circles in accepting the reality of a spirit world and the entities which purportedly inhabit it. The contribution by Edith Turner[77] provides an illustration of opinion at one end of the spectrum. She describes how during a healing ritual in Zambia she had seen,

> how the traditional doctor bent down amid the singing and drumming to extract the harmful spirit and how I saw with my own eyes a large gray blob of plasma emerge from the sick woman's back. Then I knew the Africans were right, there is spirit affliction, it isn't a matter of metaphor and symbol, or even psychology.[78]

Turner is correct in informing us that "members of many different societies, even our own, tell us they have had experience of seeing or hearing spirits."[79] Turner's acceptance of the meaning of what she perceived, however, tells us little about why that might be so. Her blunt dismissal of psychology (and semiotics) unfortunately shows no cognisance of just how powerful the psychological, socio-psychological and cultural factors within an overarching cosmology, together with physiological and environmental variables, can be in shaping behaviour, perception and inference. A brief reminder will be useful.

Examination of our own Western cultural history provides plenty of evidence. Demonic possession was commonly accepted and witnessed in late medieval and early modern Europe. The psychologist Chris French has discussed how a framework for understanding this can be couched in terms of the learned roles and stereotyped expectations which prevail under a widely accepted theocratic order. He notes, in passing, that demonic self-enactments were somewhat less prevalent in Protestant communities where demons were shunned as "sinful."[80]

Psychologist and accomplished magician Richard Wiseman[81] has added to this explanatory framework in showing how the prior expectations of witnesses can play into the hands of a skilful conjuror/magician who contrives to produce convincing demonstrations of psychic surgery. From Turner's account it is difficult to distinguish between the possibility of trickery and a potential communal apparition. But even when it comes to apparitions a significant body of evidence indicates they may be artificially induced,[82] and moreover may be shared. Furthermore, they are more likely to be reported by people with personality types associated with strong mental imagery (fantasy proneness, absorption and suggestibility) as well as being more likely to occur under conditions of stress, tiredness and suggestibility.

Here she is endeavouring to have her budding anthropologists suspend their everyday conceptions of reality and open themselves to other possibilities. There is of course an unimaginably thin line between remaining open to what experience may teach and dispensing with one's critical faculties. Undoubtedly, however, what some have called the "anthropological conversation"[83] – the attempt to utilise anthropology as an art of enquiry to shape, modify and humanise how we do science – must involve this risk. Sceptics have often gone on record demanding that extraordinary claims require extraordinary evidence. That is arguably mistaken, as what constitutes the 'extraordinary' to begin with rests on an assumed truth regarding the dominant explanatory framework. Science cannot function at its best if different standards of evidence are required according to the prior beliefs in a given area. Nevertheless, any substantive claims do require substantive evidence. This is not to deny that the world may be a lot stranger than we imagine.[84] Huxley was aware that "there is a great theatrical component to magic, entirely necessary in order to capitalise upon the power of belief"[85] but did not satisfactorily explain why trickery should be necessary in the first place if there was a real but hidden "subjective force" in play. Narby and Huxley's text contains a more thoughtful and thought-provoking contribution from Narby himself.[86] He describes a collaboration between three molecular biologists and an indigenous shaman. Extensive discussions over several days took place between them with accompanying night-time ayahuasca sessions. After due time for reflection, the scientists agreed that the experience had changed their way of looking at themselves and their "appreciation of the capacities of the human mind." In the course of the ayahuasca-induced visions all received information and advice about their own research. Two reported contact with "plant teachers" that they experienced as "independent entities." The other dissented on this point but agreed that ayahuasca was a powerful tool for exploring the human mind.

Perhaps shamanism presents us with a problem which is of greater importance than resolving the issue of whether malign and benign spiritual agencies enjoy a free-roaming existence in a mysterious immaterial world. We are always faced with the danger of seeking to reduce other modes of cultural experience to a fundamental western one. The more important lesson may concern what anthropology can do at its best. This is about accepting the other on their own terms without trying to resolve them into our own. Many languages have terms which are not translatable into other tongues. How much truer must this be of a historically situated,[87] culturally encoded, linguistically (often biochemically) and ritually mediated meaningful set of experiences! For Lévi-Strauss, "the tutelary spirits and malevolent spirits, the supernatural monsters and magical animals, are all part of a coherent system on which the native conception of the universe is founded."[88] The process and flow of experience which the shaman sets in motion is a liminal one – hovering on the borders between psychoanalysis and psychosomatic medicine – it is one utterly dependent on the acknowledged and shared cosmology within which events unfold. We would do well to learn from this in our fragmented and divided societies.

Huxley's work points to the necessity of cosmology in human affairs and its intrinsically symbolic and ritualised presence in everyday activities that function to banish or control the threat of the unseen and unknown which lurks behind the world of appearance. To Huxley the organisation of human life in all cultures, through language, custom, law, politics and conflict, has been governed by this relationship to the world beyond appearances. But just as all that glitter is not gold, all that is invisible to us is not necessarily sacred. The definable invisible realm beyond the spiritual encompasses the distal interconnected forces of social control, politics, media, law and international finance. Much therapeutic experience tells us that what we cannot see and deal with we often code as alien and disturbing.[89] Francis was also interested in what is going on when our own private worlds turn sour. He enjoyed an enduring relationship with the maverick Scottish psychiatrist R. D. Laing whom he dubbed the Shaman of Kingsley Hall.[90] We'll continue that story elsewhere in this book.

For the record, my own (RR) experience of shamans is limited. But during a trip to the Peruvian Amazon at the turn of the millennium, I had an opportunity to talk with one.[91] He explained that when someone came to him for help with a problem, he would first ingest a specific herbal potion. The spirit of the plant would then appear to him and instruct him on which plants and herbs to pick from the forest in order to treat his client. On questioning from me he told me that the spirit which so appeared was as solid and real in appearance as any person. Seeing may not be believing, but I remain impressed and puzzled.

## Notes

1. See Doja, A. (2006, pp.79–107) The Shoulders of Our Giants: Claude Lévi-Strauss and His Legacy in Current Anthropology. *Social Science Information*, 45 (1).
2. Lévi-Strauss, C. (1963) *Structural Anthropology*. New York. Basic Books.
3. See Huxley, F. (1962, pp 150–156) Which May Never Have Existed. Review of Claude Lévi-Strauss. *Tristes Tropiques. Kenyon Review*, XXIV (1).
4. 6 December 1952.
5. Tawney, R. H. (1926) *Religion and the Rise of Capitalism*. New York. Harcourt, Brace.
6. Huxley, F. (1974, p.26) *The Way of the Sacred* London. Aldous Books.
7. Ibid., p.27.
8. Rupert Sheldrake interviewed in April 2018.
9. Nietzsche, F. (2008, p.130) *Human, All too Human*. Ware. Wordsworth Classics.
10. In his Haitian fieldnotes, Huxley writes, "one needs a devotion to the something that isn't the result one expects."
11. See, in particular, Chapter 8 (Mythic Thought and Scientific Thought) in Lévi-Strauss (2016).
12. At the time of Francis' writing they were formerly known as Urubus.
13. *The Dragon* (1979). London. Thames & Hudson.
14. *The Eye: The Seer and the Seen* (1990). London. Thames & Hudson.
15. The 18th-century Scottish enlightenment thinker Adam Ferguson, for example, outlined a hierarchy of savagery, barbarism and civilisation.
16. Dibie, P. (2010, pp.327–330) Lire Francis Huxley aujourd'hui. In Francis Huxley – *Affable Souvages*. Paris. Plon Bibliotheque Terre Humains.
17. See Kuper (1997).
18. Jeremy Narby – who edited with Huxley Francis (2001). *Shamans through Time*. London. Thames and Hudson.
19. It can be noted in passing that 20th-century atomic physics provided a framework for realising the alchemical dream of transmuting lead into gold. On the biological front, D'Arcy Thomson's (1917) *On Growth and Form*, Cambridge University Press, permits one to see how topological distortions of the physical features of certain organisms reveals the similar forms of what otherwise appear as markedly different species.
20. Interviewed in February 2019.
21. Huxley, F. (1956) *Affable Savages*. Viking Press, reissued (1995) Salem. Sheffield Publishing.
22. Interview with Stephen Hugh-Jones in July 2018.

23 Kuper (1997) – see note above. Kuper attributes his unfamiliarity with Huxley and Huxley's marginal status in anthropology stems in part to the fact that his work in Amazonia was atypical in British and Australian anthropology which favoured those who worked in the former colonial hunting grounds of Africa or the South Pacific.
24 Huxley's work never found its way onto any undergraduate anthropology syllabus.
25 Boym, S. (2017) *The Off-Modern*. London. Bloomsbury.
26 25 May 1955.
27 The ties between anthropology and psychoanalysis can be traced back to Freud's (1913) *Totem and Taboo*. Huxley discusses the complex, at times inconsistent, relation between the two in his article Psychoanalysis and Anthropology (1985, pp.130–151) – in *Freud and the Humanities*. Ed. P. Horden. London. Duckworth. In this Huxley notes the tension and contention between individual and collective notions of character (the Greek notion of daemon considered as a guiding spirit), the former favoured by psychoanalysis and the latter anthropology. One may also consider the role of the structural unconscious in anthropological thought as advanced by Lévi-Strauss – see following note.
28 See Huxley, Psychoanalysis and Anthropology, p.147.
29 A failure omnipresent in classical psychoanalytic thought and a good deal of mainstream experimental psychology to this day.
30 Freud, S. (2001, p.608) *The Interpretation of Dreams*. London. Vintage.
31 Nietzsche, *Human, All too Human* (above citation, p.14).
32 Griffin (1997).
33 Revonsuo, A. (2000, pp.877–1121) The Reinterpretation of Dreams: An Evolutionary Hypothesis of the Function of Dreaming. *Behavioural and Brain Sciences*, 23.
34 Huxley, F. (1974, pp.289–301) Where the Map is the Territory. *Theoria to Theory*, 8(1).
35 Theories of collective representation were first proposed by Emile Durkheim, later elaborated by Maurice Halbwachs (1952) with his work on collective memory. More recently Sergei Moscovici has developed his theory of social representations where these are understood as

> a set of concepts, statements and explanations originating in daily life in the course of inter-individual communications. They are the equivalent, in our society, of the myths and belief systems in traditional societies; they might even be said to be contemporary versions of common sense.
> (Moscovici [1981, pp.181–209] On Social Representations. Perspectives on Everyday Understanding. In J. Forgas (Ed.), *Social Cognition*. London. Academic Press)

36 See Angelova-Igova, B. (2018, pp.334–342) When Violence Became Beautiful. *Philosophical Journal of Conflict and Violence*, 2(2).
37 *The Dragon* (p.5).
38 In John Boorman's cinematic retelling of the Arthurian legend *Excalibur*, the wizard Merlin tells a young Arthur that

> The dragon is a beast of such power that if you were to see it whole and all complete in a single glance it would burn you to cinders ... It is everywhere, it is everything, its scales glisten in the bark of trees, its roar is heard in the wind, its forked tongue strikes like lightning.

210  *Social anthropology*

In Thomas Malory's *Le Morte Darthur* (1998; Oxford University Press), Merlin's spell enables Uther Pendragon to take on the appearance of the Duke of Tintagel, Igraine's husband so that he may lay with her. Arthur is born from this union and hence is the son of a dragon.

39 A hurricane takes its name from Huracan, the dragon of the Caribbean (*The Dragon*, p.74).
40 *The Dragon* (p.11).
41 Ibid., p.10.
42 Ibid., p.6.
43 See note above on the Arthurian legend for example.
44 Ibid., p.10.
45 *The Way of the Sacred*, p.140.
46 *The Dragon*, p.6.
47 Ibid., p.31.
48 Ibid., p.11.
49 *The Way of the Sacred*, p.139.
50 *The Dragon*, p.7.
51 Huxley, F. (1966, p.9) *The Invisibles*. London. Rupert Hart-Davies.
52 Huxley, F. (1963, pp.69–83) Haiti Chérie. *Geographical Magazine*, 36(2); Huxley, *The Invisibles*; Huxley, F. (1966, pp.423–427) The Ritual of Voodoo and the Symbolism of the Body. *Philosophical Transactions of the Royal Society of London*, 251; Francis Huxley (1967, pp.281–302) Anthropology and ESP. In *Science and ESP*. Ed. J. R. Smythies. New York. Routledge & Kegan Paul.
53 The 407 pages of fieldnotes comprise observations of geography, politics and the history of Haiti; accounts of Voodoo practices and lore, herbal knowledge, folk remedies and magic; Haitian views of madness; the behavioural norms and customs in the country; the functioning of social institutions in Haiti; observations and thoughts regarding the key people Huxley encounters; and accounts of his interactions with various individuals.
54 Huxley, Anthropology and ESP.
55 He is also not shy to criticise the attitudes of some tourists who visit Haiti with the wish to be "gigolo'd" by Haitian men because of the tourists' fantasises about the size of their sexual organs. With hindsight, one cannot escape thinking there is a certain irony in Huxley's own presence as a westerner here also. The Western powers have decimated Haiti economically and then send one of their own to investigate alleged psychic abilities.
56 See Roll, W. G. (undated) Book Reviews. *The Autobiographies of Eileen Garrett*. http://citeseerx.ist.psu.edu/viewdoc/download?doi=10.1.1.675.4177&rep=rep1&type=pdf. Accessed February 2019.
57 See Cromby, Harper and Reavey(2013); and Herman, J. (1992) *Trauma and Recovery*. New York. Basic Books.
58 Collectively '*The Invisibles*' refers to all invisible spirits, the souls of the dead.
59 'Bois' may also refer to the penis.
60 *The Invisibles*, pp.208–210.
61 Ibid., p.209.
62 See Reich, W. (1975) *The Mass Psychology of Fascism*. Harmondsworth. Penguin.
63 Huxley, F. (1963) Report of a Study Conference, 29–30 March.

64 See Francis Huxley (1975, pp. 29–38) The Body and the Play within a Play. In *The Anthropology of the Body*. Ed. J. Blacking. London. Academic Press. See also Bennett, T. (2003) Stored Virtue. Memory, the Body and the Evolutionary Museum. In *Regimes of Memory*. Eds. S. Radstone and K. Hodgkin. London. Routledge.

65 Feuerbach, L. (1841/2016, p.270) *The Essence of Christianity*. Andesite Press. In this Feuerbach asserts "the true essence of religion … conceives and confirms a profoundly human relation as a divine relation" (p.iii). Feuerbach contends that our sense of the divine, of a great being beyond us and necessary for our own existence is none other than Nature. In *The Essence of Religion* (Ludwig Feurerbach (1851/2004, p.61). New York. Prometheus Books) he writes:

> Gods, the rulers over rain and sunshine, lightning and thunder, life and death, heaven and hell, owe their existence likewise only to the powers of fear and hope, which rule over life and death, and which illuminate the dark abyss of the future with beings of the imagination.

Just as Nietzsche grounded metaphysis upon the existence of dreams, Feuerbach grounds it on human fears and hopes. Revonsuo completes the circle by proposing dreams are an evolved mechanism enabling the prior simulation of threat responses. See also a discussion by Huxley on the role of hope in the origin of the miraculous virgin of Guadalupe; Huxley, F. (1959, pp.19-29) The Miraculous Virgin of Guadalupe. *International Journal of Parapsychology*, 1.

66 Introduction to *The Invisibles* (1979, p.10). Rupert Hart-Davis. London.
67 Huxley, Anthropology and ESP, p.281.
68 See Huxley, F. (1961) Marginal Lands of the Mind. In Julian Huxley (Ed.), *The Humanist Frame*. London. George Allen & Unwin, pp.169–179.
69 Ibid., p.171.
70 Huxley, Anthropology and ESP, p.282.
71 Haiti fieldnotes.
72 For a contemporary review of scientific evidence concerning the paranormal, see Groome, D. and Roberts, R. (Eds.) (2016) *Parapsychology. The Science of Unusual Experience* (2nd Edition). London. Routledge.
73 Ibid., p.282.
74 The Huxley family as a systemic context for the generation and propagation of ideas is considered in Chapter 4 of this book.
75 Narby J. and Huxley, F. (Eds.) (2001) *Shamans through Time. 500 Years on the Path to Knowledge*. London. Thames & Hudson.
76 Interview with Jeremy Narby, February 2019.
77 Training to See What the Natives See. In Narby and Huxley. *Shamans through Time* (2001, pp.260–262).
78 Ibid., p.260.
79 Ibid., p.261.
80 French, C. (2016, p.40) Possession and Exorcism. In D. Groome and R. Roberts (2016, pp. 34–47) *Parapsychology. The Science of Unusual Experience* (2nd edition). London. Routledge.
81 Wiseman, R. (2016, pp. 149–157). Psychic Fraud. In D. Groome and R. Roberts (2016) *Parapsychology. The Science of Unusual Experience* (2nd edition). London. Routledge.

82 See Moody, R. A. and Perry, P. (1993) *Reunions*. New York. Villard Books; Moody, R. A. (1994, pp.335–336) A Latter Day Psychomanteum. In Proceedings of Presented Papers, 37th Annual Convention of the Parapsychological Association, University of Amsterdam, 7–10 August 1994. Ed. D. J. Bierman.
83 See Ingold (2018, p.130).
84 Shakespeare as ever is instructive. "There are more things in heaven and earth, Horatio, than are dreamt of in your philosophy" – *Hamlet* (1.5.167–8), Hamlet to Horatio.
85 Haiti fieldnotes.
86 Narby, J. (2001, pp.301–305) Shamans and Scientists. In *Shamans through Time. 500 Years on the Path to Knowledge*. Eds. J. Narby and F. Huxley. London. Thames & Hudson.
87 From the point-of-view of both individual and group.
88 Lévi-Strauss, C. (2001, pp.108–111) Shamans as Psychoanalysts. In *Shamans through Time. 500 Years on the Path to Knowledge*. Eds. J. Narby and F. Huxley. London. Thames & Hudson
89 Smail (2005).
90 See Francis Huxley (2005, pp.185–204) Shamanism, Healing and R. D. Laing. In *R. D. Laing. Contemporary Perspectives*. Ed. S. Raschid. London. Free Association Books.
91 We spoke in Spanish.

# Part V
# The human condition

# 16 The Philadelphia Association

The Philadelphia Association (PA) was founded in London in 1965 by R. D. Laing, David Cooper, Aaron Esterson, Sidney Briskin, Joan Cunnold and Raymond Blake.[1] Its principal aim was to further the provision of residential accommodation for persons suffering from 'mental illness,' whatever that term means. The houses under its jurisdiction are intended as refuges, asylums, safe places and sanctuaries for those who need them. At the same time there is a theoretical aim to lessen suffering, and to change the facts of mental health and illness as commonly understood. What the PA of old was offering was not a new hypothesis inserted into an existing field of research and psychotherapy; the founders were proposing to change our entire perspective on the issue. Francis Huxley became a member in 1970, joining a team of four medical doctors, Hugh Crawford, Laing, Leon Redler and John Heaton. By the time Theodor entered the PA as a student in 1976,[2] there were five therapeutic communities, a general study program, individual psychotherapy training and community therapy training.[3] From 1974 to 1982, Francis was the Principal of Studies of the Philadelphia Association, London. In this section of the book, we offer some thoughts on Francis' involvement with and contribution to the PA, what the principal bones of contention, both ideological and personal, were in its daily running, and reflect on the sense some of those who were in it made of their experiences.

### Friendship with Ronnie Laing

In later years, Francis once asked: "Isn't it sometimes embarrassing to be Ronnie's friend?"[4] There are three main strands in this period of Francis' life: firstly, the friendship with Ronald David Laing, the writer, psychoanalyst and radical psychiatrist; secondly, Huxley's engagement in the PA as teacher, private scholar and curriculum organiser as well as a repository of support with his open-door policy in the hinterlands of the association; thirdly, Huxley brought the critical spirit of a social anthropologist to proceedings. One might liken his role to that of a player–coach addressing what was taking place in the theatre of the absurd. Unfortunately, a full-blown study centre or institute structure was never established. Had this happened, a necessary task would have been to establish a full-serving library. There was one in the cellar of Portland Road, where seminars and lectures were sometimes held – holding over a thousand books which Laing had donated in order to get it up and running. That act of generosity, however, was met with considerable pilfering, even by the secretary himself. For an organisation based on trust, it was an inauspicious consequence.

For Francis, the PA was an opportunity to put the wisdom he had acquired from his travels into service, drawing on his knowledge of native peoples, their developed social and cultural systems and alternative healing practices. At this time of his life, he was ready to act on two creative fronts. Firstly, as co-founder, in 1969, of Survival International. Not long afterwards, Francis was then invited to become a member of the Philadelphia Association. His good fortune, in such a short space of time, was to link arms with his fellow anthropologists and explorers to get Survival International off the ground and to pair up with Ronald David Laing, in a friendship that would last over 20 years, only ending with Laing's early death in August 1989.

Over the next decade, he would produce four books, as well as numerous articles, reviews, talks and a plethora of letters to friends and foes alike. This was a period when Huxley felt able to reflect, with some consistency, on what was taking place, whether experimental or traditional, be it popular or unpopular. The concept of intention in existential psychiatry, which he found in Laing and his colleagues' practice, led to a rejection of the notion of 'cure' and its replacement with the idea of 'healing.' Francis, ever an adventurous spirit, in his own endeavours, would seek to establish a state of social equilibrium between the person and the surrounding social actors. "So, let us change the subject." He would say, "the problem, as we said earlier, is to know when it is present time on both sides." A so-called mad person could be healed when a microcosm of thought and personal relationships is built around her or him in which that person's behaviour and experience is no longer seen as 'mad,' incongruous, anti-social or psychotic; all terms which position a person as alienated from the approved social order. Francis knew from experience, that explanations needed to be balanced by understanding. That the 'whys' and 'wherefores' of how a state of living in a particular way had come to pass, needed to parallel any notion of 'understanding' – the 'what for,' which embraced a sense of rationale and purpose – a process of discernment that uncovered, or unveiled a person's thinking habits, within which their seemingly 'mad' actions, opinions and language made sense.

As for the best-laid plans of mice and men, things are not always as smooth as they sound or might look on paper. Meeting the other as a fellow human being is a challenge, when those coming to the village of healers are initially at least, effective strangers – as certainly is the norm when it comes to 'mental health care.' Laing and Huxley followed William Blake's maxim – that to have "mental joys and mental health/mental friends and mental wealth," was paramount, whatever other "bodily riches" one may delight in. Francis, as a social anthropologist, was in the habit of following the habit of associational trains, the kind of 'nonsense' that loomed large in Lewis Carroll's poetics. The forms of absurdities found in Carroll's thought would prove to be, not infrequently, the bread and butter of the mental landscape inhabited by many of the PA's clientele. Both Huxley and Laing had the wit to both recognise and engage seriously with this.

To make sense of much of the hotchpotch of contradictory assumptions made by people who have been derailed by life, and who were looking for help, peace and sanctuary in the PA, Laing and Huxley's advice was of great help; to keep note, in a journal, of what they are and how they are experienced. This exactitude made it possible for the therapists there to build a common platform from which they could make sense of what was going on. It has an added importance in so far as the search to become a well-rounded human being, must contend with a sub-conscious, immersed in a soup of contradictory words and images. An external aid memoire may be a useful assist in keeping track of things. It may, as Jung has previously suggested, also free us of the obsession that at any one time we already know all we need to. Psychoanalysis and Anthropology, for example, can both show what happens when one attempts to interpret a body of knowledge based on inconsistent principles.[5]

Laing did not always adhere to the basic pledge, the basic principle of trust that makes psychoanalysis possible – that is the promise of confidentiality, of non-disclosure; to not breathe a word of what is confined and entrusted within the therapeutic space. For example, he told Bob Mullan, that he had met Francis' father,

> Sir Julian, via Henry Dicks, in the first place, because Julian had been given a number of electric shocks for depression ... Huxley was a world intellectual figure and I was asked to put my mind towards healing him.[6]

Laing would later tell Francis specific information from that one session with Julian, which Francis then related to his mother Juliette and friends. The issue was of course sexual in content, how could it be otherwise? How could Laing do this and why? He told other stories to students, which made one wonder whether he was caught up in his own (and others') fame?

It is appropriate that we recall that Julian, when not mentally played out, was engaged as a biologist in the interwar years with psychiatrists, psychologists and social workers developing models of the psychosocial domain. The existing Freudian and Darwinian models both posited the relationship between biological instincts and social forces to be antagonistic and estranging. What Julian Huxley did, as well as the psychoanalysts Ian Suttie and Karen Horney, and physicians like James Halliday, was to focus on the individual person and their experiences, filtered through collective organisations, be they tribes, clans or community embedded in a given society. The new concept of the 'psychosocial' would inform psychosomatic medicine, the sociology of medicine and, for the days of the PA to come, emphasise the influence of a 'sick' society on its estranged members – how it produced inauthentic human beings. According to epidemiological studies it became evident that healing body, mind and soul needed a new framework for intervention. Julian, before Francis, had realised, through his experiences of mental breakdowns, that as a species, humans are not solely biologically determined. His vision of humanism envisaged a psychosocial evolution that interacts with, and informs cultural change. Huxley's own experience thus directly informed the reform of treatment politics. John Clay sums up the crucial encounter:

> Julian Huxley had been a patient of Laing's and had invited him to give a talk at the Royal Society on "Ritualisation and Abnormal Behaviour," where Laing had met Francis. When the younger Huxley paid a visit to Kingsley Hall, Laing danced with him too, an elaborate, weaving, almost tribal dance.[7]

At the request of Professor Alec Jenner, Francis spent three months visiting the University Mental Hospital in Sheffield, to try something similar to what he had done in Weyburn with Humphry Osmond. More specifically, Francis, as a social anthropologist, was asked to look into the feasibility of moving from a large to a small-scale operational strategy, as the PA had managed to do. Jenner, on a visit to Francis' place, put it to Laing that he should not be so worked up about the techniques and theories of contemporary medical psychiatry.

> It is perfectly simple Ronnie, what we psychiatrists do it that we stop undesirable perception and experiences and undesirable conduct. And what is undesirable is what society says is undesirable. We are the people that society appoints to stop people seeing things and hearing things and feeling things that society thinks it is undesirable for them to see and hear and feel. Right?[8]

Laing told Bob Mullan that Jenner's remark crystallised, as never before, what they were dealing with.

> We use a medical model because that is the tactic that is currently most acceptable to justify this activity in our society.[9]

Psychiatric medicine then was a cover story, one concocted to justify a sinister and overt form of social and political control. In seeking to expose this, Laing was regularly accused of saying something altogether different to what he had actually said. The more he protested, the more the actuality of what he *was* saying was contorted. What he and Huxley were confronting was a deep layer of mystification supporting the medical status quo. The situation was thus more complicated than Jenner's apparently simple reveal had made out. If, as he and Francis quite rightly felt, penetrating this web of deceit was confusing enough, the resultant question of how one can change the situation, was becoming increasingly complicated. Laing himself would often appear as tantalisingly complex as the situations he applied himself to unravelling. Francis would sometimes refer to him as "the demystifying mystifier."

Lady Huxley once remarked in a conversation at Francis' flat, that his great-grandfather T. H. Huxley had said that a man's worst difficulties begin when he is able to do as he likes. Francis' astute reply was that our ancestors are, in a way, reincarnated in and through us. "But once I have redeemed them," he said, then "I can live and sing that which is genuinely fresh."[10] This was as succinct a summary of what the Laingian politics of the family had unearthed as anything and also a significant precis of the familial task which Francis faced.

When Francis and Ronnie first met, at the conference on ritualisation in 1965, Laing was 37 years old, and in private practice as a much-in-demand psychoanalyst. He also retained a position at the Tavistock Institute of Human Relations as principal investigator in the Schizophrenia and Family Research Unit, and as a Fellow of the Foundations Fund for Research in Psychiatry. *Ritualisation and Abnormal Behaviour* was the title of his conference talk. He pointed out that as social norms shift, and they certainly did in the mid-1960s, so too do the demarcation lines between what most people regard as normal and abnormal. He gave examples of para- or anti-ritualisation, private rituals that seem to be self-gratifying or self-rewarding, aiming at anxiety reduction and destructuring the usual social structure of communication. Laing told his audience, one of whom was Francis Huxley:

> On closer understanding, however, the ritual may be found not only to be self-directed but also to have a socially directed message, conveyed in a privately elaborate code. It becomes the psychotherapist's task to decode it. Sometimes, if the patients trust one enough, he will decode his signals himself, or explain them retrospectively after he has given up the ritual. Ritualisation is a formal patterning of the encounter, the meeting of human beings ... In clinical psychiatric terminology, it "deteriorates." It becomes more and more rigid, repetitious, telegrammatic, and cryptic. But then, we have not only an aberration of normal ritual, but an aberration of an aberration.[11]

Francis, 42 years old at the time,[12] had entitled his talk: *The Ritual of Voodoo and the Symbolism of the Body*. He began to describe Voodoo

> as basically a familial ancestral cult held in place, as it were, by a large pantheon of gods ... Mental crises are as common in Haiti as elsewhere, and they are not all regarded as springing from the querulous demands

of gods or ancestors. Most of them in fact come from the unrealistic demands of parents upon their children.[13]

The overlap in their thinking in these two sets of remarks is quite clear. When these two extraordinary men became friends, both had already achieved a great deal in their own respective fields. Laing once castigated Francis for not writing the social anthropology of the PA, its members, households and general scene. Francis had in fact given it a try, without Ronnie knowing, but had found it was impossible to do. Not only, in Francis' eyes, did the PA lack an identifiable cosmology but Huxley rightly saw that there were four chiefs (the medical members of the PA) and hardly a tribal culture. With so much individualism in play, it reminded him of Colin Turbull's study of "The Mountain People" – Totally individualised. It wasn't to be done. Contemporary anthropologists would likely take a different stance – James Davies,[14] for example, in recent years has conducted a fruitful anthropological study of the psychiatrists involved in compiling the *Diagnostic and Statistical Manual of Mental Disorders* (the *DSM*), but in Huxley's day, the criteria for the usual kind of anthropological study just didn't suit the set up at the PA.

Though they had related intellectual interests, in terms of their social backgrounds, Ronnie Laing and Francis Huxley were like chalk and cheese. Francis came from a culturally rich and intellectually vivid family, being the fourth generation to grow up in such a stimulating environment. As a child he had played hide and seek, while D. H. Lawrence, Aldous and Julian Huxley discussed the science of life. While he ate dinner, he could hear discussions on the frontiers of the sciences and humanities. Ronnie came from a different cultural background – the Glaswegian lower middle class. Furthermore, Francis had a brother whilst Ronnie was a single child. Both however grew up with music, books and ideas to be explored. Both could play the piano though Ronnie was the more accomplished, and would even play in Francis' home. Both wrote a lot, and yet, if one compares the texts they produced, while Laing travelled in the strange and marginalised lands of the mind, Francis was more adept as a juggler of ideas and theories, having himself travelled in the 'strange' and marginalised lands of the world. Despite the differences in their respective social entry points to the world, Laing was adamant about his friend. "There is establishment and the *establishment*," he wrote, "Francis Huxley is a friend of mine."[15]

## Responsibility

Certainly, Laing and Huxley appreciated each other intellectually, sometimes with a pinch of humour, as when Francis once said to Laing "you don't believe a word you say!" Laing for his part took Huxley seriously, quoting him for the first time in *The Politics of the Family* while discussing 'Rules and Metarules.' He writes:

One tends to assume that every negative rule (such as that against incest) implies a prior desire, impulse, propensity, instinct, tendency to do it. Don't do that, implies that one would be inclined to if not forbidden.

There is a treasure at the bottom of the tree. You will find it. Only remember not to think of a white monkey. The moment you do, the treasure will be lost to you forever. (A favourite story of Francis Huxley).[16]

In *The Voice of Experience*, Laing acknowledges fruitful discussions with Huxley on the principal theme of the book, in part two of which, on Embryologems, Psychologems, Mythologems,[17] he draws on Huxley's suggestions – first given in a talk to the Philadelphia Association in May 1977 – that many myths are symbolic recreations of the consciousness of embryological development – in that "the way that the world is created" in these myths "is the way that an embryo is created."[18] Huxley went on to contrast the way life before birth is conceptualised in the West – as a genetic plan – with the way in which various ancient traditions play with the notion of an invisible architect.

Laing also found Francis refreshing and trustworthy. The crisis in Laing's marriage with Jutta Werner in 1980 was around the issue of betrayal. Everybody around Laing knew that his wife had had a relationship with the German translator of Gregory Bateson. She was pregnant and had an abortion. Ronnie didn't know, and was not told. One evening, when Mina Semyon had been out with Ronnie, she said to him, full of awe, how she admired his cool about Jutta having an affair. She was taken aback when he asked: "What do you mean by that?" It became obvious that he didn't know. Subsequently all hell broke loose in Laing's Eton Road home. Francis was then called in to do some mediation work with the couple. During the period of this domestic and personal crisis for Laing in the early 1980s, Francis' door was open. Laing moved in as a guest, staying there for a good six months. When his relationship with Jutta finally collapsed, Laing, hit hard by the turn of events, frequently became abusive towards other people. During this time, Francis found Laing difficult to cope with. For quite different reasons, Francis resigned from the Philadelphia Association about the same time as Laing,

> I was very tired of my colleagues, that was for sure, but I was even more tired of having to be round Laing with his horrors, the way he was playing himself off against everyone without any result. I had enough of the scene, and I had to do something entirely different to establish my centre.[19]

During Laing's stay at Huxley's, there were moments of light. Others witnessed some musical interplay. Laing would play some Bach on Francis' piano and Francis would join in playing the left hand, while Laing did the right, then changing over beautifully. Francis took the PA motto, "I've set you an open door, and no one can shut it," seriously, letting Laing sleep in Mel's old room. Ronnie and Francis, two elders of the PA tribe, had a good close relationship, each doing for the other what he couldn't do for himself. And yet, perhaps inevitably, given the different orbits of celestial fame they travelled in, there was a tension present over their work. Francis put a painful question to Theodor:

> What is the trouble with my work? Why don't my books sell? Why am I seen as an anthropologist-defector? That Frenchman called me the other day, who wants a book on Anthropology and Literature of which I told you. I think I have to scorn and criticise anthropologists like La Fontaine and Douglas. You can see my family didn't read me and brother Anthony said to me recently: "Ah well you are so much more intelligent. I can't read you."[20]

Theodor replied,

> Your work is so different from Laing's, it is in no way appealing to anything "anti this or the other" and has a depth and cultural wisdom that will stay for a very long time to be read. You therefore don't write for the day … As for me, being a student of yours, your teaching and showing by example in the therapeutic events in the PA is a blessing, (is) enrichment and helps me to become who I am. For this I am for ever thankful to you.

Other students of Francis, as we shall see, were equally full of praise.

Intellectually set askance from his family, a literary rivalry of sorts with Laing was not helped by what happened when Francis last met Evans-Pritchard. Then, the famed anthropologist had given Francis a book to read about pornography, and told him that in the last 20 years, he had not read any anthropology at all. "And anyway," Evans-Pritchard continued with a twinkle in his eyes, "why do people, who go to South America, write travel stories, rather than anthropology?" Francis asked if he had read his book. "No" he replied. This may well have been the final straw for Francis, and likely stirred the self-doubt that lay behind his painful query to Theodor.

### A tale of two pities

In the series of public lectures at the Institute of Education, in May to June 1978, on the theme of "Our Approach to Psychiatry," Francis delivered an enthusiastic talk on the subject of "how people around the world have traditionally described embryonic life and the formation of the human mind in the same terms, and in relation to cosmologies, initiation ceremonies, shamanism." After each of the four lectures, the others were delivered by Laing, Frederick Leboyer and the PA member collective, a lively discussion in the packed auditorium took place.

But not all of their public appearances were delivered as part of a team. A sizeable dent in Huxley's friendship with Laing occurred when, in September

*Figure 16.1* Poster for the Philadelphia Association 1977.

1980, he was not invited to a three-week conference in Saragossa, organised by the Humanistic Therapy Association of Europe. Laing, in a display of one-upmanship, had blocked his invitation as a speaker, making it practically as well as financially impossible for him to be there.[21] Whilst there, Laing re-wrote The Testimony of Experience (later called *The Voice of Experience*). To Francis' dismay, it transpired that a good many of the PA's inner circle, collectively referred to as "the gang," attended, including Jutta, who whilst there began the affair which, back in London, led to the demise of the second Laing family and produced severe ruptures in the PA. The repercussions were felt by all; students, members of the households, students and apprentice and associate members of the PA.

As if in compensation, Francis would become a co-organiser for the International Philadelphia Association (IPA) Conference in Leuven, Belgium, a year later.[22] Together with Professor Steven de Batselier, and his team, from the Onderzoekscentrum Marginaliteit, Katholiken University Leuven, Francis managed to bring a good many voices together. This was a peak of sorts in Francis' professional life. The congress participants were professionals from all walks of life and disciplines, users, ex-mental patients, relatives of patients, politicians and journalists. All the grandees of what was by then called the anti-psychiatry movement of Western Europe were there. The intention was to set up the IPA as a valid alternative organisation and player in the developing professional field. When it came to the final meeting, chaired fatally by R. D. Laing, by then inebriated, the left-wing radical Italians, among others, led by Rotelli, Slavich and Pirella, had enough of Laing's behaviour and called it a day. Nothing unfortunately came of the IPA, although a number of prominent individuals, including Melitta Mitscherlich from Germany, Loren Mosher, of Soteria House, Felix Guattari from Paris and Erik Pennen, of the Catholic University in Leuven, as well as a host of younger attendees (Theodor included) were enthusiastic.

But the old hands like David Cooper and Laing, 'creative destroyers,' ensured a non-starter was the only outcome. Francis was appalled, the collective effort he engaged to assemble a new world view, brought to nought. Francis had spoken approvingly of the work in London, situating it a wider European context, in which a number of groups were coalescing to create an alternative paradigm in psychological healing. Francis ended his talk with a challenge to the individualism that was, and remains, rampant in the mental health field;

> This is the peculiarity that touches me, when I read that those who come to us must of necessity have access to self-determination: On closer inspection the Self cannot be understood at all so easily and described. She or he is a cosmos, that includes other people.[23]

This was an idea which he would seek to develop in later years under the guise of *The Mutual Self*.[24] In the aftermath, Laing had said to Theodor, don't "let yourself be pushed to a position when you can't do what you like to do." "Ah," said Francis:

> Ronnie can go on talking about Hegel and is a European intellectual. I think all these texts are highly poisonous with its egotism and the PA unfortunately, is now R. D. Laing incorporated. Do you see him talk about sex and love or relations between the sexes? They are not discussed. When I suggested this as a topic, there was laughter all round.[25]

Huxley's retort is germane to some of the contemporary left perspectives on mental health, which seem more preoccupied with decoding Jacques Lacan's ambiguous writings than grappling with the troubling practicalities of a mental health system in crisis.[26] "When I think of Francis, he wasn't taken in by very many things at all. He was a clear thinker," said Leon Redler. Raised in the midst of the aura of the Huxley family and its intellectual and emotional hauntings, Francis had a good grasp of the value of straight talking – that it was often preferable to any yearning to sound impressive.

> In terms of the PA relationship with Ronnie maybe he deferred to Ronnie a bit more than was necessary, but then most people did at that time. The nature of the PA was such that people were mainly attracted to Laing. Hardly anyone came to the PA because of Francis. Ronnie certainly appreciated Francis. Ronnie had the edge to this by being quite competitive. There was a deep intellectual level, level of awareness of addition and able to make a meta-level, to get some edge on Bateson. Francis had clearly something that Ronnie didn't have as well, directness, ethical sense, generous, open heartedness. I would say Francis had this in a different way than Ronnie. He was much more accessible and open to more people than Ronnie was. I think Ronnie was sometimes being the therapist, being R. D. Laing and not just Ronnie. Sometimes Ronnie wasn't necessarily trustworthy as a friend or direct or ethical in the same way as Francis usually was.

Laing once said to Redler that "the truth game isn't my game."

> He could sometimes not tell the whole truth because it sometimes didn't fit him strategically. Francis, if he would do that, they were doing it in a different way, Francis was much more trustworthy.

Francis had asked Laing: "Ronnie, do you trust yourself?" "Only if I must," Laing had replied.[27] According to Redler, Laing "could be a very bad drunk, provocative and hurtful. Francis was never hurtful."[28] Rupert Sheldrake in comparing the two men thought a large measure of Francis' sense of self was related to his family, while Laing, on the other hand, he experienced as a difficult character who, at parties, could get holed up in a dark mood and drunk.

I only saw a few times the good side of Ronnie. Ronnie, when he was drunk could be really horrible to people – extremely rude and aggressive. He could see the weak spots of people, and would hit them below the belt, so to speak. Sometimes Ronnie, like Francis, didn't really want to engage with me.[29]

Jill Purce, who had experienced Francis for longer and in different situations to her husband, pointed out, perceptibly, that he too could be

> moody and difficult. He was completely unpredictable, and then (could) be friendly and welcoming, and then he would be rude and less friendly. I feel he was definitely unfulfilled. Never really fulfilled his potentials. In the PA, Francis sort of fell through, because it wasn't clear what his role was. He fell through the cracks. He wasn't a normal academic. He wasn't a therapist either. It wasn't quite clear. He had the shamanic trickster role. Anything else he wasn't clear, what he was.[30]

Both men, each unfulfilled, though for entirely different reasons, thus brought to the theatre of radical social change a field of subterranean dynamics left over from both their past family life and the institutional rejection of their approach. For Francis, "falling through the cracks" at the PA must have been experienced as a further profound disappointment.

## Theatre of the absurd

At the beginning of their new friendship, Laing was living at Kingsley Hall, the PA's first experimental therapeutic community, set up with a five-year lease. There, he invited Francis to come and give a presentation. He duly came and spoke on *The Body and the Mind*.[31] Francis dubbed the PA households, 'Ronnie's theatre of the absurd.'

We wondered if Francis stood out in any way in the PA, and if so, how. Paul Zeal's observations reinforced the sense that even in the PA, Huxley didn't quite fit.

> He stood out as a maverick, because he wasn't a psychologist as such, he wasn't a psychotherapist. I remember Ronnie saying, something like: "You lost your place among the anthropologists, now you are here with the Philadelphians amongst us." He stood out for another kind of otherness, of the kind of knowledge. He wasn't a phenomenologist; he wasn't the psychoanalyst or psychotherapist.[32]

Kingsley Hall, in Bow, East London, has an auspicious history dating back to the first half of the 20th century, founded in 1912 by Doris and Muriel Lester. The Lester sisters took a radical stand in the political arena, maintaining strong ties with the Suffragette Movement. During the General Strike of

1926, Kingsley Hall became a shelter and soup kitchen for workers. Among many notable guests, Mahatma Gandhi stayed there in 1933, while negotiating with the British Prime Minister for Indian independence. In 1965, R. D. Laing and his colleagues asked the Lesters for use of the Hall as a community for themselves and a small number of people experiencing serious mental breakdown. Their starting point was that psychosis, was a state of reality, akin to a waking dream, and not an illness to be eradicated by psychiatry's toxic pharmaceutical payload.

At the time *The Divided Self* was out in paperback and read in the tens of thousands by an energised population of young people looking for something better. His message by now, that it was society itself which estranged the mad and encouraged the creation of false selves, was eagerly embraced. With a message for the age, he became an advocate for those whose voices were no longer heard. The Lesters gave their blessing and Kingsley Hall became home to one of the most daring and radical experiments in psychology and psychotherapy. It was an experiment which found a home in the 1960s zeitgeist.

The explosion in hope, rebellion, art and radical psychotherapy eventually spiralled down into the decade which spawned Thatcherism and the worship of the free market. But it was not entirely forgotten. When Laing died, Francis Huxley wrote the obituary for *The Guardian*. It appeared on 25 August 1989, two days after Laing's death, under the heading of *The Liberating Shaman of Kingsley Hall*. In it, Francis wrote of how Ronnie Laing had invited him to join the PA. This was

> because of my interests as a social anthropologist in such things as shamanism, which I had recently come into powerful contact with. Laing, there is no doubt, had the shamanic temperament and recognised the fact. This gift, which so often begins as a disorder, is not recognised as such in Western psychiatry, which therefore cannot use its therapeutic advantages; a fact which, of course, underlies so much of Laing's writing on radical psychiatry.[33]

In *Shamanism, Healing and R. D. Laing*,[34] Francis added to his views on Laing and the shamanic temperament. In his farewell address to Ronnie, at St. James', Piccadilly, in January 1990, Francis said: "I honour him more than I can tell you," reminding his audience of Laing's struggles, "his psychic fist hitting at the navel of insincerity."[35]

Laing's drinking habits had become well-known. Human beings, it has been noted often enough, mostly live in the ruins of their habits and Laing's habits had become increasingly public and unnerving. To the amazement of many, "Huxley noticed how even when 'lurching drunk,' he could still play Bach and not miss a note, or he would quote complicated passages from *Knots* faultlessly."[36] While Laing's problems with the bottle and his marriage were contributory factors to his problematic behaviour, one other influence should be given due mention. We've had much to say in this book of how the social-class dynamics surrounding Francis exerted a heavy toll on him and other members of the Huxley family. But class is a factor in how people responded to Laing too. And there is little doubt that a good many of the people in the PA were struck by a middle-class paralysis of English 'niceness' that could not countenance overt anger and hostility. To Laing this would have been as a red rag to a bull, his behaviour seeking to provoke a more sincere and authentic response.

Mina Semyon, who was teaching Hatha yoga in different PA houses, and going to the seminars put on by both Francis and Laing, found him,

> a bit intimidating, and so was Ronnie. Intellectually I thought he was very different from Ronnie. He seemed to be connected with people I was longing to be connected with.[37]

Meanwhile, Laing had taken to experimenting with an Aesculapian mode of incubating a client's disorder in a temple, where she or he slept and dreamt the answer to their problem.

> But this requires a priesthood, a ceremonial role that Ronnie did not like to play; nor had he a sure touch on ceremonial ordering – as I realised when, after he had been going on about households as crucibles. I remarked it was a funny kind of crucible that had no cross on its bottom, at which he sneered at me. His talent was more a matter of kicking something to pieces – divide and conquer was an unspoken maxim of his.[38]

The PA households were effectively asylums, in which freaking out could be fomented, either passively or actively, intentionally or otherwise, but the priestly/shamanic presence seemed to begin and end with Laing. Francis, was aware what the tragic consequences of that could be:

> The therapist involved meanwhile can act either as a janitor or "metteur-en-scene" of the activities in his charge, and without an exemplar to model himself on, uses his own rule of thumb to keep order, usually without knowing what it is he should be the exponent of, the usual tragic tale that goes from inspiration to institutionalisation.[39]

Francis was curious about what forms of conviviality and rejuvenation were practised in specific PA households. There were of course PA parties, where singing went on, with Laing seated at the piano; drumming too was fashionable, entertained with the hope that the assembled would find the same beat, as in tribal rituals, or even discover the counterpoint to it. Other activities included yoga, cooking organic foods together, birthing exercises, storytelling, a social-dreaming school, conversing over a cup of tea as well as collective painting. When it came to these household activities, Francis again favoured a framework in which the management of social space and social interaction took precedence over an individually oriented program. His tips to apprentice psychotherapists would be to not trespass on others, to know what you are doing before you do it. This assigns a weight not only to intuition but to confidence and experience. After all, not everything that one can do well can be verbalised. Experience was the master. To Redler, he further wrote:

> My visits to Kingsley Hall were so few, I wrote little about that, and what I did, along with similar notes about other PA houses, were mostly destroyed in the fire that ravaged my flat in 1986. That also goes for frequent efforts I made to follow the thread during PA meetings, as I had done during my fieldwork as an anthropologist with some success: for I had discovered how to remember not just the gist of an argument but the words in which stories and interchanges were conducted, according to the mode of oral (versus literary) tradition.

Leon Redler himself, on Francis' suggestion, interviewed many people who lived at Kingsley Hall. Unfortunately, they remain unpublished.[40] Redler was extremely impressed by Huxley and was saddened by the lack of appreciation and the lack of recognition of just how much he had to offer.

> I think he was probably the most underrated and unappreciated member of the PA, not by you or me, but by many. A lot of people didn't realise what a gem he was. I would say he was extremely intelligent, extremely well read, extremely generous, open hearted, gracious, sharp, sharp, he had his problems, he was sometimes depressed. He is also one of the most ethical persons I knew. Life is all about the way we treat each other. Francis was the combination of open hearted and well grounded.[41]

Redler also had something to say about what went wrong with the PA, some of it externally imposed. His comments, importantly, pinpoint a moment when the current professionalisation, commodification even, of caring and healing human relationships began. It reminds us that other possibilities, other ways of healing and sharing rooted in ordinary human interaction can still be imagined, are in fact still possible. He is aware of both the benefits and the downside of what transpired.

> Ronnie abandoned the PA (as I did) for many reasons, which I take were brought to a head when the government required therapists to professionalise their goings-on, and you'll remember that it was Heya Oakley (who reminded Ronnie at one fateful meeting that he had called her his best student) who pushed for this at that moment. With governmental regulations in place, the focus on conviviality that Ronnie so frequently invoked went with him, the professionalists took over and so the house-therapists assumed command rather than witness and support.

230  *The human condition*

What Redler identified, was part of a larger right-wing shift in political values in the UK – a shift that was at least partly responsible for the diminution of Laing's perceived importance in the 1980s.

## Sanity, madness and the PA

Francis wrote back to Redler describing the reality of Kingsley Hall as resembling a living art installation, albeit one imbued with a degree of artistic (and political) chaos that was not exactly helpful.

> My first impression of Kingsley Hall, which further experience confirmed, was that it was the stage for Ronnie's Theatre of the Absurd. I had come across this term when reading Antonin Artaud who wrote a strangely magical book about his time amongst the Tarahumara Indians of Mexico and when he returned to Paris he staged his fantasies and made a hit with the avant-garde, which eventually led to the Living Theatre which came to London in the 60s and was invited to the big Dialectics of Liberation Conference ... one attempt to recreate the situation was the Anti-University, which went bankrupt when the anarchistic members took charge by refusing to pay for the services provided, such as seminars, as you'll remember.[42]

At the Dialectics of Liberation Conference, Francis took part in the 'Challenge Seminar on Ecological Destruction by Technology' alongside Gregory Bateson, Laing and the poet Allen Ginsberg.[43] Laing in his talk on *The Obvious*, discusses having been struck by a remark made by Julian Huxley.

> He said he thought the most dangerous link in the chain was obedience. That we have been trained, and we train our children, so that we and they are prepared to do practically anything if told to do it by a sufficient authority ... It is particularly important to study the nature of obedience. Our system operates through a network of common-obedience reciprocities.[44]

But this perspicacious remark never really carried over into a self-examination of Laing's own power in the PA household. Some things, as he did note, were not at all obvious. All the magic of initiation into the PA habitat could too easily also become the invitation to a form of psychological slavery, hypnosis even, constellating around a leader like Ronnie Laing.

Questions of power, and its legitimate or illegitimate use, were always central to what Laing was hoping they would achieve.

> Attentiveness to one another is itself the key to what is called therapy ... in that respect we have people who have particular interests in anthropology, phenomenology; different sorts of mediation – any sort of skilful

means in therapy or in meditation, or through the exercise of one's body or mind, either spontaneously or in particularly directed ways, thereby in simple doing the one thing we can do best ... The metaphor there for me is the Heart ... we do our best within the limits of what is allowable or permissible.[45]

But the reality looked a bit different from the ideal Laing had portrayed. Paul Zeal put it so: "The PA equals RDL. It's very difficult to get past that." What to do about the leader, when the leader errs, or goes off the rails is a recurring feature of many significant social and intellectual movements of the past century. Its ubiquity suggests an important omission in all radical planning. Still, good friendships and respectful alliances were forged in the PA, which in reading Laing now, one can see was central to the PA's nascent aspirations. Zeal spoke in glowing terms of his relationship with Francis.

> I knew Francis in the context of those member and associate member meetings and houses. It was more a friendship, that had already begun in the social field. I didn't have a sense of him forming alliances within the PA. We saw each other quite often in the social field, which was very enjoyable ... Very interesting flat, he had, full of the most amazing curious artefacts from round the world, masks, things from many, many different cultures. It was a wonderful friendship with Francis.[46]

He was not alone, in how he saw Huxley. "Lots of people saw Francis as wonderful." Mina Semyon pointed out.

For all his eventual differences with the PA, Francis remained sympathetic to its founding spirit and the larger questions it begged. Some ten years later, in his review of Peter Sedgewick's *Psycho Politics* for *The Manchester Guardian* he would write:

> Ah yes, those were the days. How to construct another such total alternative to the inhumanity of capitalism now is the problem, which is not the same as Laing's efforts to house the mentally ill without categorising them in psychiatric term. Or is it?[47]

Unfortunately, the PA setting was full of the usual contradictions, faced by all those who have the courage to pursue and practice an authentic presence. The PA becoming an institution, however loose, left it prey to the institutional dynamics one finds in most organisations; systematic lies, gossip, envy and malice, jockeying for position in the search for individual advantage. The unsurprising result was torn relationships, which whatever the mission of the organisation sometimes remained unhealed. There were splits as in any ordinary psychoanalytic organisation.

Rebels are, sadly until they cut themselves free, still connected to what they are opposing. This is why the 'anti-psychiatry,' of Laing's other friend David

Cooper, was just a step towards a non-medical psychiatry. Cooper, an intelligent, eccentric, imposing and, for some, a disturbing figure, really posed the question as to how far one can really reject society while continuing to indulge in its benefits? One area where this came into sharp focus was the use of drugs. Hashish, LSD and Scottish medicine, were habitually put to, what was then thought, in the PA generally, good use, to alleviate the excruciating psychic pain of persons gone mad about and in this world. It was meant to be different from "Just take this pill, to help you not to shout, it takes away the life, you're better off without."[48]

Psychedelic experimentation aside, Huxley, different though he was, was no rebel in the manner of either Laing or Cooper. His attitude, honed from his anthropological travails, embodied the concept of a journey. If Cooper stood for armed revolutionary struggle, for Francis, the trek through life was one in sympathy with Taoism.

It's important to understand that despite the strength with which Laing's name was and still is associated with the PA, there was a healthy stream of ideas flowing into it from outside quarters. Isabel Hunter-Brown's reassessment of psychodynamic psychiatry in 1950s Glasgow in fact suggests that Laing borrowed widely. Two of the people from whom he did so, were D. K. Henderson in Edinburgh and his Gartnavel colleague, R. D. Gillespie, who co-authored an influential textbook of psychiatry. It was one of Henderson's students, Maxwell Jones who helped kick start the social psychiatry movement and the place of therapeutic communities.

Some of the ideas from the Scottish school even extended to critiquing our 'sick society,' a forerunner of Laing's polemic in *The Politics of Experience*. There is a very real sense therefore in which the psychiatric establishment's disavowal of Laing is a de facto repudiation of the entire influence of the Scottish school. Laing's therapeutic approach was one rooted in the finer points of existentialist philosophy merged with the openness and social concerns of the Scottish scene. It permitted him to tune into the wavelength of his "patients," allowing them to be in his presence on their own terms, rather than being drugged into silence. But another influence from north of the border was also at work – one less intellectual, one less fruitful than that bequeathed him by his Scottish colleagues. Fuelled by the demons of earlier years, he was being propelled by an unquenchable thirst, not merely for alcohol, but for fame.

Come 1984, having by now both left the PA, Laing and Huxley were at the gathering, *Awakening the Dream: The Way of The Warrior*. "Laing sees the dark side of the moon" was the lurid headline in *The London Evening Standard* referring to Laing receiving a thrashing with a collapsible shovel by a shaman apprentice and black belt. Huxley felt for him and was astonished that Laing would begin his talk the following morning on the theme of unconditional love. In Laing's life, violence and love were never far apart – and this occasion was a showcase for what was possible from their close relation. John Clay describes what happened.

Huxley was at the symposium and saw Laing's transforming effect on his audience. Huxley, familiar with the way of the shaman, and the trickster, described Laing's "technique" on this occasion as follows: First he subverted the workshop by his disruptive behaviour and his drinking, so that dissatisfaction was projected onto him and he could become the scapegoat. This enabled him to turn the tables. When he came to give his talk, the participants finally "saw" what he was really about and were affected at a profound level than might otherwise have been the case. In fact, his talk became the turning point of the conference. The audience were now receptive to his message and were hopping with energy. Violence and love had been conjoined but it was a demonstration, too, of the warrior in action – the need to act.[49]

Francis was acutely aware of Ronnie Laing's 'gift,' acquired in the course of being raised as an only child in a family with rather maddening parents. Laing had learned for his own sanity and protection – both physical and psychological – to tune into any occasion which presents itself to him, to read what his parents and others were either up to, or concealing. Francis felt that, "Laing had a blessing for all hearts and souls who would dare to live life to the outmost." To manage the mayhem which revolved around oneself was central to Laing's operation.

## Psychotherapy, mythology, initiation

Dr. Brian Evans, an academic psychologist at Middlesex University, knew Francis from his talks at the Dialectics of Liberation Congress, at the Roundhouse in the summer of 1967,[50] as well as the short-lived Anti-University in 1968.[51] This was located at 49 Rivington Street, a rather gloomy street in Shoreditch. Like Kingsley Hall, it had an association with radical politics. Brian gives some of the background.

> Prior to the election of Harold Wilson's Labour government in 1964, the UK had experienced 13 years of very dull Conservative government. The only notable political activity which I remember from my 1950s schooldays was the Campaign for Nuclear Disarmament (CND) and its annual Aldermaston marches. By the time I was finishing my PhD in the late 1960s we had swinging London and a remarkable flowering of, on the one hand, psychedelic hippy culture with its associated elements of alternative life styles and esoteric religions, and, on the other hand, Marxist and other radical political groups united in opposing the war in Vietnam. There was an interesting tension between these two phenomena, which came together at the Anti-University, at which Francis taught.[52] I enrolled for the anti-University and went to courses taught by Laing, David Cooper, Leon Redler, Morton Schatzman and Francis Huxley. Francis was the one I was rapidly looking forward to each weekend. Laing only

came once a fortnight. He had a huge crowd and it was very interesting. Francis Huxley's Sunday afternoon sessions soon became my favourite. He was absolutely marvellous, and long before the Anti-University came to an end, his talks were always packed.[53]

By listening to Francis, Brian became acquainted with anthropology. He and other listeners were learning about British anthropology as well as Lévi-Strauss among others. In his element as a raconteur, Huxley recounted many of his experiences in Haiti and the Amazonas. He encountered Francis again when Huxley came to talk at Enfield College (now part of Middlesex University) in 1977. He was there to give a talk on shamanism, which Theodor organising it had misunderstood and advertised as "shame." When he arrived at the college, Theodor pointed proudly to the posters on the wall. Huxley laughed loudly and said: "Not shame, "Shamanism!" To add to the confusion, on the day of the talk word had somehow gotten around the college that a very interesting character had been invited to Middlesex to talk about 'chauvinism.' Francis took it all in his stride and proceeded to talk about all three; shame, chauvinism and shamanism, somehow managing to contrive clear links between all three.

Brian reminisced about how Francis came to regret that he had devoted much of his life to the Philadelphia Association and Laing, thereby missing out on being in academia. As a circumspect, humorous and engaging teacher, Francis was deeply appreciated by those who were serious about their learning tasks and assignments. Murray Gordon, who came from South Africa to study in London, remembers:

> I had the great good fortune to study with Francis while I was conducting my studies in psychotherapy and education in London in the 1970s. As part of a self-defined study initiative, I had individual sessions with Francis regularly. The agenda and the syllabus were invented as we went along. Francis often surprised me with his selection of books that he recommended. I would study the recommended reading and then return a week or two later, sometimes with a paper I'd written on the subject.[54]

With Huxley having written extensively about healing and mythology, the PA students and apprentices in community therapy and psychotherapy frequenting his seminars were fortunate that he was still enthusiastically applying this knowledge to the ways and means of dealing with madness. Huxley, like almost no one else, had a zest for making mythology practical, exposing the structural possibilities in a particular person's ritual, so that one can learn to know what comes next. Therapy after all is a ritual, putting symbolic action to practical effect, alerting us to clues in a story; one that opens a door to childhood, parents and a range of ancestors.

Francis would give seminars an all sorts of challenging topics; Rhyme, Reason and Nonsense; From Substance to Revenge and Exchange;

Responsibility and Victimisation; Mythology; On Imagination; Symbolic Meaning; Anthropology of the Houses; Playing and Reality, Practice of Initiation; The Road of Excess; Meaning – the Point of its Context; Embryos and Ancestors. Whenever he wrote a lecture or was working on one of his book projects, he would share what he had so far found out. He would assign reading lists that ranged from Malinowski, via Arnold von Gennep, Ruth Benedict, Mary Douglas, Gregory Bateson, Margret Mead and Lévi-Strauss to his teachers at Oxford. Students were expected to read Freud's *Introductory Lectures* and C. G. Jung's *Symbols of Transformation*, to interrogate the meaning of therapy and report in due course in the seminars. Francis' dictum: "Never say you have read a text when you have not," was heeded earnestly. How he operated in his pedagogical capacity can be gleaned from the testimony of one of his former students. Murray Gordon's story is a fine one. It shows how Francis struck a delicate balance between encouraging and challenging those his responsibility was to educate.

> I came to discover that Francis was a great teacher himself, one who engaged with me, considered my questions and formulation of problems and gave me new food for thought, encouraging me where he agreed and provoking me sometimes when he felt I needed to look at things in a new way. One time, I wrote a paper about the Dessana tribe in the Amazon Jungles. I enthused about how they were not alienated from their natural world the way many (most) people in the Western world are. Most people in London, I pointed out, were not aware of the current phase of the moon or knew what constellations were in the sky. The Dessana however, were very aware of the natural world around them. Francis agreed with me but added a little caveat. "You know Murray that the average life span of the Dessana and tribes like that, is about 35 years! They don't have penicillin; their mathematics is not very advanced."[55]

When Francis first joined the PA and took responsibility for the General Study programme and teaching in the training sessions, he thought he had finally secured an audience and could entertain them, which no doubt it did. Nevertheless, he longed to see the PA study programme adopt a more professional level of organisation. It was clear, after he ceased being head of the study program, and was done with the PA, and Laing professionally, that he had nurtured a sense of frustration for some time. He felt that he hadn't had sufficient support and his interests were somehow treated "as a side issue." The impression was that his anthropological knowledge was treated as a kind of window dressing for the main event – which was Laing and the PA enterprise.

Huxley would encourage students to engage with writing as an art and craft, to both expand and acknowledge one's own limits. In a dream Theodor had, before leaving London after nine years, in July 1981, he heard that Francis was back in town. Coming down the round staircase of his flat, he passed Theodor and first greeted Ronnie Laing and Gregory Bateson. After a while he turned to Theodor, gave him a hug and said: "I'm not your older brother. We are equal brothers." When Theodor talked about this and other dreams featuring him, Francis responded: "I'm always at my best in other people's dreams."

That there is and will never be an Archimedean point of reference in the universe, was obvious to Laing and Huxley. Yet Laing mentioned in a discussion with Francis that people are under this desperate delusion, thinking that others can tell them what their best interests are. Psychotherapy in one form or another must contend with this longing for the unsullied, universal and wise perspective on one's life. The problem is the need to find an answer. "The hope, in therapy, that people might be released from asking questions that can't be answered." Francis was adamant that as human beings we need a cosmos. Anthropology can, with its comparative approach, provide us with a guide to how important it is to have a heaven, to which we can link up our earthly experiences, with transcendent structures that aid and facilitate the meaning of what we are doing, that this facilitates knowing what to do. As noted, Francis thought one of the issues with the PA was that it lacked an overarching cosmological viewpoint and that without it, the possibilities for healing are reduced.[56] Much of Francis' life was an inquiry into the possibility of finding such a system that could bed down comfortably in Western life.

## Notes

1  More of the history can be found in Itten and Young (2012).
2  At that time, he was a 23-year-old undergraduate at Enfield College, now Middlesex University, reading social sciences and psychology in particular. Laing's work featured in two exam questions, one in clinical and one in social psychology. In the late 1960s and early 1970s, it was difficult to become a graduate psychologist in the UK, without having at least read *The Divided Self, The Politics of Experience* or *The Politics of the Family*.
3  The Associate Members at that time were: Arthur Balaskas, Haya Oakley, Michael Yokum, Paul Zeal and Chris Oakley.
4  Addressed to Theodor, whilst jointly witnessing Ronnie's incapability to hold his chairmanship at the Louvain Conference 1981, as he was under the weather.
5  Huxley, F. (1985, pp.130–151) Psychoanalysis and Anthropology. In *Freud and the Humanities*. Ed. P. Horden. Duckworth London.
6  Mullan (1995, p.257).
7  Clay (1996, p.129).
8  Mullan (1995, p.259).
9  Ibid.
10  TLJ 26 December 1980: Christmas dinner at Francis' with Lady Huxley and other guests.
11  Laing (1966, pp.332–333).
12  Francis Huxley:

> The number 42, a number that appears two dozen times or so in Lewis Carroll's life and writings: along with a number of the most curious coincidences, all

of which has set me to see what it is about 42 that lends itself to such goings on, so that the book consists of my reflections of Carroll as much as on a number of elementary mathematical operations (about which I have made some interesting discoveries) which parallel the workings of Carroll's verbal imagination.

(Unpublished MS, FHA)

13 Huxley, F. (1966, p.423) The Ritual of Voodoo and the Symbolism of the Body. *Philosophical Transactions of RS London*, 251(772), pp. 423–427.
14 Davies (2011).
15 R. D. Laing in Conversation with Bob Mullan (1995, p.256). When the book came out, Francis said to Theodor in Santa Fe: "At least he calls me a friend."
16 Laing, R. D. (1968, p.40.) Massey Lectures. In *The Politics of the Family and other Essays* (1972, p.112). New York. Vintage Books.
17 Laing, R. D. (1982, p.111) *The Voice of Experience*. Harmondsworth. Penguin.
18 Francis Huxley (1977) *Embryos and Ancestors*. Unpublished MS, 54 pages. Evening organised by the Philadelphia Association).
19 Clay (1996, p.212).
20 TLJ 15 February 1981: Maybe the Frenchman was Paul J. Benson.
21 Relayed to Theodor by Francis.
22 All the lectures, seminar and debates are published in Erik Pennen (Ed.) (1982) *Strategie Van De Kleinschaligheid*. K. U. Leuven. Onderzoekscentrum Marginaliteit.
23 Huxley, F. (1982, p.153) Beschouwingen bij de Werking van de P. A.-London. In *Stratategie Van De Kleinschaligheid*. Ed. E. Pennen. Translated from the Dutch, by Theodor.
24 See Chapter 17 of this book.
25 TLJ 28 November 1980.
26 For an up-to-date discussion on the 'mental health crisis' see Vos, J., Roberts, R. and Davies, J. (2019) *Mental Health in Crisis*. London. Sage. With regard to Lacan, Thomas Szasz notes that Lacan was "a trained institutional psychiatrist, remained one throughout his life and was proud of it." Szasz, T. (2009, p.133) *Anti-Psychiatry. Quackery Squared*. New York. Syracuse University Press. Szasz further notes that Lacan supported the insanity defence for criminal acts, involuntary commitment and treatment. While one may consider Szasz's judgement of Lacan's prose as "impenetrable and meaningless" (p.138) harsh, his critique of Lacan's practice is valid and does raise questions about the radical left's preference, on occasion, for obscure intellectually satisfying hyperbole over tangible action and understanding.
27 As told to Theodor by Francis.
28 Leon Redler, interviewed in August 2019.
29 Interview with Rupert Sheldrake in March 2018.
30 Interview with Jill Purce in March 2018.
31 Huxley, F. (1966) 17 February 1966, MS Laing L 226.
32 Paul Zeal interviewed in March 2018, PA Library London.
33 Huxley, F. (2012, pp.283–285) The Liberating Shaman of Kingsley Hall. In *R. D. Laing 50 years since The Divided Self*. Eds. T. Itten and C. Young. Ross-on-Wye. PCCS Books.
34 Huxley, F. (2005) in R. D. Laing – Contemporary Perspectives.
35 Clay (1996, p.266). Clay told Theodor later, that it was this authentic statement, which prompted him to write his enthusiastic biography on Laing.

36 Ibid., p.183.
37 Interview with Mina Semyon, March 2018.
38 Letter to Leon Redler, Sebastopol: 28 September 2006.
39 Ibid.
40 They are accessible in the Glasgow University Special Library. www.gla.ac.uk/myglasgow/specialcollections/collectionsa-z/rdlaingcollection/
41 Interview with Leon Redler, August 2019.
42 Letter to Leon Redler, Sebastopol: 28 September 2006.
43 Cooper, D. (Ed.) (1968, p.208) *The Dialectics of Liberation*. Harmondsworth. Penguin.
44 Laing, R. D. (1968, p.29) The Obvious. In *The Dialectics of Liberation*. Ed. D. Cooper. pp.13–33.
45 Laing, R. D. (1975). What is the Philadelphia Association? Lecture 11 December; R. D. Laing Collection, University of Glasgow Library MS Laing A 78.
46 Paul Zeal interviewed in March 2018, PA Library London.
47 Huxley, F. (1982) Anti-psychiatry and Other Disorders. Review of Peter Sedzwick: *Psycho Politics*. *The Guardian*, 28 January.
48 Laing, R. D. (1976, p.46) *Do You Love Me?* Harmondsworth. Penguin; Laing's follow up book of verse to *Knots* was another essay of sorts on the tortured structures human entanglements could take.
49 Clay (1996, p.215).
50 www.cafeoto.co.uk/events/dialectics-of-liberation-reconvened/
51 Brian Evans interviewed in March 2018.
52 www.antiuniversity.org/ABOUT
53 Brian Evans interview.
54 Murray Gordon, Email from Brooklyn to Theodor Itten on the occasion of Francis' death. 7 November 2016.
55 Murray Gordon, Email from Brooklyn NY, to Theodor Itten, November, 2016.
56 Itten, T. (1979) *Myth of Madness*. A Report of a Philadelphia Association network event in summer 1979 and A Study of Francis Huxley's Work.

# 17  The late Francis Huxley

After Huxley left the Philadelphia Association and eventually London, he remained a sought-after lecturer on the international conference circuit, meeting his third wife, Adele Getty through this. Adele turned his life around radically. He married into California and spent the last 25 years of his life living in Santa Fe and Northern California. The 1980s saw no new book published, though a few successful essays made their way into the public domain. Writing may have taken a back seat in this time but Huxley continued to be an avid reader. In the 1990s he published *The Eye* and began in earnest to write *The Mutual Self*. Before eventually abandoning it, he had completed seven chapters.[1]

He lived happily in Santa Fe, as a 73-year-old, even building a new house. His third divorce entailed a rupture to his envisioned retirement in the charming hamlet of Pojoaque. Living in Santa Fe, now on his own, though it refreshed his social and cultural anthropological interests in the Anasazi Indians who had lived in the region before, was difficult. Overwhelmed as he was at times by the stresses of ongoing pain management, he contemplated calling it a day on life. At the turn of the new century, Francis spent a few months back in London, which, several times, he confessed to missing culturally. In his later years, one book did manage to see the light; *Shamans through Time* with his co-author/editor, interlocutor and enabler, Jeremy Narby. Having been invited up to Sebastopol in California by Adele, the venturesome Huxley, moved to his final 'hide out,' as he came to call his cabin, in Wagnon Road, Sebastopol.

## A personal anthropology: 1983 onwards

At the beginning of the 1980s, Francis travelled to the small coastal village of Deià in Mallorca. On his first day there he met the poet Robert Graves, a resident there since 1929. His diary entry from the time records his impressions and Graves' subsequent presence in his dream life.

> He put on his hat as he sits on the beach. Walks round on his own. Takes it off again. What's for supper. Pork and salad. He works as Julian did

in his old age. We, Avicy and I, leave very soon. That night I dream I am coming to Julian. Meeting with Graves coming into town. A week later we see him by his gate, looking down the road. Would Avice and I come for a drink! He looks askance. Hurrah! He says at something.[2]

Francis delved into Graves' life, enjoying reading the various biographies, especially Graves' passionate 14 years with the poet Laura Riding.[3] Graves' struggle with Riding to balance the passions and boundaries of love and enmity, may well have stirred in Francis, memories of his own tempestuous relationship with Joan Westcott. There were other points of correspondence between the two men in terms of their love lives. Graves' preference for young muses was also shared by Huxley. Around this time (towards the end of 1981) he wrote to Theodor;

> I've got myself a nice girl friend – but she is very young, only 25. Seems to be fond of old monster me, too, I don't deserve it. Still, only 25. I need my head examined, or the other end. I think she fears that if she really understands life she'll die. Perhaps she is right. Not that you have to understand much to feel half dead, viz yours truly. I like the bit that's alive, though. Very much.[4]

Graves, confirmed to Francis, what he had already suspected, that any answer to the riddles of life must embrace the poetic and emotional as well as the scientific. As Francis entered the last 30 years of his life, he exercised increasing caution about what he committed to paper, perhaps a prisoner of his own ever-high expectations. Our hunch is that this is one of the major reasons he abandoned many of his book projects, leaving his intellect the secondary challenge of stumbling upon poetic truths and prosaic facts. From the Gorgon's head he ruminated on masks, embryos and ancestors, meanwhile writing the mythic story of *The Eye* after *The Dragon*. Unfortunately, his work on Anthropology and Psychoanalysis was less acclaimed. Marcus Colchester, a fellow anthropologist, thought that what was most striking about Huxley was that,

> He opened up people's understanding of the complexity and depth of people's spiritual lives. He showed there were many more parallels between Western systems of belief and indigenous systems, than most of us perceive.[5]

Undeterred, Huxley the writer kept going until, in his final years, he attained a serenity which allowed him to move away from some of his previous concerns. His friend Michael Williams thought that in his latter days, it was the calculator, not the pen, that was Francis' 'best friend,' as Huxley took a step away from the poetic myth-making exemplified by Graves' '*White Goddess*' and spent innumerable hours serving the 'God' of mathematics. The crossover between myth, mysticism and mathematics was an endless source of fascination for him, as it has been for many others.

In their meeting in Basel, on the occasion of Fastnacht, Albert Hofmann would tell Francis some stories, which he said, he had rarely shared. Francis saw storytelling as a vehicle for opening up streets of communication, a means for enhancing the interpersonal ambience. "It's when you tell others from those moments, they will also tell you more sacred stories." Francis told Hofmann about how Lourival de Freitas, the Brazilian shaman, had put an empty glass over Francis' heart and one over a dying man's heart and waited. With De Freitas pressing hard, Francis eventually had to go down on his knees. The other man got up and lived for another four years. Francis found this a staggering experience, with De Freitas' 'explanation' being that he had transferred some of Francis' life force to the other man. Hofmann responded in kind with this own seemingly inexplicable tale.

> When I was a boy, my father was dying. I knew, when he is dead, we will be in absolute poverty. So, I went out on the balcony and prayed to God. For the first time I realised that God has heard me. I went back in and the doctor tending to my father was astonished, as his father got better, and lived for another six years.

He had never before told this story to any one, not even his father. Hofmann then gave Francis a copy of his book *LSD, My Problem Child*, inscribed "from Albert." Out of courtesy, Francis reciprocated with a signed copy of *The Dragon*. Hofmann, Albert, as we now called each other on first name terms, walked us back to the Basle railway station. That weekend Francis gave a seminar in Zurich, going for lunch with Hofmann and discussing, to Hofmann's evident delight, their experiences with LSD which Francis had researched in the late 1950s. He spoke about psychiatry, anthropology, social issues and Lewis Carroll in a way that Theodor had seldom heard in all the years he had known him. Over the course of the weekend, Francis would speak for nearly ten hours in all.

After the PA years had ended, Francis sensed that finding an academic place to belong to – and on his own terms at that – was never going to be easy. Without a PhD he knew there were limits, but still hoped that he might somehow secure an appointment – *sur dossier* as the French say – on the basis of collective merit. That he did not was a lasting grievance. David Napier, as Professor of Medical Anthropology at University College London, one of the most academically successful of Francis' former students, and later a friend, sensed this. They met often during the 20 years their friendship lasted, pursued a lively correspondence and shared deep feelings and thoughts together. "I would have liked to have said about Francis, that he had a life fully realised," Napier said, "but I don't think he did."[6] Asked about Huxley's legacy, Napier's generous and carefully worded response – after pausing for

*Figure 17.1* Francis Huxley with Albert Hofmann 1982, Zurich.

thought – helps us to understand more fully the pain delivered to Huxley by the lack of recognition afforded him.

> There is a formal one clearly the fact that he is probably most responsible for my ignoring the cannons of anthropology in my own life, people of my generation talk about being a minimal anthropologist. I was incited to do what I wanted in anthropology. I didn't write an ethnographic. I didn't write the usual thing of a map of the place, their customs and all that. I never tried to speak in the voice of the people. All my experiences abroad have been catalysed for other ideas. For me that's the biggest impact he had. His legacy, I think, a very personalized anthropology. The early anthropologists were spectacularly unique. Francis carried on this tradition, instead of canonising in our field. He resisted this and encouraged other people equally to resist.

This 'personal anthropology,' Napier spoke of, was grounded in Huxley's "ecumenical" insistence that "there were other ways to see the world."[7] This necessarily included the views and experience of people other than himself. To what extent this grew from an awareness that his own background was utterly atypical of that experienced by most people on the planet, we can only speculate, but his experience undoubtedly provided confirmation of it and perhaps contributed to his openness, curiosity and amicability towards others.

During the 1980s and early 1990s, Huxley kept up his appearances on the conference rounds[8] and made many a lasting impression. Andrew Feldmar, a former apprentice and Hungarian friend, who organised a number of these conferences remembers him warmly. Intrigued by Huxley's approach, Feldmar described how,

> I read everything he wrote and treasure his books very much. I thought him as open hearted and open-minded. Many anthropological reports that I read, really were colonising Europeans would go to an African or South American country, and try to assess by already formed categories, that were familiar to the anthropologist, trying to fit a different culture into pre-existing boxes. Francis didn't do that. He tried to fit into the new culture and see what it was like from their point of view.[9]

Feldmar would later invite Francis to Budapest, where they would deliver a joint seminar. The trip gave Francis the opportunity to revitalise himself, bodily and mentally, through the massage facilities at the hotel. Around this time, he had taken to Alexander Lowen's bioenergetic therapy, another offshoot of Wilhelm Reich's body psychotherapy. Francis however found Lowen's writing and his predilection for jargon uninspiring.

Notwithstanding Huxley's conference jaunts, some of his former colleagues and friends felt, whether through the lack of academic recognition, which David Napier referred to, or through his decision to decant to the USA, that Francis was disappearing off the radar. Both Napier and John Hemmings lost touch with him once Francis was in California. Robin Hanbury-Tenison's impression was that "Francis was sort of disappearing in a cloud of smoke."[10]

## Goodbye to Pond Street

Though Francis had sold the lease on his flat, he hadn't quite said goodbye to England. This followed after Juliette's death in September 1994 and the necessity to sell the family home in Pond Street. Juliette's death brought to a close the emotionally and physically draining frequent travelling between the USA and UK. Five years of impermanent living on the West Coast ended more easily, as Francis never cared very much for California or its social scene.

Having lived in various places in and around Berkeley, Adele and Francis eventually risked a move to Santa Fe, where they knew a couple of people.

Francis had previously done some anthropology there, so he went to check it out. First, they rented a temporary flat, then moved to a farm and eventually, six years later built their own home, in Pojoaque, 16 miles or so to the north. For them, Santa Fe had a much more vibrant social and anthropologically informed life. This former Anasazi settlement, and from 1610 onwards the seat of the governor of the province Nuevo Méjico, was surrounded by nature. Francis loved it there, with the added bonus that, at 2194 metres above sea level, the climate was agreeable to his joints. As in London, however, there were days when he was plagued by enduring pain and took to bed and drew the curtains.

When Francis' brother Anthony became terminally ill, he and Adele returned to London, to be with him. Anthony as the elder, had been given power of attorney over Juliette's affairs. In time Francis took over this responsibility and planned to move his mother near to his home in Santa Fe. As indicated earlier, a huge row ensued over this, between him and his niece Victoria.

Bettina and Norbert Blume bought 31 Pond Street from Francis in 1995.[11] Bettina is an organist, piano teacher and music therapist; Norbert, principal viola with the BBC Symphony Orchestra. Driving past the house, tucked away behind a beautiful holly tree, Bettina and her husband saw the estate agent's 'for sale' sign and the blue plaque commemorating Julian Huxley. She takes up the story of how they came to acquire the house.

> There were so many people interested to buy this house. There was a sealed bid. The asking price was £400,000. We had a little house in Hampstead close to Julie Dench. We thought of selling it if we could buy Pond Street. We put our bid in. We were outbid by a rather well-known pop singer. She was quite prepared to pay more as she wanted to build a music studio on top of the house.

Though the estate agent passed on the news, Francis expressed his preference for the Blumes.

> We upped a little more, to meet in the middle, of what she offered. That is how we got house. Each time I came here, in February 1995 that was, Francis, who slept on the ground floor in a sleeping bag, went into the back garden, returning to the kitchen with a big bunch of camellias and put them in my hands. Francis would tell me stories of his life and the research with Brazilian tribes.

After the deal was done, Francis brought out another bottle of whisky, placed it on the kitchen table alongside a card wishing Bettina and Norbert well. The house had been cleared, save the book shelving in the grand upstairs library of Julian and Juliette. When this was pulled out, it revealed a raft of beautiful family pictures, featuring Julian, Aldous, H. G. Wells and a picture of Julian with the Oscar which he had won for his documentary on 'The Private Life of the Gannets.'[12] These photos were scanned and the originals handed over to the Huxley family.

Another friend, fellow anthropologist and former student, David Napier was to visit often, and in appreciation of Francis and this long friendship, would dedicate his book: *The Righting of Passage: Perceptions of Change After Modernity*,[13] to him.

> We spent a lot of time talking about my work on the Gorgon, which was in correspondence with the Dragon and the monsters. We talked about the number 42, the Mutual Self, the Aldous Huxley book. I've been to the old house in Pojoaque, when they first moved there. With his little writing hut. I probably visited him four or five times. When they built their new place, I would go there every half a year, for two weeks. So, we were quite a lot of time together in Pewaukee. We spent a lot of time walking in New Mexico. It was a really important time for me.

Napier witnessed first-hand how hard it was for Francis, talking to him about how his relationship with Adele was coming apart.

> Here is Francis living in Pojoaque, all by himself. Not a young guy any longer. He must have been 76. Just built a new house and the house has problems with water coming in. It wasn't like heaven on earth. It was complicated. Francis was taken up by relatively young edge people in America, who were pretty far out, not just the Esalen (Institute) crowd.

Napier went on to say how Francis "had a love–hate relationship with this," from on the one hand being "embraced by this, because he has a certain charm," and on the other feeling that

> he wanted to exploit that. Not negatively. He had to survive and had to make some money. His father put money out for him for life. But that money decreased annually in terms of its buying power. He wasn't flying first-class, I meant that metaphorically, he had to be careful about what he did, and he needed to augment his income somehow.

Eventually their friendship of almost 20 years soured, ending in a one-sided silence. They had exchanged many warm and inspiring letters to each other. It was a good relationship for both of them. "He was my best friend for that period of time," Napier said. He would continue to honour Francis as his friend, in his book *Making Things Better*.

Being in the States once again, as the nephew of Aldous, gave Francis opportunities. The Santa Cruz University's '50 Years of LSD' gathering took place between 16 and 19 April 1993. Francis stood on stage with Laura

246  *The human condition*

Archera Huxley, reading from her chapter 'Love and Work' describing the only psychedelic session she recorded with Aldous. Francis, in this reading performance, took on the role of Aldous, playing it as accurately as he could, lending Aldous his own Huxley voice:

> There are a thousand different people going in a thousand different directions: I know there will always be – and I mean this is the extraordinary experience – at least there is somebody who knows there a thousand other people going in different directions – that there is a fundamental sanity in the world, which is always there in spite of the thousand people going in a thousand different directions.[14]

Francis, now one year older than Aldous was when he died, no longer had any need to compare himself with others, not even his illustrious uncle.

## Colleagues and appreciation

As Francis aged, he had increasing opportunities to consider how his own former students had made their way and to consider their achievements as well as his own. One of them is the present Director of Survival International, Marcus Colchester, who in 1986 founded the World Rainforest Movement. Like Francis he had experienced living for an extensive period with a tribe, enough to get wrapped up in their daily living, dream life and myths, as well as taboos. Marcus felt that someone like Francis

> was deeper in perceiving these things, than I was. In many ways he invested much more time in this than I. I was more (concerned) about land rights and material threats to these people's existence.

When the final volume of Edmund Schuster and Carl Carpenter's three-volume, 12-book series on the *Social Symbolism in Ancient & Tribal Art* was published in 1996, Carpenter had a set sent to Francis. As Adele remembers, he was very grateful, surprised and impressed. Schuster gathered extensive material, drawing on illustrations from all over the world. Francis knew Schuster personally back in London, and in *The Way of the Sacred* cited his work as "beautifully ingenious."[15] What he appreciated in Schuster's work was how he had stitched writing, interpretation, art and knowledge together, drawing from anthropologists' fieldwork with the Guarani, a southern Tupinamba tribe, to create his own bold synthesis of their art. Schuster's efforts were like music to the ears of the elder Francis, especially when Schuster once again made an important case for tribalism versus individualism. As Francis saw it, human identity is universal, and Palaeolithic art shunned personal identity. Schuster, like Francis, constructed a network of creation-myth stories about our primordial ancestors in the form of a labyrinth, a form which itself was symbolised in many of the stories. What Schuster had potentially revealed was a recursive structure in the universal symbols of cosmic creation. Lévi-Strauss, in 1935, had collected in the field a drawing of a labyrinth, made by the Caduveo of Brazil. Darcy Ribeiro of the Brazilian Indian Protection Service had also collected another example in 1947–1948. Riberio told Schuster that he refrained from including it among the illustrations for his *Arte dos Kadiueu*, because he regarded it as extraneous to Caduveo art. The woman who had drawn the design, nevertheless had insisted that it was traditional among her people and had not been introduced by the Europeans.

By coming into contact with Jeremy Narby, Francis found a younger colleague, who, like himself, was part Swiss, and, perhaps unlike Francis, possessed the virtue of getting things done. On the shelf of his father's library stood *The Way of the Sacred*. Jeremy remarked that "when I was writing *The Cosmic Serpent*, I actually tell the story looking into the book and seeing elements. They were useful to my argumentation."[16] Upon publishing *The Cosmic Serpent* in French (1995), he sent a copy of it to all the authorities he quoted, one of which landed in Francis' letter box. Narby again:

> I got this extremely long and interesting response written by him, after he had read the book in great detail in French. A lot of the authorities to whom I had sent it were Anglo-Saxon, incapable of reading French. He was an old school scholar who devoured the book in French. I began a literary correspondence, me with this English gentleman and scholar of old.

When *The Cosmic Serpent* was published in English, with an endorsement from Francis, the publisher organised a tour in 1998. It was one which was to have unforeseen consequences. It took Narby to a bookstore in Santa Fe.

> That's how we first met in person. In his kitchen, the next day, we could just sit down and talk for hours and hours and hours, talk about fascinating things, bouncing off each other's thoughts. We became instant friends. I thought there and then that we could do a shamanism "101" reader.[17] I tell the publisher that I accepted the proposition and I wanted to do it with Francis Huxley. It seemed obvious. I was the young whippersnapper. He was the old fountain of erudition. My publisher wanted me to do the book, so it would be a book by Narby and Huxley. I would do the book in the way that I wanted to do it. The goal would be to mine Francis' knowledge. And we could work on it as our friendship and complicity grew.[18]

Their co-edited book did very well in the USA and England, and was translated into various languages, enabling Francis to reach a new generation of readers he might not have otherwise had.

## A mutual knowing

One of Francis' enduring friendships developed with Loren White – a sculptor of masks – whom Francis first met at the Ojai foundation gathering, 'Way of the Warrior,' in 1984. Loren remembers his first impressions:

> Very British, a very delightful person. I do recall, when I was working in my work shed in the Happy Valley, while the conference went on, Francis would almost daily look in on me. Just be there while I sculpted. Sometimes we would talk together. It's hard to say, in hindsight on what. There was a struggle for me at that time in my life. He more or less released that for me, by just being there. There was a real acknowledgement and openness between us, which was rare in my life.[19]

They began a long correspondence, meeting regularly and sometimes spending several weeks or, in Francis' case, months with the other and their respective spouses. In 2005, Loren helped Francis wrap up his stuff in Santa Fe and crafted a mask of the 'Wounded Warrior' of and for his friend. His reflections on that time convey something of the haunted character of Francis' disposition.

> I spent a month with Francis just before he moved to California, from his Santa Fe house. We will go through stacks and stacks of papers of his father. Wrapping them up. He would say, suddenly: "You must hear this." Then he would read it, something his father had written. It was quite agonising to watch his way to get all the things from his father. Francis would ask: "Why did Julian do this? Why did he come to this?" Francis often wondered, "why he was born into the family he was born into."

Loren wanted others to know what a remarkable person Francis was – of his "remarkable intelligence" and "compassion with all the falls and the blessings." In Loren's view Huxley "lived his life according to what he saw and what he wanted." Loren, 18 years Francis' junior, had some wonderful times with him and many heart-to-heart talks. Some of his masks hung around Francis' place in Wagnon Rd.

> We talked a lot about masks and one time he wanted to know how it would look if I would make one while on ecstasy. I took ecstasy for a number of days while doing a mask. I did send him a picture of it, since he was wandering about all the aspects of creativity.

Meanwhile, Francis had cultivated a friendship with another artist, Caroline Peacock, 'Cal,' a Texas woman who he met soon after he and Adele had moved to Santa Fe. She described him as having a "little devilish look in his eyes." They picked it up together and a friendship evolved. She also had some measure of how to deal with Francis when in one of his black moods. A few years after he had left Santa Fe, Cal visited him. As she got out of her car and walked down the garden path to his cabin, she saw Francis tending his flowers.

> I say "Francis I am here, hallo." And he said, "get the fuck out of here and out of my life." I go "oh fuck yourself and give me a hug." He "oh, it's good to see you Cal, come in, have a cup of tea. How are the children?"

This can be considered either as an illustration of the therapeutic principle of 'treating like with like' or as the somewhat more prosaic and un-English one of not treating anger with niceness!

## Moving again

When Francis and Adele put their Santa Fe house up for sale, a necessary step to finance the move to Sebastopol, Francis first had to attend to the poor state of the house – despite it being only five years old. The need to carry out these repairs exacerbated his pain levels. Furthermore, he could no longer use his library, nor, except for letters, sit down and write. Meanwhile it was all dust, noise and confusion for several weeks, and, were it not for an all-purpose dragon just arrived, he wrote to Loren, "desperate thoughts of enough is enough," crept up. In his later years, Francis was in poor health, and had difficulties both in managing himself and the house. He found this discouraging and depressing. In one of his regular phone conversations with Adele, she felt anxious that he might commit suicide. Adele's husband Michael explains how

> This was the red flag for us, his trying to commit suicide. I told Adele why you don't ask him to come up here and give it a shot. She got Francis back on the phone and was talking to him about moving up here. I got on the phone and said, "I hear you're depressed and your contemplating suicide. I understand there's got to be real trouble for you. We have this land and there's an empty cabin. Why don't you come up here and give it a shot? And if you're not happy here, I will help you to commit suicide." He started laughing. I think I won him over by suggesting that. He said: "Well, I think about it." Next day he called back and said: "Okay, I do it." That started the process to help him to be on the move once again.[20]

With the move done, Francis was faced with the challenge of cultivating new friendships. To his delight he would discover a new appreciative soul not far down the woodland lane of his home in Wagnon Road.

> I would see him was walking up and down the road with Cumae, a distinguished bearing, elegance in the simple way, he never stopped. I wanted to speak to him. The mailboxes where the two roads divide, he

happened to be there once, and I too was there. Within a minute I spoke Spanish and he Portuguese. We were both Francis'. A very good sense of humour.

So begins, Professor of Spanish at Sonoma State University, Francisco Gaona's story of his ten-year friendship with Huxley.[21] They would meet regularly during the last years of Francis' life:

> Once a week we meet here in my home for tea, and the other week at his place. At five o'clock Cumae would know to get up and that was the end of the session. He loved Cumae. They were very, very close. He told me, when he was dying: "She's waiting for me." He was very, very generous and had a great sense of humour. At one point, neighbours knew that we met, and they asked my wife what do they talk about? She answered: "They mostly laugh."

The two men had many things in common, as Francisco was only nine years younger. Literature, music and etymology were favoured subjects of discussion. Professor Gaona told us how he liked Francis' spontaneity and affability, and how he still misses him. Though he did not share Francis' taste for the bizarre, the occult or LSD, they had many anecdotes to share. "He loved the I Ching and mythology. On the side of his bed, in his last days, he had lots of beautiful objects. He had a deep faith." Francis arranged, with great care, a numerology map from the I Ching for his newfound friend.

Francis was at one time struggling with an extraordinary etymological work – the first complete dictionary of Indo-European linguistic roots.[22] It is befitting of their friendship that Francis was to find in this cultural study the common etymological roots of 'friendship' and 'freedom.'[23] Francisco offered him both.

> Francis and I came from different academic relationships. I got all this rich information from him. I was delighted to be able to connect in a way, that both of us loved English literature, English thoughts. Francis was a very modest person, generous. We never spoke about the long work in writing a book. He knew how to cultivate friendships. There are many things that can happen between human beings, but he had this ability. He was suffering from arthritis and he would tell me once in a while, calling me up and say: "Look, let's not meet this afternoon, because I am not in a good mood and difficult times are here again." We never had a harsh word between us. He had a great sense of tact, attention and sensibility.

They seldom spoke about Francis' past relationships, excepting one occasion when they talked, to his fascination, about Joan Wescott, who had ended up living fairly close by. There was evidently a great camaraderie between the two gents and a fondness which Francis' death had not diminished.

Among the many letters Francis still wrote, the correspondence with his former fellow Oxford anthropologist and friend, Rodney Needham was notable. When Francis moved from Santa Fe to California, he told Rodney how he saw it as exchanging an

> arid sunny climate for one of overcast and damp. That I used to live in such a climate without much remarking on its drawbacks surprises me no end – just as I was surprised some years ago on revisiting Manaus and being taken aback by the heat, the like of which I was sure I had never before experienced.[24]

In the same letter he tells Rodney, about Cumae, his dog, and how a kind friend recently had given her a jacket marked 'In Training – Service Dog,' which meant that he could take her with him whenever he went shopping.

> If at least three people, of either sex and any age, don't say "Oh what a lovely dog, what's her name, can I pet her," we both think our time wasted. They somewhat make up for the fact that, though I have quite a few acquaintances here, of friends I have but a couple.

In a subsequent letter, two months later, he would tell Rodney, "I'm glad at heart to hear you're at peace with yourself." Then how he went to Mexico with his friends Adele and Michael,

> who have furbished a house there in a manner unobtrusively elegant: overlooking a small beach, with a grand view of the Pacific, of pelicans plunging for fish. We were entertained for several days by a solitary whale blowing, breaching and swiping its tail upon the waters, bom! bom! bom! and by sunsets playing chromatic fugues with new voices entering just when I thought all was over.[25]

The letters are a testimony to how Francis' heart remained open to cultivating and maintaining friendships, even from afar. One of his long-time friends, who had also made the transition from Europe to America was Michael Schwab, a professor of public health. Michael suggested to us that Francis might have thought leaving London had been a mistake.

> I vaguely remember references of that kind. He had put himself outside of the currents or what he was trained to be a part of, and for being in. When he left London for Adele … He got a good welcome in America. When he got married there was a huge gathering. He was so British and so intelligent, at the beginning the adoration, he loved it. He irritated people, who adored him for having a British accent. Someone would say: "I just love your accent." Francis: "Do you have anything else to say?"[26]

Michael moved in with Francis after Adele left and he himself had experienced a late divorce. Michael spoke about the rift which eventually developed between himself and Francis. As Michael saw things;

> Cal introduced me to a woman who Francis did not like at all. Her name was Seah Kris. I didn't know that Francis actually couldn't stand her. She came over and stayed for one night. The next day Francis threw me out and he said: "I don't want that woman in the house. It was time for you to go." So, I said okay. I had a long run with you, and I did know how deep it went and I left. Then he sent me a postcard he had with that famous photograph, Gare de Lyon, where the train is going off the tracks down to the street, and wrote on the backside: "*Michael our association together is over. I have no wish to renew it. Sincerely, Francis.*" He never talked to me again. Adele told me that I was not the only one, who got that treatment from him in his late years.

At a later point it occurred to Michael that this behaviour was

> a sort of kindness, for all of us who followed Francis. We defer to him. He was a doctor, father to us, and it was his way of saying: "off you go. I have done it. It's enough. Go-go." So, I told myself that story and felt better about it.

## Climate and chemotherapy

After years of living in the dry heat of Santa Fe, the damp of Sonoma County was not exactly welcome. But Francis had more pressing concerns than the Northern Californian climate. These concerned his ongoing recovery from the chemotherapy he had been receiving, following the discovery of a tumour in his throat. He was, "happy to report" that his hair was now

> growing back somewhat curly and is already thick enough to cover my pate, whose baldness had made me feel curiously ashamed. My beard is following suit – I had to shave that off so that a plastic mesh mask could be fitted over my head and clenched to the table on which I lay, an immobilised victim of radiology who then understood why I had been previously asked if I were claustrophobic. ('Occasionally' I had answered, as though they cared!)

"Oh yes," he added "and the tumour, which had grown out of the back of my nose/throat, has now disappeared – from sight, at least." Francis found solace by reading the Egyptian and Tibetan Books of the Dead, "along with other hair-raising essays on the human condition." The cancer and its treatment had entailed eight months of pills and a drastically changed diet. Three and a half months after his final dose of radiation and chemotherapy, he was told by the medics, that in another month he would be free of the vexatious after-effects of both. He was fortunate to regain sufficiently good health to permit him a return to the everyday activities of walking and letter writing. The kindness of his friends during this time often brought tears to his eyes.

Once again Francis felt comfortable being in his cabin, driving out to the beautiful Bodega Bay area for a walk with Cumae, and doing a bit of shopping on his way back. Three to four times a week, he would go up to Michael and Adele's, still the proper Englishman, to sit down for an ample meal and talk. Should there be any frictions in the new couple, "Francis would lend either a sympathetic ear." He had "a big heart and so much compassion," Michael remembers. The trust and camaraderie between himself, Adele and Michael remained strong.

## Ninety years of age: the sage with the silver stick

In 2013, the couple Dorothea Joos and Jacques Lévy, decided to drive up Wagnon Road. Looking for Francis Huxley, following the death of Joan Westcott, they had been given information that he lived somewhere in the vicinity. A routine ensued whereby the three of them would get together every three weeks. They lived a mere 15 minutes apart. Dorothea was Joan Wescott's end-of-life carer. Francis wanted to see the place in Occidental where Joan had lived and where her grave, donated by the Russian Orthodox Church, was. Dorothea experienced Francis as quite free in talking about his personal feelings and about the Huxley family. The cordiality of the meetings between the three was usually assisted by a bottle of Calvados and a cola. Francis would then loosen up. At 91 he was crystal clear and "didn't skip a beat. Francis would often repeat, the truism: "The trouble with getting old is that there's no future in it," which he thought should have a calming effect, upon one's psychic hormones, "but no, it doesn't," he would say and proceed to quote one which did exert a more positive effect on him: "Cheer up, the worst is yet to come."[27]

More often than not, Francis tired of doing nothing all day long. Regularly, until the last weeks, he would walk, with the aid of his silver-headed cane, to his letter box, picking out the weekly *Times Literary Supplement*, and the many letters he was still receiving – Francis took no interest in email. Mina Semyon was one person from former times who still exchanged letters with him and sent copies of her own books when they were published. She was very affected by Francis and always felt touched by him.

> He was a really good man. I was enjoying the last years and last years he was in my heart. I really looked forward to his cards. He always responded to my letters. I looked forward to his response, tender responses.[28]

Once Francis had picked up the post, he would settle down on his long marble desk, lean back with a joint and a cup of coffee, slightly creamed and flavoured with a spoon of brown sugar, and fully enjoy the words and stories that came his way. *The Mutual Self* had by now been long abandoned, his passion for book writing reserved for his project on the Number 42. For this, he wrote page after page of calculations and feverishly long notes, feeling duty bound to finish it. Francis was fascinated with Lewis Carroll's obsession with the number, reflected in the "42 illustrations in Alice's Adventure in Wonderland."[29] He had written previously to Peter Mayer, publisher at Overlook Books, surmising that, with Lewis Carroll,

> 42 is a number that appears two dozen times or so in his life and writings: along with a number of the most curious coincidences, all of which has set me to see what it is about 42 that lends itself to such goings on, so that the book consists of my reflections of Carroll as much as on a number of elementary mathematical operations (about which I have made some interesting discoveries) which parallel the workings of Carroll's verbal imagination.[30]

His 90th birthday eventually crept up and became a reality for which Adele and Michael arranged a fine outdoor dinner party. Many people came, some from as far afield as New Mexico. To Michael, who has taken care of people all his life, Francis was regarded as family and so was taken care of financially too. Francis had already given away his substantial share of the Santa Fe house to Adele as a gift. She, together with her new husband, who befriended Francis – were now the younger generation. Francis was very appreciative of this sense of belonging to a new family, one heightened by the occasional presence of Michael's own children and grandchildren around the dinner table, or when they would just drop in at Francis' cabin for a chat, looking out for him as Michael did. In this environment Francis became a trusted confidante to Michael. The only difficulty between them, that Michael can recall, occurred following an operation Francis had after the cancer, where he experienced a transient medicine induced 'psychosis.' Michael recounts.

> He tried to open the car door with the chopsticks. Yet he had the fucking keys in his pockets. Cumae is running up and down the highway. I opened the door and put him in the back seat, slammed the door down. Quickly I was cooling down. Francis was practising divination. He was sitting in the car, get out his chopstick to open the car. You know, during this period he was in the best moods I've ever seen him in. He was so happy, everything is love, everything is connected, and everything was beautiful.[31]

When he lost his hearing, due to age and the effects of radiation, his life drifted into that of a recluse, one of choice, as the attendant communicational difficulties in social situations bothered him. After lunch, Francis would regularly honour his habit of taking a siesta, drawing the curtains and sending out the message that he was not to be disturbed. But there were several occasions where his withdrawal from social engagement and the manner of it had distressing consequences for others.

*Figure 17.2* Wedding Picture of Francis and Adele, London 1986. From left to right: Jill Purce, Adele, Francis, Juliette Huxley and Rupert Sheldrake.

## Friends, foes and isolation

Adele recalls how Francis' retreat into social isolation began to adversely affect his relationships, even with long-established friends.

> Francis didn't do email. He didn't like talking on the phone, didn't really pick up the phone and all of that. People would come through me. They would email me: "How is Francis?" I went to Francis and told I got an email from Jeremy; he is in San Francisco. He would like to come up and see you, is that okay? He would say yeah, whatever. Apparently, Jeremy went through a very rough time with a family member dying. Basically, went out of communication and so when he arrived with his teenage son, all excited to meet and see Francis, he did not want to see him.

Jeremy Narby went to see Francis, in the company of his 15-year-old son, in 2011. As they walked over to Francis' cabin, Jeremy says that Francis

> burst out of his house and let me have it for five minutes or so. Then he went back into the house. I was there, shell-shocked, and my son was looking at me. I told Adele this was unacceptable; we would not stay; we were going to leave immediately. "No" she said, "you can't leave."

Jeremy told her what was going on in his life. She was fuming and went to his cabin:

> "Francis, I am mad. I just can't believe you did this to a friend. Do you know what is happening in Jeremy's life, do you know about the death of his father and long illness of his mother?" Francis said: "horrible; I better come up and apologise to Jeremy for that." The next thing Jeremy remembers is that Francis came back out of the house, and said "okay now let's have dinner."

It made for a very awkward meeting around the dinner table. For his former co-writer this felt like Francis was saying:

> "I let you know why I was unhappy with you. Now that's done and now we'll just continue and have dinner together." The problem for me was that this was hard to accept ... I think he was generally annoyed that I hadn't done another book with him. He felt that I let him down on that count. We had a strong friendship, and ours was a strong intellectual encounter. In my view, sometimes you come together, and other times you move apart.

Adele saw that the damage done had been permanent.

> I don't know if they ever had any communication afterwards. Francis felt like rejected by Jeremy in some way that caused him to react this way.

Michael, felt bad for Jeremy Narby and sad that this heartfelt person who had so much compassion and a wonderful sense of humour could be "really fucking difficult to other people." He found it "remarkable that he and I never had these kinds of rows."

Rupert Sheldrake and Andrew Feldmar were other long-time friends to incur Francis' wrath. Adele thought that

> Francis had the feeling he was being talked to, rather than engaged in conversations, which was extremely important to him. He didn't care how smart you were (or) your levels of success are whatever. If you were just a narcissist, going on all morning all about your own stuff and not asking a question, like: "What about you Francis, what you think?" That dynamic was extremely important for Francis.

For Adele, Francis' rejection of old friends was disturbing, not least because "all these people were also part my life as friends." If they were no longer welcome, she and Michael would miss them. She actively sought to challenge Francis on his behaviour, asking him, with little success.

> "Why are you no longer engaging with your long-time friends. What ends a relationship. Surely, even if they've done something to you to insult you

or ignore you. Whatever it is, is it worth breaking the connection?" He would just stonewall me. He would say nothing to the point, he wouldn't engage around this. A field sample: A friend from Santa Fe calls Francis. Francis goes: "Who is this?" "Well, it's Victor." Francis: "What do you want?" Victor: "To see how you're doing?" Francis: "Well, it's none of your business."

Another one who remembers how he tried to distance her is Cal. How she handled him was not only a master-class in the art of being both direct and unphased by seemingly rude behaviour, but how to see past the behaviour and reach in for the person. Few of Francis' friends who felt his ire could muster this resource. Francis was in this respect perhaps a little like Laing. Once he had passed 90, the truth was that Francis could catch very little of any conversation. His hearing aids were dated and Michael's offer to get new ones was declined. At their final joint-Christmas-dinner, he said to Theodor, "since I can't really hear and follow the conversation, I prefer to talk. You can also lean back. Do enjoy talking less."

## Home care, marijuana and ghost dances

When Francis was 88 years old, Diana Conn Darling, who lives in Santa Rosa, was asked by Adele to find someone to be Francis' driver and companion. Diana decided to take the job herself.

> I would give him an opportunity to be ordinary, if he wanted to. If that turned out to be relaxing for him, it was just great. I was not quite a friend, not quite staff, but somewhere in between.[32]

For the last four years of Francis life, Diana came in two days a week, doing paid social work for Francis. She would arrive at 9 or 10 in the morning, as arranged, and hang around the cabin as Francis played solitaire or read something, after which he would take his seat in the car and be driven to Sebastopol, where he would do some shopping, mostly at Organic shops round town. At home, even when it looked chaotic, he was well organised, and did not take kindly to Diana picking up books and looking at them.

> He wanted me to leave things the way they were, because he was involved in the process ... (an) Englishmen working on his numerology thing.

His three cabin rooms were mostly, though not always, tidy and clean. Francis would buy groceries and put the vegetables down on top of previously old food, with the result that "a new life was evolving in Francis' refrigerator. He wouldn't let me clean it out. He would refuse." Adele and Michael, however, would come in, when Francis was out with Diana, and do the cleaning. In case he found out, his 'guardez le silence' saved domestic peace. He would then laugh when he discovered the outcome. Diana describes him as a very grounded, earthy person. He told her how grateful he was to Adele and Michael for taking care of him.

When Diana, as a former editor of various journals, offered to help him with his unfinished books – Adele encouraged her in this direction – in order that Francis complete his writings, he showed no interest. The only thing he was interested in was *Esmeralda Fufluns*, a story for children and grown-ups he had written and narrated in earlier years. He no longer had a recording or a copy of the script. Diana was successful in securing both for him, something which pleased him immensely. When she had a chance to finally read *Affable Savages*, she began to understand

> the magnitude of Francis' contribution to the world anthropological attitude. The shift from objects to subjects. He treated all those people, like fellow people and not exotic creatures of some kind. He got in with them and had respect for them, even if their folly is plenty.[33]

Huxley refused to take painkillers fearing the effect they would have in clouding his brain. The pains, however, grew worse with each passing year. Francis wanted to smoke a spliff every morning, just as Freud used to indulge his own daily love for cigars. The marijuana helped ease the pain caused by the tooth plate he had to wear.[34]

In the woods behind Francis' cabin is a spring, which he considered as the 'source' of the place. He would walk down the steeply wooded, meandering path, perform libations there, light a candle and do as he spiritually pleased. Cal remembers how Francis made some feather adornments and prayer sticks. In his final weeks he was unable to make any further offerings owing to the risk of a fall. Cal offered to be his emissary.

As we were chatting with Cal, along came Michael Stuart Ani, author of the book *The Ghost Dance*. That book was his key to Francis and their short friendship. Eight months before Francis died, Michael Stuart, who lived close by in Wagnon Road, brought along his book manuscript. No longer reading much, Michael read the manuscript aloud to Francis. Stuart Ani acknowledges his friend in the published book, "the ground-breaking anthropologist and co-founder of Survival International, Francis Huxley, for his deep insight into the book and my soul."[35] Together they talked passionately about their respective experiences in the Brazilian jungle, and with animated faces, would begin the incantation of native songs. They undertook a few ritual ceremonies together, with Francis saying to Michael: "Until you and I are done, I'm not going anywhere."[36]

## Recollections and farewells

Whether as uncle, godfather or family friend, Francis was at home with children. Victoria and Susie would write to him to keep him abreast of family news, as when their mother died.[37] Aldous' grandson Trevenen, talked of how great Francis was "when we were kids. I'm great with kids too. So, we have something in common, getting down to kids' level talking."[38] Susie Huxley recalls how "he was always very affectionate, but he could also be quite scary. He loved to tell stories to children."[39] Playing about was always very much a Huxley thing. Rupert Sheldrake too, praised Francis and Adel, for how funny they were with his sons Merlin and Cosmo. Cosmo experienced his father and Francis as being very close, and he had an interesting perspective, not just on their relationship but on their respective approaches to the sacred. He thought

> they represent two different ends of the spectrums. Francis was in the dark. His imagination was tickled by the dark. Whereas my dad tends to go to the light side of things. Francis had a slightly morbid sense of humour. He and my dad, they were teasing each other.[40]

Francis agreed to be godfather to Theodor's first born, Dimitrij Emanuel.[41] They would exchange cards and occasional letters, once Dimitrij was older, and Francis was in California or Santa Fe. In one of his last letters to Dimitrij, who had asked Francis about a paper he had written on Dadaism, for his A-Levels, the godfather answered:

> Yes, I know something of Dada, mostly from that book by Roger Shattuck, "The Banquet Years," and I can't say I'm surprised that dada made your energy go down, there's something hilariously self-defeating about it. And then, as you say, you've been an outsider in some ways, and none of them your doing: and how to be looking after oneself under such circumstances is no easy matter, as I know for myself & as do a lot of my friends. I'd like to see you as and when you find it possible to come visiting.[42]

Thanks to Dimitrij's insistence on visiting Francis a final time – previous visits had been during the summer months of 1995 and 1997 – the Itten Family visited for what turned out to be Francis' final Christmas celebration. Coincidentally, Dimitrij's brother, Raphael, was in Los Angeles for an exhibition of his street art, at about the same time and was also able to come. Raphael has memories about visiting Francis in Santa Fe (1995/1997),

> where we were living in this beautiful environment with him and Adele. As a child it really felt like being in a movie. Going to this area where I could recognise the authentic America with indigenous roots with all the sculptures and the landscape. Especially I remember from that trip that with Francis we build that dyke and having a horse ride in the desert.

As for Christmas 2015, it was idyllic and fairy-tale like, with Francis in that small cottage surrounded by that nature. A warm welcoming ceremony with a lot of laughter, tears, emotions great conversation and again drinks and pot. Christmas night was again incredibly hilarious, as we started at Francis' cottage, followed by a quite weird Christmas dinner.

On New Year's Day before departing, Raphael Itten recalled how

it was a great honour to have a final chat with him, showing him my animal sketchbook. I really saw and felt how fascinated he was and supported me to continue my art and maybe work with stained glass. Should I have blockages while I'm at work, it would be helpful to visit parks and zoos. "Never forget listening to enough Johann Sebastian Bach," he tipped me on this very emotional goodbye ceremony.[43]

**Fair-well**

Some people would ask Francis to come back to them in visions and let them know how life after death was. Francis was of course appalled. He said to Stuart Ani: "That's disgusting, I'm leaving. I'm not coming back." Stuart Ani was with Francis the day before he died. Adele had put a chair beside the bed.

I spoke and sang for him our chants. I thought he wasn't even there. Right before I left, his hand crept over and touched my hand. "You are such a fine gentleman, a good boy," that was the last, he said.[44]

The final night that came to Francis was nothing we can truly know of. Adele left their guest room quietly at 10 AM having spent all night with him. It was 29 October 2016, a Saturday. Back in London, it had been his favourite day of the week, a day when he would stroll around the Portobello Road flea market – a sweet must. The assembled care team including Michael, Cal and Adele, were all exhausted. Half an hour later, Francis John Heathorn Huxley died in the midst of a thunderstorm. "He was, just gone!"[45]

Francis did not miss his last boat. The following Monday the body of the late Francis Huxley had to be at the crematorium for 4 o'clock in the afternoon. The atmosphere in the house was quiet and subdued. A simple fair-well ceremony was arranged and conducted with a few other people coming along. Adele instructed Cal what objects she wished to be placed with the body in the casket. "Put the white buffalo in," Adele's voice said to her. It was a piece which had been given to Francis by a young woman, Rosily, on the occasion of her last visit, an enamelled disc of a white buffalo. It's not something Adele would have consciously thought was important. Nevertheless, it was put into the casket.

Michael put the lid on, put the casket on the back of his pickup and drove to the crematorium. When Adele picked up the ashes the following day – they were the only ashes for that one day – the mortuary attendant remarked that

*Figure 17.3* Francis' cabin in Wagnon Road and Grave 2020. Courtesy Dawn Heumann.

there was something with the body, if she would like to see it? Consenting, she was handed the aforementioned disc of the White Buffalo. On one side it used to have an enamel painted Greenland scene. The attendant asked Adele whether she knew what was on the other side. "No" was her reply. The burned disc changed hands and on the back was written, in words previously covered by enamel, "I am solid."

Besides, Francis was leaving his widely travelled Bagdad chest behind in their possession, full of photos of several Huxley lifetimes. Loren Eugen White, took back his adze he gave to Francis in 1984, melted it down and forged a fair-well shield, decorating the tombstone on the grass connecting the two cabins on Wagnon Road. David Napier's generous moving obituary[46] appeared in *The Guardian*, which had been a publishing home for over 20 years of Francis' reviews, concluding: "Above all, Francis will be remembered for his insatiable desire to know things and for his wholesome and robust laugh."[47] A longer version was published in *Anthropology Today*[48] giving due recognition to Huxley's innovative reflexive ethnography. Francis was "never one to boast about his intellectual privilege, the truth that he had these in abundance always emerged unexpectedly." Good humour was his medicine to cope with whatever life dished up, be it the ingredients for a further joke and/or a challenge to be appreciated as a gift from Fortuna. Like the poet Wordsworth, whom he admired for his industrious practice, he often longed to be the 'odd one in,' jesting, fooling, humouring and employing humour as a platform from which one could somersault through the imagination. Fun and love, were for Huxley, essential to both life and enquiry. As fully a man of his time it is also true to say that Francis was at the same time a man out of his time – perennially pursuing unconventional ideas, and exploring off the beaten track, "The very new has a strange way of looking like the very old," he had written. Perhaps he can be considered the first 'off-modern' anthropologist, one well-seasoned in the art of life and the necessity to feed the heart. His work and his approach to it deserve appreciation and have lessons to impart beyond the span of his own life. We take leave here with his final words: "Thank you, thank you! Let's go, let's go."

**Notes**

1 On 15 July 2013, Francis sent a disc with seven chapters and a covering letter to Theodor, for him and Ron to use as much as they like for The New Politics of Experience, for which he would write an endorsement. In the letter he wrote,

> for you to see for yourself what remains of the Mutual Self, an unsatisfactory reminder of what seemed a good idea at the time, but which 15 years later fills me with "oh deceive me," not to mention the fact that Thames & Hudson gave me an advance on the prospect of £2,000.

2 Tuesday, 29 April 1980. Francis Huxley Journals 1977–1984. FHA.
3 From 1926–1940, Graves and Riding built a joint home 'Canellun' in the early 1930s.
4 Letter to Theodor Itten on 19 November 1981.
5 Marcus Colchester interviewed in August 2018
6 David Napier interviewed in August 2018.
7 Ibid.
8 A very notable one was taking place between the 10 and 14 July 1985, in Interlaken, Switzerland, where he appeared alongside the Dalai Lama, Levin-Goldschmidt, Jean Huston, Joan Halifax, Rupert Sheldrake and Irina Tweedie. Being invited to the conferences opened up the possibility to earn some money, but Adele Getty noted "Francis never earned good money in those places, I guess about $1000. Mostly you get a paid for keeps and travel fair and you get a stipend of some kind, not enough to make a living." A. Getty interviewed in April 2018
9 Andrew Feldmar interviewed in July 2018.
10 Robin Hanbury-Tenison interviewed in January 2018.
11 Interview with Bettina and Norbert Blume in March 2018, in 31 Pond Street, London.
12 It was made in 1938, the first movie about wildlife – the Northern Gannets of Grassholm, a small, rocky islet off the western tip of Pembrokeshire, Wales – to win an Academy Award. Julian Huxley was the producer and director, and Ronald Lockley, the writer.
13 Napier, A. D. (2004) *The Righting of Passage: Perceptions of Change After Modernity*. Philadelphia. University of Pennsylvania Press.
14 Huxley, L. A. (1975), www.youtube.com/watch?v=qqKAdK29jGE (50:00 – 1:13:32).
15 Huxley, F. (1974, pp. 157–158) *The Way of the Sacred*. London, Aldus Books.

16　Jeremy Narby interviewed in February 2019.
17　"The publisher Jeremy Tarcher had asked me to write a 'Shamanism 101 reader.' '101' refers to the basic introductory university-level course in the US. An accessible but serious compilation of texts. And the 60%/40% division of proceeds was in my favour (as I was to do most of the work). The book has sold 12,000 copies in the US to this day, fewer in the UK (perhaps 2,000), with 10,000 copies in French."
18　Narby interviewed in February 2019.
19　Loren Eugen White interviewed in April 2018.
20　Michael Patrick Williams interviewed in 12 April 2018.
21　Interview with Francisco Gaona, Sebastopol, April 2018.
22　Watkins, C. (Ed.) (2011) *The American Heritage Dictionary of Indo-European Roots.* Houghton. Mifflin Harcourt.
23　Francis' interest in etymology was long standing. When Theodor left London, in the summer of 1981, he asked Francis which book he should take with him, given a choice of one when needing to flee? His reply: "Origins!" This was referring to E. Partridge's (1966) *Origins: A Short Etymological Dictionary of Modern English.* 4th Edition. London. Routledge & Keagan Paul.
24　Letter to Rodney Needham, Sebastopol, 31 January 2006. FHA.
25　Letter to Rodney Needham, Sebastopol, 31st March 2006. FHA.
26　Interview with Michael Schwab in July 2019,
27　LTI 1 January 2003, Francis uses this quote by Philander Chase Johnson from 'Shooting Stars,' a story Johnson published in Everybody's Magazine, 1920. "It sums up Ronnie's attitude too, don't you think."
28　Interview with Mina Semyon in March 2018.
29　Wilson, R. (2009, p.164) *Lewis Carroll in Numberland.* London. Penguin Books.
30　Letter to: Dear Peter Mayer, 5 December 2003.
31　Michael Patrick Williams interviewed in April 2018.
32　Diana Conn Darling interviewed in April 2018.
33　Ibid.
34　A physician's letter from Dr. P. Lovejoy dated 6 January 2014 confirms "the therapeutic value of cannabis" for the "serious medical condition" which Francis suffered from.
35　Stuart Ani, M. (2017, p.278) *The Ghost Dance – An Untold History of the Americas.* San Bernadino. Penoaks.
36　Michael Stuart Ani interviewed in April 2018.
37　Victoria's card to Francis from 2 February 2016, with the Commemoration Programme of the life of Ann Huxley, 2 November 1920–2 January 2016. FHA
38　Trevenen Huxley interviewed in April 2018.
39　Susie Huxley interviewed in March 2018. She fondly remembers when Francis came back from his travels, showing her, Lucinda and Victoria, spears, headdresses and voodoo artefacts.
40　Interview with Cosmo Sheldrake in March 2018.
41　Born in 17 December 1981, the year Theodor returned to Switzerland.
42　Letter from Francis, Santa Fe, 15 November 2004. FHA.
43　Memories of Francis, Raphael Itten, 16 October 2017.
44　Michael Stuart Ani interviewed in April 2018.
45　"I have to say, when Francis died, he was just gone." Adele Getty interviewed in April 2018.

46 The *Daily Telegraph* promised to print an obituary written by Theodor but missed the right time and let it lay. 16 January 2017.
47 Napier, A. D. (2016, p.37) Francis Huxley – Anthropologist and Writer Fascinated by Myth and Shamanism. Obituary. *The Guardian*, Wednesday, 21 December.
48 Napier, A. D. (2017, pp.28–29) Francis Huxley (1923–2016). Obituary. *Anthropology Today*, 33(1), February.

# 18 Francis Huxley and the human condition

> Francis Huxley was the most intellectually adventurous person that I've ever met.
>
> (David Napier)[1]

When Francis Huxley died in October 2016, his life and work left behind a string of unanswered questions, questions which in many ways his life had posed. How then to sum up his life's achievements and/or the achievements of a lifetime such as his? Huxley – the "feral intellectual" as he was described – was enormously quizzical about the human condition. He, like others before him, was aware of the inadequacies of any one discipline to confront it. Many commonly suppose – wrongly so – that psychology is best fitted for the academic study of human beings. But those of us within it know only too well its shortcomings. Chief among these, as Svetlana Boym suggested, was that it lacks the time and space within it to tell nuanced individual stories. Both the time and the space have been subverted by the imperative to be both quintessentially scientific and respectable to the dictates of the academic cum corporate marketplace. To be sure, storytelling can still be found amongst its ranks – located as often as not amongst the marginalised, struggling to have their voices heard and their existence recognised – but an additional issue is the nature of the stories which beg to be told – and what contexts they are sheltered within. As one further extends the boundaries within which tales are told, psychological enquiry comes increasingly to resemble social anthropology and its preferred strategy of reductionism becomes less and less successful.

Social anthropology itself, Huxley intuited, needed a narrative psychological dimension more than it required a mathematical one and sought wherever possible to supply it. "God," he wrote, "as William Blake remarked, is not a mathematical diagram."[2] In some respects, trapped within the intellectual fashions of the day, psychoanalysis was entertained as that dimension, capable of supplying the unconscious gel that would bind together healing rituals, religion, the symbolism of the sacred, family structure, the sexual politics of human groups and, finally, the body as the mediator for the journey undertaken by thought from the murky depths of the unconscious into the full blossom of social life. The figure of the shaman perhaps personified better than any other, this bond between the subterranean chaos of the mind and the terrestrial well-being of the social group. But a key function of the shaman, no less vital than the ritually ordained mystical voyage into mental worlds unchartered by Western science, concerns attending to, transforming and healing the social and individual wounds of community members, and at some risk to the shaman. The cosmic elements which are brought into active play in the course of ritual are simultaneously symbolic and actual, agents of transformation which cross the Cartesian divide and bridge the gaps – as we perceive them – between mind and body, the present and the past, the material world and the spirit world. Because of this ability to unify, what to us cannot be unified, shamanism was of fundamental interest to Huxley, who recognised not only the need for social anthropology to systematically engage with the subject of disordered minds and alternative mental states, but to do so that it may bring back something of value for us to reckon with in our own blighted realms of personal and social fragmentation.

Unusual for an anthropologist of his time, Huxley had no interest in utilising Western colonialist categories of thought in order to mould the customs, habits and practices of other cultures into a form suitable for assimilation into the preferred cerebral comforts of our own world. He saw it as his task to adapt to the mental templates of others and to see the world through their eyes. Laing described the terror which people may have of what their own and others' psyches may produce as 'psycho-phobia' – something which he thought was a characteristic of most psychiatrists. For Huxley, the remedy for such psycho-phobia was not only to embrace others' ways of seeing, but to travel in altered states of consciousness, one form of which, he considered madness to be. This he practiced first hand, and in both therapeutic and informal contexts assisted others to safely do likewise, exercising at all times due care. To embrace others' ways of seeing however entails more than just a shift in perspective. It is a political act which works in two directions. It questions the validity of the opposition between self/us and other, for by embracing the position of the 'othered' it ceases to be 'other,' simultaneously marking the dissolution of the familiar comforts of 'home.'

Viewed in relation to psychological crises, breakdowns or breakthroughs, the shamanic ritual is a promise to rectify what cannot otherwise be rectified within the given cosmic order. The promise to heal, rather than the mere hope of it, is almost, though not entirely, absent in psychotherapeutic culture – a reason both why traditional psychiatry is "toxic" as Peter Breggin[3] described it and why Western culture is almost devoid of shamans, save of course the growing business of neo-shamanic cults, devoid of any set cosmology and lacking any tribal context. The adherence to an extreme form of materialism is also a factor here. Medicine and psychoanalysis/psychotherapy nevertheless remain our only cultural cousins to shamanism – possessing a ritual/sociological structure delineating a rite of passage to and from distress. The potential path from chaos and despair to order and hope is enshrined within it. Before one even considers the 'ritual' insults which comprise treatments within biologically oriented psychiatry, however, the profession falls at the first hurdle with its regular pronouncements that certain conditions are 'life-long,' 'intractable' or 'resistant to treatment' and that people who have been seriously traumatised will invariably be 'scarred for life.' Throughout, any failure to heal is located in the intransigent other, never the putative healer of the mind – neither the way of the shaman, nor of the warrior. In shamanism a failure to heal may entail the shaman paying with their life!

Shamanism also speaks to the fragility of the human condition, our vulnerability to dislocation, grief, threat, illness, pain, madness and death. That the shamanic voice can cast its net so widely is not merely because shamans wield an "ensemble of techniques for knowing," but because they are "sophisticated producers of meaning."[4] Rationalism and its partner in dogmatic crime, individualism, in the guise of striving for self-sufficiency, decision-making command and control are not only in denial of this, they have failed to offer a satisfactory 'Weltanschauung' that gives meaning and purpose to life. In both the symbolic and the real world, we, all human beings, *are* in need of all the help we can get, something Francis Huxley easily recognised. It is in hindsight that one sees his meeting with the maverick Scottish psychoanalyst R. D. Laing as almost inevitable – their two paths destined to merge. But there are other reasons *that* meeting of minds also seems pre-destined, which we shall come to shortly.

But if Huxley's twinning of the 'anthropologised' and othered with madness was bold, there is a very real sense, hardly a surprising one, in which it did not go far enough. Huxley certainly challenged the colonial imprint abroad, though its domestic variant, racism at home, went unrecognised, untheorised and unchallenged throughout the entire radical movement to oppose institutional psychiatry. Awareness of the pernicious effects of racism was, during the 1960s, largely confined to its victims and yet there is also a real sense in which an opportunity was missed. At the Dialectics of Liberation conference in 1968 in which Huxley, Laing and David Cooper were visibly present, the Black Power advocate Stokely Carmichael spoke of the "mental violence" and "psychological murder" inflicted by the White West – not just on the peoples of Africa, but on Black Americans in the USA and their consequent need to develop a "revolutionary" and "resistance" consciousness to oppose both their external oppression and their internalisation of it.[5] Carmichael was clear, that by opposition to the violence, he didn't meant adjustment to it. Despite this, the sources of 'psychiatric' disturbance were predominantly theorised in terms of existential-phenomenological and familial influences, stretching in Laing's case to an awareness that the wider systems in which family life was embedded, including the global capitalist system were an integral part of the context. Carmichael insisted that what he was talking about was "a system of international white supremacy coupled with international capitalism."[6]

Racism thus remained 'beyond words' and far from 'obvious' to those crusading against psychological despair and psychiatric tyranny.[7] Laing's key intuition that he was involved in the study of situations, not individuals, and Huxley's insight that there were meanings of madness which could usefully be imported from abroad somehow were unable to effectively come together – perhaps because both were already fully occupied, fighting against their own effective marginalisation from their respective host disciplines, psychiatry and anthropology. In this context we may better understand why Huxley's contribution to the Philadelphia Association, to some extent, went under the radar. Francis was otherwise well-equipped to make the leap, and was acutely aware of the misgivings which had emerged in the 1960s. He was appreciative of Talal Asad's *Anthropology and the Colonial Encounter*,[8] and took a strong independent line rooted in a democratic ethos, a line which would bear later fruit. Toni Morrison, some years later summed up what had been overlooked. "The trauma of racism is, for the racist and the victim" she wrote, "the severe fragmentation of the self, and has always seemed to me a cause (not a symptom) of psychosis."[9]

Even with the added parameters, which Freud and his heirs supplied to the anthropological enterprise then, something profoundly important was missing from it. The failure to explicitly map racism was not the only problem. Huxley's Oxford talk on 'Anthropology and Psychoanalysis' highlighted a number of excesses in the psychoanalytic universe which led to problems in the relationship between the two fields – prominent among them, Freud's insistence on the universality of the Oedipus complex. Although sympathetic, Francis had no hesitation in labelling psychoanalysis a "caricature of … a philosophical system"[10] which had logical inconsistencies with anthropology. A critical dimension, for both Huxley and Laing, was the necessity to add a practical political element to what they were critiquing. This practical engagement would occupy them both for years.

Laing and Huxley were also able to intuit that while the facts of life appear plain enough from a distance – we are born, we age, love, mate, work, play, fight, create and eventually die – these facts do not so much define us as a species as highlight the biological, social, emotional and creative imperatives which fine tune our existence. Some facts – love, sex, birth and death – in their intangible enormity, point to an inescapably spiritual aspect to being human, as well as provide the ontological edifice on which psychoanalysis was arguably erected. For ineffable mystery, politics and the ontology of unending change, however, psychoanalysis substituted the failed aesthetics of a predictable clockwork biology, predicated on Newtonian mechanics. It did so for reasons which continue to haunt intellectual endeavour in the modern academy – the craving for acceptance in the halls of establishment thought. Perhaps more than most, Huxley was acutely aware that shamanism is anchored in a fundamentally different view of reality that favoured in Western epistemologies. To his credit, he was prepared to work with the ambiguities which come from living and practising in two seemingly incompatible systems.

As for all these facts, contingencies and wonders we encounter, we do so as an organism with an evolved, highly complex sensibility, equipped to utilise our curiosity and capacity to question what we see around us, and intrinsic to the quality of life which is possible. Endowed with this, we are unavoidably tasked with making sense, imposing an order of meaning, on the changing world, landscapes, people and relationships that make up the journey. Our fledgling individual attempts to craft meaning out of this are paralleled by the intellectual, psychological and artistic challenges to make sense of the human condition in its entirety – where all these individual strivings merge into a collective whole, a puzzle bound by geographical, cultural and historical variations; nothing less than the full range of conditions in which we humans are present, and both shape and in turn are shaped by the world.

What Huxley and Laing both realised is that essential as such disciplined attempts are, they necessarily come up short in the face of the inexplicable givens of our existence – both material and existential; what Rebecca Solnit described as "the mystery in the middle of the room, the secret in the mirror ... what has been there all along."[11] We must confront this fact of the world and our own presence in it as ultimately mysterious and that an awareness of this sublime mystery is one of the conditions of being. Many writers have referenced the celebration of this as underpinning what Abraham Maslow called peak emotional experiences. For Baudelaire, it was "the fantastic reality of life," for Boym, "the ordinary marvellous," for Arendt, the "miracle" of freedom and for Benjamin "the renewal of existence in a hundred unfailing ways."[12] The mysterious nature of being may also lie behind Freud's concept of the uncanny, a realisation of the fundamental strangeness of existing in the world.

Within the broader mystery of the fact of existence, outlined above, are attendant others; our experiential entry and exit points from the world vis-à-vis the birth and presumed death of consciousness, the nature of experienced time and the place of love in the fabric of the world. These are central to our experience and understanding of life and cannot be resolved by rational means alone – they rather invite an engagement with one's total being, one that in Huxley's words "must be acted out in order to be experienced and experienced if one is to make it one's own."[13] In several works he dived headlong into these waters, charting the symbolic roadmaps of world culture and documenting its riches without ever seeking to reduce the map to the semblance of anything more rudimentary. The mysterious, though soaked in the world of appearance, is not synonymous with it. Huxley's charting of divine iconography and mythic symbolism stands as his answer to the question – what is the world? It is the world, ready-made, and replete with its own history and people that we encounter when we are thrust into the world newly born; a phenomenology of human sacred symbolism.

The requisite attitude behind a good deal of Huxley's work is thus a reverence for the unknown, an attitude that is antithetical to the epistemologies currently ordained and worshipped in the church of academia. Huxley's respect for indigenous peoples, their right to define their own life in the way they choose, their right to be heard, for their voices to be carried into Western academic and political discourse speaks of a demand for knowledge to be allied to justice. Huxley also accorded people the right to experience the world in a manner consistent with their own customs. Though we now consider it a distinctly post-modern slant, Huxley long saw a place for granting different cosmologies rights of co-existence. Raised as he was in the socially privileged bosom of the Huxley clan, educated at Gordonstoun School and Oxford University, the distance he covered intellectually and emotionally, in rejecting the ideologically constructed norms which bolster the mirage of Western superiority cannot be underestimated. A substantial part of this book has been devoted to unravelling the matrix of intellectual, emotional and social possibilities which are passed from one generation to another. For Huxley, as for all of us, escaping that web is impossible but weakening and mitigating its effects in some directions is not. We can cultivate how to live within the strictures of the given, choose to some extent, using one's inbuilt and acquired resources, what outside influences may enter. He rejected aspects of eugenic thought which his favoured uncle and father endorsed; challenged, both in his narrative anthropology and with the creation of Survival International, some of the cultural accoutrements of colonialism and white supremacy; rejected the monotheistic centrepiece of respectable English society; stood apart from the scientism of his esteemed father and the literary bolthole of his uncle and tried to forge his own way in the world.

Huxley challenged the instrumental bent of knowledge in another crucial manner. His LSD experiences accorded love a pivotal place in the human place in the cosmos. Like Chagall, he believed "the meaning of life and art" was "provided by the colour of love."[14] One can too easily dismiss this as a hangover from the pop philosophy which coursed through the veins of the 1960s. One should look past such fashionable dismissal. Huxley was extremely well-read in cultural anthropology and comparative religious thought as well as the extant literature on psychedelia, and did not make his pronouncements lightly. He was drawing attention to an experiential truth which has pervaded world thought for millennia; one which may be as crucial for our own survival and the well-being of the biosphere as the material logistics of selfishness, promoted under conditions of extreme capitalism as a central plank of neo-Darwinian thought. What Darwin imputed into nature, for all its genius, Huxley intuited as coming from Darwin's own masculine-tinged view of the world. Huxley was strongly influenced by the suffering his mother endured in her marriage and took a keen interest in the iniquities which women in the world faced. Unlike many men of his time, he was domestically cultivated, did his own chores and promoted a feminine aesthetic. For him, this meant an artistic, even existential appreciation of nature was needed to compliment the excesses of an impersonal view of the natural world. With the intellectual heritage of his great-grandfather weighing heavily on his shoulders, Francis used his anthropological experience and awareness of the often, personal nature of

### Francis Huxley and the human condition 271

non-Western cosmologies, to balance the formative Huxley picture. His essay on Darwin remains bold, original and fully contemporary for our age.

Perhaps what may be most important in understanding Francis Huxley, the man, from an anthropological perspective is an awareness that his own life unfolded from a central point within a mythical structure – that mythos, the all-embracing grand narrative, being the unquestioned positing of the entire Huxley family as a repository of hereditary intellectual genius. The potent symbols of this myth, we might surmise, comprise the collected works of T. H. Huxley, Julian, Aldous and Andrew, but more important than these are the strength of the circulating beliefs which testify to the family genius – and for these we have a host of powerful social institutions and artefacts to bolster the belief. Our research for this book suggests that for several generations, members of the Huxley family have been subject to the pressures of this mythical canon.

Francis, throughout his life, exhibited a deep fascination with masks, those he brought back from his field studies – which he hung on his wall – and those he made. He tried on various occasions to enlighten other family members to their other-worldly allure, not always with success it must be said. Victoria Huxley, his niece, recalled Francis putting them into play during games of charades. She found it "frightening." Francis' fascination however was shared by David Napier, whose PhD thesis, *The Interpretation of Masks*, he examined. The wearing of a mask performs multiple functions. In the first place the mask represents an 'other' that cannot be directly seen but whose influence (real or imagined) pervades a community and pervades it often through the production of fear. Secondly, masks hide what can be seen – they occlude the face of the person wearing it. In both instances the mask marks a boundary between what is known and what can only be inferred. To put on a mask is to undergo a personal transformation in which one becomes the unknown/feared other. One may suppose that in such role-playing, the wearing of masks marks the beginning of theatre.[15] Within this theatrical arena, masks not only signify and comment on the nature of identity, they provide a forum for hiding intentions as well as identity. This is principally because unlike a living human face, the facial features of a mask are essentially frozen, unchanging in the 'face' of the dynamic reality they inhabit.

Such disguised intentions and identities have a long history as perceived threats to ruling elites. In the late 18th century, the Carnival of Venice was outlawed and the use of masks rendered strictly forbidden. In our own times political demonstrators wear masks to evade identification from mass surveillance, while the politicians they disdain adopt their own form of camouflage according to their publicity consultants. The masquerade, furthermore, provides a commentary of sorts on the philosophical conundrum of what is real or actual versus what merely represents or disguises the real. The issue of what masks a person wears crops up repeatedly in psychotherapy. The issue is inseparable from the question of authenticity. Psychotherapy, when it is effective and sufficient safety is in play, permits the gradual uncloaking or 'demasking' of a client's defences until a naked 'original' face is free to be displayed. The removal of one's defences may be experienced as a form of death and hence the death mask may symbolically represent a version of the self that is felt to be closest to home.[16] It is of more than passing interest that an iconic figure in US popular culture – the Joker/clown is so often paired with chaos, death and destruction. From its beginnings in ancient theatre, the art of masquerade – the human play on illusion, delusion and reality – has developed to such a point that in the 21st century it has taken on its most unsettling and destabilising form – the simulation of reality – or even as Baudrillard argued – the murder of reality.[17]

In the context within which this biography is situated, the mask or 'persona'[18] of the Huxley 'tribe' is to display intellectual standing, worthy of the family name. With the Huxleys, the identifying mask is supplied by society – the name itself is taken as sufficient evidence of what lies beneath it, no evidence necessarily required. And yet, as Napier argued, the mask-wearer is at the centre of a paradox. One carries the mark/mask of distinction – the Huxley name – whilst sooner or later the wearer fears that forthcoming evidence of its veracity may be required. Francis' ambiguous relationship with academia, his skirting around what Rupert Sheldrake referred to as the central theoretical and metaphysical dilemmas could in the present light be construed as a form of protective self-sabotage to avoid being judged.

Masks then, as icons, can be representative and protective, but also persecutory. No wonder Francis saw his membership of the family as some kind of curse, even as it opened doors of opportunity. Perhaps buried within the mythos of the Huxleys lies a deep desire, a dream of a return to normal life – "a thirst for the ordinary life of an ordinary person"[19] – one essentially publicly uncategorised – one from which they sprang, before T. H. Huxley's dream time exploded everything. How hard or impossible must it be, to be oneself authentically, to be "a different sort of person" to the one whose life has been dreamed by others when one awakens to life, living within a nexus of other dreamed people and their beliefs.[20]

Francis was at times aware that he was trapped, and in various ways sought to escape. In many ways his life is a calling card to abandon the traditional premises on which intellectual merit is assessed and on which higher education is founded. In an earlier work, one of us (RR) called for psychology to be reimagined as a form of enquiry into the human condition.[21] One can imagine a similar clarion call for an anthropology of the future, in which investigators' researches are fully embedded in their own conditions of living. In hindsight one can see Huxley's life and work, as a fully lived enquiry into the conditions of his own existence – familial, cultural, symbolic and religious, a self-designed anthropological programme pursued largely outside of academia. Its outcome is an answer to the twin questions of 'what is the nature of the world?' and 'how do I wish to be known in it?' One can posit this exploration as one's own declaration that without oneself, the world would be incomplete!

Part of his own educational deprogramming in this regard was aided by the prior psychedelic experimentation of his uncle, Aldous, though Francis took these experiments substantially further and saw greater significance in the worlds which might be revealed in the pharmacologically discoverable hinterlands of the mind. He extended his own re-programming as a resource to others, practising teaching by apprenticeship, paying careful attention to experience. All this begs important questions regarding the pursuit of knowledge. Just what kind of knowledge, what kind of enquiry, what programs of learning, what kinds of academics and researchers subscribing to what kinds of values do we want? Does it all have to be safe, obedient, careful, following laid down procedures, capable of guaranteeing pre-ordained results within a specified time period? If so, it will remain the case that the existential and metaphysical dimensions of our existence, not to mention truly liberating commentary or art, will remain off-limits from the academy. Then, there will be no place for the Francis Huxley's of this world and any vision for what the fruits of intellectual life can deliver will be correspondingly diminished.

## Notes

1. Interview with David Napier in August 2018.
2. Ibid., p.6.
3. Breggin, P. (1991) *Toxic Psychiatry*. New York. St. Martin's Press.
4. See Huxley, F. and Narby, J. (2001, p.6) *Shamans through Time*. London. Thames and Hudson.
5. Stokely Carmichael (1968) Black Power. In *The Dialectics of Liberation*. Ed. David Cooper. Harmondsworth. Penguin.
6. Ibid., p.150.
7. 'The Obvious' and 'Beyond Words' were contributions to the conference by Laing and Cooper respectively.
8. See Assad (1973).
9. Toni Morrison (2019, p.177) *Mouth Full of Blood*. London. Chatto & Windus.
10. Huxley, F. (1985, pp.130–151) Psychoanalysis and Anthropology. In *Freud and The Humanities*. Ed. P. Horden. London. Duckworth.
11. Solnit (2006, p.202).
12. See Boym (2005, p.583); Baudelaire, C. (2010, p.20) *The Painter of Modern Life*. London. Penguin; Benjamin, W. (1999, p.63) *Illuminations*. London. Pimlico.
13. Huxley, F. (1974, p.31) *The Way of the Sacred*. London. Aldus Books.
14. Marc Chagall quoted in *Newsweek* (1985), 8 April.
15. See Napier, A. D. (1986) *Masks, Transformation and Paradox*. London. University of California Press.
16. Wilhelm Reich contended that one's psychic and bodily defences are effectively the same. The job of the psychotherapist, in Reich's view, was to break down one's physical bodily armour wherein emotional pain was stored in the form of rigid muscular tensions.
17. See Baudrillard, J. (2008) *The Perfect Crime*. London. Verso.
18. In Ancient Greece, the persona was a mask used in theatre to denote a character. Our contemporary notion of personality as what is essentially true of a person, therefore reflects an inversion of the original meaning of the word.

19 The sentiments of Chekhov's narrator in his novella *The Story of a Nobody*. See Checkov, A. (2012, p.92) *The Story of a Nobody*. Richmond. Alma Books.
20 "A different sort of person" – Chekhov (2012, p.8)
21 Laing engaged for a year in a spirited attempt to render the human sciences more artful. A favoured play on words of his was whether the attempt to understand human beings might swing from being 'truthful' to 'trothful' – i.e. from one rooted in facts to one faithful to the human condition.

# Appendix 1: Huxley's bibliography

## Books

1956 *Affable Savages* – An Anthropologist Among the Urubu Indians of Brazil. Rupert Hart-Davis, London.
1957 Scientific Book Club, Hardcover. London.
1957 The Travel Book Club, Hardcover. London.
1957 The Viking Press, New York.
1958 Prijazni Divljaci (*Affable Savages*. Translated by Konstantin Milles) Epoha Zagreb.
1960 Amiables Sauvages. Traduit de l'anglais par Monique Lévi-Strauss. Plon, Paris.
1960 The Travel Book Club, Hardcover. London.
1961 Second Edition. Prijazni Divljaci – Il izdanje. Epoha Zagreb.
1963 A Harvest Book, Paperback. London.
1963 Selvagens amávei. um antropologista entre os indios Urubus do Brasil. (Translated by Japi Freire). Companhia Editora Nacional, São Paulo.
1966 Capricorn Books Edition, New York.
1973 Aimables sauvages. Couverture rigide. Terre Humaine. Plon, Paris.
1980 Aimable sauvages, Hardcover. 2nd Edition. Terre Humaine. Plon, Paris.
1985 Poche, Paperback. Plon, Paris.
1995 Sheffield Publications, Salem, Wisconsin.
2010 Affable Souvages. Lire F. Huxley aujourd'hui, par Pascal Dibi. Bibliotheque Terre Humane, Plon, Paris.
1964 **Peoples of the World**. Blandford Press, London. Reprinted, 1971, 1975.1964 Littlehampton Book Services Ltd, Chester Springs, Pennsylvania.
1964 A Sun book paperback. Walker Publisher.
1965 *Les peuples de la Terre*. Fernand Nathan. Paris.
1966 **The Invisibles**. Rupert Hart-Davies, London.
1969 *The Invisibles – Voodoo Gods in Haiti*. First US edition published by McGraw-Hill. New York.
1973 **Tribes of the Amazon Basin in Brazil 1972**. (with E. Brooks, R. Fuerst, and J. Hemming), Hardcover & Paperback. Charles Knight & Co. London.

1974 Hardcover, Transatlantic Arts. London.
1974 Doubleday and Company. First US edition.
1974 *The Way of the Sacred.* Aldus & Jupiter Books, London.
1976 Paperback. A Laurel Edition. Dell. New York.
1977 *Sagrado e o Profano. Duas Faces da Mesma Moeda.* tradução de Raul José de Sá Barbosa. Rio de Janeiro. Editora Primo.
1978 *Symbolen Van Het Mysterie.* Amsterdam Boek.
1989 Hardcover. Bloomsbury Books. London.
1976 Harper & Row. New York.
1976 *The Raven and the Writing Desk.* Thames and Hudson. London.
1979 Collier Books, Macmillan, Inc., New York & Canada.
1979 *The Dragon – Nature of Spirit, Spirit of Nature.* Thames and Hudson. London.
1980 Star Book Paperback, W. H. Allen & Co. London.
1982 Japanese Edition. Heibonsha. Tokio.
1989 *El dragón. naturaleza del espíritu, espíritu de la naturaleza.* Debate. Madrid.
1992, 1994 reprints.
1989 *Mitos Dioses Misterios – El Dragon.* Mercado Libre. ediciones del prado, Hardcover. Argentina & Mexico.
1990 *The Eye – The Seer and the Seen.* Thames and Hudson. London.
1992 *L'Oeil – Mythes et metamorphoses.* Seuil. Paris.
1992 *Me no sekai gekijō. seisei o utsusu kagami.* Japanese Edition, Translation by Hiroshi Takayama. Heibonsha. Tokio.
1997 *Dragão – Natureza do Espírito, Espírito da Natureza.* Rio de Janeiro. Del Prado.
2001 **Shamans Trough Time** *– 500 Years on the Path to Knowledge.* (Ed. with J. Narby) J. P. Tarcher/Putnam, New York/Thames and Hudson. London.
2002 *Chamanes – Cinq cents ans sur la piste du savoir.* Editions Albin Michel. Paris.
2005 *Chamanes a través de los tiempos. Quinientos años en la senda del conocimiento.* Biblioteca de la Nueva Conciencia. Barcelona.
2005 *Samanok.* Hungarian Translation. Budapest. General Press Kiado.
2009 *Anthologie du chamanisme. Cinq cents ans sur la piste du savoir.* Editions Albin Michel. Paris.
2017 *Chuan yue shi guang de Saman. tong wang zhi shi de wu bai nian zhi lü.* Translation by Jie Yuan. Chines. Bejing.
2018 *Anthologie du chamanisme.* Reissue, A.M. ESP.LIBRE.

**Translations**

1962 *Africa Before the White Man.* Translated from French by Francis Huxley. Labouret, Henri (1946) L 'Afrique precoloniale. Walker. New York. Published simultaneously in Canada by George J. McLeod, Limited, Toronto.1963 Reprint Hardcover.

1963 *The Origins of Life.* Translated from French by Francis Huxley. Jules Carles (1950) Les origines de la vie. Walker and Company. New York. Published simultaneously in Canada by George J. McLeod, Limited, Toronto.

**Unpublished book manuscripts (Francis Huxley Archive)**

1957 *Darwin Film.* Planned together with Ellen Huxley for National Educational TV.
1965 *Body and Mind in Anthropology.*
1977 *Embryos and Ancestors.*
1978/2003 *Forty Two.*
1988 *Aldous – A Film about the Life of Aldous Huxley* (with Mary Pjerrou).
1997 *The Mutual Self.*
1998 *A Huxley Family Album.*

**Book chapters**

1961 Marginal Lands of the Mind. In *The Humanist Frame.* Ed. Julian Huxley, pp.169–179, George Allen & Unwin. London.
1961 States of Suggestibility. Conference on Parapsychology and Psychedelics (November 1958, New York) Parapsychology Foundation, Inc. The Colonial Press. Clinton. Massachusetts, pp.19–21.
1961 Increases in Awareness and Suggestibility. Conference on Parapsychology and Psychedelics (July 1959, St. Paul de Vence, Fr) Parapsychology Foundation, Inc. The Colonial Press. Clinton. Massachusetts, pp.72–73.
1962 Who and Why? In *What is the Human Race up to?* Ed. N. Mitchinson. pp.273–288. Victor Gollancz. London.
1963 The Religious Significance of Experience under Hallucinogenic Drugs. In *Hallucinogenic Drugs and Their Psychotherapeutic Use.* Ed. Crocket, R. et al. pp.174–178. Charles C. Thomas. Springfield.
1967 Anthropology and ESP. In *Science and ESP.* Ed. J. R. Smythies. pp.281–302. Routledge and Kegan Paul. London.
1970 Which May Never Have Existed. In *Claude Lévi-Strauss – The Anthropologist as Hero.* Ed. E. N. Hayes. pp.61–69. MIT Press. Cambridge. Massachusetts.
1971 Anthropologe und Psychologe im Kreuzverkehr – Francis Huxley und Max Lüscher. In *Rauschmittel und Süchtigkeit.* Ed. Gottlieb Duttweiler Institute. pp.133–139. Herbert Lang. Bern.
1971 Experimente mit Halluzinogenen. In *Rauschmittel und Süchtigkeit.* Ed. Gottlieb Duttweiler Institute. pp.89–94. Herbert Lang. Bern.
1974 Die Frage der Erhaltung der menschlichen Kulturen. In (Ed. Rivière) *Südamerika – Die Völker der Welt.* Europa Verlag, Zurich. pp.8–11.

1975 The Body and the Play within the Play. In *The Anthropology of the Body*. Ed. J. Blacking. pp.29–38. Academic Press. London.

1982 Beschouwingen bij de Werking van de P. A.-London. In *Stratategie Van De Kleinschaligheid*. Ed. E. Pennen. pp.148–153. K. U. Leven. Flanders. Belgium.

1985 Psychoanalysis and Anthropology. In *Freud and the Humanities*. Ed. P. Horden. pp.130–151. Duckworth. London.

2005 Shamanism, Healing and R. D. Laing. In *R. D. Laing – Contemporary Perspective*. Ed. S. Raschid. pp.179–198. Free Association Books. London.

2007 Shamans through Time. Tricksters, Healers, Voodoo Priests and Anthropologist (with J. Narby and J. Mohawk) In *Visionary Plant Consciousness. The Shamanic Teachings of the Plant World*. Ed. J. P. Harpignies. pp.24–38. Park Street Press. Rochester.

2012 The Liberating Shaman of Kingsley Hall. In *R. D. Laing 50 Years since The Divided Self*. Ed. T. Itten and C. Young. pp.283–285. PCCS Books. Ross-on Wye.

**Articles (incomplete)**

1947 Nesting and Breeding Habits. Birds of Jan Mayen. Oxford Goes Exploring.

1949 The Oxford Viewpoint Journal, by Francis Huxley, Peter Heyworth Bernard Smith.

1949 Exploration in Gambia. *The Geographical Magazine* 22, pp.271–277.

1951 Os indios do Maranhao e do Pará. Palavras de um etnologo – Histori as de um indio loiro e um ataque nao realizado. *A Gazeta*, Sao Paulo. 21 December.

1951 Resenha de "A Organização Social dos Tupinambá." *Sociologia*, 13 (3), pp.289–297.

1952 The Affaire Guajaja. *World Review*, August, pp.35–47.

1953 In the Brazilian Jungle. *The Geographical Magazine*, 1st March 1953 pp.553–563.

1955 The Rawdon Syrinx. *Liverpool Bulletin*. 5 (1/2), p.17.

1959/1960 Charles Darwin – Life and Habit. *American Scholar*, 29 (1), pp. 85–93.

1959 The Miraculous Virgin of Guadalupe. *International Journal of Parapsychology*, 1, pp.19–29.

1960 Substance and Method in Zen Practice. *International Journal of Parapsychology*, II (2), Spring 1960.

1963 Haiti Chérie. *The Geographical Magazine*, 36 (2), pp.69–83.

1966 The Body and the Mind. *R. D. Laing Collection, Special Collections Department, University of Glasgow Library*, MS Laing L 226.

1966 The Ritual of Voodoo and the Symbolism of the Body. *Philosophical Transactions of RS*, London, 251 (772), pp.423–427.

1967 Stop/Go with LSD – Behind Every Work of Art Lies the Human Body. *The Geographical Magazine*, 40, pp.17–18.
1970 An Antidote to Lévi-Strauss. *Encounter*, 34 (5), May, pp.71–77.
1972 Madness and Mysticism – Comments. *Contact* 38, Summer 1972, pp.12–14, University of Edinburgh.
1974 Where the Map is the Territory. *Theoria to Theory*, 8 (1), pp.289–301.
1980 Charles Darwin – Life and Habit. Part I & II. *Theoria to Theory*, 14, pp.27–42, 107–124.
1992 World Culture. *International Synergy Journal*, Santa Fe. 6 (2), pp.5–10.
1993 Und redet wie ein Drache. *Manuskripte – Zeitschrift für Literatur*, 33 (121), pp.50–58.

## Thesis

1949 The Social Mechanism of a South American Tribe. An account of marriage, war and exchange among the Tupi-Guarani of Brazil, with comparisons drawn from South American Tribes. Thesis presented for the degree of Bachelor of Science at the University of Oxford. p.108. Unpublished. FHA.

## Poems (incomplete)

1950 Marco Polo. *World Review*, October, p.50.
1950 Poem. *World Review*, October, p.30.

## Forewords

1993 Foreword. In *Star Warrior, The Story of Swiftdeer*. Bear & Company. Rochester.
1997 Foreword. In A. Getty, *A Sense of the Sacred*. pp.VI–VIII. Taylor. Dallas, TX.
1998 Praise for *The Cosmic Serpent* by Jeremy Narby. J. P. Tarcher/Putnam. New York.
1999 Aldous. In *Aldous Huxley Recollected*, by Dunaway, D. K., Preface pp.v–xiii, Alta Mira Press, Sage. Walnut Creek.
1999 Foreword to "Dear Juliette." In *Letters of May Sarton to Juliette Huxley*. pp.13–16, Ed. Susan Sherman. W. W. Norton & Company. New York.

## Reviews (incomplete)

1955 The Taming of the Demons. *African Folktales and Sculpture*, by Paul Radin, Elinore Marvel and James Johnson Sweeney. *Encounter*, April, pp.83–84.
The Endless Worm. *The Return of the King*, by J. R. R. Tolkien. *The New Statesman and Nation*, 50, 5 November, pp.587–588.

## Appendix 1

1960 Frazer within the Bloody Wood. *The Golden Bough*, by James George Frazer. *The New Statesman*, 16 April, p.561.

1961 *Clinical Theology*, by Frank Lake. DLT. *Contact*, 19, January, pp.30–32.

1963 All Done with Mirrors. *The Ambidextrous Universe*, by Martin Gardner. Allan Lane. *The New Statesman*, 40.
Light Through Darkness, by Henry Michaux. *The New Statesman*, No. 31.
Phallic Fungus. *The Sacred Mushroom and the Cross*, by John Allegro. Hodder & Stoughton. *New Society*, pp.17–18.

1964 Destroyer of the Mind. *Light through Darkness*, by Henri Michaux. *The Observer*, 9 February, p.27.

1976 Ay, There's the Rub. *Life After Death*, by Arnold Toynbee and Arthur Koestler. The New Statesman, 6 August, p.183.
The Gene Machine. *Who Do You Think You Are?* by Oliver Gillie. *The New Statesman*, 19 November, pp.716–717.

1977 Prison of Thought. *Discipline and Punish*, by Michel Foucault. 24 November, p.16.

1978 A Shaman and his Circus. *The Origin of Table Manners*, by Claude Lévi-Strauss. *The Guardian*, 2 November, p.9.
Jung and some Freuds. *Jung. Man and Myth*, by Vincent Brome. *Sigmund Freud. His Life in Pictures and Words*, complied by Ernst Freud, Luci Freud and Ilse Grubrich-Simitis. *The Guardian*, 30 November, p.17.

1979 This Holy Terror. *The History of Sexuality*, by Michael Foucault. *The Sadeian Woman*, by Angela Carter. *The Guardian*, 29 March, p.10.
Dr. Dodgson and Mr. Carroll. *The Letters of Lewis Carroll*, edited by Morton Cohen, 2. Vols. *The Guardian*, 13 September, p.10.
On the Fringe. *Natural Medicine*, by Brian Inglis. *The Guardian*, 1st November.
Married to the Sphinx. *Freud, Biologist of the Mind*, by Frank J. Sulloway. Psychoanalytic Politics, by Sherry Turkle. *The Guardian*, December, p.7.

1980 A View of Dark Places. *The Return of Eva Peron*. V. S. Naipaul. *The Guardian*, 26 June, p.9.
Beastly Welfare. *Great Zoos and the World, Their Origin and Significance*, edited by Lord Zuckermann. Sunday Times, 1st June.
Thirsting for the Absolute. *Bricks to Babel* by Arthur Koestler. *The Guardian*, 30 November.

1981 One Myth Only. *The Naked Man. Introduction to a Science of Mythology*, volume 4, by Claude Lévi-Strauss. *The Guardian*, 24 September, p.16.
Our Own Disease. *The Diseases of Civilisation*, by Brian Inglis. *The Guardian*, 5 November, p.18.
A Wonderland of Books. Edward Giuliano. *Lewis Carroll. An Annotated International Bibliography 1960–1977*. Harvester Press. *TLS*, November, p.1334.

1982 Anti-Psychiatry and Other Disorders. *Psycho Politics*, by Peter Sedgwick. *The Guardian*, 28 January, p.19.
No such Thing. *The Sexual Fix*, by Stephen Heath. 17 June, p.8.
1983 Raining Cats and Dogs. *Living Wonders*, by John Michell and Robert J. M. Rickard. *The Spectator*, 8 January, p.20.
Defender of the Faith. *Ernest Jones. Freud's Alter Ego*, by Vincent Brome. *The Guardian*, 3 February, p.10.
Story telling in Samoa. *Margret Mead and Samoa*, by Derek Freeman. *The Guardian*, 3 March, p.10.
In Two Minds. *A Biography of Jonathan Miller. The Guardian*, 14 April.
1984 Anthropology of Joy and Woe. *The Human Cycle*, by Colin. M. Turnbull. *The Guardian*, 22 March, p.19.
Black Blood Legacy. *The Haunted Mind*, by Hallam Tennyson. *The Guardian*, 17 May, p.18.
Good for the Soul. *The Way of the Animal Powers. Vol. 1 of the Historical Atlas of World Mythology*, by Joseph Campbell. *The Guardian*, 5 July, p.19.

## Obituary

1989 Liberating Shaman of Kingsley Hall. R. D. Laing Obituary, *The Guardian*, 25 August.

## CD

1967 *Esmeralda Fufluns*. A story for children and grown-ups only. Written and told by Francis Huxley. Music by Julian Hayter. A Dragon Record. www.youtube.com/watch?v=Cz66C1dL1yE

## Broadcasting (not conclusive)

1948 Oxford University Gambia Expedition. Amateur film 1948, 45 minutes. Silent.
1948 Rocks and Birds of Jan Mayen. Science Survey. BBC Home Service. 29 January.
1952 A Game of Hide and Seek. Three talks. BBC Home Service. 22 April, 29 April, 6 May.
1954 Ghosts, Gods and Tortoises. BBC North of England Home Services. 14 December.
1955 Jaguars in Brazilian Jungle. BBC Home Service. 16 November.
1955 Snakes, Spells and Dolphins. BBC North of England Home Services. 17 October.
1960 Recording by Francis Huxley on visit to Bank Street Unitarian Church, 9 July 1960, FH "Summary of Sunday morning church observations, 1960 compared ..."
1962 Perspective – Francis Huxley, anthropologist discusses some taboos of death. BBC 15 February.

1963 Voodoo and Illness. BBC European English Services. 6 May.
1976 English, Sound, Other Sound Edition. Other Worlds [sound recording]/ compiled and presented by Peter Fry and Malcolm Long for ABC Special Projects. 6 Other World. Sydney. Australian Broadcasting Commission. Myth, Magic and Mystery/compiled and presented by Peter Fry and Malcolm Long for ABC Special Projects. Eliade, Mircea, 1907–1986. Francis Huxley and Nevill Drury.
1981 BBC Woman's Hour. 15 February 1981. Conversation with an Anthropologist.
1985 Tantra of Gyüto. Sacred Rituals of Tibet. A film by Sheldon Rochlin and Mark Elliott. Narrated by Francis Huxley and the Dalai Lama. (Video recording). First issued by Allied Artists and Snow Lion Communications as motion picture 1974. Narrators, Francis Huxley, Dalai Lama.

**Interviews and press**

1951 Estuado os indios barsileiros. Estudo social e anthropologico – Claracoes do sr. Francis Huxley. "A Gazeta," São Paulo, 1st March 1951.
*Folha Vespertina*: Misterio No Paradeiro do Cientista Huxley. Belem – Pará, 14 November 1951.
Os indios do Maranhao e do Para – Fala-nos Francis Huxley. A GAZETA – Sao Paulo, 21 December 1951.
1987 Töten wir Mutter Erde? Francis Huxley in St. Gallen. Ostschweizer AZ, 30. Juni, by R. Gaston Sutter.
Das Falsche Selbst. Zur Anthropologie von Francis Huxley, by Theodor Itten. St. Galler Tagblatt Fri 3. Juli, Horizonte, p.4.
Der Natur entfremdeter Mensch. Francis Huxley, ein Wissenschaftler und Mystiker gegen die Umweltzerstörung. Ostschweizer AZ, by Roger Gaston Sutter. Friday, 10 July.
1989 Was ist Wahnsinn? Ronald Laing-Gedenkveranstaltung mit Francis Huxley. St. Gallen Tagblatt, Kultur, by Peter Surber. Friday, 22 September III/3.
1991 Profile. Faces behind Ideas. Francis Huxley & Adele Getty. *International Synergy Institute*. 2 (2), pp.3–7.

**Reviews of Francis Huxley books**

*Affable Savages*

1956 In the Jungle, by Harold Nicolson. *Observer.* 23 December.
1957 Visitor Finds Brazil Indians Affable Lot, by Max Herzberg.
Other New Books. Affable Savages, by Raymond Mortimer. *Sunday Times.*
Mr. Huxley Reports on the Urubus, by H. C. Brearley.

'Savages' Fine Tale. L. A. Mirror News. 18 February.
Affable Savages, by Charles Wagley. *Nat. Hist. Magazine*, February.
Affable Savages. *The New Yorker*, 16 February.
Under the Blue Derby. *Time*, 18 February.
Affable Savages. *The New Yorker*, 16 February.
The Urubus, Tireless Jungle Gossips, by Edward A. Bloom. *Providence Sunday Journal*, 17 February.
Lessons in Civilization, by Wilton M. Krogman. *Chicago Sunday Tribune*, Magazine of Books, Part 4 – p.3.
Amorous Cannibals, by Burns Singer. *Encounter*, Books, April, pp.77–78.
Noble Savages, by A. V., Coton, *The Spectator*, 22 February, p.36.

1958 Affable Savages: An Anthropologist among the Urubu Indians of Brazil, by Allan R. Holmberg. *American Anthropologist*, 60, pp.388–389.

1961 (after French first Edition in 1960)
L'homme face à sa raison d'être. *Dernière heure d'Alger*, 2 January.
Je Reviens D'Eldorado, by Kleber Haedens. *L'Intransigeant*, 11 January.
Séjour Parmi Les Primitifs, by I. G. *Progrès Égyptien*, 17 January.
Libertinge Urubu, by Robert Jaulin. *Lettres Nouvelles*, April.
Naguère encore ils étaient cruels, by Roger Teneze. *Voix du Nord*, May.
Un Idien sait être un Sauvage, san pour autant manquer de principes, by Dr. J. Petitot. *Le Génie Medical*, May.

## *The Invisibles*

1966 Among Black Magicians, by H. D. Ziman. 11 April.
Close-up of Voodoo Priests Seen by a Scientist. *The Times*. 14 July.
Voodoo. *TLS*, 18.8.
In Search of Voodoo, by Geoffrey Gorer.

1968 Mr. Huxley's Tape-recorder Approach. *Kirkus Review*. 1st February.

1970 Voodoo Gods in Haiti. Francis Huxley, Erika Bourguignon. *American Anthropologist* 72 (2), pp.415–417.

## *Esmeralda Fufluns*

1967 Games that Dragon Play. *Sunday Times*, 12 December.

## *The Way of the Sacred*

1974 Multi-Faith, by R. L. R. *Church Times*. 3.11.
Rites of Man, by Philip Toynbee. *Observer*. 22.12.
For Seekers, by Maurice Richardson. *New Statesman*. 27.12. p.938.
Rites for a Reassembling God, by I. M. Lewis. *TLS* 14.2., p.173.

1977 The Oldest Most Ancient Truths of Humanity, by Andrew Feldmar. *What's On*. 13 January. p.37.

## The Raven and the Writing Desk

1976 Flamingos and Mustard, by Geoffrey Grigson. *The Guardian*, 25 November, p.13.
The Liddell Riddle, by Eric Korn. *The New Statesman*, 3 December, pp.802–803.

1977 Only Connect, by Edward de Bono. *The Spectator*, 8 January, p.23.
A Ceremony of Carrolls, by Peter Heath. *Virginia Quarterly Review*, 53 (3), pp.534–540.
Lewis Carroll. Various Fits, by Brian Alderson. *The Times*, 17.2.
The Nonsense Game, by J. S. Atherton. *TLS*, 25.2., p.217.

1978 Jerome Bump, Univ. Of Texas at Austin; *Victorian Studies*, 21 (4), pp.521–523.
James R. Kincaid, Univ. Colorado; *Nineteenth-Century Fiction*, 33, pp.272–276.

## The Dragon

1979 The Dragon, by Gabriel Wedmore. *Journal of Geomancy*, 4 (1), October.
1979 Dragon Power, by Peter Redgrove. *The Guardian*, 23 October.

## The Eye

(No reviews discovered)

## Shamans Trough Time

2001 Reviewed by Ian S. MacIntosh, *Cultural Survival Quarterly Magazine*.
2001 Reviewed by Lauren Russel, *Evergreen Monthly*, October.
2002 Sur la piste du savoir Chamanique. Patrik Dasen. *Le Courrier*, Samedi, 6 April, p.20.
2004 Black mass observation. Shoel Stadlen. *TLS*, 30 July.

# Appendix 2: General bibliography

Literature on the Huxley family in particular is extensive. What follows is necessarily select, though provides more than useful background for anyone wishing to delve a bit deeper. The material cited in the sections on Anthropology and Psychiatry provide a useful illustration of the range of material consulted and which we have found useful in assessing the context in which Francis Huxley worked and the interpretation of the ideas which he worked with.

## The Huxleys

Baker, J. R. (1976) *Julian Huxley. Scientist and World Citizen*. Paris. UNESCO.

Bates, S. and Winkler, M. G. (1984). The Papers of Julian Sorell Huxley. A Guide. Woodson Research Centre Fondren Library. Houston Texas. Rice University.

Bedford, S. (1973) *Aldous Huxley. A Biography. Volume One 1994–1939*. London. Chatto & Windus.

Bedford, S. (1979) *Aldous Huxley. A Biography. II. The Turning Points*. London. Quartet Books.

Bibby, C. (1960) *T. H. Huxley – Scientist, Humanist and Educator* (with forewords by Sir Julian Huxley and Aldous Huxley). New York. Horizon Press.

Bisbee, C., Bisbee, P., Dyck, E., Farrell, P., Sexton, J. and Spisak, J. W. (Ed.) (2018) *Psychedelic Prophets. The Letters of Aldous Huxley and Humphry Osmond*. Montréal and Kingston. Gill Queens University Press.

Bradshaw, D. (1995) *The Hidden Huxley*. London. Faber & Faber.

Clarke, R. (1968) *The Huxleys*. London. Heinemann.

Collie, M. (1991) *Huxley at Work: With the Scientific Correspondence of T. H. Huxley and the Rev. Dr. George Gordon of Birnie, near Elgin*. London. Palgrave.

Deese, R. S. (2015) *We Are Amphibians. Julian and Aldous Huxley on the Future of Our Species*. Oakland. University of California Press.

Desmond, A. (1994) *Huxley: From Devil's Advocate to Evolution's High Priest*. New York. Perseus Books.

Dronamraju, K. R. (1993) *If I Am To Be Remembered: Correspondence of Julian Huxley.* Totteridge-London. World Scientific.

Dunaway, D. K. (1995) *Aldous Huxley Recollected.* New York. Carroll & Graf.

Getty, A. (1990) *Goddess: Mother of Living Nature* (Art and Imagination Series). London. Thames & Hudson.

Hoban, M. (2019) *An Unconventional Wife – The Life of Julia Sorell Arnold.* Melbourne. Scribe.

Huxley, A. (1927) *Proper Studies.* London. Chatto & Windus.

Huxley, A. (1959/2004) *Brave New World Revisited.* London. Vintage.

Huxley, A. (1954/2004) *The Doors of Perception.* New York. Vintage.

Huxley, A. (1989) Julian Huxley – A Family View. The Galton Lecture for 1987. In Keynes, M. & and Ainsworth Harrison, G. (Ed.) (1998) *Evolutionary Studies. A Centenary Celebration of the Life of Julian Huxley.* London. MacMillan, pp. 9–25.

Huxley, A. (2009) *Perennial Philosophy.* New York. Harper Perennial.

Huxley, J. (1935) *T. H. Huxley's Diary of the Voyage of HMS Rattlesnake.* Edited from the unpublished MS. London. Chatto and Windus.

Huxley, J. (Ed.) (1961) *The Humanist Frame.* London. George Allen & Unwin.

Huxley, J. (Ed.) (1965) *Aldous Huxley. A Memorial Volume.* London. Chatto & Windus.

Huxley, J. (1970) *Memories.* London. George Allen & Unwin.

Huxley, J. (1973) *Memories II.* London. George Allen & Unwin.

Huxley, J. (1986) *Leaves of the Tulip Tree.* London. John Murray.

Huxley-Archera, L. (1975) *This Timeless Moment. A Personal View of Aldous Huxley.* Milbrae. Celestial Arts.

Huxley, L. (1908) *Life and Letters of Thomas Henry Huxley. Vol. I–III.* London. Macmillan.

Morrell, O. (1975) *Ottoline at Garsington. Memoirs of Lady Ottoline Morrell 1915–1918.* (Ed.) R. G. Gathorne-Hardy. New York. A. A. Knopf.

Nicholls, C. S. (2003) *Elisabeth Huxley, A Biography.* London. Harper Collins.

Rosenbaum, S. P. (Ed.) (1975) *The Bloomsbury Group.* Toronto. University of Toronto Press.

Sherman, S. (Ed.) (1999) *Letters of May Sarton to Juliette Huxley.* New York. W. W. Norton.

Smith, G. (Ed.) (1969) *Letters of Aldous Huxley.* London. Chatto & Windus.

Thody, P. (1973) *Aldous Huxley. A Biographical Introduction.* London. Studio Vista.

Trever, M. (1973) *The Arnolds – Thomas Arnold and His Family.* London. The Bodley Head.

UNESCO (1975) *Julian Huxley in Memoriam.* London. UNESCO House.

Waters, C. K. and Van Helden, A. (Ed.) (1992) *Julian Huxley. Biologist and Statesman of Science.* Houston. Rice University Press.

Watt, D. (Ed.) (1975) *Aldous Huxley – The Critical Heritage.* London. Routledge & Kegan Paul.

Weindling, P. (2012) Julian Huxley and the Continuity of Eugenics in Twentieth-century Britain. *Journal of Modern European History*, 10 (4), pp.480–499.
White, P. (2003) *Thomas Huxley – Making the "Man of Science."* Cambridge. Cambridge University Press.

## Anthropology

Assad, T. (1973) *Anthropology and the Colonial Encounter.* New York. Prometheus Books.
Ballée, W. (1994) *Footprints of the Forest. Ka'apor Ethnobotany – The Historical Ecology of Plant Utilization by an Amazonian People.* New York. Columbia University Press.
Bateson, G. (1980) *Naven.* London. Wildwood House.
Benedict, R. (1971) *Patterns of Culture.* London. Routledge & Keagan Paul.
Blacking, J. (Ed.) (1975) *The Anthropology of the Body.* London. Academic Press.
Brooks, E. Fuerst, R. Hemming, J. and Huxley F. (1972) *Tribes of the Amazon Basin. Report for the Aborigines Protection Society.* London and Tonbridge. Charles Knight.
Corry, S. (2011) *Tribal Peoples for Tomorrow's World.* London. Freeman Press.
Douglas, M. (1980) *Evans-Pritchard.* London. Fontana Modern Masters.
Evans-Pritchard, E. E. (1951) *Social Anthropology.* London. Cohen & West.
Faradon, R. (1999) *Mary Douglas.* London. Routledge.
Fortes, M. (1983) *Oedipus and Job in West-African Religion.* Cambridge. Cambridge University Press.
Gardner, K. and Lewis, D. (2015) *Anthropology and Development.* London. Pluto Press.
Geertz, C. (1988) *Works and Lives. The Anthropologist as Author.* Stanford. Stanford University Press.
Guppy, N. (1961) *Wai-Wai – Through the Forest North of the Amazon.* Harmondsworth. Penguin Books.
Hanbury-Tenison, R. (1973) *A Question of Survival – For the Indians in Brazil.* London. Angus and Roberstson.
Hemmings, J. (2003) *Die if You Must. Brazilian Indians in the Twentieth Century.* London. Pan.
Hemmings, J. (2019) *People of the Rainforest.* London. Hurst.
Ingold, T. (2018) *Anthropology. Why it Matters.* London. Polity.
Keynes, M. and Ainsworth Harrison, G. (Ed.) (1998) *Evolutionary Studies. A Centenary Celebration of the Life of Julian Huxley.* London. Macmillan.
Kuper, A. (1997) *Anthropology and Anthropologists. The Modern British School* (3rd Edition). London. Routledge.
Kuper, A. (2003) The Return of the Native. *Current Anthropology*, 44 (3), pp.389–402.

Kuper, A. (2016) Meyer Fortes. The Person, the Role, the Theory. *The Cambridge Journal of Anthropology*, 34 (2), Autumn, pp.127–139.
Leach, E. R. (1984) Glimpses of the Unmentionable in the History of British Social Anthropology. *Annual Review of Anthropology*, 13, pp.1–23.
Levi-Strauss, C. (2011) *Tristes Tropiques*. London. Penguin.
Lévi-Strauss, C. (2013) *Anthropology Confronts the Problems of the Modern World*. Cambridge. Harvard University Press.
Lévi-Strauss, C. (2016) *We Are All Cannibals and Other Essays*. New York. Colombia University Press.
Loyer, W. (2015) *Lèvi-Strauss*. Paris. Flammarion.
Mair, L. (1969) *Witchcraft*. London. Weidenfeld and Nicolson.
Narby, J. (1998) *The Cosmic Serpent, DNA and the Origins of Knowledge*. London. Victor Gollancz.
Riberio, D. (1996) *Diarios Indios – Os Urubus-Kaapor*. Sao Paulo: Companiha Das Letras. S.
Rivière, P. (Ed.) (2007) *A History of Oxford Anthropology*. New York & Oxford. Berghahn Books.
Thambiah, S. J. (2002) *Edmund Leach – An Anthropological Life*. Cambridge. Cambridge University Press.
Wescott, J. A. (1962) The Sculpture and Myths of Eshu-Elegba, the Yoruba Trickster: Definition and Interpretation in Yoruba Iconography. *Africa*, 32 (4), October, pp.336–353.

## Psychiatry/psychoanalysis/Philadelphia Association/science/philosophy

Boym, S. (2005) Poetics and Politics of Estrangement: Victor Shklovsky and Hannah Arendt. *Poetics Today*, 26 (4), pp.581–612.
Clay. J. (1996) *R. D. Laing – A Divided Self*. London. Hodder and Stoughton.
Cooper, D. (1968) *The Dialectics of Liberation*. Harmondsworth. Penguin.
Cromby, J., Harper, D. and Reavey, P. (2013) *Psychology, Mental Health and Distress*. Houndmills. Palgrave Macmillan.
Davies, J. (2011) *Cracked. Why Psychiatry is Doing More Harm than Good*. London. Icon Books.
Dyck, E. (2010) Spaced-Out in Saskatchewan. Modernism, Anti-Psychiatry, and Deinstitutionalization, 1950–1968. *Bulletin of the History of Medicine*, 84 (4), pp.640–666.
Feurerbach, L. (1851/2004) *The Essence of Religion*. New York. Prometheus Books. p.61.
Frosch, S. (2013) *Hauntings: Psychoanalysis and Ghostly Transmissions*. New York. Palgrave Macmillan.
Griffin, J. (1997) *The Origin of Dreams*. Trowbridge. Redwood Books.
Holt, N. J., Simmonds-Moore, C., Luke, D. and French, C. J. (2012) *Anomalistic Psychology*. New York. Palgrave Macmillan.

Itten, T. and Young, C. (Ed.) (2012) *R. D. Laing 50 Years since* The Divided Self. Monmouth. PCCS-Books.

Itten, T. and Roberts, R. (2014) *The New Politics of Experience and the Bitter Herbs.* Monmouth. PCCS-Books.

Laing, R. D. (1966) Ritualization and Abnormal Behaviour. *Philosophical Transactions of the Royal Society London*, 251 (772), pp.331–335.

Laing, R. D. (1970) *Knots*. London. Tavistock.

Laing, R. D. (1972) *The Politics of the Family and Other Essays.* New York. Vintage Books.

Laing, R. D. (1987) Laing's Understanding of Interpersonal Experience. In R. L. Gregory (Ed.) *The Oxford Companion to the Mind.* Oxford. Oxford University Press. pp.417–418.

Levine, G. (2011) *Darwin the Writer*. Oxford. Oxford University Press.

Medawar, P. (1969/2008) *Induction and Intuition in Scientific Thought*. London. Routledge.

Mullan, B. (1995) *Mad to be Normal. Conversations with R. D. Laing*. London. Free Association Books

Osmond, H. (1952) On Being Mad. Saskatchewan. *Psychiatric Service Journal*, 1 (2), September, pp.63–70.

Raschid, S. (Ed.) (2005) *R. D. Laing. Contemporary Perspectives*. London. Free Association Books.

Voss, J., Roberts, R., Davies, J. (2019) *Mental Health in Crisis*. London. Sage.

# Appendix 3: *Affable Savages* and Monique Lévi-Strauss

*Affable Savages* was translated into French by Monique Lévi-Strauss, first published in 1960 as *Amiables Sauvages*. It went into various reprints in hard cover as well as paperback. When we wrote to his publisher Plon in Paris, we learned that from Marguerite Mignon-Quibel that "Plon sold approximately 13,000 pieces of the book, throughout the different prints of the book."[1] Monique Lévi-Strauss gratefully responded to our request for any further information:

> *Francis and I did correspond while I was translating his book, but that was sixty years ago, and I did not keep our letters. I am not aware of a correspondence between FH and CLS. My husband had great esteem for FH and he thought his work was most valuable. He would not have advised me to translate his book had he thought otherwise. I cannot remember FH's presence among the guests when my husband received his honorary degree in Oxford in 1964. We never visited Sir Julian and Lady Huxley in London, but I do remember meeting Sir Julian at a formal reception at UNESCO in Paris. Francis did visit us in our apartment in Paris. I have forgotten the conversation but am pretty sure we talked about the translation of his book.*
>
> *The remark I care to volunteer is that Francis was against the title AIMABLES SAUVAGES. So was I, so was Claude. But Malaurie, who was our publisher at PLON, told us we had to follow the advice of the commercial direction. Claude tried to convince him it was a poor title, in vain. Francis never believed I had done my best to avoid this title and preferred the English one, that reads well in French. He never wrote to me again, did not thank me for the translation. I was hurt and I never forgave Malaurie. You can imagine my surprise when the last reprint of the French translation came out two years ago bearing the title I had asked for.*
>
> *I hope I am not disappointing you. Best wishes,*
>
> *Monique Lévi-Strauss*[2]

## Notes

1 Marguerite Mignon-Quibel, Directrice Commercial and Marketing Email: März 2018, 11:41.
2 Email: Monique Lévi-Strauss, November 2018.

# Index

*Note*: Figures are shown in *italics*, as is the family tree. Footnotes are indicated by an "n" and the footnote number after the page number e.g., 272n30 refers to footnote 30 on page 272.

18 Belsize Park Gardens, London NW3 6
18b Wedderburn Road, London NW3 134, 135
31 Chemin Bel Air, 2000 Neuchâtel 11, 12–13, 15, 82
31 Hillway, Holly Lodge Estate, Hampstead 3, 21–22
31 Pond Street, Hampstead 7, 14, 28, 126, 133–135, 175, 183, 243–246
60th birthday, of Francis Huxley 6, 53–54
65A Belsize Park Gardens, London NW3 6, 46, 127, 128, 182
70th birthday, of Francis Huxley 7
90th birthday, of Lady Juliette Maria Baillot-Huxley 43
1105 Wagnon Road, Sebastopol, California 7, 90, 136, 239, 249, 257
1960s xv, 40, 153, 170; and the human condition 267, 268, 270; Philadelphia Association 219, 227, 233; St. Catherine's College, Oxford 174, 178, 183

Abinger Hill School 3
Aborigines' Protection Society 6, 189
Abrahamic religions 197
academic world 59, 173, 188, 193, 199, 226; Francis Huxley in later life 241, 243, 250; Oxford University 95, 96–97, 104, 105, 175, 176, 178
adaptation 143–144, 145
Aesculapian mode of incubation, of R. D. Laing 228

*Affable Savages, The* 148, 175, 176, 179, 199, 258, 290
affairs xvi, 23, 26, 42, 44, 108–139, *110*, *127*, *137*
*Africa Before the White Man* 6
aid, to Brazil 189, 190
Alexander, F. M. 36, 204
alternative healing 170, 181, 216
Ani, Stuart 258, 259
anthropology: as means to contend with family issues 152; Gambia *see* fieldwork, anthropological; Haiti *see* Haiti, fieldwork; the Ka'apor *see* fieldwork, anthropological; LSD contribution to 158–159; narrative xiv, 105, 147, 270
*Anthropology and the Body* 6
*Antic Hay* 32, 44
anti-psychiatry 160, 224, 231–232
Anti-University 6, 120, 180, 186, 230, 233–234
apparitions 206
appearances 31, 152, 195–197, 207
Arendt, Hannah 269
aristocracy of the mind 63, 64, 65
Arnold, Julia Sorell *4*, 16, 17
Arnold, Thomas *4*
Arnold, Thomas (the younger) *4*, 16–17, 67
Arnold-Huxley, Julia Francis *4*, 17, 18, 19, 32, 35, 44, 78
Arnold-Huxley, Margaret *4*, 19, 32, 41–42, 44, 71n30, 78

Index    293

*Awakening the Dream: The Way of The Warrior* 6, 132, 133, 232, 248
ayahuasca sessions 207

Baillot, Alphonse *4*, 11, 12, 13
Baillot-Huxley, Lady Juliette Maria *4*, 11, 12–13, 20, *83*; death of 56; on Francis' final theatrical role at school 86; Julian Sorell Huxley 19, 57; 90th birthday of 43; on son's prospective partners 57; stories told about her by granddaughters 14; tale of Captain Middleton of HMS Ramillies 90; on weight of expectation on Matthew 58
Bair, Deirdre 37
Baker, J. R., memoir of Julian Huxley by 55
Balaskas, Meloma *4*, 6, 21, 128
Balliol College, Oxford 5, 32, 53, 77, 90, 92, 93–95
Bateson, Gregory 81, 151, 181, 221, 230
BBC (British Broadcasting Corporation) 89, 98, 175, 183–186, 244, 281–282
Bedford, Sybille 43
Benjamin, Walter 269
Bergson, Henri 68
Berkeley Hills, San Francisco 134, 243
biological theory 61, 62, 145, 200, 217, 268
biologically oriented psychiatry 267
"black dog" 24–25, 57
Blake, William 3, 216–217, 265
Bloomsbury Group 13, 14, 33, 34, 42, 59
Blume, Bettina 148, 244
Blume, Norbert 244
*Body and Anthropology* 182–183
*Body and Mind in Anthropology, The* 176, 181
Boym, Svetlana 197, 199, 265, 269
Brains' Trust episode, on HMS Ramillies 89–90
*Brave New World* 31, 63, 65
*Brave New World Revisited* 64, 65
Brazil xiii, xiv, 5, 6, 7, 39, 103, 121, 126; aid to 189, 190; fieldwork in 144, 145, 147–150, *149*; Government of xiii–xiv, 5, 6, 189, 190
British Broadcasting Corporation (BBC) 89, 98, 175, 183–186, 244, 281–282
Bruce, Rosalind 3, *4*, 44
Butt Colson, Audrey 95, 103, 175, 177, 182, 183, 184–185, 187

Byron House Preparatory School 3, 22, 78

cancer 7, 17, 47, 125, 252–253, 254
cannabis 164, 177, 257–258, 263n35
capitalism 53, 196, 231, 267, 270
car accident 7
Carles, Jules 6
Carroll, Lewis xvi, 17, 35, 184, 236n12, 241, 254
cataract operation 7
Chagall, Marc 270
*Charles Darwin – Life and Habit* 5
chemotherapy 7, 252–253
Chichele Lecture 6
*Chrome Yellow* 33, 34
City of Liverpool Public Museum 5, 112
Clarke, Ronald 54
Clay, John 200, 232–233
Colchester, Marcus 240, 246
collective memory 54, 201, 203
colonialism 69, 270–271
common meaning, frameworks for making 150
communicative memory 60–61, 71n42
consciousness 47, 168, 169, 196, 202, 221, 266, 267, 269
*Cosmic Serpent, The* 205, 247–248
cosmologies 66, 164, 168–169, 175, 195–212, 220, 222; and the human condition 266, 270, 271
cosmos 168, 169, 224, 236, 270
creative thinking 105
cultural misattribution bias 66
Cunard, Nancy 43–44

Darling, Diana Conn 257–258
Darwin, Charles 5, 114–115, 164, 174, 198, 270, 271; haunting 51, 52, 62, 68
de Freitas, Lourival 121, 241
demonic possession 206
Diablerets 3
diagnosis, Haitian 170
Dialectics of Liberation Conference 6, 70, 230, 233, 267
Dieudonne 171
*Divided Self, The* 227
divine iconography 269
Dodgson, Charles L. xvi, 17, 35, 184, 236–237n12, 241, 254
doors of perception, opening the 46, 66, 161
*Doors of Perception, The* 40, 161

double lovers 23–24
Douglas, Mary 103, 185
dreams 171, 200, 202, 211n65, 236
*Dragon – Nature of Spirit, Spirit of Nature, The* 6, 198, 240, 241
dragons 143, 183–184, 201–202, 209–210n38, 210n39, 245
Dunaway, David King 42, 55, 58; on suicide of Trevenen Huxley 71n30
dynasty, Huxley xv, 50, 54–61, 56, 66

Eamonn Andrews Show 6, 186
Ecole Superieure des Jeunes Filles 12
elite thinking 63, 64, 65
embryological development 221
energy, in human beings 180
epistemology xiv–xv, 103, 168–169, 268, 269–270
*Esmeralda Fufluns* 183–184, 258
ESP (extra-sensory perception) 164, 172, 180–181, 203, 204, 205
etymology 56, 200–204, 250, 263n24
eugenics 61–66
evacuation, of Francis Huxley to Wales 5, 81, 82, 85, 87n7, 87n14
Evans, Brian 120, 186, 233
Evans-Pritchard, Edward 5, 102–104, 111, 177, 178, 222
*Everybody's Got Something to Hide Except for Me and My Monkey* 153
evolutionary biology 47, 51, 61, 62–63, 67, 68, 193, 218
existential psychiatry 216
expectations xv, 28, 55–60, 56, 61, 144, 206, 240
extra-sensory perception (ESP) 164, 172, 180–181, 203, 204, 205
*Eye – Seer and the Seen, The* 7, 198, 239, 240
*Eyeless in Gaza* 44

fame, phenomenology of 59
family life, dynamics of 60, 226, 267
family name 51, 58–59, 60, 61, 67, 272
family pressures 58–59, 71n30
family tree 4, 16, 56, 205
*Farewell to Eden* 58
farewells 258–260
fear 12, 26, 60, 61–66, 112, 211n65, 271; cosmology and the sacred 201–202, 203–205
Feldmar, Andrew 133, 243, 256
Festschrift for 70th birthday 7

fieldnotes 38, 84, 104, 148–149, 169, 180, 202, 208n10
fieldwork, anthropological: Gambia xiii, 5, 84, 99–102, 100, 143; Haiti *see* Haiti, fieldwork; Ka'apor *see* Ka'apor fieldwork; Saskatchewan 5, 113, 151–165
Fordham, Kathleen 24
Fortes, Professor Meyer 5, 103, 104, 111, 145–146, 147, 177, 199, 200
"frame of mind", behind a story 150
French structuralism 105
Frensham Heights School 3, 78
Freud, Sigmund 19, 181, 200, 202, 258, 268
Fuerst, René 126, 190, 193n6
functionalism 198

Gambia fieldwork xiii, 5, 84, 99–101, 100, 143
Gaona, Professor Francisco 250
Garrett, Eileen 37, 38, 41, 67, 167–168, 172, 203
Garsington Manor 3, 13–14, 33–34
genius, social construction of 55
Getty, Adele Marie 4, 6, 7, 26, 132, 134, 239, 262n8, 263n46
*Ghost Dance – An Untold History of the Americas, The* 258
ghost dances 257–258
Gordonstoun School 5, 77–87, 81, 83, 87n7, 109, 110, 270
Graves, Robert 31, 162, 239–240

Hahn, Kurt 77–78, 79, 80–81, 82, 86
*Haiti Chérie* 175
Haiti: fieldwork 5, 38, 84, 153, 165, 167–173, 234; cosmology and the sacred 198, 201–202; love and history 113–114, 116–117; St. Catherine's, Oxford 176, 182; Voodoo *see* Voodoo, Haitian
hallucinations 40–41, 152, 160, 164, 180
Hanbury-Tenison, Robin 126, 185, 177, 178, 243
haunting 50–73, 56
healing 122–123, 157, 158–159, 170, 171, 203, 205, 265–266; Philadelphia Association 216, 217, 218, 224, 227, 229, 234, 236; St. Catherine's College, Oxford 180, 181, 182, 185
health 183; of Francis Huxley 3, 22, 248–249, 253; mental 59,

## Index

159, 160, 185, 190, 215, 216–217, 224–225, 237n26
Heathorn, Henrietta Anne *4*, 51
Hemmings, John 188, 189, 190, 193n6, 243
herd mentality 64–65
Heywood, Rosalind 122, 180
Hitler, Adolf 63, 64, 77
HMS Ramillies 5, 88–90
HMS Rattlesnake 51
Hoberstone, Kate 191–192
Hoffer, Abram 160, 167
Hofmann, Albert 41, 152, 164, 241, *242*
Hollywood Heights fire 46
home care 257–258
Hong Kong, Francis in *91*
Hovde, Ellen *4*, 45, 46, 114, 151
Howard, Ernst 108
Howard, Ferelyth 5, 13, 54, 108, *110*
Howard, Jean 108–109
human potentialities, search for 47–48
Huxley, Aldous: death of 47; early life 31–32; Ellen Hovde 45; emotional detachment of 66; eugenics 63, 65, 66; eye infection/eyesight 32, 36, 43; fire at Hollywood Heights 46; at Garsington Manor 33; influence on Francis 37; literary career 36; LSD/mescaline experimentation 39; perennial philosophy of 39; as public intellectual 47; as screen writer 55
Huxley, Andrew Fielding *4*, 7, 45, 54, 271
Huxley, Ann *4*, 7, 110
Huxley, Anthony Julian 3, *4*, 7, 27
Huxley (née Hovde), Ellen *4*, 37, 40, 45, 46, 114–118, 134, 171, 175; Saskatchewan 151–152, 154, 155–156, 157, 158, 163–164
Huxley Francis: Adele Marie Getty *4*, 6, 7, 132, 135, 239, 262n8, 264n46; Adriana Paula Santa Cruz *4*, 6, 108, 125–126, *127*, 127; Aldous' influence on 37; Balliol College, Oxford 93–107, *100*; birth of 20; City of Liverpool Public Museum post 5, 112; death of 260, 263; dragon mythology 143, 183–184, 201–202, 245; Ellen Hovde 45, 46, 114, 152; farewells 258–260; Ferelyth Howard (first love) 5, 13, 75, 108, *110*; Gambia expedition 99; at Gordonstoun School 79; human condition 66; independence of 25; Jan Mayen expedition 98; Joan Westcott *see* Westcott, Joan; Lapland expedition 84; in later life 239; LSD experimentation *see* LSD; Meloma Balaskas *4*, 6, 21, 128; ornithology 96; 'other' (people categorised as) 69; paranormal 29n21, 67, 120, 121–122, 168, 169, 204–208; pedagogical capacity 235; practical political element to critiques 268; psychedelia *see* psychedelia; as a recluse 254–257; recollections 258–260; research fellowship 97, 177; R. D. Laing friendship 178, 207, 215–220, 221–222, 224; serving in Royal Navy 88–90, *91*; St. Catherine's College, Oxford 97; St. John Society 83; science mentors 96–98; 70th birthday 7; 60th birthday 6, 53–54; social anthropology *see* social anthropology; theatrical roles 85; ultimately mysterious world 269; Weyburn mental hospital 5, 153, 157, 158, 159, 160, 163, 170, 218; zoology *see* zoology
Huxley, Sir Julian Sorell 3, *4*, 5, 6, 7, 13, 15, 33, 35, 54–55, *56*, *83*; Anthony Julian's qualms about him according to his daughter Victoria Huxley 26; "black dog" 57; cultural misattribution bias 66; death of 6; belief in disembodied spirits 67; eugenics 61, 62–63; expectations of 57; fellowship at New College, Oxford 3, 20–21; Ferelyth Howard 109; *LIFE* magazine on 31; love affairs 42, 44; LSD 153–154; marriage to Juliette Maria Baillot 19, 34, 69; Mary Ward cared for him after Julia Arnold Huxley's early death 19; May Sarton (lover) 23–24; mental health of 24–25, 154, 217–218; mescaline 153–154; move to London 21–23; nervous breakdowns 24–25; on obedience 230; politics of 63, 65; and politics of the family 20–21; Professor of Zoology at King's College, Oxford 21; as public intellectual 47; relationship with Francis 86, 89, 97, 136; as scientist 17, 32, 35–36; UNESCO Director General xiii, 17; as "walking contradiction" according to Adele Getty 26

Huxley, Juliette *see* Baillot-Huxley, Lady Juliette Maria
Huxley, Laura Archera *4*, 38, 42–43, 44, 45, 46, 47, 113, 245–246
Huxley, Leonard 3, *4*, 17–19, 20, 22, 44, 53, 57, 94, 108
Huxley, Margaret *4*, 19, 32, 41–42, 44, 71n30, 78
Huxley, Mel 128, 129, *130*, 131, 137
Huxley, Susie 44, 56, 58, 110–111, 125, 258–259, 263n39; recollections of Francis Huxley's parents 12, 14, 23, 26, 28
Huxley, Tessa *4*, 45, 114, 116
Huxley, Thomas Henry (T. H.) xiii, *4*, 5, 9, 16, 17–18, 19, 36, 53; Balliol College, Oxford 94; "black dog" 24–25, 57; death of 60; belief in eugenics 61, 62; evolutionary biology 61, 67; search for new "human potentialities" 47–48; legacy of 60; as public intellectual 47; pugnacious genius 57; understanding of working classes 52
Huxley, Trevenen (Trev) 3, *4*, 18, 19, 24, 57–58, 115, 116, 258–259; Aldous Huxley 32, 36, 43, 44, 45, 46
Huxley, Victoria *4*, 14–15, 26, 27, 58, 59, 244, 258–259, 271; love and history 108, 110, 111, 125–126, 128, 132
Huxley dynasty xv, 50, 54–61, *56*, 66
Huxley family mythos 152
Huxley myth 53, 271

identifying mask 272
Ilma, Viola 3, 22
indigenous peoples 144, 188, 190–191, *191*, 192, 194n16, 270
individualism 220, 224, 246–247, 267
inheritance 44, 53–55, 56, 66, 171
institutional power 106
institutional psychiatry 237n26, 267
intellectual aristocracy 31, 63, 105
intellectual elitism 63, 64, 65
intellectual hauntings 61–66
intelligence xvi, 14, 39, 70–71n19, 133, 205, 248; haunting 55, 56–57, 63, 64
interests, personal *see* personal interests
international capitalism 267
International Philadelphia Association (IPA) Conference, Leuven, Belgium 224
international white supremacy 267

*Invisibles, The* (Haiti fieldwork) 6, 171, 175, 179, 202–204; *see also* Haiti, fieldwork
IPA (International Philadelphia Association) Conference, Leuven, Belgium 224
Isherwood, Christopher 55
*Island, The* 41
Izumi, Kiyoshi (Kyo) 158, 159
Izumi-Osmond-Sommer design, for mental hospitals 160

Jenner, Professor Alec 6, 218
Jones, John 93
Joos, Deborah 123
Joos, Dorothea 253
Jung, C. G. 144, 200, 217, 235
justice 270; social 188–193, *191*

Ka'apor fieldwork xiii, 5, 69, 103, 147–150, *149*, 179, 199; anthropology and its challenges 144, 145
Karaya children *191*
King, Dr. Truby 21
King's College, London 3, 21–22
Kingsley Hall experimental therapeutic community 226
kinship systems 105, 168, 195, 196
*Knots* 119
Korea conference on shamanism 7
Kuper, Adam 199

Labouret, Henri 6
LaGuerre, Gerard 171
Laing, Ronald David (R. D.): Aesculapian mode of incubation 228; Anti-University 233–234; *Awakening the Dream: The Way of The Warrior* 232–233; in comparison to Francis Huxley 220; Dialectics of Liberation Conference 230–231; Francis Huxley's views on 227–228; friendship with Francis Huxley 178, 207, 215–220, 221–222, 224; Kingsley Hall 226, 227; marriage to Jutta Werner 221; memorial gathering 7; obituary by Francis Huxley 7, 227; "Our Approach to Psychiatry" *223*; Philadelphia Association (PA) 207, 224–225, 226, 227, 228, 232; practical political critique 268; on psycho-phobia 266; Scottish school, of psychiatry 232; ultimately mysterious world 269

*Laing and Shamanism*, lecture by Francis Huxley on 7
Lapland, expedition to 84–85, 87, 143
Le Bon, Gustav 64–65
Leach, Edmund 104–105, 175–176
*Leaves of the Tulip Tree* 7
Lennon, John 153
*Letter to Francis Huxley, A* 7
*Letter to Humphry Osmond* 154
Lévi-Strauss, Claude 86, 103, 105, 149–150, 185, 192, 234; cosmology and the sacred 195, 197–198, 201, 207
Lévi-Strauss, Monique 290
Lévy, Jacques 253
Lewis Carroll Society 6
*Liberating Shaman of Kingsley Hall* 7, 227
London Zoo 13, 23, 27, 68, 88
LSD 39–41, 118, 171, 172, 182, 232, 241, 245–246, 250, 207; as anthropology practice 152; as healing agent 170; mental hospital designs 158; as model psychosis 163; Saskatchewan 151–152, 153–155, 156–157, 158, 160, 161, 163–165
*LSD, My Problem Child* 241
lysergic acid diethylamide *see* LSD

magic skirt, of HMS Ramillies 90
Manaus, Amazonas, Brazil 7, 251
marijuana 164, 177, 253–255, 257–258, 263n35
*Marriage Among the Trio, A Principle of Social Organisation* 175–176
masks 130, 231, 240, 248, 271–272
Maslow, Abraham 269
materialism 67, 68, 196, 205, 266
mathematics 195, 197, 235, 236n12, 240–241, 254, 265
Mead, Margret 235
Medawar, Peter Brian 97–98, 99, 167
medical model 218
mediumship 67, 164, 165, 167, 168, 182–183
ménage à trois, with May Sarton 23
mental health 59, 159, 160, 185, 190, 237n26; nervous breakdowns 6, 24–25, 69, 154; Philadelphia Association 215, 216–217, 224–225
mental illness 152, 165n23, 170, 203, 215, 227, 228; *see also* Philadelphia Association (PA)
mescaline 39–40, 151, 152, 153–154, 164

Middleton, Captain Gervase Boswell 89, 90, 92n6
militant materialism 205
military career, of Francis Huxley 88–90, *91*
model psychosis, LSD as 163
modern psychiatry 158, 218
modernity 192
money 36, 44, 125, 135, 173n13, 188, 203, 245, 262n8; Haiti fieldwork 167, 171, 173
moral imagination 191
Morrell, Lady Ottoline 3, 13–14, 21, 33–34, 38
Morrison, Toni 191
motifs 198–200
Mr. Gray 80, 81
*Mutual Self, The* 7, 67, 224–225, 239, 245, 253–254, 262n1
mysticism 47, 67, 241
myth: creation- 246–247; of hereditary genius 57, 271; Huxley 53, 271
mythic symbolism 269
mythology 6, 53, 119, 143, 151, 171, 176, 233–236; cosmology and the sacred 198, 199, 200–202; Francis Huxley in later life 241, 246, 250; the Ka'apor 147–148, 150; Oxford University 104, 105
mythos 152, 271, 272

Napier, David 241–242, 243, 245–246, 265, 271, 272
Narby, Jeremy 7, 199, 205, 206–207, 239, 247, 255–256
narrative anthropology xiv, 105, 147, 270
natural selection 174, 180
Needham, Rodney 251
neo-Darwinian thought 68, 270
neo-fascism 64
neo-shamanic cults 266
nervous breakdowns 6, 24–25, 69, 154
Neuchâtel (31 Chemin Bel Air, 2000) 11, 12–13, 15, 82
New College, Oxford 3, 20, 98
Nietzsche, Friedrich 65, 197, 200, 211n65
non-medical psychiatry 232
noumenal world 195
numerology 15, 250, 257
nutritional psychiatry 160

obedience 230
*Obvious, The* 230

Ogston, A. G. "Sandy" 93–94, 96–97
old eugenics 62
ontology 196, 198, 268
*Origins of Life, The* 6
ornithology 96
orthodox psychiatry 159, 266
Osmond, Dr. Humphry 39, 40, 41, 114, 172, 218; Saskatchewan 151–152, 154, 155, 156, 157, 158, 159, 160–161, 163, 164
"Our Approach to Psychiatry" 222, *223*
Oxford Journals 111–112
Oxford University, Francis Huxley at 93–106, *100*

PA (Philadelphia Association, The) 6, 128, 160, 186, 215–236, *223*, 268
paranormal 29n21, 67, 120, 121–122, 168, 169, 181, 204–208; *see also* Voodoo, Haitian
Parapsychological Institute, New York 5
parapsychology 37, 41, 67, 167, 172
Peacock, Caroline 248
*Peoples of the World* 6, 175
perennial philosophy, of Aldous Huxley
personal anthropology, of Francis Huxley 239–243, *242*
personal interests xiii, 9, 26, 37, 66, 150, 190, 239; Philadelphia Association 220, 227, 230–233, 235; St. Catherine's College, Oxford 177–178, 179, 182
personality traits 57
phenomenal world 195
phenomenology 40, 59, 195, 230–233, 267, 269
Philadelphia Association, The (PA) 6, 128, 160, 186, 215–236, *223*, 268
Pojoaque, New Mexico 7, 135, 136, 239, 244, 245
*Politics of Experience, The* 39, 232, 262n1
politics of the family 19–21
*Politics of the Family and other Essays, The* 220–221
populism 64
psychedelia 66, 150, 205, 232, 233, 246, 270, 273; Aldous Huxley 36, 40, 41, 47; Saskatchewan 151, 153, 155, 158, 160, 164
psychiatric medicine 218–219
psychiatric treatment, LSD contribution to 160, 163–164

psychiatric wards, anthropological study of 158
psychiatry 29n21, 151, 160, 232, 241, 268; anti- 160, 224, 231–232; biologically-oriented 267; existential 216; institutional 237n26, 267; modern 158, 218; non-medical 232; nutritional 160; orthodox 159, 266; psychodynamic 232; radical 227; social 232; Western 227
psychoanalysis 156, 200–202, 207, 209n27, 240, 265–267, 268; R. D. Laing's breaching of confidentiality 217
*Psychoanalysis and Anthropology* 6
psycho-anthropology 182–183
psychodynamic psychiatry 232
psychological well-being 190
psycho-phobia 266
psychosis 163–164, 227, 254, 268
psychosomatic medicine 25, 192, 200
psychotherapy xv, 36, 41, 128, 152, 183, 204, 243, 273n16; Francis Huxley in later life 266–267, 271–272; Philadelphia Association 215, 219, 227, 229, 233–236
Purce, Jill 132, 226

qualities 66, 146, 182

racism 62, 72n46, 267, 268
radical psychiatry 227
Ramillies, HMS 5, 88–90
rationalism 68, 267
rationality 67, 68, 69, 199
Rattlesnake, HMS 51
*Raven and The Writing Desk, The* xvi, 6, 35, 180
recollections 258–260
Redler, Leon 215, 225, 229, 230, 233
reform eugenics 62
Reich, Wilhelm 36, 273n16
religion 17, 154, 190, 233, 285–286; Aldous Huxley 35, 39; cosmology and the sacred 196, 197; haunting 67, 68; *see also* Haitian Voodoo
*Religion without Revelation* 80–81
responsibility 220–222
Ribeiro, Darcy 5, 247
rites 6, 104, 168, 169, 174–175, 181
*Ritual of Voodoo and the Symbolism of the Body, The* 219
ritual symbolism 169

*Ritualisation and Abnormal Behaviour* 6, 178, 218, 219
rituals 29n21, 132, 133, 171, 177, 219, 228, 265–266; cosmology and the sacred 203, 204; Oxford University 101, 104; Saskatchewan 159, 160, 164
Rivière, Peter 175–176, 176–177, 178, 179–180
Royal Navy 5, 27, 37, 88–90, *91*, 111
Royal Society 5, 6, 51, 53, 218

sacred, the 17, 35, 67, 174, 195–197, 269
St. Catherine's College, Oxford 6, 94, 97, 173, 175
St. John Society 83, 84
Santa Cruz, Adriana Paula *4*, 6, 108, 125–126, *127*, 127
Santa Fe 7, 113, 134–135, 136–137; Francis Huxley in later life 239, 243, 244, 247, 248, 249, 251, 252, 254, 257, 259, 260
Santa Isabel, Aragonia River *191*
Sarton, May 22, 23, 24, 88
Saskatchewan fieldwork 5, 113, 151–165
Schwab, Michael 26, 113, 125, 251
science mentors 96–98
Scottish school, of psychiatry 232
Secretary House, Zoological Gardens 5
self-directed evolution 47
Semyon, Mina 221, 228, 231, 253
sensory information 195
70th birthday, of Francis Huxley 7
sexual infidelities 20
sexual liberation 14, 47
sexual morality 111–112
sexual mores 42, 43
sexual politics 36, 184, 265–266
sexual prey 24
sexual reconfiguration 152
sexual relationships 24
sexuality 20, 23, 43
shamanism 121–122, 152–153, 169, 170, 205, 207, 247, 266, 267
*Shamanism, Healing and R. D. Laing* 227
*Shamans Through Time – 500 Years on the Path to Knowledge* 7, 136, 199, 239
Sheffield University Mental Hospital 6, 218
Sheldrake, Rupert 132, 136, 197, 199, 225, 256, 259, 272; haunting 58, 59, 62–63
Simpson, Avice 6, 133

60th birthday, of Francis Huxley 6, 53–54
social anthropology 5, 6, 95, 96, 102, 103, 104, 105, 143–146; *see also* cosmology; Gambia fieldwork; Haiti fieldwork; Ka'apor fieldwork; sacred, the; St. Catherine's College, Oxford; Saskatchewan fieldwork; Survival International
social control 65, 207
social Darwinism 62, 68, 198
social elite 65
social heritage 61
social justice 188–193, *191*
social organisation 70, 175–176, 190, 193, 196, 198
social planning 62
social position 61
social psychiatry 232
social systems 196
Sommer, Robert 158, 159, 160
spiritualism 47, 67, 68
spirituality xiv, 23, 118, 119, 152, 189, 240, 268; cosmology and the sacred 196, 198, 203, 207; St. Catherine's College, Oxford 179, 180, 181–183
structural anthropology 105
structuralism 105, 195
*Study of Precognition: Evidence and Methods, The* 37
supremacy 61–66; white 267, 268
Survival International 6, 58, 68, 126, 148, 186, 188–193, *191*, 216, 270; Francis Huxley in later life 246, 258
"survival of the fittest" 61

Tante Juliette *4*, 11, 12–13, 20, *83*
therapeutic relationships 183
transgenerational aspects of family 11, 15, 42–45
tribal peoples xiv, 68, 150, 188, 189, 194
Tribes of the Amazon Basin in Brazil (conference) 6
*Tribes of the Amazon Basin in Brazil* (publication) 6
Trinity College Cambridge 5
Tupinamba (Tupi) xiii–xiv, 145, 246

unconscious, the xv, 35, 47, 120, 152, 209n27, 265–266; cosmology and the sacred 200, 202; haunting 60, 61, 64
UNESCO (United Nations Educational, Scientific and Cultural Organization) 5, 17, 24, 31, 54, 68, 290

unity of difference (between Aldous Huxley and Francis Huxley) 34–36
University Mental Hospital, Sheffield 6, 218
unorthodox therapies 183

Viking Fund Grant 5
*Voice of Experience, The* 221, 224
Voodoo, Haitian 116, 169, 170–171, 219–220; cosmology and the sacred 198, 202, 203–205; rituals for re-enacting bodily memories of past tensions and conflicts 204; St. Catherine's College, Oxford 176, 171, 186; see also *Invisibles, The*

Wagnon Road, Sebastopol, California 7, 90, 113, 124, 136; Francis Huxley in later life 239, 248, 249, 252, 253, 258, 260, *261*
Ward, Arnold 19
Ward, Mary 19
*Way of the Sacred, The* 6, 31, 132, 157, 187n30, 196, 205, 246, 247
Way of the Warrior conference 6, 132, 133, 248

well-being: psychological 190; of tribal and indigenous peoples *see* Survival International
Werner, Jutta 221
Westcott, Joan 6, 118, 119, 120, 123, 178, 184, *184*; Francis Huxley in later life 240, 250–251, 253
Western psychiatry 227
Weyburn Mental Hospital, Saskatchewan 5, 153, 157, 158, 159, 160, 163, 170, 218
White, Loren Eugen 248, 249, 261
*White Goddess* 240
white supremacy 267, 270
Williams, Michael Patrick 7, 20, 127, 240
Wiseman, Richard 206
*Women in Love* 33
Woolf, Virginia 13, 14, 23, 33, 68, 73n79
workshops, on mythology and rites 6

Zeal, Paul 119, 226, 231
Zeitlin, Jacob 55
Zoological Society of London 5, 22, 54, 88, 109
zoology xiii, 3, 5, 20, 21, 51, 66, 135; Oxford University 94, 95, 97, 98, 100, 102